THE BEAKER PHENOMENON?

Sidestone Press

THE BEAKER PHENOMENON?

Understanding the character and
context of social practices in Ireland
2500-2000 BC

NEIL CARLIN

© 2018 Neil Carlin

Published by Sidestone Press, Leiden
www.sidestone.com

Imprint: Sidestone Press Dissertations

Lay-out & cover design: Sidestone Press
Photograph cover: Old Head of Kinsale, foto: Robert Fudali via Adobe Stock.
    Pottery drawings by Eoin Grogan.

ISBN 978-90-8890-463-9 (softcover)
ISBN 978-90-8890-464-6 (hardcover)
ISBN 978-90-8890-465-3 (PDF e-book)

This publication was financially supported by the University College Dublin School of Archaeology.

Contents

Acknowledgements		9
Preface		11
1.	**Introduction: querying the Beaker Phenomenon?**	13
	1.1 Understanding the Beaker complex?	13
	1.2 'Similar but different'?	15
	1.3 Local worlds: people, places and things	16
	1.4 Structure, scope and methodology: a road map	17
2.	**New versions of old stories**	21
	2.1 Introduction	21
	2.2 Beaker 'culture' and cultural-historical approaches	22
	2.3 Early 1900s: Beaker-free Ireland says No to Romans	23
	2.4 The 1930s: the first Irish Beaker boom	24
	2.5 The 1940s and 50s: the arrival of Beaker invaders	25
	2.6 The 1960s and 70s: new beginnings	27
	2.7 The 1980s and 1990s: Irish Beaker elites – the 'Lunula lords'	28
	2.8 The 2000s: Beaker excavation boom – data vs knowledge	29
	2.9 Shifting chronologies: the legacy of Lough Gur and Newgrange	31
	2.10 Fragmentary pasts: non-integrated typologies	33
	2.11 Problematising prestige and recent developments	34
	2.12 Post-colonial Beaker-rich Ireland	36
3.	**A settled past**	39
	3.1 Beaker pottery in Ireland	39
	3.1.1 The distribution of Beaker pottery	40
	3.1.2 A context for Beakers	45
	3.2 Infamous Beaker 'settlements'	47
	3.2.1 Lough Gur	47
	3.2.2 Newgrange	49
	3.2.3 Knowth	51
	3.2.4 Monknewtown	53
	3.3 Settling some issues?	55
	3.4 Dwelling on the evidence?	60

4.	**Remembering everyday life**	**65**
	4.1 Introduction	65
	4.2 Beaker-associated pits	65
	4.3 Spreads and middens	80
	4.4 Fulachtaí fia	87
	4.5 Connecting spreads and pits	89
	4.6 Ideologically significant depositions	91
	4.7 Beaker settlement in Ireland in its wider context	92
5.	**Fragments of the Dead?**	**95**
	5.1 Introduction	95
	5.2 Beaker deposition in wedge tombs	96
	5.3 Beaker deposition in court tombs	107
	5.4 Beaker deposition in passage tombs	110
	5.5 Beaker deposition in portal tombs	112
	5.6 Beaker deposition in cists	113
	5.7 Beaker deposition in ring-ditches and ring-barrows	120
	5.8 Beaker deposition in pit graves	120
	5.9 Understanding deposition in mortuary and megalithic contexts	122
	5.10 Wedge tombs and cists as Beaker burials?	124
	5.11 A wider European context?	129
6.	**Commemorations of Ceremonies Past?**	**135**
	6.1 Introduction	135
	6.2 Beaker deposition in timber circles	137
	6.3 Beaker deposition at timber circles	147
	6.4 Beaker deposition in earthen enclosures	148
	6.5 Understanding Beaker ceremonial deposition	150
7.	**Transformational acts in transitional spaces**	**153**
	7.1 Introduction	153
	7.2 Beaker-related objects in bogs, rivers and lakes	154
	7.3 Beaker-related objects in dryland 'natural places'	156
	7.4 Identifying depositional patterns and practices	157
	7.5 Beaker-related objects in 'natural places' in Europe?	158
	7.6 Understanding deposition in boglands in Ireland	159
8.	**A time for Beakers?**	**161**
	8.1 Introduction	161
	8.2 Methodology and date selection criteria	161
	8.3 The dating of the Irish Beaker phenomenon	164
	8.4 Dating depositional practices	169
	8.5 Comparing Ireland to Britain?	170

9. Everything in its right place? — 173
- 9.1 Introduction — 173
- 9.2 Beaker Pottery — 173
- 9.3 Polypod bowls — 177
- 9.4 V-perforated buttons — 179
- 9.5 Wrist-bracers — 181
- 9.6 Copper Daggers — 185
- 9.7 Sun-discs — 186
- 9.8 Lunulae — 189
- 9.9 Gold bands and basket-ornaments — 191
- 9.10 Battle Axes — 192
- 9.11 Identifying depositional patterns and practices — 193

10. The Beaker phenomenon in Ireland and Beyond? — 197
- 10.1 The genomic transformation of north-west Europe? — 198
- 10.2 External influences? — 200
- 10.3 Continuity and change? — 202
- 10.4 Beaker pots: commemorating the domestic — 206
- 10.5 The meanings of Beaker-related objects? — 207
- 10.6 Personhood and 'personal possessions' — 208
- 10.7 Transformation rituals — 208
- 10.8 Supra-regional cosmologies? — 209
- 10.9 Rites of passage in sacred places? — 212
- 10.10 The Beaker transformation? — 213
- 10.11 The Beaker Phenomenon? — 215

Bibliography — 217

Acknowledgements

This book would not exist in its current form without the support, encouragement and input of Karen Dempsey, my partner in life and of course, archaeology. Much of what is expressed here comes from our discussions and shared passions, as well as her constructive feedback on ever-changing draft chapters. Thanks to Kerri Cleary who read, commented on and copy edited the manuscript. Her observations have greatly clarified and enhanced the text, though the faults it still has are entirely mine. Alex Guglielmi assisted greatly with the bibliography. Thanks also to Karsten Wentink and Corné van Woerdekom of Sidestone Press for all their patience and help.

The research for this book was originally undertaken as a doctoral study in the University College Dublin, School of Archaeology and the Humanities Institute of Ireland, with the support of a UCD Ad Astra scholarship under the supervision of Jo Brück. I am grateful to Jo and the examiners of my PhD thesis, Harry Fokkens and Gabriel Cooney, whose astute critique and probing questions provided the basis for this book.

I am pleased to acknowledge the support of my friends and colleagues in the School of Archaeology at University College Dublin, particularly Gabriel Cooney and Graeme Warren for their interest, encouragement and support and Conor McDermott for his help with creating and editing many of the illustrations in this book. I would also like to formally acknowledge my gratitude to the School of Archaeology for their financial contribution. During a break from teaching in UCD, this book was completed in Reading, where Karen is currently a Research Fellow. Thanks to all those in the Department of Archaeology at the University of Reading who made me feel so welcome while I was there, particularly Duncan Garrow.

I wish to thank Jim Mallory for originally encouraging my interest in the Beaker phenomenon. I am also grateful to all my colleagues whom have shared and discussed their work with me, particularly Mary Cahill, Neil Wilkin, Alison Sheridan, and Stuart Needham. Thanks to Tom Booth for so generously sharing his time and knowledge with me. Our discussions have considerably improved my understanding of aDNA.

My sincerest thanks to the community of archaeologists, consultancies, directors, and other heritage professionals who kindly contributed their time and shared the results of their investigations with me over the 15 years. Without them and the high quality of their work, this research would not have been possible. I am especially grateful to Helen Roche and Eoin Grogan who examined the pottery from over 95 of the unpublished sites included in the study and whose reports were of strategic importance to this project. My own analysis was made possible by their reports containing highly detailed analysis of these ceramic assemblages which they so generously shared and discussed with me.

Many people and organisations very kindly provided images and/or gave permission for these to be reproduced in the book including Tracy Collins and Frank Coyne of Aegis, Jacinta Kiely and Eachtra, Rob Lynch and IAC, Mel McQuade, Billy O'Brien, Richard O'Brien and Transport Infrastructure Ireland, Ros Ó Maoldúin, Jessica Smyth, Maeve Sikora and Matt Seaver of the National Museum of Ireland, Kara Ward, Fintan

Walsh, as well as Ann Woodward and the late Fiona Roe. Thanks to Mary Fannon for bringing her eye for detail to these.

Finally, thank you to all my family and friends, old and new, for their encouragement, support and understanding of my endeavours. I very much appreciate it.

Preface

This book is a completely true account of what people were doing with Beaker pottery and other associated objects in Ireland… Or at least, it is as true as any account of the adoption and adaptation of the so-called Beaker phenomenon in Ireland can be, when based upon the fragmentary evidence that people left behind through a very select range of activities over 4000 years ago.

It all began one day in May 2003, when I was part of a team of archaeologists working on a construction site in Kilgobbin townland, near Stepaside in County Dublin. I trowelled back the surface of a deposit to reveal the then unfamiliar orange sherds of Beaker pottery – its colour and decoration stood out against the grey/brown of other prehistoric ceramics that I had found before. Ines Hagen, the director of the excavations, shared her books on the topic with me, but these did not make things any clearer; the more I read, the more questions I had. During chats with my colleagues, at break-times and during afterwork get-togethers, I learned that this pottery was showing up on sites more and more often, but for many reasons, these new discoveries of Beakers were not mentioned in any of the published literature. This book is a response to all the unanswered questions I had then. It is a reaction to the past approaches taken to Beakers in Ireland and beyond. It provides a synthesis of information from older sites as well as the 'grey literature' of modern excavations. It is also a tribute to the generosity of the archaeological consultancy sector in Ireland, who shared full details of their excavations and took time to talk them over with me.

The research for this book was originally undertaken as a doctoral study in the University College Dublin, School of Archaeology and the Humanities Institute of Ireland, with the support of a UCD Ad Astra scholarship under the supervision of Joanna Brück. That PhD thesis contains catalogues detailing the sites and artefacts featured in this book and is freely available to download from the UCD Research Repository: http://hdl.handle.net/10197/9438. The results and discussions in this book are based on data available to the author before December 2009. Since the research for this book was first completed a very small number of new discoveries of Beaker pottery have been made in Ireland, however, they are not considered here on the basis that their inclusion would not have significantly changed the conclusions reached. This book therefore represents one way of telling the story of the Beaker phenomenon in Ireland – which has its faults (and these are very much my own) – which endeavours to capture some of the complexities of the human past.

1

Introduction: querying the Beaker Phenomenon?

1.1 Understanding the Beaker complex?

During the mid-third millennium BC, diverse groups of people across much of Europe adopted and adapted differing aspects of an international suite of novel material culture and social practices typified by distinctive ceramics known as Beaker pottery. This suite frequently included the burial of crouched inhumations with grave-gifts such as stone wrist-bracers, arrowheads and early copper or gold objects. Archaeologists have labelled this the Beaker *phenomenon*, because so many aspects relating to the rapid and widespread transmission of this assemblage have defied explanation. Numerous theories, including migration and the development of a prestige-based economy, have been developed to explain this phenomenon and its relationship with contemporary social and technological change (*e.g.* Clarke 1970, 271; Burgess and Shennan 1976; Harrison 1980). Yet the nature and social significance of these material traits, as well as their exact origin and methods of distribution, remain matters of debate. Recent aDNA studies have resulted in a resurgence of explanations involving large-scale people movement (Olalde *et al.* 2018), but so far we have not managed to answer fundamental questions such as: how did this happen? Why did it happen? What was the allure of these objects and practices? What did they represent?

This book aims to investigate these questions by providing an innovative approach and distinctly Irish perspective on the Beaker phenomenon. It does so through a regionally specific study of the character, context and dating of the practices and objects forming the Beaker phenomenon in Ireland. This provides the basis for an exploration of how and why these cultural innovations (including copper metallurgy) were brought to this island and then adopted/adapted, and how this compares with other parts of north-west Europe. It also assesses the evidence for transformations in social practices and people's lives that may have occurred in tandem with the appearance of Beaker-associated novelties. One of the key aims of this study is to create a fuller account of the social agency of Beaker-related objects and to better understand their role in constructing, negotiating and representing people's social reality, including their values, identities and relationships with other people, places and things.

Geographically, the island of Ireland is simultaneously connected to and cut off from the European continent by the sea (Fig. 1.1). This discrete and naturally defined land mass therefore represents a suitable case study in which to explore issues relating to the spread and adoption of cultural innovations such as the Beaker phenomenon in the deep past. Despite appearing to be the westernmost outpost of the Beaker phenomenon, a considerable number and range of stone and metal Beaker-related objects have been found here, suggesting an unusually high level of interregional interaction in the latter half of the third millennium BC (Case 1995; 2004a; O'Brien 2004; Carlin and Brück 2012; Carlin and Cooney 2017). Many were uncovered through activities

Fig. 1.1: A twenty-first century view of Ireland's location on the western edge of the European continent (© Sémhur / Wikimedia Commons / CC-BY-SA-3.0).

such as agricultural works, peat-cutting, antiquarian investigations and archaeological excavations during much of the twentieth century. The building boom in the Irish economy from 1997 to 2007, however, resulted in a decade of intensive developer-led archaeological investigations and an exponential increase in discoveries of Beaker pottery from apparent settlement contexts across the island (Fig. 1.2). In 1996, Beaker pottery had only been found at 65 sites in Ireland, most of which were excavated in the 1930s and 1940s, but by 2007, pre-construction excavations had resulted in the discovery of at least 150 new sites producing this ceramic (see Chapter Two). This study was therefore prompted by this upsurge in Beaker discoveries and the questions that these raised about the nature of the Beaker phenomenon in Ireland and how it has been regarded.

Traditional characterisations of the Beaker phenomenon in Ireland have considered it as radically different from elsewhere in Europe, where Beaker vessels are stereotypically found as part of funerary assemblages with single burials (*e.g.* Clarke 1976, 472-3; Burgess 1979, 213; Vander Linden 2006a; 2006b; Needham 2007, 44). Ireland is generally depicted as being rich in Beaker-associated settlement evidence with a minor funerary component consisting primarily of collective burials in primary and secondary contexts in mega-

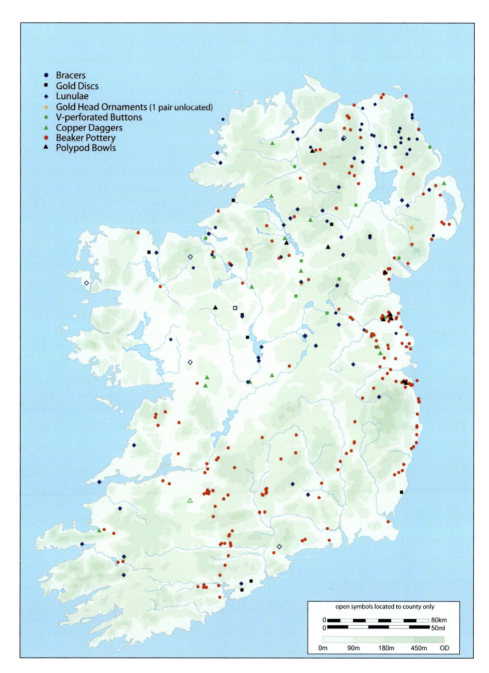

Fig. 1.2: The distribution of all Beaker pottery and related objects in Ireland.

lithic tombs. Most notably, the classic Beaker burial seems to be totally absent and crouched inhumations only appear in graves with Food Vessels (a distinctively Irish and British form of pottery) and a range of other objects after 2200 BC (Burgess 1979; Case 1995a, 19; 2004c; Needham 1996, 128; Cooney and Grogan 1999, 87; O'Brien 2004, 565). From this perspective, the Irish version of the Beaker phenomenon seems puzzlingly different from everywhere else. Many of the same types of objects that occur with burials in other parts of Europe have also been found in Ireland, but in non-funerary contexts. What is the explanation for this? How can this be understood?

1.2 'Similar but different'?

A very important point needs to be made here; this scenario of Ireland being different rests upon the false assumption that elsewhere the Beaker complex was culturally homogenous and represented the same practices or values everywhere because some highly uniform aspects such as the pottery were so widely shared throughout much of Europe. It is increasingly recognised, however, that the Beaker phenomenon is in fact characterised more by its regional variability than uniformity (Vander Linden 2007a, 185-6; 2013; Fokkens 2012a, 24-7). This has been succinctly encapsulated by the phrase, 'similar but different', which was used as the title for an innovative book highlighting the

INTRODUCTION | 15

Beaker complex's blend of regional differences and broader similarities (Czebreszuk 2004). This heterogeneity is illustrated by the highly discontinuous distribution of varying components of this complex, which do not correspond with the distribution of Beaker pottery. For example, around the Tagus Estuary in southern Portugal, where Beakers probably first appeared, these pots are mainly found with arrowheads and palmella points, the latter of which are seldom found with Beakers in other parts of Europe (Salanova 2002, 2004; Case 2004b. Many of the artefacts that supposedly form key elements of the Beaker panoply, including copper tanged daggers and wrist-bracers, are rare in Portugal and other Atlantic regions like northern France (Salanova 2002; 2004, 73). Indeed, this reflects the fact that wrist-bracers were a Central European contribution to the Beaker complex and therefore absent from early Beaker burials in western Europe (Harrison and Heyd 2007, 203, 205; Turek 2015, 31).

Certain early Beaker-associated burial practices (dating c. 2600-2300 BC) display an incredible level of uniformity and seem to have been highly standardised across many parts of Europe, including Britain and the Netherlands. These early Beaker-associated graves repeatedly comprised sex-differentiated single inhumations and a restricted set of objects, all of which were aligned and arranged in accordance with a specific set of rules (Fokkens 2012b; Garwood 2012). These indicate that some commonly understood ideas and practices were widely shared, but it is important to highlight that these early standardised burials are quite rare and have a very uneven distribution (Fokkens 2012b; Garwood 2012; Heise 2016). Beaker-associated burial practices were regionally variant in many other places such as Portugal or north-western and southern France, where collective burials were to the fore, or in Hungary where cremations were the main form of burial (Harrison 1980; Salanova 1998a; Vander Linden 2006b, 318-9).

Similarly, the earliest copper artefacts in western Europe represent a recurrent, but restricted selection of objects made from highly distinctive compositions of metal, some of which have been found alongside Beaker pottery (Brodie 1997; 2004; Roberts 2009). This gave rise to the view that the transmission of metallurgy was intrinsically linked with that of the Beaker phenomenon (*e.g.* Childe 1925; Sheridan 2008a and b; Fitzpatrick 2009). There is, however, a growing realisation that copper metallurgy pre-dates Beaker pottery across much of Europe and that the strength of the link between these has been exaggerated (Roberts 2008a; Vander Linden 2013). The Beaker repertoire (including a Beaker vessel, dagger and wrist-bracer) does not comprise a distinct formalised assemblage or technological package that emerged within the same cultural milieu (Salanova 2004, 73).

Archaeologists have struggled to identify a single geographical area of origin for the Beaker complex precisely because they have been wrestling with a synthetic phenomenon. This comprises the archaeologically detectable materialisation of interactions across large tracts of Europe involving a highly dynamic collection of novel materials, objects, ideas and practices that originated independently in various regions and were circulated through the movement of people and overlapping exchange networks (Turek 2013, 9; Vander Linden 2013). The manifestation of these material traits in each region would have been influenced by factors including the position of each place in relation to the various exchange networks, the structured nature of the relations between different areas, the dynamics of each society, the pre-existing traditions of each area and the way these innovations were introduced (Salanova 2000; 2004, 75; Vander Linden 2007a, 187; 2007b, 346-50). This accounts for why traditional pan-European single-factor explanations of the Beaker phenomenon involving a social event, group or process have failed to explain the spread of Beaker-associated objects and practices.

The idea of a highly uniform Beaker phenomenon is a relic of the cultural-historical migratory approaches to the past that were prevalent when this topic first began to be studied (see Chapter Two). At that time, it was thought that the Beaker phenomenon was the product of ethnic migrations. The repeated co-occurrence of objects such as wrist-bracers, or copper tanged daggers with Beaker pots in graves, provided the required evidence of a recurrent range of objects that formed a distinct and cohesive assemblage or 'culture' across the extent of its distribution. As a result, the Beaker pot became reified as the type-fossil of this 'culture', the uniformity of this complex was over emphasised, regional variation downplayed, and an almost exclusive focus upon the funerary domain developed (Clarke 1976; Vander Linden 2016, 9). This created a legacy that continues to this day, whereby most studies of the Beaker phenomenon have been based on the evidence from the funerary sphere, particularly the pottery and/or the burials with which it is sometimes found, while the occurrence of Beaker-associated objects in contexts such as settlements or natural places has received very little attention (see Case 2004c, 201). This bias has resulted in a very narrow understanding of the role of Beaker-related objects in other aspects of life in prehistoric Europe.

1.3 Local worlds: people, places and things

Many of the issues that arise in consideration of the Beaker phenomenon are of key importance for understandings of wider European prehistory, the adoption of cultural innovations over millennia and archaeology itself. The archaeologically confusing ways in which widely exchanged supra-regional innovations were locally integrated during their transmission is not unique to the

Beaker phenomenon. Similar archaeological phenomena with distinctive ceramics and highly characteristic burial practices were also present across Europe during the third millennium BC, including the Corded Ware, Yamnaya and Globular Amphora complexes (Harding, A. 2000; Fokkens 2012b, 123; Furholt 2014). All of which raise the fundamental questions of how and why did diverse groups in different places across such wide areas and long distances come to adopt and adapt similar cultural practices, ideas and objects in regionally distinctive ways? Of key importance here are the ways in which people in the past (just like today) used objects, materials and monuments as symbols and metaphors to represent other people, places or things, to enable them to communicate meanings or values and to construct their social identities.

International exchange and interactions involving the movement of people, objects or ideas were not a new phenomenon that suddenly developed in the latter half of the third millennium BC. These kinds of interconnections are imperative for biological, social and material reproduction (Mauss 1990; Lévi-Strauss 1949; 1987, 47). The widespread distribution of specific prominent artefacts or traditions across western Europe is entirely consistent with much of the continent's prehistory. For example, the extensive occurrences of Neolithic megalithic tombs throughout Europe indicate that humans have continuously adopted novel material culture over millennia in accordance with local needs. Similarly, the exchange of Beaker-associated innovations parallels other previous traditions, such as the distribution of jadeite axes from the western edge of the Alps as far west as Ireland during the late sixth to early fourth millennium BC (see Pétrequin *et al.* 2008; 2009).

Yet, there is still something distinctively curious and complex about the ways that widened interregional interactions became so prominent and material traits converged so much across such vast swathes of Europe in the third millennium BC (see Vander Linden 2016, 8-11; Furholt 2017). While sets of ideas, symbols and objects were shared between many different regions, it cannot be assumed that these had the same meaning or significance to all people in each place (see Kopytoff 1986; Gosden and Marshall 1999, 170). The values associated with some of these may have been changed or rejected as part of their translation from one region to another. Indeed, the varied treatment of Beaker-associated objects in different parts of Europe indicates that these did not possess fixed monolithic meanings that travelled with them. Because of these factors, an awareness has developed that regional studies are needed to increase our knowledge of the idiosyncratic manifestation of the Beaker phenomenon in each area (*e.g.* Barrett 1994; Fokkens 1997, 362; Garwood 1999, 281; Vander Linden 2013). This approach enables the traditions and practices that are shared with other regions to be identified, as well as those that are not. Most importantly, to better understand this widespread phenomenon, it must be considered in terms of the various local worlds of the small-scale societies that were connected together by supra-regional elements. Grand narratives are certainly necessary and useful, but it is at the micro-scale of everyday social life, including settlement and ceremonial activities, that international elements were enacted to fit within the context of local frameworks (Cooney 2000, 232; Cleal and Pollard 2012, 330).

To better understand the varied meanings that Beaker-related objects held for people (and the ways that people used these to construct or reinforce meanings), we must examine their roles in social practices and consider these in relation to their contexts, functions, place and time, as well as their connections with other objects (Hodder and Hutson 2003, 172, 192). A significant proportion of the archaeological record is a direct reflection of people's depositional activities, which were often selective and intentional acts involving choices regarding materials and context (Thomas 1999; Fontijn 2002; Pollard 2002). Deposition provided a scheme for the negotiation and reproduction of cultural values and social relations (see Needham 1988; Fontijn 2002; Pollard 2002, 22). In other words, it was a strategy people used for making sense of their lives and the world in which they lived. The examination of multiple components of Bronze Age depositional practices as part of an inter-related framework reveals patterns representing actions that were widely repeated across time and space, from which the wider beliefs and ideological values of the people in these places can be inferred (*e.g.* Bradley 1982; Needham 1988; Vandkilde 1996; Fontijn 2002). This is well illustrated in a Dutch context by David Fontijn (2002), who has demonstrated that the Bronze Age deposition of metalwork, grave-gifts and settlement materials represented interconnected exchanges, between people, ancestors and the supernatural, that were related to various stages in human life-cycles. A contextual analysis of the objects forming the classic Beaker assemblage throughout Europe, one that considers the contexts in which these artefacts are present and absent, as well as the objects that they are found with and without, is certainly needed to develop a deeper appreciation of their meanings and roles in each region. Yet this approach has not been sufficiently applied.

1.4 Structure, scope and methodology: a road map

This book aims to remedy this gap in our research by interlinking the analysis of Beaker pottery and various Beaker-associated object types (that have traditionally been studied in isolation) with their context of discovery and depositional treatment within an Irish context. This approach enables me to identify the typical ways in which different object types were deposited and characterise their roles in social practices within settlements, funerary monuments, ceremonial settings and 'natural places'. It takes advantage of the very significant quantities of evidence for Beaker-associated activities in non-mortuary contexts from Ireland to provide insights into aspects of the social lives of Beaker-related objects in a range of contexts that have traditionally received little attention.

One of the ways in which this study achieves this is through a detailed examination of the deposition of Beaker ceramics. This includes an assessment of the total number of Beaker pots and sherds, as well as the number of sherds per vessel in each feature. Information about the condition of the pottery, including the degree of fragmentation, surface and edge-wear, as well as other forms of abrasion, is noted where such observations had been made by the ceramicist who analysed the assemblage. Efforts were made to use the ceramics to detect evidence for material connections between different features, such as the occurrence of sherds from the same pot in different contexts, which might suggest that the deposits had been obtained from the same aggregation of materials. This analysis provides insights into the treatment of this pottery prior to and during deposition, including whether the pot was used prior to deposition or made especially for this purpose, and whether this pottery was deposited as soon as it was broken or if it had been in another context after breakage but prior to its eventual deposition. Based on this analysis, the patterning in these deposits is used to infer the past social practices that resulted in the formation of the deposits in which the pottery was found. This operates on the basis that the form, condition and context in which we find Beaker pottery is (to a large extent) a direct reflection of the depositional activities of people in the past, even if this is affected by taphonomy or issues of preservation. Although this perpetuates the reification of Beaker ceramics, this approach is dictated by the fact that the pottery is often the only element of the Beaker assemblage to have been deposited in the contexts being examined.

This study also examines the depositional treatment of many of the objects routinely found with Beaker pottery either in Ireland or elsewhere in Europe, as well as those that can be linked to Beaker pottery on stylistic grounds, such as wooden and ceramic polypod bowls, copper tanged daggers (Needham 1996; 1998; 2005), wrist-bracers (Woodward *et al.* 2006; Fokkens *et al.* 2008), V-perforated buttons (Shepherd, I. 2009), gold sun-discs, lunulae, basket-shaped and other sheet gold head ornaments (Clarke 1970; Case 1977a and b; 1995a; Taylor 1980; 1994; O'Connor, B. 2004; Needham 2005; Needham and Sheridan 2014), as well as barbed and tanged arrowheads of Conygar Hill, Green Low and Sutton type, and hollow-based arrowheads (Green 1980, 141-2; O'Hare 2005; Woodman *et al.* 2006, 134-8; Nicolas 2017).

Although most of these objects are broadly contemporary with Beaker pottery, both lunulae and V-perforated buttons have date ranges of 2300/2200-1900 BC, which means that some examples probably post-date the currency of Beakers in Ireland (Shepherd, A.N 2009; Needham 2011; Cahill 2015; Fitzpatrick *et al.* 2016). Nevertheless, the decoration on V-perforated buttons is very similar to that found on the base of Beaker pots and gold discs. Similarly, it has been argued that lunulae and Beaker pottery share motifs as well as similarities in terms of their compositional symmetry (Taylor 1970, 59-64; 1994, 42) and that these collars represent Beaker-associated goldwork (Needham 1996, 130; 2000, 30). This is supported by their occurrence with gold discs in Portugal and Ireland (Cahill 2015). These are all included here to facilitate an examination of the Beaker phenomenon in its widest possible sense and achieve a more integrated understanding of the social role of these items. As mentioned above, the study also includes objects that have been found in contextual association with Beaker pottery, labelled here as Beaker-associated artefacts.

This study is primarily concerned with synthesising information about the frequency and nature of the deposition of Beaker pottery and Beaker-related objects in various contexts. This includes assessing the context and the artefactual content of deposits in terms of type, quantity, condition of these objects, their associations and the manner of their deposition. While typological aspects of the various artefacts are used to provide a secure chronological platform, no detailed stylistic analysis or first-hand examinations of the physical characteristics of any artefacts has been undertaken. As such, this study is heavily reliant upon the work done by various specialists. All stone tool types occurring alongside Beaker pottery have been recorded as part of this study, including the presence of debitage. However, my analysis of these focuses primarily on the types and quantities of each of the various stone tools such as scrapers and arrowheads. I have excluded stone tools lacking contextual associations with Beaker pottery and those that have not been demonstrated by radiocarbon dating to have been contemporary with this ceramic. This is because of difficulties in accurately ascribing date ranges to lithics based solely on typological or technological characteristics. For the purposes of this study, a distinction is maintained between single finds, hoards and multiple finds. The latter category is considered to comprise a set of objects that have been found together but (unlike most hoards) may not have been the product of a single depositional act.

Other contemporary objects, such as copper axes and halberds, were probably made by people who used Beakers but have been excluded from this research because they are not generally regarded as forming part of the Beaker assemblage and have never been found with this pottery. Their exclusion raises important questions about how the European Beaker assemblage is defined. This is an issue returned to at the end of the book, but these questions seem especially pertinent in an Irish context where so many of the classic Beaker-associated items have been found as chance discoveries without any accompanying Beaker pottery. As the depositional treatments of copper axes and halberds have previously been elucidated (see O'Flaherty 1995; 2002; Becker 2006), these patterns are referred to here for comparative purposes.

Despite reservations about the suitability of applying the term 'Chalcolithic' to Ireland for the period 2450-2200 BC (see Carlin and Brück 2012), it is employed in this book because it facilitates comparison with Britain and serves as a convenient shorthand for a time when Beaker pottery was the only ceramic in use in Ireland. Beaker pottery rapidly replaced Late Neolithic Grooved Ware shortly after 2500 BC and there is nothing to suggest the level of overlap between these two ceramics that is argued for southern Britain (*e.g.* Garwood 1999; Needham 2005; 2007, 44). The term 'Chalcolithic' also distinguishes the floruit of Beaker pottery from the changes that happened at the start of the full Early Bronze Age, c. 2200 BC, including the advent of bronze metallurgy, Food Vessels and the adoption of crouched single burials across large parts of Ireland. It is important to highlight, however, that the analysis of the dating of the Beaker phenomenon, as presented in Chapter Eight, reveals that the currency of Beaker pottery in Ireland was from 2500-2100 BC, thereby outlasting the Chalcolithic by 100 years.

Though the occurrence of artefacts from the European Beaker assemblage features in overviews of Irish prehistory (*e.g.* O'Kelly 1989; Waddell 1998; Cooney and Grogan 1999), this study provides the first major reconsideration of the nature of their manifestation in Ireland and includes a reassessment of the information from older discoveries to bring them up to date with current understandings (see Chapter Two). It uses relevant information from pre-existing studies and catalogues that were either purely typological or conducted as part of investigations into the deposition and hoarding of metalwork, but included Beaker-related objects (*e.g.* Harbison 1969; 1976; Taylor 1980; O'Flaherty 1995; Eogan, G. 1994; Becker 2006). Most of these studies were not concerned with how or why so many Beaker style objects occur in the Irish archaeological record in the manner that they do; it was necessary in many cases to supplement these records with further contextual details.

Most of the evidence that this book is based upon has been discovered in the last 15-20 years and much of it is as yet unpublished. A key aim for this book is thus to synthesise as much of this data as possible, while also integrating it with the updated information from older discoveries. This means that there is variability in the quality and quantity of the data used in this study, because the information that it is based on was generated by a wide range of different people over a long course of time during which the approaches taken to the discovery, recording, excavation and examination of artefacts and sites changed greatly (see Chapter Two).

Most of the non-ceramic objects featured in this study were found during nineteenth century agricultural activities rather than by archaeologists during recent excavations. Consequently, many of these are lacking reliable information on their provenance, context or find circumstances, particularly those that were discovered as single finds rather than in hoards. As a result, we only have a partial picture of the depositional treatment of these objects and it is difficult to ascertain quite how representative this is.

Many of the excavations featured in this study were conducted prior to 1980 and the quality of recording or analysis is highly variable and often lacking detailed contextual data. This limits the level and value of the information that can be extracted. Attempts were made to overcome these problems by interrogating the information within the published accounts of these excavations, however, examination of the primary archive for these older excavations might have yielded better results. Similarly, some of the artefactual assemblages from these excavations remain in need of (re)assessment by relevant specialists as part of future studies.

There were also some problems with the data from excavations conducted since 1980, such as the availability of completed reports. While most of these investigations have been conducted in accord with a uniformly high standard, divergences in excavation, recording and sampling strategies, as well as approaches to the production of the excavation report and/or the various specialist reports on aspects such as pottery, lithics, charcoal and bone, have certainly affected the character of the insights that have been achieved (see McCarthy 2000).

As a result, the limitations of the available evidence are almost certainly replicated in the current research. These limitations must be accepted and considered when interpreting the data. While a quantitative approach has been employed, the calculated totals and percentages should not be seen as definitive. No attempt has been made to demonstrate the statistical significance of any of the patterning identified in this study because the data is simply not robust enough. I am not despondent about this, nor am I worried that these detract from the identified trends in social practices. After all, the degree to which we can ever aspire to accurately (re)construct the past is restricted (see Hall and Brück 2010, 85; Brück 2015), but I am optimistic that this study will add to ongoing conversations about the Beaker phenomenon.

Although approaches to the Beaker phenomenon have changed dramatically from the early twentieth century to the present day, there is a strong connection between some of the current problems in our understandings and the approaches that have been taken towards it. These issues are explored in Chapter Two, which reviews how previous scholarship has shaped our knowledge of the Beaker Phenomenon, both in Ireland and at the wider level.

Some of the following chapters employ the various categories that have traditionally been used to label the contexts in which Beaker pottery or other object types have been found. These categories include settlements (Chapters Three and Four), funerary and megalithic contexts (Chapter Five), and ceremonial settings, particularly timber circles (Chapter Six), as well as 'natural places' (Chapter Seven). Although this approach facilitates the discussion of the results of this study within manageable sections, the contexts in which the artefacts occur often defy simplistic characterisations of this kind. These clear-cut contextual categories mask the true complexity of the evidence and are unlikely to reflect the worldview of Chalcolithic people. At that time, activities seem to have been conducted as part of a spectrum of practices across a range of different contexts. The sacred and profane were inextricably interlinked, civil ceremonies, secular rites and religious rituals were probably part of everyday life and thus it is not possible to draw a clear division between the ceremonial and the mundane in past societies (Bell 1992, 38; Brück 1999a, 325-7; Bradley 2005a). In recognition of these issues, this study focuses upon the identification of social practices, rather than labelling things as simply residential or ceremonial (Bell 1992; Berggren and Nilsson Stutz 2012).

To explore these issues further, the very well-known occurrence of Beaker artefacts in what have generally been interpreted as settlement contexts such as that from Newgrange in County Meath are examined alongside the rest of the Irish evidence for Beaker-associated houses and the deposition of Beaker-associated materials in 'domestic' structural contexts, including postholes, stakeholes, and slot trenches (Chapter Three). Large numbers of pits have been found to contain Beaker pottery in Ireland, which are generally assumed to represent settlement activity. The deposition of Beaker pottery within these and other non-structural contexts including spreads, middens, and the burnt stone mounds also known as *fulachtaí fia* are analysed in Chapter Four. In Chapter Five the deposition of Beaker artefacts and associated human remains in megalithic or funerary contexts in Ireland, including earlier Neolithic megalithic tombs, contemporary megalithic monuments known as wedge tombs, as well as cists and cairns are examined. In Chapter Six the occurrence of Beaker pottery and other typical Beaker-related objects in ceremonial contexts, particularly within circular timber and earthen monuments is assessed. The deposition of Beaker-associated artefacts in 'natural places' such as bogs, mountains, caves and rivers almost certainly had a ceremonial aspect, but represents a distinct form of activity that is explored within Chapter Seven.

In Chapter Eight, the radiocarbon dating of the Beaker phenomenon in Ireland is reviewed to establish a new understanding of the chronology of Beaker pottery and Beaker-associated practices. All radiocarbon dates cited in this book are calibrated date ranges equivalent to the probable calendrical age of the sample and are expressed as BC dates, calibrated at two sigmas (95% confidence levels). These determinations were calculated using the calibration curve of Reimer *et al.* (2004) and the computer program OxCal (v4.1.7) (Bronk Ramsey 1995; 1998; 2001; 2009). Then, the focus widens to explore the full range of contexts in which each type of Beaker-related artefacts occurs in Ireland and their spatial distribution. Attention is given to highlighting their highly selective depositional treatment. Finally, in Chapter Ten, we return to reconsider the issues that have already been highlighted here, and all the various strands of evidence from the previous chapters are woven together to produce a very different narrative of how and why people in Ireland used Beakers and Beaker-related objects in Ireland.

2

New versions of old stories

2.1 Introduction

While some of the broader European scholarship on Beakers has tended to consider Ireland alongside Britain as part of the 'British Isles' (*e.g.* Czebreszuk 2004, 478; Vander Linden 2013, 75), most Irish archaeologists have tended to emphasise that Ireland is different to Britain. Instructive in this regard, is the way in which that term of reference, the British Isles, is considered in an Irish context to be highly political (see Cooney 1995; 1997a). The Beaker phenomenon in Ireland is often presented as being rich in settlement evidence yet lacking in a funerary component – most notably the classic Beaker burial – and to have had a prolific copper industry mainly producing so-called "heavy" objects including axes, halberds and daggers that largely occur in hoards (Case 1995a, 19-23; O'Brien 2004). This situation has often been contrasted with a characterisation of Britain as a place where Beakers were deposited in single graves and the earliest copper items predominantly consist of "light" objects such as blades, awls, or ornaments (Burgess 1979; Thomas 1999; Needham 1996, 126-8). Thus, the Irish Beaker tradition is argued to be more like that of the Atlantic region, while the British Beaker complex is considered part of the north-western European tradition, with closer links to the Netherlands (Burgess 1979; Thomas 1991; Case 1995a, 19; 2004a; Needham 1996, 128; Cooney and Grogan 1999, 87; O'Brien 2004, 565).

The very explicit way in which narratives of the Beaker phenomenon in Ireland have been conducted with reference to its nearest neighbours and former colonizers is illustrative of the fact that much of our (mis)understandings about the pan-European Beaker phenomenon directly reflect the ways it has been studied, both in Ireland and beyond. This should not come as a surprise given that archaeology as a practice is always set within its present and so the contemporary context of interpretation plays a significant role in shaping views of the past (Shanks and Tilley 1987; Hodder and Hutson 2003). This does, however, raise questions about the potentially problematic ways that archaeologists have reached their conclusions about the Beaker phenomenon and the ways these have changed over time. As Clarke (1976, 460) put it: "Dare we suspect, that the Beaker 'problem' is a philosophical artefact of our own manufacture, an unreal problem, an insoluble problem or perhaps a problem not worth the effort of solution?… [T]he problem is not a matter of data but a matter of … theory". This view was recently echoed by Marc Vander Linden (2013), who characterised the entire history of European Beaker scholarship as the repetitive application of problematic interpretative approaches that have yielded few advances in understanding. He highlighted the need for novel approaches to be taken to this subject, just as Clarke had done 37 years earlier, but the very fact that it remained necessary to repeat Clarke's clarion call suggests that a better understanding of past approaches is required to avoid repeating old mistakes.

To understand how previous interpretations of the Beaker phenomenon were reached, it is necessary to situate past works within the social, political and intellectual context of their creation (see Hodder 1986; Shanks and Tilley 1987). Therefore, this chapter chronologically and thematically reviews the genesis and development of knowledge of the Beaker phenomenon from the late nineteenth century onwards, but with a particular focus on Ireland and its broader European context. This serves to examine the legacies that have been created by past scholarship and to highlight those aspects that remain as implicit premises which influence(d) subsequent interpretations. This reflects my own concerns regarding the ways in which archaeologists have inserted their concerns and values into their narratives of the past, which are then used to legitimise these views within the present. Given that we are all influenced by our situatedness (within our present world), questions can be raised about what aspects of my worldview I am contributing here (Hodder and Hutson 2003, 196-234). While we may struggle to see the flaws created in our own dispositions, we can still be clear about how and why we want to (re)construct the past. My dissatisfaction with aspects of our current society, including widespread inequality and the privileging of the individual over the community, certainly motivates much of the critique presented here. This is especially true of my approach to critiquing the widely held idea that we see the emergence of self-aggrandising individualistic elites during the third millennium BC. On a personal level, I have a strong awareness of the highly fluid ways in which we construct our various social identities, due to my childhood experiences of living in various parts of Ireland and my subsequent attempts to define where I am from.

Related to this is a strong interest in the ways in which we use material culture to make our worlds and ourselves. Undoubtedly, my anxieties about doing things the right way and my desire to have order in my life have both piqued my interest in the rulebound nature of Beaker-associated depositional activity. Without going into further detail here, it is already clear that there is much of me to be found in this book. However, it is important to note, that by admitting to my lack of complete objectivity, I am not advocating a relativism that undermines the basis of my arguments. I am content that I have woven together the various strands of the available evidence as cohesively as is now possible "to make a coherent story" (Wylie 1993; Hodder 2004, 28) and that these knowledge claims have been critically evaluated by my peers.

2.2 Beaker 'culture' and cultural-historical approaches

Most of the problematic approaches taken to the Beaker phenomenon have their roots within earlier twentieth century archaeological frameworks, when this pan-European enigma was first studied (Clarke 1976, 460; Vander Linden 2013). At that time, archaeology was largely focused on providing a cultural-historical sequence of human groups that were defined through their material culture. In the absence of the precise chronologies afforded by radiocarbon dating (which had not yet been developed), archaeologists had to rely solely upon typologies of objects like Beaker pottery to produce timelines and evolutionary cultural sequences for prehistory (Roberts and Vander Linden 2011). The assumed progenitors for each object type, their areas of origin and the extent of their distribution were identified to chart their subsequent circulation through time and space. As part of this process, certain material culture traits were selectively grouped together (based on their similarities and recurrent associations) to form discrete spatio-temporally bounded archaeological units of classification known as 'cultures' (see Shennan 1989; Jones 1997). The application of this approach to the recurrent discovery of Beaker artefacts in Britain and continental Europe – as part of a highly distinctive burial rite including weapons such as daggers and arrowheads – during the nineteenth and twentieth centuries created the impression of a distinct and cohesive Beaker culture. This resulted in the reification of the Beaker pot and the classic Beaker burial.

It was generally assumed that the spread of these 'cultures' from their origin-point reflected the past movement of human groups of a particular ethnicity. In the case of the Beaker culture, the seemingly rapid and widespread dispersal of Beaker grave assemblages and apparent absence of any associated settlements provided evidence for the migration of a distinctive ethnic race of exceptionally mobile 'Beaker Folk' (see Harrison 1980, 11; Brodie 1994). In the words of Hawkes and Hawkes (1947, 54): "once arrived, these several waves of energetic conquerors soon occupied the greater part of Britain, ruthlessly dispossessing the Neolithic communities of their best pastures, and also no doubt of their herds, and sometimes their women". One very prominent advocate of this approach was Vere Gordon Childe, who at various times envisaged these 'Beaker people' as warriors, beer drinkers, itinerant metallurgists, traders and gypsies (Childe 1925; 1949, 119; 1950, 130; 1958, 213-28). These 'Beaker Folk' were considered to have been taller with shorter and broader heads and to have been physically and technologically superior than Neolithic people (*e.g.* Abercromby 1902; 1912). Nowadays, most of these physical differences, including head-shape, are recognised as being largely reflective of social practices such as infant head-binding (Parker Pearson *et al.* 2016). Until the late 1970s, this cultural-historical paradigm remained dominant in Beaker studies; these almost exclusively focused on using typology to recognise the identity, movements and origins of putative Beaker "folk" across Europe, rather than examining the reasons behind these (*e.g.* Sangmeister 1966; 1972; Clarke 1970, 277; Case 1977a, 71). When the relationships between cultures were discussed, this was done almost exclusively through the prism of historical terminology such as invasion, colonization and trade. This had a significant impact on archaeological discussions of the past, an impact that continues to this day.

The emergence of these cultural-historical approaches was very much a product of the intellectual and political milieu of the nineteenth and early twentieth century. In tandem with the upsurge of nationalism in Europe around this time, the past was increasingly being used as a political tool to legitimize the existence of a series of newly emerging nation states (Trigger 1984; Geary 2002). This resulted in the application of evolutionary and taxonomic approaches to identify the 'culture' of past ethnic groups through their physical remains and highlight the enduring character of their distinctive identities (Trigger 1984; Shennan 1989, 5-7; Vander Linden and Roberts 2011). This approach endured unchallenged until the 1960s, probably because it fitted with many of the dominant paradigms of thought during a turbulent period in Europe that included two world wars and the rise of fascism. As we will see, this is certainly true of Ireland, where cultural-historical approaches dominated from the 1920s until quite recently (see Waddell 1978; 1991; 2005; Cooney 1995; 1996) and syntheses of Irish prehistory have mainly comprised descriptive sequencing of events (*e.g.* Herity and Eogan 1977; Harbison 1988; O'Kelly 1989). With the foundation of the Irish Free State in 1922, archaeologists sought to anchor this newfound political entity within the distant past and accentuate its status as separate from, yet equal to Britain, its former colonizer (see Cooney 1996, 158).

2.3 Early 1900s: Beaker-free Ireland says No to Romans

In Ireland, examples of Beaker pottery remained virtually unknown on this island until the 1930s (*e.g.* Mahr 1937, 372) and the Europe-wide 'Beaker culture' was considered not to have extended so far westward (Abercromby 1912; Macalister 1921, 201-2; Mahr 1937, 372). To some extent, this reflects the traditional unidirectional, *Ex Oriente Lux* models of thought that were dominant at this time, which held the view that Ireland only passively received European innovations long after other regions had (*e.g.* Childe 1925). The first Irish discovery of this ceramic occurred in 1885, during an antiquarian investigation of a wedge tomb at Moytirra, Co. Sligo (Cremin Madden 1968), though these were not recognised as Beakers at this time. Subsequently, in Abercromby's (1912, 114) catalogue of British and Irish Bronze Age pottery, the Moytirra wedge tomb was listed as one of only two sites to have produced this pottery in Ireland. The other example was a pot from Mount Stewart, Co. Down, which had been published as a Beaker in the *Dublin Penny Journal* of 1832. Abercromby (1902; 1912) considered these sherds to represent insufficient evidence that the 'Beaker invaders' who colonised Britain had also

ventured to Ireland. This view was maintained by R. A. S. Macalister (1921, 201-2; 1928, 52) in his books, *Ireland in Pre-Celtic Times* and *The Archaeology of Ireland*, which were among the earliest syntheses of Irish prehistory. Macalister explained the presence of these few Beaker sherds as reflecting "the work of captive women" that had been enslaved during an Irish raid of Britain. He speculated that they must have been females due to the small size of the finger imprints upon these pots. His approach is highly reflective of attitudes to women in Ireland and Britain at this time, who despite having achieved partial suffrage, were not afforded the same privileges as most men (McAuliffe 2014).

Interestingly, Macalister had already discovered Beaker sherds himself, along with a wrist-bracer, during the excavation of a cist grave at Longstone Furness, Co. Kildare, in 1913 (Macalister *et al.* 1913), but these were not recognised as Beaker at the time (see Chapter Five). While the pot from Mount Stewart, which had first been published as a Beaker in the *Dublin Penny Journal* of 1832, was subsequently reclassified as a Vase of the Food Vessel tradition (Evans and Megaw 1937). Issues regarding the correct identification of pottery were of considerable significance and had major consequences given the typological approaches of the time, but errors such as these continued to be made as Irish studies of Beakers developed. This is due in part to the fact that, for much of the twentieth century, there was little awareness that Beaker pottery in Ireland often lacks any or much decoration.

The apparent paucity of Beaker material culture in Ireland in the early twentieth century served the needs of Irish nationalism in its construction of a distinctive postcolonial Irish identity. This may also partially explain the reluctance to positively identify the ceramic on this island. Beakers were added to the list of 'races', including the Romans and the Anglo-Saxons, that were considered to have invaded Britain but avoided Irish shores. Their perceived absence from Ireland was hailed as evidence for the existence of fundamental dissimilarities between Irish and British people (*e.g.* Bremer 1928; Macalister 1928, 52).

The Irish Sea and any evidence for connections across it with Ireland's politically unattractive neighbours in Britain were downplayed (Waddell 1991, 29-30). In contrast, the significance of the Atlantic seaways was emphasised to demonstrate Ireland's illustrious history and accentuate links with continental Europe (see Cooney 1995, 271; Waddell 2005, 205). For example, Macalister (1928, 52) argued that: "for all that the two islands are so near together, Britain is essentially an island of the North Sea, Ireland of the Atlantic Ocean; and this difference is fundamental throughout the whole history of their mutual relations". Present-day connections with continental Europe were also prioritised alongside those of the past. This is illustrated by the successive appointments of German and Austrian archaeologists, Walther Bremer and Adolf Mahr, as Keeper of Antiquities in the National Museum of Ireland in 1925 and 1927 (Crooke 2000, 142; Wallace 2008, 169). Both gentlemen advanced the construction of a separate Irish national identity through their work. For example, Bremer (1928, 27-8), who served as an officer in the German army during the First World War, argued that the Moytirra pottery was most closely related to Breton Beakers and proclaimed that, "only two Beakers of the English type have been found in this country".

2.4 The 1930s: the first Irish Beaker boom

The 1930s was a time of intense archaeological investigation led by prominent male archaeologists on the island of Ireland (Cooney 1995; 1996). Excavations were encouraged and financed by the newly independent political entities of Northern Ireland and the Irish Free State, both of which were eager to use archaeology to forge and complement their own national identities (Cooney 1995, 267; 1996, 158). Thus, Adolf Mahr (1937, 262) was able to boast in his presidential address to the Prehistoric Society of the "enormous amount of fresh evidence" that had been uncovered through large-scale systematic excavations undertaken during the previous five years.

Two significant developments occurred in 1932 that resulted in new discoveries of Beaker pottery. The Harvard Archaeological Expedition, which conducted Ireland's first comprehensive scientific excavations (see Waddell 2005, 217-20), and a special employment scheme to create jobs in the Irish Free State were both established. The employment scheme enabled many significant investigations including those at Lough Gur, Co. Limerick (see Section 3.2.1), through the provision of labour and much needed financial support (Cooney 1995, 267; Waddell 2005, 214). Beaker pottery was also unknowingly found during the Harvard excavations of the cairn at Poulawack, Co. Clare, in 1934 (Hencken 1935), and the court tomb at Creevykeel, Co. Sligo, in 1935 (Hencken 1939). Also in 1934, the first scientific excavation of a wedge tomb was conducted by Harold Leask, the then inspector of National Monuments, at Labbacallee, Co. Cork (Leask and Price 1936). The sherds from this dig were shown to none other than Vere Gordon Childe, who (as we will see below) exerted a considerable influence upon the development of Beaker studies in Ireland. Though Childe did not recognise any of these as Beaker, one vessel was subsequently identified as such by Case (1966).

In 1933, a landmark paper by Lily Chitty in *The Antiquaries Journal* drew attention to several previously unpublished and unrecognised Beakers found in Northern Ireland, at Bushmills, Murlogh Bay and Whitepark Bay, all in County Antrim, and Mount Stewart in County Down. Its publication seems to mark the beginning of an increased rate of discovery of Beakers in Ireland. Yet, this paper has very rarely been cited. This may be partially reflective of the political differences that existed at this time between archaeologists operating in the jurisdictions of Northern Ireland and the Irish Free State and the fact that she was a British archaeologist may have resulted in her work being ignored in the latter part of Ireland. Unfortunately, this may also be considered a result of gendered discrimination; the author was a woman, and so would not have been afforded the same respect and privileges as men in this period.

By 1936, Seán P. Ó Ríordáin had begun his intensive excavations of a wide area around Lough Gur, Co. Limerick (Fig. 2.1), which continued until 1954 (see Cooney 2007, 215). As a consequence of these investigations, it could no longer be claimed that Beaker vessels were lacking in Ireland. Beginning in 1938, with his highly significant discovery (and identification) of Beaker pottery in a wedge tomb at Lough Gur (Ó Ríordáin and Ó hIceadha 1955), his activities in Limerick uncovered at least 6000 sherds of Beaker pottery from as many as 14 different sites, including the large stone circle at Grange (Ó Ríordáin, S.P. 1951), Lough Gur Sites C and D (Ó Ríordáin, S.P. 1954), Rathjordan (Ó Ríordáin, S.P. 1947; 1948), Rockbarton (Mitchell and Ó Ríordáin 1942), Ballingoola (Ó Ríordáin, S.P. 1950) and the enclosed occupations on Knockadoon, a peninsula around which lies the horseshoe-shaped lake, such as Circles J, K, L and Sites 10 and 12 (Grogan and Eogan 1987). These transformed understandings of Beakers in Ireland (although they were mainly misidentified as Beaker settlement enclosures; see Section 3.2).

Meanwhile in Northern Ireland, Estyn Evans, Ivor Herring and Oliver Davies had also begun excavating wedge tombs. Initially, they targeted these monuments because they were highly visible and thought to have been built by newcomers (see Waddell 2005, 201-3). After the fortuitous discovery of Beakers at the Largantea tomb in County Derry (Herring 1938), Davies (1939, 254) deliberately set about excavating other wedge tombs with the specific aim of finding more of this pottery. Thus, the 1930s became a golden age of Beaker discoveries in Northern Ireland. Considerable quantities of this pottery were discovered during the excavation of other wedge tombs including Kilhoyle (Herring and May 1937) and Boviel (Herring and May 1940), both in County Derry, as well as Loughash (Davies 1939) and Cashelbane (Davies and Mullin 1940) in County Tyrone. While the Beakers at Kilhoyle were not recognised as such at the time of excavation, those from Largantea were positively identified by Childe and then heralded as "the first definite beakers to be found in Northern Ireland" (Herring 1938, 171). This proclamation seems to have overlooked the previous identification of Beakers from Counties Antrim and Down by Chitty (1933), thereby absenting her contribution to scholarship.

Fig. 2.1: Excavation of Lough Gur wedge tomb in 1938 (after Ó Ríordáin 1955, Plate IV).

2.5 The 1940s and 50s: the arrival of Beaker invaders

While Ireland's neutrality protected it from the heavy destruction that many European counties suffered during the Second World War; the resulting economic stagnation had a serious and lasting impact on the island. State-funding for archaeology decreased in both jurisdictions during the 1940s and 50s (see Waddell 2005, 220, 288), Beaker pottery continued to be discovered, albeit at a much lesser rate than in the previous decade. S.P. Ó Ríordáin continued his programme of excavations at Lough Gur and under his influence others conducted concurrent investigations in the locality that also yielded Beakers, for example, at the Caherguillamore rock shelter (Hunt 1967) and the settlement at Ballingoola (MacDermott 1949). In 1948, Ó Ríordáin's former student, Michael J. O'Kelly, recovered Beaker pottery during the excavation of a cist and cairn at Moneen, Co. Cork (O'Kelly 1952). This is noteworthy because O'Kelly would subsequently strongly influence understandings of Beakers in Ireland through his excavations at Newgrange.

The very first Beaker pottery to be found in the east of Ireland was discovered in 1945 during an excavation of Ballyedmonduff wedge tomb, Co. Dublin, financed by University College Dublin (Ó Ríordáin and de Valéra 1952). This was soon followed by the unearthing of Beakers nearby, at Dalkey Island off the coast of County Dublin, during excavations conducted from 1956 to 1959 by G. D Liversage with the assistance of George Eogan. A large quantity of Beaker ceramics was recorded within a midden at Site V, in what would then have been an unusual context to find Beakers (Liversage 1968). Elsewhere around this time, Beakers were found at a few other sites including Baurnadomeeny wedge tomb, Co. Cork (O'Kelly 1959), and a possible cemetery at Gortnacargy, Co. Cavan (Ó Ríordáin, B. 1967). Meanwhile, in County Down, "the first probable Beaker sherds from an Irish horned cairn" were recorded within Ballynichol court tomb (Collins 1956, 118). The occurrence of Beakers in other court tombs was, however, almost totally unrecognised until Michael Herity conducted a review of the finds from these megaliths several decades later (Herity 1987). Cumulatively, these various discoveries over the course of the 1930s, 40s and 50s led to a scenario whereby Máire de Paor (1961, 653) declared to a European audience in 1958 that Beaker pottery was widespread in Ireland (perhaps proudly, given that Ireland was increasingly becoming a recognisable member of the political world-stage, having exited the British commonwealth and officially become a republic in 1948). Macalister's Beaker-free island now seemed a very distant proposition.

Archaeologists in Ireland employed a cultural-historical approach throughout much of the twentieth century that exclusively relied upon migrations to explain all changes in material culture. It was only upon the realisation that Beaker pottery was definitely present across the island that they fell into step with their European counterparts by attributing its introduction to the influx of a new race. Subsequently, there was considerable acceptance that the introduction of Beakers to Ireland represented one of the more significant waves of invasion in Irish prehistory (Herring 1938, 185; Ó Ríordáin, S.P. 1954, 452; Apsimon 1969, 28-33; 1976, 27; Harbison 1973, 93-7; 1975, 113; Sweetman 1976, 71; Herity and Eogan 1977, 111-17, 131; Eogan, G. 1984, 320; 1991, 117; Grogan and Eogan 1987, 485-9; Eogan and Roche 1997, 25). This narrative switch is illustrated by Macalister's shift from completely denying any traces of Beaker influence (1921, 201-2; 1928, 52) to his description of these 'invaders' who "exterminated the men, or at least reduced them to slavery" which appeared in the revised edition of his synthesis, *The Archaeology of Ireland* (1949, 87-8). Such was his belief in the existence of a large-scale Beaker-associated intrusion into Ireland that Macalister (1949, 87-8) supported Abercromby's (1912, XI, 99) suggestion that the migration of Beaker people was responsible for the spread of an Indo-European language to Ireland, as well as Britain. This was subsequently echoed and expanded upon by several other Irish archaeologists (*e.g.* Harbison 1975, 115).

Childe's theories about the spread of archaeological cultures, including the westward migration of ethnic Beaker folk, were clearly very influential in Ireland and these migrants were soon credited with introducing a wide range of novelties including copper metallurgy (Case 1966; Cremin Madden 1968; Apsimon 1969). It was Humphrey Case (1966) who wrote the most influential paper on this topic entitled '*Were the Beaker people the first metallurgists in Ireland?*', in which he suggested that Beaker people introduced copper working to Britain and Ireland. This followed on from his previous analysis of early metallurgy, in which it was argued that the earliest copper working probably started in the Cork/Kerry area (Coghlan and Case 1957, 99). Interestingly, it was Childe who recommended to Case (while studying at the Institute of Archaeology in London) that he should tackle the question of Beaker metallurgists. Case's Childean hypothesis was to be subsequently echoed by many Irish scholars (Case 1966; 1977a; Cremin Madden 1968; Apsimon 1969; Herity and Eogan 1977).

Due to the by-now substantial number of discoveries of Beaker pottery in Ireland, it became increasingly implausible to use its perceived absence to serve the needs of Irish nationalism. Instead, the particular type of Beakers found here were now held up as evidence that Ireland was very distinct from Britain. An Atlantic European origin was sought for Irish Beaker pottery and this was hailed as the point of departure for those putative people who had brought this pottery to Ireland's shores (Macalister 1949, 87-8; Ó Ríordáin, S.P. 1954, 452; Harbison 1973, 93-7; 1975, 113; Herity and Eogan 1977). As well as metallurgists, these Beaker arrivistes were also seen as megalith builders who brought the wedge tomb concept to Ireland from northern France, where it's supposed proto-types – *Alleés Couvertes* – were located (De Valera 1951, 180; De Valera and Ó Nualláin 1961, 115; Herity 1970, 13; Herity and Eogan 1977, 122). The co-location of both wedge tombs and copper metallurgy in the south-west of the island was taken as evidence that an Atlantic group of Beaker immigrants had landed there, bringing metallurgy and a new type of society with them (Herity and Eogan 1977, 117-22).

Reacting to the hunt for European connections and origins in Irish archaeology, Estyn Evans (1968, 7), who was a Belfast-based geographer, slammed this as unduly nationalistic and declared it as a "kind of Sinn Fein movement in prehistoric studies". He expressed his frustration at the unwillingness of Irish archaeologists to accept the reality of a British influence upon Ireland's past (see Evans 1981, 112). At the same time, however, and in a very similar fashion, archaeologists based in the newly founded Northern Ireland (including Evans) were seeking to legitimate its status as a region that was distinct from the rest of Ireland and had a long-lived unity with Britain (see Cooney 1995, 271; Waddell 2005, 216). Operating within a cultural-historical framework, they sought exclusively British parallels for Northern Ireland's Beaker phenomena and argued that Beakers had come to Ireland from Britain via a northern Irish point of entry (*e.g.* Chitty 1933, 26; Herring 1938, 186; Davies 1939, 261; 1940, 148-54). Thus, discoveries of Beaker pottery in Northern Ireland served to affirm a unionist identity. Clearly, the strong ethnic slant of cultural-historical Beaker studies combined with the supra-regional nature of this phenomenon made it a very suitable vehicle for political interpretation, such as these competing readings of the past.

2.6 The 1960s and 70s: new beginnings

The 1960s was an important decade in the development of Beaker studies in Ireland. The first in-depth examination of Irish Beaker pottery and its contexts was undertaken by Aideen Cremin Madden for an MA thesis in 1964, and published in 1968. This was shortly followed by an overview and reappraisal of the Beaker finds from Northern Ireland by Arthur Apsimon (1969). Although only a small number of new Beaker sites were found during the sixties, two major excavations commenced during this decade that would subsequently dominate understandings of the Irish Beaker phenomenon. In 1962, George Eogan and Michael J. O'Kelly both began their respective campaigns at Knowth and Newgrange in *Brú na Bóinne* (Boyne Valley), Co. Meath. The results of these major excavations, as well as those conducted by David Sweetman at Monknewtown, revealed evidence for intense Beaker-associated activity in the Boyne Valley that radically changed the perception of the Beaker complex in Ireland in the 1970s (Sweetman 1971; 1976; 1985; 1987; O'Kelly *et al.* 1983; Eogan, G. 1984; Eogan and Roche 1997).

This major switch in perspective was due to the fact that most of the Beaker-associated features uncovered in *Brú na Bóinne* were interpreted as the remains of Beaker occupations. Previously, the general perception of Beakers in Ireland was that these pots were mainly found in a funerary setting, particularly collective tombs (*e.g.* de Paor 1961, 659; Cremin Madden 1968, 12). Strangely, this view that Beakers in Ireland were mainly used for funerary purposes had continued even though supposed Beaker settlements containing large quantities of this pottery had already been discovered at Lough Gur and at Dalkey Island (see Sections 2.4 and 2.5). That reluctance to accept the extent of the non-sepulchral evidence in Ireland was probably due to the pervasiveness of the contemporary European belief that Beakers were a funerary-ware. The findings from the Boyne Valley complex, however, combined with those from other concurrent excavations of Beaker habitations at Ballynagilly, Co. Tyrone, by Arthur Apsimon (1969; 1976), and at Tullywiggan, Co. Tyrone, by Helen Bamford (1971), ensured a change of narrative. Henceforth Ireland was seen as a place where Beakers were mainly found in settlements (*e.g.* Case 1977a, 77; Mercer 1977; Burgess 1979, 213), though these settlements were considered to be quite rare (Brindley, A.L. 1995, 6; Case 2004a, 375; O'Brien 2004, 480).

This switch to viewing the Irish Beaker complex as non-funerary was relatively minor compared to the changes in perspective on the Beaker phenomenon and prevailing archaeological frameworks that were happening internationally. Since the 1960s, the emergence of radiocarbon dating had highlighted serious issues with cultural-historical typological and diffusionist arguments and there had been an increasing realisation that its approaches were based upon flawed assumptions (Shennan 1989, 5). Awareness grew of the problems with a normative view of 'culture', whereby recurring associations of artefacts expressed a human group's shared set of practices and beliefs that all members of that social or ethnic entity conformed to. It was recognised that humans actively and selectively participate in cultural traditions in diverse ways, rather than automatically reproducing cultural traditions by default (see Binford 1965; Clarke 1968; Renfrew 1977; Shennan 1989). Furthermore, the classification of these 'cultures' as coherent entities involved highly arbitrary groupings of cultural traits within a chosen spatial temporal area that concealed differences and exaggerated similarities (Binford 1965, Hodder 1978, 1982; Shennan 1978). This had a homogenising effect that rendered large tracts of the past static, thereby creating the need for false 'transition moments', usually in the form of a sudden migration event, to account for change. This tendency to attribute all material developments to external influences without adequate explanation of how and why these developments happened became heavily critiqued (*e.g.* Binford 1962; 1972; Clarke 1968; 1978; Renfrew 1972).

Archaeologists sought to remedy the failings of cultural-historical approaches through what became known as 'New Archaeology' and then as 'processualism'. This new framework sought to explain change by focusing almost exclusively on local adaptations and the internal dynamics of society from economic, political, scientific, and social evolutionary perspectives (Trigger 1989, 264-88). A hallmark of this approach was its emphasis on formulating universal rules of human behaviour and employing cross-cultural analogies (*e.g.* Renfrew 1973). Migration's role was largely abandoned as a vector of change and replaced by acculturation processes, often featuring economic management systems whereby material culture operated as symbols of rank. These developments had a very significant impact upon the direction of Beaker studies, resulting in new interpretations of this phenomenon.

The idea of a 'Beaker culture' in central and north-western Europe that was spread by large-scale movement of new people was convincingly critiqued by Stephen Shennan (1976; 1977), Colin Burgess (Burgess and Shennan 1976) and David Clarke (1976). They highlighted that this was a social phenomenon because a coherent Beaker assemblage (comprising a restricted set of repeatedly associated artefacts) only occurred in funerary contexts and apart from a burial type, few of the typically recurrent aspects of archaeological cultures, such as a house type or subsistence economy, could be identified. They argued that Beaker pottery and its associated artefacts represented a 'package' or 'set' that was spread across Europe through exchange and interaction between newly emerging elites who considered this assemblage desirable and valuable (Shennan 1976; 1978). In Burgess and Shennan's (1976) 'Cult Package' model, they explained this as being due to the Beaker pot's role within a male beer-drinking cult. Here they drew upon early interpretations of Beakers as drinking vessels (*e.g.* Abercromby 1912) and cross-cultural analogy with a peyote cult that spread across North America in the nineteenth century.

As an interesting aside, one of the earliest adaptations of Burgess and Shennan's cult package model was by a Northern Irish archaeologist, Brian Scott (1977a), who gave it a novel twist. Arguing that sufficient evidence to support the assertion of a drinking rite was lacking, he proposed instead that a European-wide Beaker sect had been based on the use of plant-derived hallucinogens such as *A. muscaria* (a variety of mushroom) or *Cannabis sativa* that could have "provided visionary ecstasy in prehistory" (ibid., 29-30). Perhaps inspired by 1960s counterculture and an increased awareness of illicit drugs in Ireland, Scott suggested that the Beaker pot served as a hallucinogenic urinal, whereby a mushroom-based infusion would be drunk and then through the medium of a Beaker pot could be "offered in solution in urine from persons who had previously ingested it".

Following on from the processualist critiques of Beaker 'culture', it was widely accepted that Beaker-related objects were obtained to confer and symbolise power as part of a newly developed prestige goods economy (Clarke 1976). The idea that these played a key role in the development of social ranking became (until recently) a rarely challenged and self-evident orthodoxy in Anglophone Beaker studies (*e.g.* Clarke 1976; Burgess 1980; Harrison 1980; Whittle 1981; Gibson, A. 1982; Shennan 1982; Bradley 1984; Braithwaite 1984; Thorpe and Richards 1984). This was partially based on the idea that the appearance of the Beaker package with the earliest 'single' graves in many European regions reflected a wider social evolutionary trend whereby collective burials were replaced by individual ones. Alongside the development of early metallurgy at the dawn of the Bronze Age, this was commonly considered to reflect major social changes, including the demise of a Neolithic egalitarian or communal value-system and the emergence of a new globalised economy, increased social stratification and institutionalised inequality (*e.g.* Renfrew 1973; 1976; Harrison and Heyd 2007; Kristiansen 2015). According to this model, individual status was achieved by the exchange and/or display of exotic goods, thus competition for control of exchange systems led to attempts by both the existing elite and their challengers to find ever more novel types of prestige goods to exchange (*e.g.* Renfrew 1974; Thorpe and Richards 1984; Clarke *et al.* 1985). Ultimately, this apparently resulted in the entry of these emerging elites into the European Beaker exchange network to avail of a wider range of high-value exotic objects and technologies in the form of pottery and metallurgy to maintain and display their supremacy. These acquisitions were then used as 'symbols of power' to adorn these wealthy individuals, hence their occurrence in "rich" or "high-status" graves. Of course, how these putative elites or this Beaker exchange network emerged is never considered. These are some of the many problems that undermine the credibility of this enduring interpretation and which we will discuss in more detail towards the end of this chapter.

2.7 The 1980s and 1990s: Irish Beaker elites – the 'Lunula lords'

As we have seen, during the 1970s a view developed in Ireland that most Beakers were found in settlements and indeed very few Beaker discoveries were made in that decade or in the 1980s, apart from the continued excavations at *Brú na Bóinne*, all of which were interpreted in this new light. George Eogan's excavations at Knowth uncovered more Beaker-associated features and David Sweetman (1985) also made new discoveries of this ceramic at Newgrange, where he excavated a large pit circle that he considered to be a Beaker-associated construction. Within this monument, Beaker pottery was found in a spread that he interpreted as a habitation. He went on to find more Beakers at Newgrange during his partial excavation of a probable timber circle (Sweetman 1987). Despite relating these features to Beaker settlement activity, he was aware that these represented what was then a rare discovery of Beakers in a clearly ceremonial context in Ireland. Sweetman (1985, 216) stated that "the excavation of the pit circle at Newgrange adds a new dimension to our knowledge of the Late Neolithic/Beaker settlement in the Boyne Valley, … it gives an insight into the technological skills and the rituals of the people who, up to relatively recently, have been associated in Irish archaeology only with the wedge-shaped gallery graves". While Sweetman compared his findings to several well-known Final Neolithic monuments in Britain, such as Stonehenge and Durrington Walls, he followed his predecessors by consistently emphasising the uniqueness of the Newgrange discoveries (*e.g.* Sweetman 1987, 294).

During the 1980s, the introduction of Beaker pots on this island remained synonymous with the adoption of copper metallurgy (Scott 1977a; 1977b; Sheridan 1983), though in keeping with wider trends both developments were now considered as products of social rather than ethnic developments (Case 1977a; Waddell 1978, 125;

O'Kelly *et al.* 1983). By this time, culture-historical frameworks had generally been rejected in favour of more processual approaches and a far greater emphasis placed upon recognising evidence for continuity of people and place in the prehistoric record (*e.g.* Waddell 1978; O'Kelly *et al.* 1983; Cooney 1987; Grogan 1989; Cooney and Grogan 1999, 78). As one of Ireland's earliest and most prominent processualists, M.J. O'Kelly exemplifies these approaches. He was instrumental in obtaining the first radiocarbon dates in Irish archaeology and advocated the scientific testing of hypotheses through reconstructions such as those at Newgrange (O'Kelly 1982, 73, 86), which he himself considered as an example of 'new archaeology' (ibid., 73). He also stressed the evidence for continuity of activity and the lack of change associated with the use of Beakers outside Newgrange (O'Kelly *et al.* 1983), though this was based on a misreading of the chronology of various pottery types (see Section 2.9).

An important advancement for Irish Beaker studies in the 1980s was the radiocarbon dating of human bones from wedge tombs by A.L. Brindley and Jan Lanting (Brindley *et al.* 1987/8; Brindley and Lanting 1992). This confirmed that some skeletal remains were broadly contemporary with the deposition of Beaker pottery and that these monuments were almost certainly constructed by users of this ceramic. Prior to this, the only published radiocarbon dates for wedge tombs were from Island, Co. Cork, and dated to the Middle Bronze Age (O'Kelly 1958). Consistent with the non-migratory approaches of the time, these were no longer seen as evidence for invaders or ethnic groups. Gabriel Cooney and Eoin Grogan (1998, 84) highlighted their structural similarities to earlier Neolithic tombs and argued that wedge tombs form part of a longer Irish megalithic tradition. While William O'Brien (1999, 251-61) related their construction to localised territorial land claims within the context of internal social dynamics.

By the 1990s, the by-now mainstream (in Britain at least) interpretations of Beakers and early metals as prestigious or exotic objects associated with increased social ranking and emphasis upon the individual had been adopted in Ireland, despite the absence of Beaker-associated individual burials (*e.g.* O'Kelly 1989, 71-2; Waddell 1998, 121-3; Cooney and Grogan 1999, 83-93; O'Brien 1999; 2004). Cooney and Grogan (1999, 90-93) attempted to adapt the prestige goods model to better suit an Irish setting by arguing that in Ireland (unlike Britain), Beaker pottery conferred and created status within settlements, rather than in funerary settings (see Section 2.11). Problematically, this was largely based upon Ó Ríordáin's excavations at Lough Gur, which seemed to indicate a high level of continuity of population at the end of the Neolithic alongside the emergence of a Beaker-using elite. It was believed that this new social hierarchy was indicated by Beaker-associated enclosed settlements that produced larger quantities of Beaker pottery and 'personal ornaments' compared to nearby unenclosed occupations (Grogan and Eogan 1987, 467-89; Cooney and Grogan 1998, 471; 1999, 78). Later, however, it would be realised that these enclosed settlements were constructed in the Late Bronze Age (see Section 2.9).

O'Brien (1999; 2004, 570-2) also argued for the existence of elites, but this was based upon the results of his investigations in the early 1990s at Ross Island copper mine in County Kerry. There he found Beaker ceramics at an ore-processing camp associated with the mine, which was dated to 2400-1800 BC (see Chapter Three). This confirmed the existence of Ireland's long-suspected Beaker-associated copper industry. This mine was probably the sole source of the low-arsenic A-metal used to produce all the copper objects, mainly axes and halberds, that occur in Ireland (Case 1995a, 19-23; O'Brien 2004). This copper was also widely exchanged across the Irish Sea, where it was used to create much of the earliest British metalwork and is known from some southern British Beaker burials (Northover 1999, 214; Northover *et al.* 2001, 28; Needham 2002, 105; 2004). Inspired by this, O'Brien argued that the advent of copper metallurgy in the south-west of Ireland resulted in the emergence of powerful elites; "lunula lords', who controlled the production and supply of copper and used gold lunulae as badges of their wealth and status. They lived within "fixed social territories" recognisable today by the presence in north Kerry of Beaker pottery, lunulae and copper production, as well as the construction of henges and the absence of wedge tombs (but see Chapter Nine for critique). O'Brien (2004, 572) proposed a social division between these Beaker users and another group based in the south-west of Counties Kerry and Cork who also used this pottery, but continued Neolithic practices such as reciprocal exchange and the construction of megaliths in the form of wedge tombs. We will return to this interpretation later in the chapter.

2.8 The 2000s: Beaker excavation boom – data vs knowledge

Irish archaeology underwent fundamental changes from the late 1990s onwards when pre-development archaeology began to grow in tandem with the economy. This resulted in such a dramatic surge in the number of excavations conducted per annum that it became difficult to synthesise the results of these investigations and convert this into new knowledge (Doyle *et al.* 2002, 13; Cooney *et al.* 2006, 15). This development-led archaeological activity peaked from 1997-2007, before declining greatly as Ireland's economy entered a recession (Fig. 2.2).

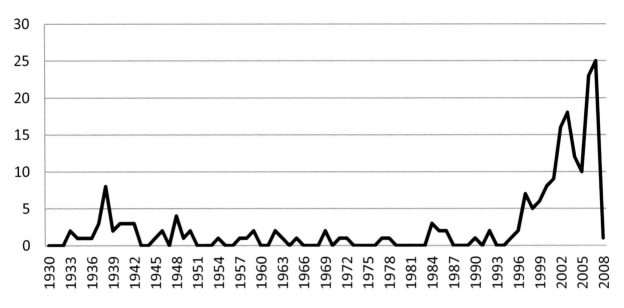

Fig. 2.2: The number of excavations that have yielded Beaker pottery per year showing notable peaks in 1938, 1997, 2003 and 2007.

As a result of that boom in excavations, Beaker pottery was discovered on 150 new sites across the island, representing a very considerable increase on the number of previously known find spots. Almost all these new discoveries were made on green-field sites with no above ground expression of the archaeological features that lay below. They indicated a much greater distribution and range of evidence for Beaker-associated activities than previously suspected, though most were interpreted as the remnants of settlements (see Chapters Four and Nine). This large body of new information generated from 1997 onwards had great research potential but its implications for pre-existing understandings of the Beaker complex were not explored, until my research on this topic began (Carlin 2005a; 2011a; 2011b; 2013; Carlin and Brück 2012; Carlin and Cooney 2017).

At this time, Irish archaeology was predominantly focused on meeting the needs of economic development by ensuring that archaeological remains were suitably recorded in advance of construction. For much of the noughties there was a significant shift in the focus of Irish archaeology away from museum or university-led research (Cooney *et al.* 2006). In what has been described as "the fetishization of excavation" (Waddell 2007), emphasis was almost wholly placed upon the collection of archaeological data with the aspiration that it would be 'analysed or interpreted at a later stage'. Underlying this obsession with excavation seemed to be a belief that the acquisition of more data and artefacts would bring archaeologists closer to understanding what the past was really like (Clarke 1978, 3). This empiricist and objectivist approach overlooks the fact that the past still needs to be translated into the present. It represents a direct continuation of the traditions of Irish archaeological practice, which originated within a cultural-historical framework (see Cooney and Grogan 1999, 1; Woodman 1992a, 295; 1992b, 38; Cooney 1995, 268). Indeed, Adolf Mahr's 1937 declaration that "the basis for future archaeological research must be saved before it is destroyed" (Mahr 1937, 262) seemed to form a mantra for future generations of Irish archaeologists. Mountains of new archaeological data were generated, but most of this was presented solely within the so-called grey literature comprised of unpublished stratigraphic reports. This made it extremely difficult to stay abreast of new findings, let alone conduct any syntheses or create any research benefit from this material (Anon 2006, 12; 2007; Bradley 2006; Cooney *et al.* 2006; Wilkins 2010).

In more recent years, this situation has begun to be remedied, through the wider publication of the results from road schemes and other large-scale development-led projects (*e.g.* Stanley *et al.* 2017). Research such as the Cultivating Societies project (Whitehouse *et al.* 2014) and Smyth's (2014) synthesis of Neolithic settlement have drawn heavily upon the evidence from developer-led excavations. In that regard, this book, which is based on the author's PhD research, is of fundamental importance in tackling the lack of synthesis of Beaker sites in Ireland. This forms part of a recent upswing in research on the Beaker phenomenon in Ireland along with two other PhD theses that have subsequently been completed on aspects of this subject (Ó Maoldúin 2014; McVeigh 2017). Related to this, a renewed interest in wedge tombs is indicated by Ros Ó Maoldúin's recent excavations of a cluster of these monuments in the Burren, Co. Clare (Fig. 2.3).

Fig. 2.3: Excavations at Parknabinnia wedge tomb on the Burren, Co. Clare, during the summer of 2017 by The Irish Fieldschool of Prehistoric Archaeology (photo reproduced by permission of Ros Ó Maoldúin).

2.9 Shifting chronologies: the legacy of Lough Gur and Newgrange

Despite the large array of new data relating to Beakers in Ireland from development-led excavations, understandings of the Irish Beaker phenomenon remain strongly influenced by discoveries of Beaker pottery prior to the 1980s. Excavations conducted at Lough Gur from 1936 to 1954 and at Newgrange from 1962 to 1975 have especially dominated most accounts of Beakers in Ireland (*e.g.* Harbison 1988; Waddell 1998; Cooney and Grogan 1999). Ó Ríordáin's problematic typo-chronological sequencing of the ceramics from the Knockadoon peninsula strongly impacted on interpretations of the Lough Gur sites and on Irish Beaker studies generally. Most of Ó Ríordáin's work pre-dated the invention of radiocarbon dating, and so like all other Irish archaeologists of the time, he envisaged a very short chronology for the Neolithic (see Waddell 2005, 211, 227). Based on the (vertical) stratigraphic relationships of the various ceramics at Lough Gur, Ó Ríordáin considered a particular coarse flat-based form of pottery – "Lough Gur Class II" – to date to the end of the Neolithic (Ó Ríordáin, S.P. 1954, 451-4, fig. 55). This resulted in the conclusion that Beakers represented one of the latest types of pottery present on the Knockadoon sites (*e.g.* de Paor 1961, 659; Cremin Madden 1968, 15) and that the Class II ware must be a contemporaneous reaction to Beakers by the indigenous Neolithic population (*e.g.* Harbison 1973, 95).

Although Eamon P. Kelly had argued in 1978 that Class II ware could not be Neolithic and must be of Late Bronze Age date, only recently did this view gain widespread acceptance (*e.g.* Cleary, R. 1993; 1995; Roche 2004; Grogan 2005a, 318). It was also subsequently recognised that many of the Lough Gur stone-built structures thought to reflect Beaker-associated activity (*e.g.* Simpson 1971; Gibson, A. 1987), are in fact later Bronze Age constructions (Cleary, R. 2003; Grogan 2005b, 52-62; Cooney 2007, 220) and that most of the Beaker pottery occurring there was residual (see Chapters Three and Five). The date for the construction of the embanked stone circle at Grange has been similarly revised (Roche 2004), but debate about this continues (see Cleary, R.

2015; Section 6.4). With hindsight, it can be seen that the presence of large quantities of Beakers within the Late Bronze Age settlement enclosures at Lough Gur was merely a reflection of the added protection from more recent plough-damage that the enclosures afforded to these earlier deposits (see Section 3.2). These chronological errors had enduring consequences for subsequent interpretations of Beakers in Ireland because of an over-emphasis upon the Lough Gur sequence in approaches to Irish prehistory and perhaps an unwillingness to accept criticism of Ó Ríordáin's Class II hypothesis.

Consequentially, when Beaker pottery was discovered at sites like Dalkey Island (Liversage 1968), Monknewtown (Sweetman 1976) and Newgrange (O'Kelly *et al.* 1983), in various admixtures of material of different dates that included much older Early Neolithic as well as much younger flat-based pottery, it was not recognised that the Beaker sherds were in a disturbed context. Instead these layers were regarded as chronologically secure deposits that matched the ceramic sequence from Lough Gur in which Beaker pottery represented the latest stage in a short phase of activity. In retrospect, the Beaker activity at these sites formed only one aspect of a much longer sequence of occupation. This was not, however, appreciated at the time. This is exemplified by the ongoing tendency (*e.g.* Mount 1994; McCormick 2007) towards verbatim readings of the reports on the faunal assemblage from so-called 'Beaker layers' at Newgrange (Van Wijngaarden 1975; 1986) as if they did not represent an admixture of materials formed over at least one millennium (see Section 3.2).

Significantly, these misinterpretations form part of a wider trend and were not unique to the Boyne Valley and Lough Gur. As observed by Peter Woodman (1992a, 308), there was a tendency until the 1990s to regard many sites in Ireland that post-dated the building of passage tombs but pre-dated iron metallurgy as Beaker-related. This is especially true of later Bronze Age sites as indicated by the manner that stone circles, such as the Great Stone Circle at Newgrange, and ceremonial enclosures, such as Monknewtown or Grange, as well as copper mines and boulder burials were considered alongside wedge tombs as part of a Final Neolithic Beaker floruit (*e.g.* de Paor 1961, 655; Herity and Eogan 1977, 132; Waddell 1998, 112-13; Cooney and Grogan 1999, 86-9; see Chapters Three, Five and Six for more detailed discussion). With the benefit of hindsight and ever more precise chronologies which mean that we no longer rely entirely on typology for site dating, we can see how these conclusions would have been reached. Archaeologists operating within a cultural-historical framework that considered all innovations to have had an external source would have turned towards the 'Beaker Folk' in a bid to relate a new site-type to a significant migration event, one that occurred between the apparent influx of farmers in the Neolithic and Celtic warriors in the Iron Age.

Given his non-migrationist stance, O'Kelly (1989) argued for a considerable degree of continuity between passage tombs and Early Bronze Age monuments such as wedge tombs, as well as between Neolithic and Beaker-associated activity outside Newgrange, which he considered as evidence for ongoing occupation. In an approach that was widely followed, he employed the phrase 'Late Neolithic/Beaker' to characterise this putative period. His interpretation of some of the external features at Newgrange as the vestiges of Beaker-associated 'domestic' structures gained much traction (*e.g.* Cooney and Grogan 1999, 79-81; Roche and Eogan 2001; Grogan 2004a; 111-2; Carlin 2005a, 2012b). Rather than being considered an exceptional site (see Section 3.2.2), it became de rigueur to compare new discoveries of Beaker-associated features to those at Newgrange and to follow O'Kelly's lead by interpreting these as the remains of settlements (*e.g.* O'Brien 2004, 475; Johnston *et al.* 2008). O'Kelly's interpretation of the activity at Newgrange was, however, strongly influenced by the perception that the time-gap between the zenith of the passage tomb complex (then thought to be Late Neolithic but now considered as Middle Neolithic) and the adoption of Beakers was very short. Again, this partially reflects the enduring influence of the problematic typo-chronological schemes previously developed by scholars like Ó Ríordáin before radiocarbon dating existed.

Although Grooved Ware pottery, dating from the Late Neolithic, had long been known in Ireland (*e.g.* Ríordáin, S.P. 1951; Liversage 1968), it was only in the 1990s that it started to be widely identified (Cleary, R. 1983; Roche 1995; 1999; Sheridan 1995; Brindley, A.L. 1999). This resulted in a delayed appreciation of the existence of a distinct pre-Beaker Late Neolithic, associated with the use of Grooved Ware and post-dating the construction of passage tombs (Eogan and Roche 1997, 256; Cooney and Grogan 1999, 75-94; Cooney 2000a; Roche and Eogan 2001). This negatively impacted Irish understandings of the Beaker phenomenon. Many apparently dramatic changes in social practices and material culture, such as the demise of the passage tomb complex and the construction of open-air enclosures, were falsely attributed to the adoption of Beakers rather than Grooved Ware 500 years earlier (*e.g.* Herity and Eogan 1977; O'Kelly 1989; Eogan, G. 1991; Cooney and Grogan 1999, 78, 92; Roche and Eogan 2001, 139, though see Carlin 2017).

As a consequence of these revisions of Irish chronological frameworks, the treatment of the Beaker phenomenon in Ireland within existing syntheses of Irish prehistory became quite outdated (*e.g.* Harbison 1988; O'Kelly 1989; Waddell 1998; Cooney and Grogan 1999). This situation was subsequently exacerbated by the large number of new Beaker discoveries made after 1997 (see below). One of the hallmarks of Irish Beaker studies that emerges here is an overly strong reliance on the findings from just one or two landmark excavations and a reluctance to re-evaluate these, despite knowing that they were a product of their time and pre-dated more recent breakthroughs (see Chapter Three). This is something that is characteristic of wider approaches to Irish prehistory (see Woodman 1992a, 295) and is perhaps indicative of a deferential attitude towards prominent male archaeologists such as Ó Ríordáin, O'Kelly and Eogan. Given that Ireland is a relatively small island with quite a small archaeological community, this would be unsurprising.

2.10 Fragmentary pasts: non-integrated typologies

While the various approaches taken to Irish prehistory have certainly had a strong impact, the distinctive character of the Irish archaeological record has also shaped the way in which the Beaker phenomenon has been studied here. Many of the typical aceramic Beaker-related objects such as V-perforated buttons, copper tanged daggers and wrist-bracers were discovered in significant quantities in Ireland, long before Beaker pottery was perceived to be present (in any significant quantity). These objects were, however, rarely found with each other or even in the same types of contexts and thus, the way they were studied reflected the character of their discovery (see Chapters Seven and Nine). Perhaps treating each of these artefacts separately was justified by the absence of the pottery, which represented the essential ingredient of 'Beaker culture' and provided a unifying link between these discrete discoveries. Unfortunately, the legacy of this fragmentary approach persisted long after Beakers were recognised in Ireland and the possibility that the depositional treatments of these objects may have been interrelated was ignored.

Most of the aceramic Beaker artefacts, such as metal daggers or wrist-bracers, have been the subject of detailed typo-chronological studies resulting in the creation of extensive catalogues (*e.g.* Harbison 1969a; 1976). These consider the various types of Beaker artefacts in isolation from one another and the contexts in which they have been found, with little attention given to their depositional treatment. Separate typological studies of Beaker pottery have continued since Cremin Madden's work in the 1960s. Case (1993; 1995a; 2001; 2004a) conducted several highly important short synopses of Beaker pottery from older excavations in Ireland and produced straightforward typological schemes for the characterisation of Irish Beaker pots. More recently, A.L. Brindley (2004) also provided a succinct and up-to-date overview of Beaker ceramics from older excavations. The exclusion of the large number of recently discovered vessels, however, left a lacuna that has been partially filled by Eoin Grogan and Helen Roche's (2010) synthesis of Irish prehistoric pottery in light of newer excavations.

One of the persistent trends that unites studies of aceramic Beaker-related objects, pottery, and accounts of the Beaker phenomenon, is the very fragmentary and non-integrated way in which they have all been considered. This is exemplified by overviews of the Beaker phenomenon within each of the various syntheses of Irish prehistory (*e.g.* Harbison 1988; O'Kelly 1989; Waddell 1998; 2010; Cooney and Grogan 1999). These also treat Beaker pottery in complete isolation from all the other aspects of the Beaker assemblage. Metal objects like copper daggers and golden ornaments are generally discussed in separate sections on metallurgy with little or no reference made to the Beaker complex, while wedge tombs also tend to feature in different sections of these books, often discussed alongside earlier Neolithic megalithic tombs. This kind of non-integrative approach is also clearly present in most of the published accounts of Beaker-associated discoveries at particular sites. For example, the locations of the various Beaker deposits at the Knowth passage tomb complex were never considered in relation to one another or to their site location (Eogan, G. 1984; Eogan and Roche 1997; see Chapter Five). On the few occasions that the find-spots of Beaker pottery were indicated on Knowth site plans, pre-existing Neolithic features, such as the passage tombs, were removed from these illustrations (presumably because they represented a different part of the site's cultural-historical sequence). A notable exception to this non-integrative approach is provided by Case's (1977a; 1995a; 2001) overviews of the Irish Beaker complex, which included considerations of the contexts and associations of a wide range of objects.

Aside from the very discrete nature of Beaker deposition, a predisposition towards treating objects and data by type or period divorced from their wider context has long been characteristic of prehistoric studies in Ireland (see Woodman 1992a, 295; 1992b, 38; Cooney and Grogan 1999, 229; for critique of Irish obsession with accumulating and sorting data rather than understanding it). This is particularly true of Irish Bronze Age studies which until recently (*e.g.* Grogan 2005a; 2005b; Cleary, K. 2007; Ginn 2014, 2016; Leonard 2015) had focused almost exclusively on singular aspects such as Early Bronze Age burials, ceramics or metalwork deposition without integrating data from other settings such as settlements (*e.g.* Eogan, G. 1983; Waddell 1990; O' Flaherty 1993; 1995; Mount 1997a; Brindley, A.L. 2007). A more contextual approach has now been applied to many aspects of Irish prehistory, with greater attention being paid to depositional patterning in recent decades (*e.g.* Cooney and Grogan 1999; Cooney 2000a; Becker 2006; 2013; Bradley 2006). However, a contextual approach to the Beaker phenomenon in Ireland has only recently begun to be applied through the integrated relational research that I have conducted (see Carlin 2011a and b; Carlin and Brück 2012; Carlin and Cooney 2017).

2.11 Problematising prestige and recent developments

Despite critiques of the prestige goods theory (*e.g.* Bintliff 1979; Brodie 1994; 1997; Fontijn 2002; Brück 2004a; 2006a; 2006b; Vander Linden 2006b; 2007a; Fokkens *et al.* 2008; Brück and Fontijn 2013; Fowler 2013), the view that powerful entrepreneurial individuals acquired exotic objects to show off their wealth has become deeply embedded in Beaker discourse (*e.g.* Sheridan 2008b; 2012). As we have seen, this theory was originally formulated to explain cultural changes such as the spread of the Beaker phenomenon through internal social mechanisms rather than population movements, but in doing so, a range of highly problematic assumptions were made. The prestige goods model drew heavily upon structural Marxist anthropology, which is characterised by its strong interpretative emphasis on economic systems and economic value, as well as modes of production (*e.g.* Godelier 1977; Frankenstein and Rowlands 1978; Rowlands 1980). Consistent with the processualist methods of the time, cross-cultural analogies and one-size-fits-all social evolutionary typologies were employed to support the assumption that progressively more hierarchical forms of society must have developed towards and after the end of the Neolithic, resulting in the rise of elite groups of powerful wealthy individuals (male chiefs) (*e.g.* Renfrew 1973; 1976).

In many ways, despite the attempt to improve upon the shortcomings of cultural-historical approaches, the prestige goods model simply replicated nineteenth-century social evolutionary perspectives (as evident in archaeology's three age system) that assumed a linear social progression from the distant past to modern western society in a highly flawed manner (see McIntosh 1999; Fowler 2013, 74-5). A feature of this kind of belief in universal cross-cultural stages of evolution is the problematic assumption that completely different historical contexts, which are separated by time and space, can be considered comparable (see Barrett and Fewster 1998; Spriggs 2008; Roscoe 2009). The prestige goods model was based on ethnographic analogy with eighteenth- and nineteenth-century African and Oceanic/Pacific societies like the Kongo of west central Africa and Melanesian groups; their comparison with European Chalcolithic and Early Bronze Age groups was therefore false because those societies had been strongly influenced by colonial contact (Gosden 1985; McIntosh 1999, 2-3). As a result, anthropological studies such as Sahlin's classic Melanesian 'Big Man', and exchange systems such as Malinowski's Kula ring exchange in New Guinea, reflect modern capitalism and lack any time-depth (Spriggs 2008). These are not as relevant to prehistoric Europe as has been assumed and do not support the hypothesis that a prestige goods economy existed in the deep past. Furthermore, Chris Fowler (2013, 85) has argued that Renfrew and others fundamentally misunderstood the way in which Polynesian and Melanesian 'Big Men' gained social status from their ability to give away rather than acquire possessions. Underlying the prestige goods model there seems to be an a priori assumption that the desire to pursue power and prestige is a cross-culturally recognisable motivation for all humans.

As a result of these flawed approaches, it seems to have been presumed that the Beaker exchange network developed (whereby Beakers were competitively acquired by newly emerging elites) in the same way everywhere, simply because this was the next natural and inexorable step in a longer chain of evolutionary developments (for which nobody was specifically responsible). The reasons why the Beaker package was desirable, or these putative elites rose to prominence are never explicitly explored (see Vander Linden 2013). The particular or general underlying social conditions or processes in any region where this new social order is thought to have emerged were not examined, despite the clear differences that existed across Europe at the time (Fokkens 2016, 301). As Vander Linden (2013) has astutely observed, the prestige goods model negated itself by serving as both a cause and effect of the spread of the Beaker phenomenon across Europe. In effect, the Beaker package hypothesis largely just replaced large-scale population movement with elite individuals as the prime mover in explaining the widely shared aspects of this phenomenon. Despite the stated intentions of various processualist archeologists and the switch away from a migratory perspective, this new framework for interpreting the Beaker phenomenon maintained many of the pre-existing problems of the cultural-historical approach *e.g.* a typological methodology that did not take fuller account of regional diversity, revise how this phenomenon was defined or provide an answer as to how or why it developed (Vander Linden 2013).

Just as cultural-historical archaeologists in the nineteenth and twentieth centuries had focused largely on the highly distinctive Beaker burial, so too did the advocates of the prestige-based Beaker package (*e.g.* Shennan 1976; 1978). This theory paid little attention to evidence from non-funerary contexts and completely overlooked the fact that classic Beaker inhumations are just one aspect of a very diverse range of Chalcolithic mortuary practices (Gibson, A. 2004; 2007). It relied heavily upon a simplistic reading of the so-called high status or 'rich' Beaker burials (see Brodie 1997, 300; Fowler 2013, 81-93). This involved the naïve assumption that objects in the grave were personal possessions directly reflecting the lived identity of the deceased individual and that burials served almost exclusively to create and maintain hierarchical divisions (despite the highly equivocal nature of the evidence). It has been convincingly reasoned that the objects deposited in single graves did not belong to the deceased and actually inform us about the construction and depiction of social relationships (*e.g.* Brück 2004b, 317-8). It has also been contended that the burial ceremony was so highly transformative that the highly contrived form of identity visible in a Beaker grave may have nothing to do with the life of the deceased (*e.g.* Garwood 2011, 268; 2012, 300-301; Fokkens 2012b; Fowler 2013, 103).

It is quite revealing that ethnographic groups who had been influenced by mercantile capitalism were specially selected to justify the prestige goods model. According to this ethnocentric viewpoint, the exchange of objects, ideas or knowledge was seen very reductively and almost exclusively in terms of modern-day western economic concepts. Beakers and other objects were seen merely as passive commodities whose value was linked to their scarcity; a form of disposable and displayable wealth that were traded as strategic capital for economic gain (Barrett 2012; Brück and Fontijn 2013). From this perspective, material differences across time or space, especially those concerning objects that were rare or foreign, can only be understood very narrowly in terms of social inequality and conflated with elites and/or displays of power (Vander Linden 2007a, 179-82; Fowler 2013, 89).

The prestige goods model reduces objects to being passive and inanimate, falsely assuming that there is a clear distinction between people and things. It also imposes a post-enlightenment conception of the self, which overlooks the fact that an individual becomes socially constituted as a person through their relationships with other people and things (Brück 2001; 2004; Fontijn 2002, 81; Fowler 2004; Brück and Fontijn 2013). It frames all social relations as being hierarchical and self-aggrandizing because it imposes a false division between economic and social value systems and privileges one over the other (Barrett and Needham 1988; Brück and Fontijn 2013). This overlooks the fact that many things and ideas would have been deemed valuable for a wide range of social reasons that are difficult to appreciate within a modern capitalist framework (Graeber 2001; Needham 2008, 326; Brück and Fontijn 2013). Many objects were treated in much the same way as humans and were probably considered as social entities in the European Bronze Age (Thomas 2002, 47; Brück and Fontijn 2013; Fowler 2013, 87). There is strong evidence to indicate that objects were exchanged through non-antagonistic gift-giving at this time (Needham 2008, 319-20). These exchanges were of fundamental importance to the creation and maintenance of social relations and personhood. To reductively view these as being only about prestige is to miss the important point that the social meaning of objects was often more important than the economic value because of the central role played by these objects in the construction of social identities and relationships (Brück 2016). This raises important questions about how objects were valued in the Chalcolithic (see Graeber 2001; Fokkens 2016, 301) that we will return to in the final chapter.

In reality, this prestige goods interpretative framework imposes modern, western liberal capitalist economic values into the past (Barrett and Needham 1988). This is evidenced by the model's emphasis on bounded competitive individuals who freely pursue their own self-interest (see Fontijn 2002, 19; Thomas 2004a; Brück 2006b, 75, 93; Brück and Fontijn 2013). It is interesting to note that these prestige-based interpretations rose to prominence in Anglophone parts of the world during an era that would ultimately be dominated by the "greed is good" political agenda of Thatcherite Reganomics. John Bintliff (1979, 73) characterised as "Conservative propaganda" the theory that all social change in European prehistory was due to the rise and subsequent actions/strategies of an upper class elite minority of ambitious political actors. Bintliff also highlighted that Colin Renfrew, one of the leading proponents of this approach (*e.g.* Renfrew 1973), stood for election as an MP for the Conservative Party and subsequently in 1991 became a Conservative Peer. Indeed, it can be suggested that the prestige goods model legitimises the status quo of the present day by creating the narrative that society was patriarchal and competitive in the past and that inequality is universal and normative.

As a result of the issues with prestige, aspects of this theory have subsequently been revised and developed. Foremost among these has been the idea that the widespread use of a similar range of Beaker pots and other associated objects reflects a broadly shared ideology or ethos (*e.g.* Shennan 1993; Strahm 1998; 2004; Vandkilde 2005; Heyd 2007; Vander Linden 2004, 41; 2015, 612; Fokkens *et al.* 2008; Garwood 2012). This is based on the idea that there seem to have been commonly shared cosmological concepts that involved using the symbolism of hunting and warfare to construct very particular and uniform categories of identity for a selection of the dead who were probably never warriors or hunters (Case 2004b, 29; Fokkens *et al.* 2008; Needham 2008; Fokkens 2012b, 123). Vander Linden (2012; 2013) has observed that like the Beaker package hypothesis from which it developed, very little explanation has been given of how or why this Beaker ethos developed or spread. This premise has a somewhat circular argument because this Beaker-associated set of beliefs is posited as both the mechanism and the motivation for the spread of Beaker-associated objects and practices.

In the last decade or so, there has been a revitalised interest in the type of questions that were originally a feature of cultural-historical approaches, such as the origins of the Beaker phenomenon and the role of human immigration in its transmission. This has occurred in tandem with the development of bioarchaeological techniques such as strontium and oxygen isotopes, as well as ancient DNA analysis, which have enabled the detection of human mobility in ways that were previously not possible. Initially, isotope analysis confirmed that some small-scale people movement, as exemplified in southern England by the Amesbury Archer and Boscombe Bowmen, certainly occurred among some of those who used Beaker pottery (*e.g.* Price *et al.* 2004; Bentley 2006; Evans *et al.* 2006; Evans and Chenery 2011). In particular, the discovery that the Amesbury Archer was born on the continent, probably in the Alpine Region, before travelling to England, played a key role in reopening old debates about Beaker migrations.

Recently, aDNA studies have contributed much new information about large-scale migration and population change during the third millennium BC, including the very significant discovery that so-called Steppe genes from central Eurasia were newly introduced to Europe during this timeframe (*e.g.* Allentoft *et al.* 2015; Haak *et al.* 2015; Mathieson *et al.* 2015). Previous research (Cassidy *et al.* 2016) had identified the presence of this same ancestry in three individuals on Rathlin Island, off the coast of Northern Ireland, by 2000 BC. A new aDNA study, however, revealed that from c. 2400 BC some Beaker burials in Germany, the Czech Republic, southern France, northern Italy and Britain have high levels of this same Steppe ancestry (Olalde *et al.* 2018). Based on this, the study claims to have identified major Beaker-associated westward migrations into north-west Europe, which is most evident in Britain, where apparently 90% of the Neolithic gene pool was replaced by Steppe genes over a few hundred years, in tandem with the introduction of Beaker-associated material culture (ibid.). As a result, debates about the implications of aDNA analysis, including the scale and nature of human mobility in the third millennium BC (*e.g.* Vander Linden 2016; Fultorf 2017) and the extent to which the spread of the Beaker complex was a population-based process, have just begun (*e.g.* Callaway 2018). This is an issue to which we will return in Chapter Ten. For now, it suffices to say that currently we have more questions than answers and that the causes of the Beaker phenomenon remain as unclear as ever.

2.12 Post-colonial Beaker-rich Ireland

At the start of this chapter, we observed that Irish accounts of the Beaker phenomenon in Ireland tend to highlight its 'unique' character, with a particular emphasis placed on its difference to Britain. An examination of Irish Beaker studies through time have shown how it has consistently been interpreted in a manner that served the needs of cultural nationalism in Ireland. The origins of this lie in Ireland's struggle during the earlier part of the twentieth century to become a nation-state separate from Britain. Many archaeologists accentuated the exceptional nature of Ireland's past to provide a clear basis for the construction of a national(ist) Irish identity with associated origin myths, thereby emphasising a glorious pre-colonial past (Cooney 1996; 1997a). In the National Museum of Ireland, the very lavish central display of Bronze Age gold objects, including Beaker-associated artefacts, emphasising that these were all made in Ireland, can be seen as an illustration of how nationalism continues to be a thematic driving force in Irish archaeology. Doubtlessly, this reflects the fact that the question of Ireland's relationship to Britain and Europe, and developments in Northern Ireland, remain as major preoccupations in Irish politics. On the other hand, some presentations of the exceptional nature of Irish prehistory were a direct reaction against longstanding Anglocentric approaches, which denied the regional diversity of prehistoric Ireland and Britain (see Cooney 1995, 272; 1997a, 29; 2000b; 2003; Brophy and Barclay 2009).

Ironically, despite Irish archaeologist's long-standing assertion of the distinctively regional character of Irish prehistory, models of understanding from other countries, especially Britain, have been consistently abstracted from their context and projected onto the Irish archaeological record. As observed by Peter Woodman (1993, 640): "In spite of the effort and interests of individuals, traditionally we have been users of the theory of others rather than the innovators of our own." Throughout the study of Beakers in Ireland, there has been a reluctance to use the Irish evidence to argue against the predominant Anglophone interpretative paradigms or to construct completely new readings of such a European phenomenon. This is particularly well-illustrated by Irish archaeologists' adoption of the prestige goods theory as a social approach to explaining the spread of Beakers, despite the lack of evidence for any elites (see Carlin and Brück 2012) and the well-known absence of the stereotypical "rich" Beaker burials from Ireland, upon which this theory was based (*e.g.* Waddell 1998, 132; Cooney and Grogan 1999, 78, 90-93; O'Brien 2004). O'Brien's hypothesis typifies Irish archaeology in following Childe (1925) and others in the conflation of technological changes with social developments and in viewing metal as a form of economic wealth that was interconnected with the transmission of Beakers (Case 1966; 1977a; Cremin Madden 1968; Apsimon 1969; Herity and Eogan 1977; Scott 1977a; 1977b; Sheridan 1983). It has since been contended that the introduction of copper metallurgy by Beaker users may have been coincidental rather than an integrated aspect of the Beaker complex. The importance of metal has been overemphasised through the imposition of modern technocentric and social evolutionary values onto the past (Hodder and Hutson 2003). In reality, it is just one of many contemporary changes in material culture that did not cause major transformations in social practices in Ireland (Carlin and Brück 2012).

Perhaps the adoption of such unsuitable interpretative models in the late 1980s and early 1990s reflects the eagerness of a new generation of Irish archaeologists to transcend traditional cultural-historical approaches and employ a more up-to-date social perspective. Despite the replacement of migration as the main mechanism for explaining cultural change, the particular models of acculturation that were employed appear to have also been influenced by nationalism. As a young nation-state finding its place in the world, the continued development of an Irish cultural identity at the end of the twentieth century involved grappling with this island's past relationship with Britain.

Ireland was still characterised as having been subject to a succession of foreign influences, but now the distinctively insular and uniquely successful ways in which past people adopted, adapted and perfected external innovations was highlighted, including the Beaker phenomenon, gold and copper metallurgy and the passage tombs constructed at Knowth and Newgrange (see Fontijn and Van Reybrouck 1999). Long-term continuities of people, place and practice throughout Irish prehistory were stressed, while developments like the adoption of Beaker pottery were characterised as changes that had less impact on insular practices than elsewhere (*e.g.* Cooney and Grogan 1999). This approach echoes a longer standing historical tradition of considering more recent arrivals to Ireland, such as the Vikings or Anglo-Normans, as having a very considerable impact before being integrated into a pre-existing Irish cultural continuum (Robb 1999). In this way, Irish archaeology delicately counterbalances the impact of external forces on the island without denying their existence, while bolstering Irish pride and creating an enduring sense of Irishness that is rooted in the deep past. This has the effect of providing a sense of timeless permanence to Irish identity while simultaneously acknowledging and minimising the impact of others, including that of British colonial power, upon Irish people and their cultural traditions in the more recent past. Readers may well form the opinion that this book also falls into this category.

Returning to the observations of Clarke (1976, 460) and Vander Linden (2013), which were highlighted at the start of this chapter, we can see that the foundational approaches to the study of the 'Beaker phenomenon' have strongly influenced subsequent thinking on the subject on this island and beyond, and continue to do so. In Ireland, a range of factors including the needs of Irish nationalism; the legacy of pre-radiocarbon archaeology; the traditional penchant for migratory explanations for all cultural changes; the false imposition of the prestige goods model; the delayed recognition of a Grooved Ware-associated Late Neolithic; and a tendency to look at Beaker-associated activities and objects in Ireland in isolation from one another, have all contributed towards a particularly impaired knowledge of the Irish version of the Beaker phenomenon. This book aims to redress all of these issues by providing a revised narrative of the Beaker complex in Ireland and its wider European context that takes full account of recent advances in both knowledge and theoretical approaches.

3

A settled past

3.1 Beaker pottery in Ireland

This study was prompted by a significant increase in the discovery of Beaker pottery in Ireland, particularly since 1997, and the questions these discoveries have raised. Based on all discoveries made before 2010, at least 21,772 sherds of Beaker pottery have been recovered from a total of 219 sites in Ireland (excluding 25 sites where Beakers have been found in a residual or uncontexted position).[1] To begin, it is essential to provide some more background to this assemblage by briefly outlining the character of this pottery, its distribution across the country and the contexts in which it occurs.

In Ireland, Beaker pottery generally occurs in a highly fragmentary condition that often impedes the identification of their original form or style (Brindley, A.L. 2004, 335; Needham 2005, 179). A high proportion of these vessels are also undecorated, meaning that decorative elements cannot be used for this purpose (Case 1993, 251; Grogan and Roche 2010, 36; Eoin Grogan, pers. comm.). While some broad observations can be made, the duration of use represented by many assemblages is unknown and therefore it has proved difficult to devise typo-chronological schemes for the development of Beaker pottery in Ireland (Brindley, A.L. 2007, 250).

Only a small number of continental-styled Beakers with classic All-Over-Ornament (AOO) or All-Over-Cord (AOC) are known from Ireland and these are thought to represent the earliest Beaker pottery introduced to this island (Case 1993, 248; Brindley, A.L. 2004, 334; Grogan and Roche 2010, 36). Instead, most of the Beakers found here exhibit a typical Bell-Beaker S-shaped profile, have generally rounded or pointed rims, and simple formal horizontally arranged zonal ornamentation (Fig. 3.1). These combine elements of the early Atlantic tradition, as well as more north-western European and British influences, to form a hybridised style that seems to have developed at an early stage (Case 1993, 265; 1995a, 14, 23; Brindley, A.L. 2004; Grogan and Roche 2010). In Ireland, the most common forms of these pots belong to Clarke's (1970) European Bell Beaker, or his Wessex/Middle Rhine types; Stages 2 and 3 in Lanting and van der Waals (1972) scheme for the development of British Beakers (Brindley, A.L. 2004, 334), as well as Case's (1993; 1995a) Style 2, which are considered to date from c. 2450-2200 BC (see Chapter Eight). Plain vessels without decoration but occasionally with cordons are also quite widespread in Ireland and are routinely found with the other decorated types (Case 1993, 251; Grogan and Roche 2010, 36).

Late-styled Beakers (Case's (1993) Style 3 and (2001) Group B2) that generally comprise inturned rims, waisted profiles and vertically arranged motifs, particularly triangles and cross-hatched lozenges, are seldom found in Ireland (Brindley, A.L. 2004, 334; Grogan and Roche 2010, 33). The examples that are known are highly comparable to Long-Necked, Short-Necked and Weak-Carinated Beakers in Britain

---

[1] All the data analysis in this book is based on information pre-dating 2010. However, very few new discoveries have been made since then.

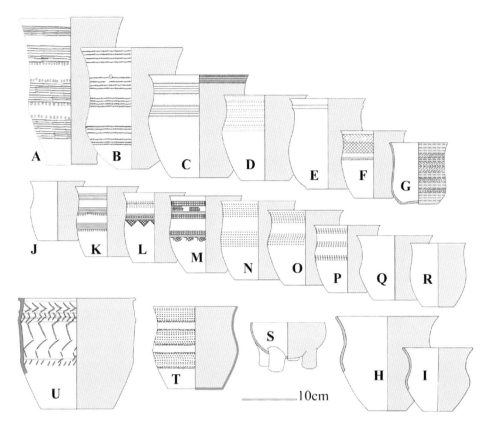

Fig. 3.1: Illustration of assorted styles of Irish Beaker pots
(A–B, H–I) Windmill, Co. Tipperary;
(C–D) Farranamanagh, Co. Tipperary;
(G) Dalkey Island;
(E, J–L) Mell, Co. Louth;
(F, M–R) Newtownbalregan 2, Co. Louth;
(S) polypod bowl from Newtownbalregan;
(T–U) Kilgobbin, Co. Dublin
(after Grogan and Roche 2010).

which post-date 2250 BC (Needham 2005; Wilkin 2009; Curtis and Wilkin 2012).

Humphrey Case (2004c, 375) observed that early Irish Beaker pottery displays a wider and richer set of international contacts than Beakers from Britain. While this may be true, it is important to note that the cross-pollination of western Maritime Beakers and eastern Corded Ware traditions seems to have occurred in continental Europe (most probably in present-day northern France), before any or many aspects of this phenomenon were introduced to Ireland and Britain (Brodie 1998, 50; Salanova 2002; Case 2004a; Needham 2005, 182).

Irish Beakers range in size from the smallest example at Ballyglass, Co. Mayo, which had a height of 9.2cm (Roche forthcoming), to much larger examples such as that at Parknahown, Co. Laois (external rim diameter: 29cm and vessel height: 29cm; O'Neill 2007) and Ballybriest, Co. Derry (external rim diameter: 36cm and vessel height: 50cm; Hurl 2001). Although most of these pots are thin-walled, thicker-walled larger Beakers are also common. A distinction has often been made between the former representing 'fine' Beakers and the latter, which are referred to as 'domestic' vessels because they are generally larger and/or coarser or more informally decorated. These often occur, however, on the same site and occasionally within the same context and both belong to a single ceramic repertoire comprising a spectrum of different-sized Beaker pots that served a range of purposes (see Grogan and Roche 2010, 36). Large bucket-shaped containers with cordons below the rim – often referred to (in an Irish context) as 'Rockbarton pots' and which may have served as storage vessels (Case 1961; Grogan and Roche 2010) – represent a form of 'domestic' Beaker that is particularly common in Ireland.

Petrological examinations have been conducted on Beaker pots from a range of sites including Newgrange (Cleary, R. 1980), Monknewtown and Knowth (Brindley, J. 1984), all in County Meath, Dalkey Island, Co. Dublin (ibid.), Ross Island; Co. Kerry (Ixer 2004), Lough Gur, Co. Limerick (Brindley, J. 1984; Cleary, R. 1984) and Ballincollig, Co. Cork (Mandal 2006). All of which have revealed that early and late types of Beakers were made using locally available materials, suggesting it was the idea behind the pots, rather than the pottery itself, which was brought to Ireland.

3.1.1 The distribution of Beaker pottery

Largely due to excavations over the last two decades, particularly during the earlier 2000s, the known extent of Beaker-associated activity in Ireland has been radically transformed. This pottery has now been found across most of the country indicating that the use of this ceramic was much more widespread than previously realised (Fig. 3.2). These newer discoveries of Beaker pottery have greatly extended its distribution into regions such as mid-Munster or south

Fig. 3.2: The distribution of Beaker pottery in Ireland.

Leinster and along the western Atlantic fringe.[2] Intensive Beaker-associated activity have now been identified at places such as the northernmost foothills of the Dublin – Wicklow Mountains, the Dundalk Bay area of County Louth or the Blackwater Valley in County Cork (Fig. 3.3). There seems to be a particularly strong concentration of Beaker sites in the eastern part of the country, which may be a reflection and continuation of historic settlement patterns as well as the location of modern developments. For example, these new discoveries have also augmented the status of the Lower Boyne Valley as the greatest concentration of Beaker sites in Ireland (Fig. 3.4). Almost half of all the Beaker pottery found in Ireland now comes from this area, most of which occurred in the artefact-rich spreads at Newgrange, Knowth and Monknewtown (see Chapter Three).

At an island-wide scale, most discoveries of this ceramic have been made in coastal or riverine locations. Movement by water may have been a major mode of travel in prehistory with rivers serving as prehistoric communication arteries (*e.g.* Condit and O'Sullivan 1999; Grogan 2005a, 27-8). This is exemplified by the numerous sites producing Beaker pottery that have been recorded along the fringes of the eastern coastal lowlands and also within the major river valleys such as the Barrow, Nore, Suir, Blackwater and Lee in the south of the country. The concentration of Beaker sites along these valleys suggests that these places were preferentially selected as locations for settlement, perhaps to facilitate interaction with other communities. The wide

---

2   Reference is made here to the four present-day provinces of Ireland because these provide a convenient way of referring to discrete regions of the island: Connacht in the west, Ulster in the North, Leinster in the east and Munster in the south. This is not to suggest that these regional divisions existed in the Chalcolithic.

A SETTLED PAST | 41

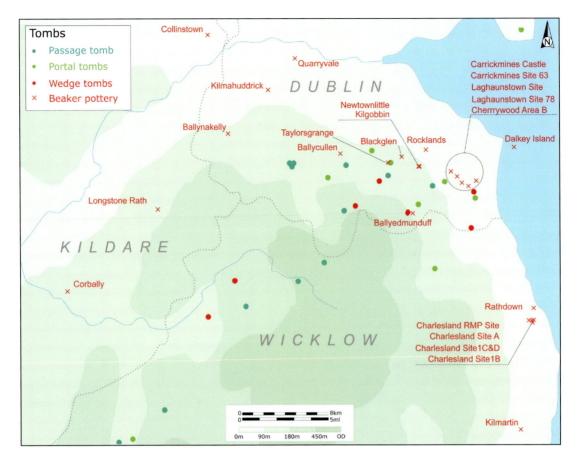

Fig. 3.3: The distribution of Beaker pottery in south Dublin and the surrounding area.

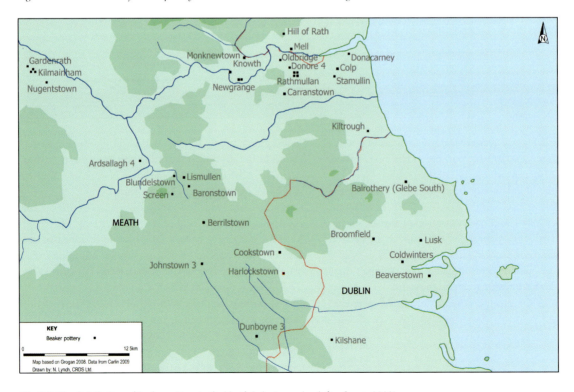

Fig. 3.4: The distribution of Beaker pottery in the North Leinster region (after Seaver 2008).

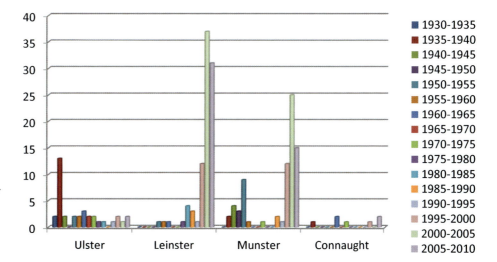

Fig. 3.5: The number of excavations in each of the four provinces of Ireland to have produced Beaker pottery over a series of five-year periods dating from 1930 to 2010.

dispersal of supra-regional items such as copper daggers, wrist-bracers and gold discs throughout Ireland indicates that movement and communication between different groups was an important activity (Fig. 1.2).

The present-day distribution of sites producing Beaker pottery in Ireland is very much an artefact of the methods and circumstances by which these sites have been found and is likely to change in the future (Becker *et al.* 2017). Most of the assemblages found over the last 30 years were uncovered during excavations conducted in advance of construction works, especially linear developments such as such as the new roads constructed under the auspices of Transport Infrastructure Ireland. For example, most Beaker-associated discoveries in Leinster (86%: 80 out of 93) and Munster (66%: 50 of 76) have been made after 1996 and exclusively because of commercial, residential and infrastructural development. The engineering requirements of these infrastructural developments means that wetland and upland topography including marshes, bogs, and steep terrain are generally avoided. This has greatly influenced the distribution patterns of Beakers we see today, which comprises clearly visible linear patterning that largely reflect the location of recent developments to service the needs of present-day population centres. Similarly, upstanding monuments and other known sub-surface archaeological sites, as well as areas that are archaeologically-rich, are also avoided because of legislative protections to ensure their preservation. This means that sites such as these are rarely excavated and Beakers appear relatively scarce in these contexts. In contrast, the most commonly excavated discoveries consist of pits lacking any above ground expression, which have been found in slightly elevated positions within low-lying locations (see below and Chapter Four). This is largely a reflection of the location of modern development activity and so, this study merely reflects where Beakers are known to have been found rather than all the places where they were deposited.

So then, we must ask if the distribution of Beaker pottery in Ireland is genuinely reflective of past patterning? Are these distributions a product of the differential survival of the archaeological record and of the different means by which this record is revealed? Despite the growth of new discoveries over the past decade, some gaps in the distribution of Beaker ceramics remain. This is most notably the case in the midlands where Cappydonnell, Co. Offaly, represents the only known site to produce this pottery. Elsewhere, Beakers have rarely been found in western Galway, the south-west coastal fringe and north-eastern Ireland, particularly County Antrim. Given these distribution patterns, it seems appropriate to question whether the paucity of this pottery from these places is merely a reflection of a lack of research or excavation in these areas or something else?

In contrast to Munster or Leinster, the majority of Beaker sites from Ulster are not recent discoveries, with only 13% (5 out of 36) found since 1996 (Fig. 3.5). Half of all those Beaker sites were found between 1930 and 1945 during research excavations of upland megaliths by a small group of archaeologists based in Northern Ireland (see Chapter Two). Owing to their concentrated efforts, Beaker sites in Northern Ireland predominantly consist of monuments, particularly wedge tombs located on elevated positions within Counties Tyrone and Derry. Comparatively few examples of this ceramic have been found in sub-surface features on lower terrain.

Given that the north-east of Ireland has a long tradition of settlement, as revealed by excavations at places such as Donegore Hill in County Antrim (Mallory *et al.* 2011) and Armalughey in County Tyrone (Carlin 2016), the apparent paucity of Beaker discoveries in this area seems curious. Significant assemblages of early and middle Neolithic pottery have long been known from this region (see Case 1961; Sheridan 1995; Grogan and Roche 2010) and a few sites have produced Late Neolithic Grooved

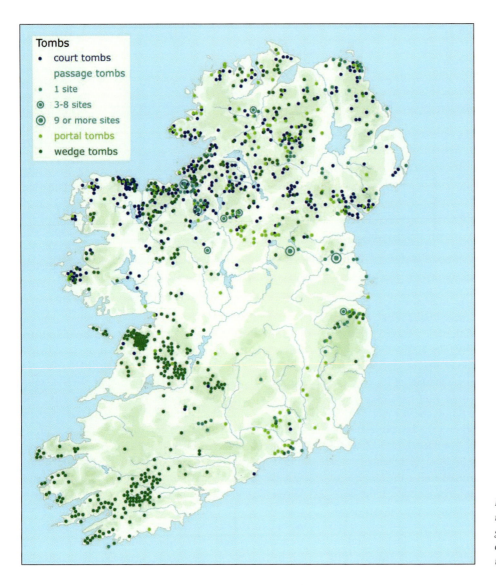

Fig. 3.6: The location of all megaliths in Ireland. A large gap in their distribution occurs in the midlands where these tombs are largely absent.

Ware (see Brindley, A.L. 1999; Eogan and Roche 1999). Yet unlike elsewhere in Ireland, where most locales with a history of Neolithic settlement have produced Beaker pottery, this is not the case in this area (see Chapter Three; Carlin 2005a). A large concentration of Food Vessel burials occurs in the north-east (Waddell 1990, 37; Grogan and Roche 2010, 41, illus. 8), however, and an exceptionally large number of wrist-bracers have also been found there. This certainly suggests that this region was inhabited, in the latter half of the third millennium BC, by people highly aware of the Beaker tradition and so the paucity of Beakers in the north-east is highly anomalous. This apparent 'gap' primarily reflects the limitations of my own social-archaeological network which is based around my work in the Republic of Ireland. I am less familiar with the archaeologists working in Northern Ireland; therefore, my access to unpublished reports from that jurisdiction is not comparable and it is likely that more Beakers have been found during the last 20 years, particularly in Counties Antrim and Down.

The absence of Beakers from the south-western coastal fringe is also notable and perhaps surprising given the presence of Beaker pottery at Ireland's earliest copper mine at Ross Island, Co. Kerry, and the dense concentration of wedge tombs occurring in some parts of this region. There has, however, been relatively little investigation of the large numbers of wedge tombs in the south-west of the country, apart from a few examples such as Toormore and Altar, Co. Cork that did not produce any Beaker pottery (Herity 1966; 1967; 1970; O'Brien 1999). The absence of evidence for any Chalcolithic activity from these excavations suggests that some of these wedge tombs were built after this pottery's use had ceased c. 2050 BC (see Section 5.2 and Chapter Eight). Indeed, there has been relatively little archaeological excavations of any kind in the extreme south-west of the country. With its coastal uplands and rugged terrain, this area has not been subject to large-scale development projects. This is probably the main reason for the current lack of Beaker pottery from this region and future investigations will probably result in more Beaker discoveries.

Unlike north-eastern Ireland, the archaeology of the midlands has received very little scholarly attention. Apart from Counties Meath (Moore, M. 1987) and Laois (Sweetman *et al.* 1995), the archaeological inventories for the counties in the central lowlands remain unpublished. Although some aspects of this area's archaeological record have been examined as part of wider studies (*e.g.* Cooney 1987; Mount 1997a), little or no synthesis has been conducted and overall understanding remains poor. This might suggest that the paucity of Beaker pottery from the midlands is due to a lack of investigation. In recent times, however, several large-scale archaeological examinations have been conducted prior to the construction of residential developments and linear infrastructure including the M4 motorway (Carlin *et al.* 2008), the M6 motorway (Anon 2006), and the gas pipeline to the west (Grogan *et al.* 2007). Despite these excavations, very few Beakers or other earlier prehistoric ceramics have been found and megaliths are also largely absent (Fig. 3.6). Most of this region appears to have been largely devoid of evidence for human activity in the Neolithic, particularly the wetter poorly-drained portions with heavy soils, which may not have been best suited to early prehistoric agricultural technology (Grogan *et al.* 2007, 137-9; O'Carroll and Mitchell 2013).

Thus, it seems that the central lowlands remained sparsely populated until after the start of the Early Bronze Age, when a major expansion of settlement into lower-lying areas began (Cooney and Grogan 1999, 105). In some locales, particularly in County Westmeath, significant concentrations of burials were placed, c. 2100 BC, along the broad moraine ridges that criss-cross the otherwise low-lying landscape (see Cooney 1987, 131; Waddell 1990). For much of the midlands, however, evidence for human activity increased slightly, but remained quite limited during the third millennium BC, apart from some trackways across boglands and some pyrolithic/water-boiling sites known as *fulachtaí fia* (O'Carroll and Mitchell 2013; see Chapter Seven). Present evidence seems to indicate that the paucity of Beakers from the midlands is a genuine reflection of the low level of inhabitation of this landscape at that time, but our knowledge of settlement in this region is too poor to allow for any certainty. This is particularly so as it is difficult to reconcile this idea of very low settlement density with the concentrations of other Beaker-related objects occurring in various parts of the midlands, including lunulae, copper daggers and V-perforated buttons, indicating that this area was certainly not devoid of human activity (Fig. 1.1). This is reinforced when one also considers the concentrations of copper axes and halberds from this region, although it may be significant to note that these mainly occur as single finds and that there is a lack of copper hoards in the region (O'Flaherty 1995, 25-7; Becker 2006, 91-2).

The discrete and selective spatial patterning that we see in this region is at least partially reflecting the specific depositional practices of the area. This is an issue that we return to towards the end of Chapter Nine, but this patterning may also be reflective of the fact that people seem to have gone to 'natural places' to deposit particular kinds of objects (as discussed in Chapter Seven), particularly bogs that were located away from areas that were intensively occupied. This raises questions that require further research about whether people travelled from other areas to conduct or witness depositional activities in the midlands. One potential way forward would be to undertake comparative case-studies that integrate the available paleoenvironmental evidence with the settlement, burial and depositional record within specific locales, so that they can be considered within their landscape context as exemplified by Eoin Grogan's North Munster project (*e.g.* Grogan 2005a and b).

3.1.2 A context for Beakers

Now that we have seen what this pottery was typically like and where it was found across the island, let us turn to the types of contexts from which it has been recovered. Settlements (mainly comprising pits, spreads and postholes) appear to represent the most common type of site (79% of 219) to produce this pottery; Beakers represented by 14,541 sherds (67% of 21,772) from at least 1099 vessels (88% of 1245) have been discovered within this context (Fig. 3.7). Funerary contexts represent the second most common type of site (17% of 219), however, this category has merely produced 3% of all Beaker sherds and 8% of all Beaker vessels. Only a small share (1%) of all the Beaker sites in Ireland is formed by the category of 'natural places' and this context has produced no more than a few sherds from five vessels (less than 1% of all Beaker pottery), all of which came from caves (see Chapter Seven). Beakers have only rarely been discovered on what can be regarded as ceremonial sites (3%), such as those comprising deposits at Late Neolithic timber circles, but the four recorded incidents of this have produced 6534 sherds, which represents a rather sizeable proportion (30%) of all this pottery in Ireland.

The Beaker-associated settlement sites generally comprise deposits of occupational debris within features such as pits, spreads, postholes and stakeholes. It is rare to find stakeholes or postholes containing Beakers without an associated contemporaneous pit or spread that also contains Beaker pottery (see Section 3.3). At most of these sites, pits are the only definite Beaker-associated feature, which makes untangling whether other features should be considered contemporary challenging. This is especially so because they typically occur (72%) on multi-period sites that are dominated by Early Neolithic and/or later Bronze

Age activity that often includes the remains of houses from these periods. This has often affected the way the Beaker-related features have been investigated because the few pits containing Beaker-pottery can appear to represent a minor component of the archaeological record. Such features have not traditionally received much attention from archaeologists and in the context of excavations, where time and money are always a limited resource, these pits have often been deemed less worthy of being radiocarbon dated compared to the remains of an Early Neolithic or Late Bronze Age house.

It has been observed that Beaker settlement sites are generally located in slightly undulating topography on a gentle south or south-east-facing slope between 6m and 120m above sea level and within 1km of a river (Carlin 2005a). Although some of these sites are in low-lying locations, mostly they occur in locally elevated positions. A clear preference was observed for free-draining and fertile soils such as Brown Earths and Grey Brown Podzolics that could be used for either pasture or tillage (Carlin 2005b). These locations would certainly have been suitable for occupation, as is emphasised by their regular occurrence on sites that include both Early Neolithic and Late Bronze Age houses. Yet does this mean that the pits containing Beaker pottery, along with associated postholes and stakeholes, directly represent settlement activity? These issues are explored in detail here and in Chapter Four, which studies the pits and spreads in much more detail.

That the majority of Beaker pottery seems to occur in what have been regarded as settlement or domestic contexts in Ireland is initially unsurprising. After all, the best-known Beaker-associated activity in Ireland has been found in what has usually been interpreted as a settlement context outside the passage tombs at Newgrange (O'Kelly *et al.* 1983) and Knowth (Eogan, G. 1984; Eogan and Roche 1997). These and other putative Beaker habitations from a few other landmark excavations have dominated current understandings of the Irish Beaker phenomenon (see Chapter Two). They have contributed significantly towards the view that unlike anywhere else, Beaker pottery on this island predominantly occurs in what have been considered habitations and rarely in funerary contexts (Clarke 1976, 472-3; Burgess 1979, 213; Case 1995a, 19; Needham 1996, 128; Brindley, A.L. 2007, 250).

Yet, as we saw in the previous chapter, our knowledge of the third millennium BC, including the dating of various artefact and site-types, has changed radically since these earlier excavations were conducted. Many of the characterisations of the sites and features containing Beakers have been based upon a false dichotomy between settlement and ceremonial, as well as ritual and 'domestic' activities (see Brück 1999a; Bradley 2005a). This means that the nature of the Beaker-associated activity at many of these putative settlement sites is less clear-cut than often assumed and so it is necessary to reconsider the interpretation of these Beaker-associate deposits.

To better understand the processes and activities associated with the creation of these deposits, and to elucidate what they can inform us about past settlement practices, a detailed exploration is required of the deposition of Beaker-associated artefacts in structural contexts such as postholes, stakeholes and slot trenches. This includes an appraisal of the essential qualities of each of these features, such as their quantity, shape, size, and their relationship to other Beaker-associated features occurring on the same sites. The range, frequency and manner of deposition of Beaker-related materials, as well as the form, quantity and condition of these artefacts are also examined. This includes an assessment of the total number of Beaker pots and sherds deposited in each context. Several structures in Ireland have been claimed to represent Beaker houses and so these are reviewed in detail here as part of this examination.

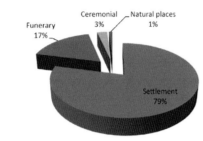

number of sites

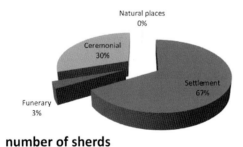

number of sherds

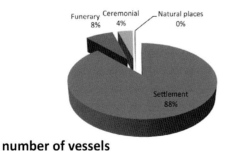

number of vessels

Fig. 3.7: The percentage of sites of different categories to produce Beaker pottery, as well as the percentage of Beaker sherds and vessels found in each category.

3.2 Infamous Beaker 'settlements'

It is appropriate to start by reconsidering some of the more well-known Beaker 'settlement' sites in light of subsequent advances in knowledge, as highlighted in Chapter Two. This includes the putative Beaker settlements at Knockadoon, Lough Gur, Co. Limerick (Ó Ríordáin, S.P. 1954; Grogan and Eogan 1987) and three other sites, all of which occur within the *Brú na Bóinne* monument complex in County Meath. These comprise the passage tombs at Newgrange (O'Kelly *et al.* 1983; Sweetman 1985; 1987) and Knowth (Eogan, G. 1984; Eogan and Roche 1997; Roche and Eogan 2001), as well as inside a large earthen circular monument known as an embanked enclosure or henge at Monknewtown (Sweetman 1971; 1976). As we will see, the evidence for Beaker-associated settlement was overstated and many features on these sites were wrongly considered to represent activity associated with this pottery's use.

3.2.1 Lough Gur

At Lough Gur, Seán P. Ó Ríordáin discovered Beaker pottery from as many as 14 different sites, some of which were incorrectly thought to represent Beaker-associated settlement structures. These include Sites C and D (Ó Ríordáin, S.P. 1954), and the enclosed occupations on the Knockadoon peninsula such as Circles J, K, L and Site 10 (Grogan and Eogan 1987; see Cleary 2003, fig. 2 for a map of these sites). As detailed in Chapter Two, a coarse flat-based form of pottery discovered during excavations at Knockadoon – termed "Lough Gur Class II" – was considered by S.P. Ó Ríordáin (1954, 451-4, fig. 55) to represent an indigenous response to Beaker pottery and was used alongside the European-styled ceramic at the end of the Neolithic, both of which were considered to represent the latest pottery present at Knockadoon (*e.g.* de Paor 1961, 659; Cremin Madden 1968, 15; Harbison 1973, 95). Over time, it has gradually been recognised that 'Lough Gur Class II' is a form of Middle or Late Bronze Age pottery (Kelly, E.P. 1978; Cleary, R. 1993; 1995; Roche 2004; Grogan 2005a, 318) and that many of the features thought to be of Neolithic or Beaker date at Lough Gur (*e.g.* Simpson 1971; Gibson, A. 1987) represent later Bronze Age activity (Cleary, R. 2003; Grogan 2005b, 52-62; Cooney 2007, 220). A small amount of this assemblage has also been identified as Grooved Ware (Roche 1995; Grogan 2005b, 88).

At Site C, a small assemblage of Beaker pottery (Ó Ríordáin, S.P. 1954, 340) was found in a deposit along with two barbed and tanged arrowheads, as well as Early and Middle Neolithic ceramics, Food Vessels and Class II pottery (ibid., 321-41; Grogan and Eogan 1987, 336-462; Grogan 2005b, 50-53). This layer was thought to have formed during a series of continuous occupations dating from the Early Neolithic to the Beaker period (Ó Ríordáin, S.P. 1954, 342); however, the presence of the Late Bronze Age Class II pottery at the lowest levels of this deposit (ibid., 343) indicates that this represents chronologically mixed strata and very few conclusions can reasonably be drawn, other than that the Beakers are in a residual position. Three circular post-built structures were identified from a scatter of postholes, pits, hearths and other features found during the excavation (Ó Ríordáin, S.P. 1954). Two of the buildings (Houses I and III) were considered by Alex Gibson (1987) to represent Beaker dwellings, but these have generally been ascribed a Neolithic date (Grogan 1989; 1996; 2002; 2005b; Cleary 2003; Cooney 2007, 222; Smyth 2007; 2010; 2014). There is, however, absolutely no evidence available from the excavation to confirm any of these hypotheses. Due to the thin soil cover, the stratigraphic relationships between the deposit and the features discovered on this site are unclear (Kelly, E.P. 1978) and it is unlikely that the coherent structural remains represent Beaker-associated activity (see Section 3.4).

At Site D, 2000 Beaker sherds were found mainly within a deposit of habitation debris containing an admixture of different pot types including Early Neolithic and later Bronze Age 'Class II' ceramics, as well as a Lough Ravel copper axe and a small undecorated gold disc (Ó Ríordáin, S.P. 1954, 410-11; Eogan, G. 1994, 19). This deposit, which was considered Beaker in date, was sealed under a terrace wall that S.P. Ó Ríordáin (1954, 390) also dated to the Beaker period. This wall can, however, be directly paralleled by later Bronze Age walls excavated by Rose Cleary (2003, 141) at a neighbouring site on the Knockadoon peninsula, it therefore seems much more likely to have been constructed during that period. This is supported by the presence of chronologically earlier and later pottery, including later Bronze Age ceramics alongside the Beaker pottery. This also indicates that the Beaker materials under this wall were in a disturbed context. As such, it is not possible to ascertain the nature of the Beaker-associated activity in this location. Certainly, the accepted view that the copper axe and gold disc were deposited with habitation debris (*e.g.* Case 1993, 241) needs to be reconsidered. While it has been argued that structures II and III at Site D are Beaker houses (Simpson 1971; Gibson, A. 1987, 7), there is little evidence to support the attribution of a Beaker date. These buildings have traditionally been regarded as earlier Neolithic constructions (Ó Ríordáin, S.P. 1954, 390; Grogan and Eogan 1987, 481; Grogan 2002; 2005b; Smyth 2007; 2010) because of S.P. Ó Ríordáin's (1954, 390) observation that the deposit immediately overlying these structures were almost exclusively associated with Early and Middle Neolithic pottery.

At Site 10, 570 sherds from 29 Beakers, as well as arrowheads of the hollow-based and barbed and tanged variety, were discovered within an extensive 'habitation layer' containing Early Neolithic pottery, Vases of the Food Vessel tradition and Cordoned Urns (Grogan and Eogan 1987, 453-4; Grogan 2005b, 51). An enclosure wall overlay this chronologically mixed deposit, but based on morphological comparisons as well as the presence of Class II pottery, it was probably built during the later Bronze Age (Cleary, R. 2003, 147). It is difficult to ascertain what artefacts on this site are residual and so very few conclusions can be drawn about the character of Beaker deposition there.

Excavation of the enclosed settlement site at Circle L resulted in the discovery of two distinct stratigraphic phases of activity. The earlier of these was considered to date to the Neolithic, while the later was regarded as Beaker-associated (Grogan and Eogan 1987, see below). Over 1110 Beaker sherds from 38 Beaker vessels, as well as Early Neolithic, Middle Neolithic and Class II (later Bronze Age) pottery were recovered, but the contextual details for some of these is vague, due to the poor preservation of the excavation archive (Grogan and Eogan 1987, 391). The stratigraphically later activity comprised a central structure within a walled enclosure (Grogan and Eogan 1987, 418-20), whose double-kerbed construction was also very similar to the later Bronze Age enclosure walls excavated by R. Cleary (2003).

The central building within the enclosure apparently displayed two stages of construction. The first consisted of a layer of habitation soil that was defined on one side by a line of postholes. The second construction stage comprised an overlying stone-built oval structure which is described as producing a predominantly Beaker assemblage (Grogan and Eogan 1987, 482), though smaller quantities of Earlier Neolithic and later Bronze Age (Class II) pottery were also present. The exact context of these finds remains unstated, but is likely to have been an artefact-rich deposit that was found overlying or within the house (ibid., 429). In this regard, Grogan and Eogan (1987, 437) clearly state that "it was impossible to establish any precise sequence for the pottery because of the disturbance caused by the prolonged and intensive occupation on the site". Nevertheless, the stone-built oval structure was regarded as a Beaker house for several reasons (Grogan and Eogan 1987, 413-5; Grogan 1989, 79). Of all the pottery associated with this building, Beaker pottery was considered to represent the youngest type; there was also more of this ceramic than any other and it occurred at a higher level in the deposits associated with the house (Grogan and Eogan 1987, 437, 482).

It is difficult to maintain this interpretation now that we know the pottery from the stone-built structure and the rest of the site comprised an admixture from chronologically disparate periods rather than short-lived continuous activity. The apparent association of Late Bronze Age pottery with the house suggests that it was built at that time. Rose Cleary (2003, 146) has highlighted the very strong similarities between this oval structure and the stone-built oval example (House I) from Site D (Ó Ríordáin, S.P. 1954, pl. XLI) to which S.P. Ó Ríordáin (ibid., 146) ascribed a Middle Bronze Age date due to its association with clay and stone moulds. She has also remarked on the parallels between the enclosing walls at these and other later Bronze Age sites at Lough Gur. In light of this, R. Cleary (2003, 146) suggests that the later house and enclosing wall are later Bronze Age constructions that disturbed a previously unenclosed habitation site dating to the Neolithic and Beaker periods.

The earliest phase of activity at Circle L was thought to comprise a large number of postholes, hearths and pits that were interpreted as defining at least three circular structures (Grogan and Eogan 1987, 437). These features were overlain by an occupational layer that the wall of the enclosure had been constructed over (ibid., 413). Ceramic finds from this deposit, and the features associated with it, included Early and Middle Neolithic, Beaker and later Bronze Age pottery, then known as Lough Gur Class II ware (ibid., 437). Although the exact contextual relationships are unknown, the structural remains were deemed to be at the same horizon as the Earlier Neolithic material and have been widely regarded as Neolithic houses (Grogan 2002, 521; 2005b, 50; Cooney 2007, 222; Smyth 2007). The deposit was considered to be contemporary with the layer representing the first phase of the central structure, mentioned above (Grogan and Eogan 1987, 415).

The Beaker pottery was interpreted as intrusive because it was thought to post-date the other ceramics (Grogan and Eogan 1987, 437). An assumption seems to have been made that if the stratigraphically later phase of activity on the site was Beaker-associated, then logically, these earlier features must represent pre-Beaker, Neolithic settlement. However, the presence of pottery dating from between 4000-1000 BC suggests that the older artefacts are likely to have been found in residual contexts. Indeed, based upon what we now know from the other sites in the locale, the earlier Neolithic and Beaker materials were probably displaced from their original contexts during later Bronze Age activity. This is supported by the fact that different sherds from the same Beaker vessels were repeatedly found in each of the different layers on this site (ibid., 407-8, 415, 423, 429). Apart from the Beaker pottery in chronologically mixed deposits, there is no credible or discernible evidence for Beaker-associated settlement activity on this site.

Outside the enclosure known as Circle K, an earlier Neolithic structure (House 1) was found to be sealed by a layer of habitation debris containing most of the Beaker pottery (394 sherds) from the site (see Grogan and Eogan 1987, 336-462). This deposit was subsequently disturbed by the construction of the enclosure, which almost certainly occurred in the later Bronze Age, as indicated by the exclusive presence of Class II pottery within the infill of the enclosing wall (see Cleary, R. 2003, 146).

In summary, most of the Beaker-related objects found at Lough Gur were either in a residual or disturbed position and very few conclusions can be reached about their original context. These artefacts predominantly occurred in quite large quantities within above ground deposits, thereby suggesting that they had originally been deposited in midden-like surface-accumulations that were subsequently disturbed by later Bronze Age activity. Ironically, the construction of the later Bronze Age buildings and enclosures that disturbed so many Beaker artefacts was also responsible for their survival in these locations. These upstanding remains fortuitously provided protection to these surface deposits from the threats posed by both the natural elements and modern-day agricultural practices such as plough-damage. We will return to consider these kind of midden-like surface-accumulations in more detail in Chapter Four.

3.2.2 Newgrange

Excavation of 40% of the periphery of the principal passage tomb at Newgrange revealed Beaker-associated activity which it has been argued, includes evidence for metalworking, spreads of occupation debris and up to 18 possible structures associated with stone hearths (Fig. 3.8); (O'Kelly *et al.* 1983; Cooney and Grogan 1999, 80). Numerous factors relating to the excavation at Newgrange impede our ability to discern the Beaker-associated element on this multi-period site. Notably, the absence of detailed contextual information (for the artefacts found outside the tomb) from published accounts of the site makes it difficult to argue for associations between artefacts and features. The fabric-driven methods of classification originally employed in the analysis of the ceramics at Newgrange (Cleary, R. 1980), which treated the pottery as a single contemporaneous assemblage, also hinders the identification of where each pottery type was found (Brindley, A.L. 1999, 33). While R. Cleary (1983, 100) did identify some Grooved Ware from the excavation, other Grooved Ware was originally considered as Beaker, including 'undecorated Beaker-associated bowls' and 'rusticated Beaker ware' (Cleary, R. 1980, groups 20, 21b, 25a, 27-9; Roche 1995).

Removal of the so-called 'cairn slippage' from the front of the main passage at Newgrange revealed a chronologically mixed deposit described as the 'Beaker layers' (O'Kelly *et al.* 1983, 27-9, fig. 9). This primarily occurred in five main concentrations focused upon the entrance to the tomb (Figs. 3.9-3.10). These 'Beaker layers' overlay (and extended outwards beyond) an extensive layer of quartz and granite stones that flanked the tomb's south-eastern perimeter for 50m either side of the tomb's entrance (Cleary, R. 1983, 58-117). This quartz and granite stone layer had originally been interpreted as slippage from the mound's façade that occurred long after the monument had been built (O'Kelly 1982). It has subsequently been convincingly argued that this quartz-granite layer represents the remains of a platform deliberately constructed during the use-life of the tomb (Cooney 2006; Eriksen 2006; 2008; Stout and Stout 2008; Carlin 2017, but see Hensey and Shee Twohig 2017 for a contrasting perspective).

Investigation of these layers produced a mixture of Middle Neolithic Impressed Ware, over 2000 sherds of Late Neolithic Grooved Ware, and other materials dating to as late as the Iron Age, including a large faunal assemblage of unknown date but which included Iron Age horse bones (van Wijngaarden-Bakker 1974; 1986; Cleary, R. 1983, 58-117; Mount 1994; Bendrey *et al.* 2013; Ó Néill 2013; Carlin 2017). Mixed among these were 3600 Beaker sherds from 200 vessels including two polypod bowls as well as many small convex scrapers (Lehane 1983, 131-3), three barbed and tanged arrowheads (one Conygar and two Sutton B types; Lehane 1983, fig 64, nos E56: 781, 675 and 1025), two serpentine disc beads and a Killaha-type bronze flat axe (O'Kelly and Shell 1979).

The extent to which these 'Beaker layers' represent a chronologically insecure deposit formed over millennia is reinforced by the occurrence of the 'Beaker layers' both under and over a bank of yellow boulder clay (see O'Kelly *et al.* 1983, figs. 9, 11, 13) that inscribes the mound to the west of the tomb entrance and sealed some of the hearths (ibid., 27-9, 35-9, fig. 9; Cooney 2006, 705; Carlin 2017). O'Kelly *et al.* (1983, 27-9; 39) suggested that the bank may have been specially created to cover earlier features, such as hearths, and regarded its construction as contemporary with Beaker activity precisely because of this stratigraphic relationship. The bank has subsequently been interpreted as part of a sequence of deliberate constructions that were built to enclose the tomb and has been compared to the banks of nearby embanked enclosures (Mount 1994, 435; Cooney 2007, 705-6; Carlin 2017). The exact date and function of this bank, however, remain unknown. Nevertheless, it remains unlikely that Beaker-associated settlement debris could occur both below and above such a monument. Overall, the dating and interpretation of these deposits at Newgrange are problematic and it is particularly difficult to disentangle the Grooved Ware activity from that associated with Beakers.

Although the large faunal assemblage from Newgrange clearly does not represent a single chronological horizon, patterning indicative of ceremonial feasting has been identified including a very large amount of pig bone, whose calorific content had not been fully exploited (Mount 1994). Cattle bones were also present and the age

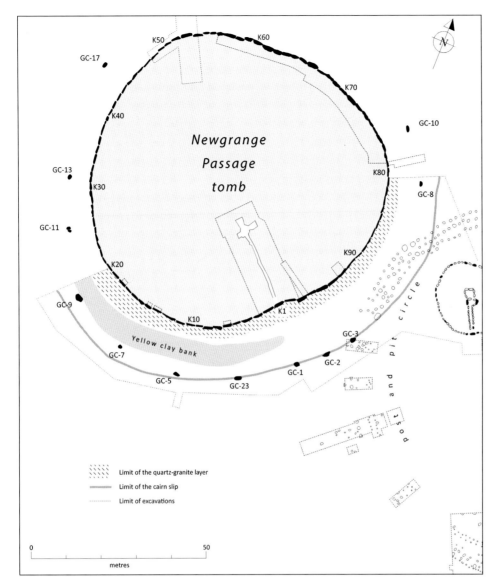

Fig. 3.8: Plan of Newgrange passage tomb and adjacent features showing the location of the 'cairn slippage' which sealed the chronologically mixed deposit described as the 'Beaker layers' which overlay the quartz and granite layer (after Lynch 2015, fig. 2).

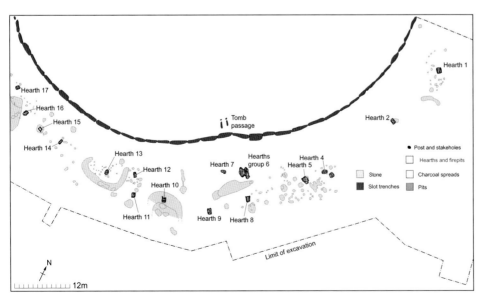

Fig. 3.9: The stone hearths and associated features in the central area at the entrance to the passage tomb at Newgrange (after Smyth 2014, fig. 5.15; courtesy of Jessica Smyth).

structure of these suggested that fattened mature animals had been specially selected and brought to the site. Further investigation including the radiocarbon dating of these bones is, however, necessary to ascertain whether this reflects Neolithic, Bronze Age or Iron Age activity.

The discovery of the Killaha-type bronze flat axe in these 'Beaker layers', near a putative metalworking area that produced hammer-stones, a polishing stone and a possible metalworker's anvil, was regarded as evidence for Beaker-associated metalworking in a 'domestic' setting (O'Kelly and Shell 1979; Stout and Stout 2008, 91). However, the axe type, is understood to date from 2200-2000 BC, which post-dates the currency of Beakers at Newgrange and furthers the argument that the strength of association between these various artefacts is very weak and that the chronological integrity of these layers is questionable (Needham 1996, 130; 2000, 37-8; see Chapter Eight).

The rectangular stone-lined formal hearths and the features that were spatially associated with them and the so-called 'Beaker layers' were widely regarded as the remains of Beaker-associated circular structures, representing dwellings some 5-6m in diameter, comprising arcs of post or stakeholes and lengths of possible foundation trench (Grogan 1996, 44; 2004a, fig. 9.3; Cooney and Grogan 1999, 80-1). This interpretation seems to have been based upon the presence of Beaker pottery within some of the hearths – such as Hearth No. 1 in the 'Eastern Area' (O'Kelly et al. 1983, 15) – as well as in the pits that surrounded them, alongside the mistaken belief that the overlying 'Beaker layers' represented a single phase of Beaker-associated activity. While Beaker pottery was present in some hearths, Grooved Ware was present in others. Furthermore, a similar rectangular stone hearth was present at the centre of the Grooved Ware-associated timber structure at Slieve Breagh in County Meath (de Paor and Ó h-Eochaidhe 1956). These are comparable to the distinctive hearths found within Orcadian dwellings (Richards 2005; Smyth 2010, 25-27) and suggest that at least some of these features represent Late Neolithic activity (see Roche and Eogan 2001, 132; Carlin and Brück 2012; Carlin 2017). Given that many of the features at Newgrange represent a palimpsest and that the only consistent component of each putative structure was a hearth, it remains unclear whether the other features in the vicinity were genuinely contemporary and if they really did represent the remains of buildings.

While there is no doubt that much Beaker-associated artefacts were deposited outside the entrance to the passage tomb at Newgrange, many of the features that were previously attributed a Chalcolithic date represent earlier or later activity. Although these have traditionally been interpreted as 'domestic' in character (*e.g.* Stout and Stout 2008, 91), it is extremely difficult to identify distinct 'domestic' and ritual spheres during this period (Brück 1999a) and it is no longer clear that the Beaker-associated deposits represent the remains of a settlement at that location. The multi-period nature of the deposits outside the tomb, as well as the construction of the large Grooved Ware-associated timber circle immediately to the south-east and the possible timber circle containing Beaker pottery to the west (Fig. 3.8), all suggest that the exterior of this Neolithic monument remained a focus for ceremonial activities during the third millennium BC and beyond (see Carlin 2017). It may be best to view the Beaker-associated activity within that context and these issues are returned to in Chapters Four, Five and Six.

3.2.3 Knowth

At the passage tomb cemetery at Knowth, very small quantities of Beaker pottery were found in the passages of Tombs 2 and 15 (Eogan, G. 1984, 308-12; see Chapter Five) and several pits, but much larger amounts were discovered within five large surface deposits of culturally-rich occupational debris – labelled as Concentrations A-E – described as "spreads of dark earth that had developed from occupation refuse" (Roche and Eogan 2001, 131). Each was at least 15m long and 10m wide and occurred in widely

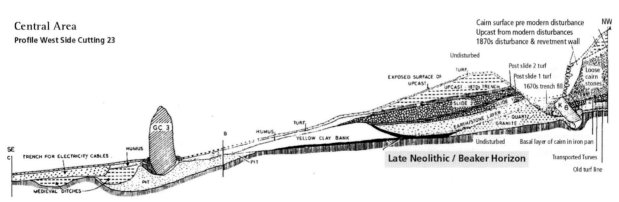

Fig. 3.10: Section showing 'cairn slippage' overlying the 'Beaker layers' at Newgrange (after O'Kelly et al. 1983, fig. 9).

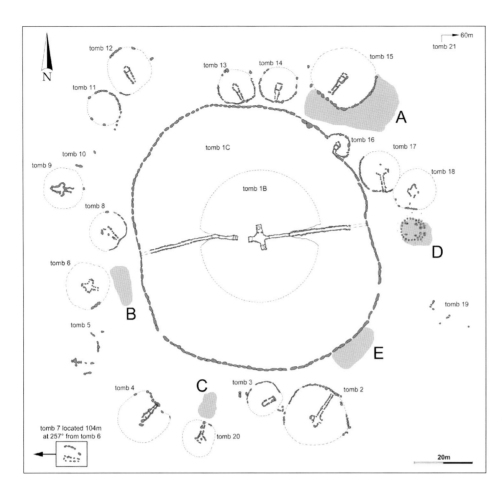

Fig. 3.11: The five large Beaker associated deposits (Concentrations A-E) found at the passage tomb complex at Knowth, Co. Meath (Drawn by Conor McDermott, after Eogan and Cleary 2017).

separated areas surrounding the perimeter of the large centrally-located passage tomb known as the main mound or Tomb 1 (Fig. 3.11). These spreads produced a total of 4307 sherds from 293 Beakers, as well as 1500 lithics comprising debitage and 198 modified tools, including 160 scrapers and three (two barbed and tanged and one hollow-based) arrowheads (Eogan, G. 1984, 286-304; Eogan and Roche 1997, 223-60).[3] These deposits display much greater chronological integrity than at Newgrange; Concentrations' B, D and E only produced Beaker-associated materials, while Grooved Ware also occurred within Concentrations A and C (Eogan, G. 1984, 245-86; Eogan and Roche 1997, 202-7; Roche and Eogan 2001, 129-37).

These Beaker-rich layers have been interpreted as the product of 'domestic' activity (Eogan, G. 1984, 313; Roche and Eogan 2001, 131) that may represent "the remains of homesteads" (Eogan and Roche 1997, 256). The evidence for this is, however, highly ambiguous. While the deposits certainly relate to occupation, there is little to indicate what the nature of this was or whether the activity from which this debris was original-

ly generated occurred at Knowth or elsewhere. This issue is explored in Chapter Four.

Each of the deposits of culturally-rich occupational debris was situated at or near the entrance to a passage tomb (Fig. 3.11). Concentration A surrounded the entrance and much of the southern and western perimeter of Tomb 15; Concentration B was located directly outside the entrance to Tomb 6; Concentration C was situated directly opposite the entrance to Tomb 20; and Concentration D overlay the Grooved Ware-associated timber circle opposite the entrance to the eastern passage of Tomb 1 (Roche 1995, 39; Roche and Eogan 2001, 137). Concentration E occurs opposite the entrance to Tomb 2 (but at a distance of 8m) and overlay a circular stone setting situated beside the kerbstones (Nos 27-28) of the main mound (Eogan and Cleary 2017, 240-43). These kerbstones are decorated with megalithic art featuring two 'eye-like motifs' whose gaze is thought to be directed towards another ornately decorated kerbstone (K52) at the rear of the Newgrange passage tomb (ibid., 242).

Similar to Newgrange, the locations of these deposits were deliberately chosen to continue to refer to particular aspects of the monuments, notably their entrances and exteriors that had been emphasised through architecture

---

3 Recently, an additional 66 lithics were analysed from these spreads, but these have not been included here (Little and Warren 2017).

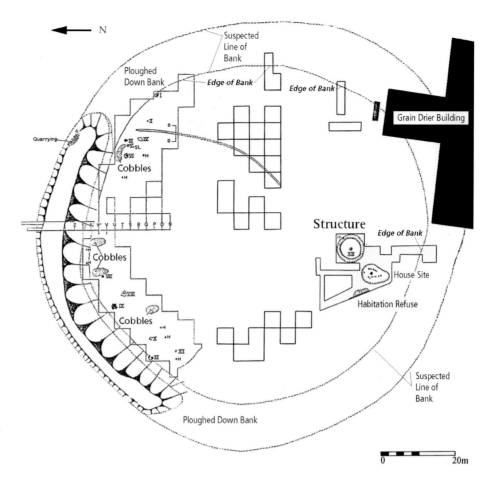

Fig. 3.12: The partially excavated embanked enclosure at Monknewtown, Co. Meath (after Sweetman 1976).

and depositional activity since these monuments were first built (Carlin 2017; see Chapter Ten). Given that the placement of Beaker-associated materials was almost exclusively and consistently focused on these locations within the entire complex, this activity certainly seems to have been commemorative of the past events conducted there. The relationship of these large piles of occupational debris to *in situ* settlement is vague, however, and it is plausible that these represent the remains of communal gatherings and ceremonial undertakings, including feasting that involved the collection and deposition of settlement material (see Chapters Four, Five and Six).

3.2.4 Monknewtown

The partial excavation of the embanked enclosure at Monknewtown, ahead of agricultural development, resulted in the recovery of evidence for multi-period activity including 5000 Beaker sherds, as well as Early Neolithic, Middle Neolithic and Middle Bronze Age pottery from features within its interior (Fig. 3.12). The dating of the enclosure and the chronological relationship of these various phases of activity to the monument remain unclear (Sweetman 1971; 1976; Roche and Eogan 2001, 135). While no unambiguous evidence was excavated to clarify the date of its construction, it has generally been assumed to be Late Neolithic (Stout 1991; Condit and Simpson 1998; Cooney and Grogan 1999, 87-91).

The extended duration of human activity at this place was not recognised at the time of excavation; Beaker pottery was thought to represent the youngest ceramic on the site, while the Middle Neolithic activity was considered to overlap with the currency of Beakers and so, as Sweetman (1976, 39) acknowledged, all the finds from the site were treated as a single contemporaneous assemblage. Consequently, all features were considered "as part of the Beaker culture" (ibid., 25), even though many represented Middle Bronze Age (or even later) activity (see Roche and Eogan 2001). The published accounts of this excavation only consider most of the finds at a site-level, however, and so it is difficult to retrospectively attribute artefacts to their contexts of discovery. Future analysis of the site archive may help to remedy this.

In the south-western part of the site, the excavation revealed an extensive spread of occupation debris, referred to as "a habitation" and consisting of dark charcoal-rich soil, up to 0.6m deep, which produced most of the 5000 Beaker

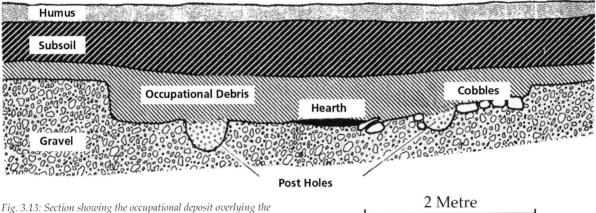

Fig. 3.13: Section showing the occupational deposit overlying the putative Beaker structure at Monknewtown, Co. Meath (after Sweetman 1976).

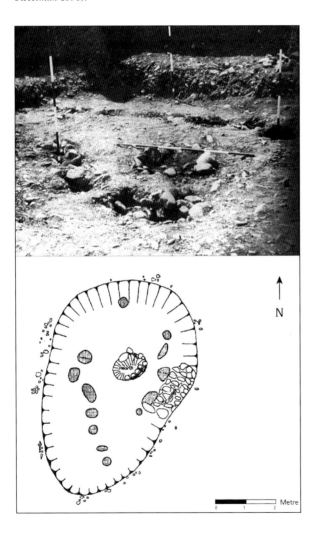

Fig. 3.14: The features forming the putative Beaker house at Monknewtown (after Sweetman 1976).

sherds (Sweetman 1976), as well as an admixture of pottery dating from between the fourth and second millennia BC. While this spread has traditionally been assumed to represent Beaker activity, the inclusion of these other ceramics may indicate that the Beaker pottery is not within its final depositional context. If so, then this deposit would only indirectly reflect Beaker-associated activity.

Underneath this deposit, was a putative Beaker structure comprising a large oval depression (6m by 4m by 0.5m), described by the excavator as an "egg-shaped pit dwelling" (Sweetman 1971, 139). This had a flat floor, steep sides and a centrally located hearth (1m in diameter) defined by vertical flagstones (Figs. 3.13-3.14). Thirteen stone-packed postholes were found along the western side of the pit, although these displayed no obviously recognisable or convincing structural pattern. This oval hollow was filled by the same multi-period deposit detailed above, indicating that this putative house was created before that deposit existed in that location. Combined oak and birch charcoal found within this deposit in the area around the hearth returned a radiocarbon determination of 2459-2136 BC (UB-728; 3810±45 BP; Smith *et al.* 1974, 269); however, we cannot be certain that this charcoal was associated with the use of the hearth or the putative structure (in the unlikely event that it existed) or if it is even associated with the formation of this deposit. Furthermore, none of the postholes produced Beaker pottery; instead these were filled with sterile material resembling the natural subsoil (Sweetman 1976, 38). We do not, therefore, know when any of the features thought to form this structure or the deposit that fills the hollow were created. Given the evidence for post-Beaker activity at Monknewtown, it is possible that this feature could have been dug after the demise of Beakers in Ireland

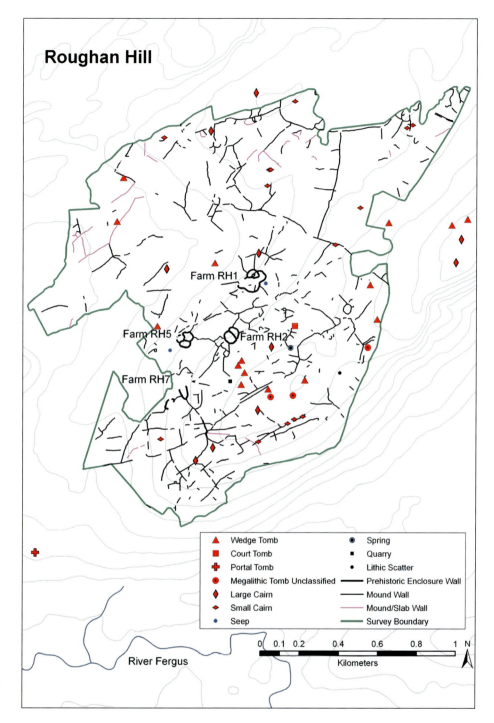

Fig. 3.15: Map showing the location of the 'Beaker settlement' at Roughan Hill, Co. Clare, including the field walls and enclosure labelled here as "Farm RH1" (courtesy of Carleton Jones).

and then backfilled with a deposit containing residual or disturbed Beaker sherds, as well as Neolithic and Bronze Age artefacts. At present, the only conclusion that can be drawn about this Beaker activity is that Beaker-associated habitation debris was deposited at Monknewtown and shares a spatial relationship with the embanked enclosure. Whether this represents settlement or ceremonial activity remains unknown, though it may represent both. This issue is considered further in Chapter Six.

3.3 Settling some issues?

Having reconsidered the interpretation of these highly influential excavations that dominated subsequent narratives of the Irish Beaker complex, we turn our attention to a related issue. More recent excavations at Roughan Hill, Co. Clare, Ross Island, Co. Kerry and Graigueshoneen, Co. Waterford have identified evidence for Beaker houses, but their interpretation may have been influenced by the likes of Newgrange or Lough Gur, and so they are evaluated here.

A SETTLED PAST | 55

At Roughan Hill, Co. Clare, survey work in the Burren by Carleton Jones (1996; 1998a) revealed an extensive prehistoric landscape including ancient field walls, enclosures, structures and Ireland's densest concentration of wedge tombs (Fig. 3.15). A cluster of four enclosures, interpreted as contemporary farmsteads, were found to be at the centre of a network of radiating field divisions defined by low, grass-covered stone-work representing collapsed walls, described as 'mound walls' (Jones et al. 2010, 37). These 'mound walls' overlie the limestone karstic terrain of the Burren, thereby protecting the bedrock from erosion. This results in the survival of preserved pedestals of bedrock underneath each wall and thereby higher than the surrounding unprotected limestone, which has become more eroded over time.

The measurement of the heights of the bedrock plinths under the various walls enabled the development of a relative chronology for these field-divisions. The 'mound walls' had higher pedestals than many of the other walls in the locality, such as the Iron Age examples that were constructed differently or the early medieval walls associated with ringforts, thereby indicating that these 'mound walls' pre-dated those features (Jones, C. 1998a; 2008, 42; Jones et al. 2010, 37). One of the large 'mound wall' field-systems circumscribed an area of 75 acres and was centred upon a kidney-shaped enclosure with a mound wall (labelled 'Settlement 1'/ 'Farmstead 1'), thought to represent a Beaker-associated farm (Jones, C. 1996, 17; Jones et al. 2010; 52). Both this and a neighbouring large 'mound wall' enclosure ('Farmstead 2') displayed a similar morphology and identical pedestal heights, suggesting that these were broadly contemporary.

Partial excavation of the middle of the enclosure of 'Farmstead 1' revealed at least two distinct periods of occupation. The earliest habitation is dated by the presence of Beaker pottery within a centrally located midden deposit. The excavation recovered 254 Beaker sherds, a sherd from an Irish Bowl, thumb-nail scrapers, hollow-based arrow heads, flakes from polished stone axes, saddle querns, hammer-stones and retouched stone tools (Jones, C. 1996, 19). The second main phase is represented by Iron Age activity associated with the remains of a stone structure that seems to indicate various episodes of rebuilding on the same spot over an extended duration (Fig. 3.16). This may have re-used the structural materials of a former Beaker house and may also have been re-used in the medieval period (Jones, C. 1998b, 33). Artefacts associated with the Iron Age use of this structure include iron objects, a large grooved sandstone block and blue glass beads (ibid., 35).

The stratigraphic relationships established between some of the surviving structural remains and the Beaker-associated midden indicate that these walls were built on top of the Beaker-associated midden materials (Jones, C. 1998a; 1998b, 36). A post-Beaker date for these walls is supported by the discovery that the bedrock under these parts of the structural remains had low pedestals, indicating that these walls were younger than the 'mound wall' of the kidney-shaped enclosure. During this Iron Age phase three smaller pits and a large pit were dug into the midden, while some other parts of this midden were disturbed to create a level surface for the construction of a house phase (Jones, C. 1998a; 2008). The large pit contained both Beaker and Iron Age artefacts and materials that returned three distinct radiocarbon determinations of 2288-2140 BC (UB-10258; 3784±25 BP), 1900-1699 BC (UB-10257; 3492±32 BP) and 193-54 BC (UB-10477; 2106±23). The latest of which was obtained from a charred hazelnut shell, confirming that at least some of this activity belongs to the Iron Age.

The kidney-shaped 'mound wall' enclosure – whose high pedestals indicated that it pre-dated the Iron Age and early medieval wall – which encircled the midden and the buildings was also assigned a Beaker date and considered to be functionally related to the Beaker-associated midden. The evidential basis for this was supplied by excavations at 'Farmstead 2', the neighbouring 'mound wall' enclosure. Here, a midden-like deposit that contained sherds of Vase and Bowl Tradition pottery was also identified in two separate locations immediately inside the enclosing mound wall (Jones, C. 1998b, 36; 2015, 91-2). This argument, however, leaves some issues unresolved regarding the exact functional and chronological relationship between these middens and the large enclosures which encircle them. Due to the difficulties of recovering evidence for clear-cut stratigraphic relationships in a landscape like the Burren, where prehistoric soils are so depleted, these issues seem unresolvable. Based on the available evidence, however, the enclosures are more likely to have been built in the later part of the third millennium BC than at any other time.

Returning to whether there was a Beaker house within the enclosure of 'Farmstead 1', convincing evidence is lacking. The multiple phases of re-use displayed by this central stone-built house prevents the recognition of its earlier outline, which could have been associated with the use of Beaker pottery (Jones, C. 1998b, 33). Yet, the fact that it was not possible to determine the form of a Beaker-associated structure results in an important level of doubt as to whether a stone-built house was in this location during the Chalcolithic. The absence of any such house from the neighbouring contemporary enclosure only adds to these doubts.

At Ross Island, Co. Kerry, overlooking the lakeshore of Lough Leane, excavation of an escarpment platform outside the copper mines, in an area known as the 'Western Shelf', revealed ten possible Beaker structures, as well as 456 sherds from 25 Beaker pots, stone tools and animal bone (O'Brien 2004, 173-215; fig. 53). Occurring immediately adjacent to the mines, this is thought to represent the remains of

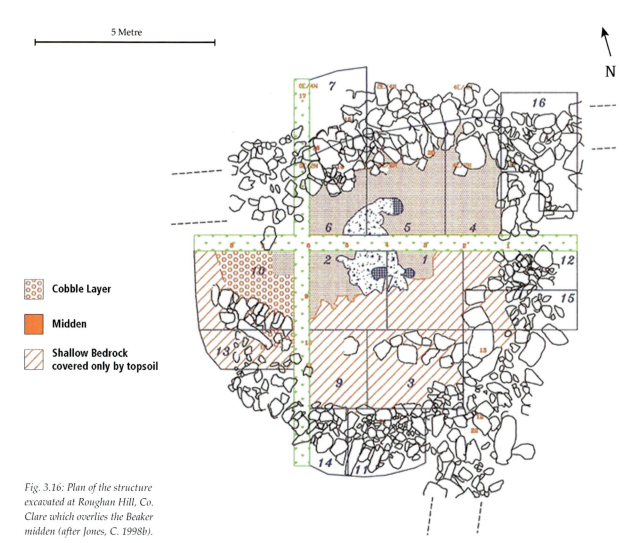

Fig. 3.16: Plan of the structure excavated at Roughan Hill, Co. Clare which overlies the Beaker midden (after Jones, C. 1998b).

a Beaker camp associated with ore-processing and other metallurgical activities (ibid.). This habitation comprised two surface deposits that were found to overlie each other and the ground level. The uppermost deposit consisted mainly of ore-processing sediments but also contained hammer-stones and anvil blocks, bone fragments, a quern-stone and a polished stone axe, as well as sherds from 13 Beaker vessels and an Irish Bowl (ibid., 358-9, fig. 166). Six radiocarbon determinations obtained from charcoal and bone samples within this deposit returned dates ranging between 2457 and 1527 BC: 2457-2142 BC (GrN-19627; 3820±35 BP), 2345-2025 BC (GrA-7512; 3760±50 BP), 2289-1978 BC (GrA-7009; 3730±50 BP), 2136-1782 BC (GrA-7010; 3610±50 BP), 2028-1755 BC (GrA-7513; 3560±50 BP) and 1870-1527 BC (GrA-7007; 3380±50 BP). The lower layer, which was interpreted as a trampled occupation surface, comprised a thin dark silty deposit containing 182 sherds from 18 Beakers and additional sherds from the Bowl mentioned above, as well as hammer-stones, bone and flint debitage (ibid., 171). Three radiocarbon dates were obtained from materials within this deposit: 2470-2206 BC (GrN-19628; 3875±45 BP), 2467-2147 BC (GrN-19624; 3845±40 BP) and 2139-1828 BC (GrA-7552; 3620±50 BP).

These deposits sealed the structural features that O'Brien (2004, 173-214) interpreted as forming at least ten Beaker huts, Structures A–K (Figs. 3.17-3.18). These features include pits, 400 stake and postholes, and six slot trenches that were all dug into the old ground level. Structure A was a small (2.85m by 1.75m) oval building comprising a short curvilinear slot trench, an arc of 15 stakeholes and several postholes (ibid., 183, fig. 78). Structure B consisted of an assortment of 27 stakeholes, also thought to represent the outline of a small sub-circular hut with a diameter of just 1m. Four other putative 'Beaker structures' (G, H, J and I) comprised a very similar collection of spatially associated features, which are all interpreted as the remains of huts (ibid., fig. 82). The identification of these structures from the complex array of features in this area does, however, seem rather speculative. None of these structures display clearly defined, coherent or readily definable lay-outs. No artefactual or other dating evidence was recovered from any

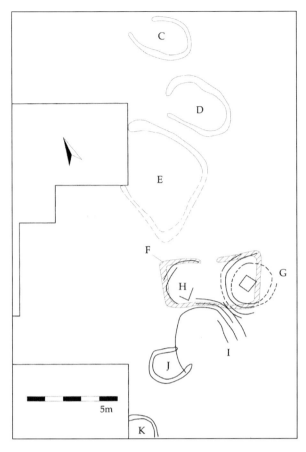

of these features to confirm that they were Beaker-associated or contemporary. In each case, there is little evidence to suggest that they should be regarded as forming elements of the same structure.

The foundations of a small sub-circular (3.15m by 1.8m) hut – Structure C – was comprised of two short curvilinear slot trenches containing stakeholes. One of these trenches produced three Beaker sherds, a hammer-stone and an animal tooth. The Beaker pottery was not of a late-style and so would typically date from 2450-2200 BC (Brindley, A.L. 2004, 338; see Chapter Eight). The other trench contained fragments of hammer-stones and cattle bone that returned a radiocarbon determination of 2140-1786 BC (GrA-7530; 3620±50 BP) post-dating the use-life of these sherds. Either these features were not contemporary or the deposits within them are not chronologically secure. Similarly, Structure D also consisted of a short curvilinear slot trench and 22 stakeholes thought to be the remains of a sub-rectangular (3m by 2m) hut. The curvilinear feature contained hammer-stone fragments, animal bone, copper ore, a lump

Fig. 3.17: Simplified outline plan of the key features forming Structures C - K at Ross Island (after O'Brien 2016, Fig. 8.25; reproduced with permission of Billy O'Brien).

Fig. 3.18: Structure C at Ross Island (photo by and reproduced here courtesy of Billy O'Brien).

58 | THE BEAKER PHENOMENON

of copper-sulphide ore and a hollow-based flint arrowhead. Beaker sherds and a hammer-stone fragment were also discovered in a surface-deposit occurring inside the putative dwelling. Structure E was a comparatively large (5m by 4m) trapezoidal building comprising a long slot trench on one side and an assortment of post and stakeholes. Finds from the trench included hammer-stones, two Beaker sherds and cattle bone that returned a radiocarbon date of 2271-1937 BC (GrA-7523; 3690±50 BP). Another rectangular building plan (5m by 2m), known as Structure F, was discerned from a concentration of 60 stakeholes, none of which produced any artefactual or dating evidence.

While the surface deposits of occupational debris clearly represent the remains of Beaker-associated activity, the structural features do not convincingly form the remains of distinctly recognisable Beaker dwellings, as has been claimed. Nor is it clear that all these features reflect activity dating from the third millennium BC, despite occurring outside the earliest copper mine in Britain and Ireland. There are issues with the evidence that raise the possibility that the few Beaker sherds from structural contexts at Ross Island are in a disturbed or residual context. Foremost among this is the contradiction between the stratigraphic and chronological relationships of the structural features and the surface deposits. Very similar artefacts were found within the various structural features and the two surface deposits, but four of the radiocarbon dates from the surface deposits pre-date those from the structural features, even though the deposits are stratigraphically younger. Given the presence of both Food Vessels and post-Beaker radiocarbon dates on this site, it seems quite possible that the reason for this chronological incongruity between the surface deposits and the structural features is that the trenches, post and stakeholes post-date the layers. If these features were dug into the Beaker spread and then backfilled with this same material, it would be almost impossible to detect during excavation until the surface deposit had been removed. A radically different interpretation is that the Beaker materials were deposited just outside the entrance to the copper mine at Ross Island during ritualised forms of activity relating to the dangerous transformative work associated with the mine. This would certainly be consistent with the kind of Neolithic activity observed at axe quarry sites and the placement of Beaker debris outside other significant places, like the entrances to passage tombs (see Section 5.4; Cooney 2005).

At Graigueshoneen, Co. Waterford, a sub-oval structure consisted of three concentric rings of stakeholes (0.2m by 0.25m) measuring 7.6m in external diameter, with a probable north-eastern entrance that was 2m wide (Johnston *et al.* 2008). The inner ring of 22 small stakeholes was the most complete, though spacing between them varied. The stakes of the outer two rings (comprising 18 and 11 stakeholes) were placed at a wider distance from one

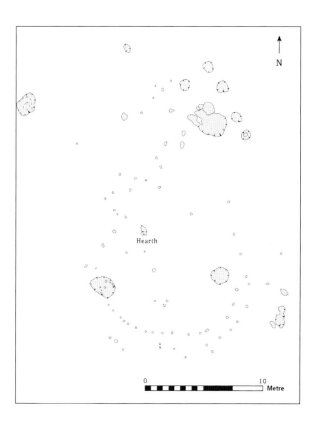

Fig. 3.19: The stakehole-built sub-oval structure from Graigueshoneen, Co. Waterford (after Johnston et al. 2008; fig. 1).

another and may have functioned as an enclosing element, a support for the roof, or may have been remnants of wall repairs (Fig. 3.19). The excavator suggested that the house consisted of a possible double layer wattle and daub wall supporting a straw roof. A total of 15 Beaker sherds came from three different structural stakeholes. One of these contained two small Beaker sherds, occasional burnt clay, a worked flint, two grains each of barley and wheat, a sorrel seed, a probable redshank seed and charcoal (species unidentified) that returned a radiocarbon date of 2860-2490 BC (Beta-170161; 4110±40 BP). Two pits, several ancillary stakeholes and a hearth were recorded in the north-eastern interior of the structure and these produced sherds from seven Beaker vessels and occasional pieces of worked flint and chert. One of the two pits was located within the inner arc of stakeholes. It was filled by two deposits containing charcoal, burnt clay, burnt stone, seven sherds from a Beaker pot, a worked quartz crystal, seven hazelnut shell fragments, 77 barley and 18 wheat grains, as well as charcoal that returned a date of 2460-2200 BC (Beta-170160; 3860±40 BP). This is by far the least ambiguous example of a Beaker-associated structure and we will discuss this further towards the end of the chapter. Before we do that, we need to examine the character of the structural features from other sites that contain Beaker deposits, namely postholes, stakeholes and linear features, in more detail.

Site name	No. of Beaker features	Beaker features
Ardsallagh 4	1	one posthole
Dunboyne 3	2	one posthole and one pit
Moanduff 2	2	one posthole and one spread
Danesfort 8	2	one posthole and one pit
Curraheen 1	2	one posthole and one pit
Caherabbey Upper 103.1	2	one posthole and one pit
Caherabbey Upper 185	3	one posthole and two pits
Ballydrehid 185.5	4	one posthole and three pits
Skreen 3	5	one posthole and four pits
Newtownlittle	9	one posthole, seven pits and a spread
Laughanstown Site 35	12	one posthole, four pits, a hearth, a stone surface, a spread
Beaverstown	4	two postholes and two pits
Charlesland Site A	5	two postholes and three pits
Rathwilladoon	6	two postholes and four pits
Mell	6	two postholes, a spread, two pits, a slot trench
Kilmainham 1C	14	two postholes, nine pits, three spreads
Newtownbalregan 5	10	five postholes, three pits, a slot trench
Kilgobbin	14	six postholes, six pits, a spread, a slot trench
Rathwilladoon	7	one stakehole, four pits, two postholes,
Barnagore 2	2	one stakehole and one pit
Graigueshoneen Field 3	5	three stakehole and two pits
Ahanaglogh Field 2 Area 13	2	one slot trench and a pit
Haggardstown Site 13	7	one slot trench, five pits and a spread
Kilbride	2	two slot trenches and a spread
Rathmullan Site 10	8	two slot trenches, four pits and a spread
Ross Island	5	three slot trenches, two spreads and a pit

Table 3.1: The number of Beaker-associated postholes, stakeholes and slot trenches and other Beaker- associated features occurring on the same site.

3.4 Dwelling on the evidence?

Excavations have uncovered at least 34 postholes on a total of 19 sites that contained Beaker pottery, as well as five stakeholes on three additional sites. These postholes and stakeholes are circular- or oval-shaped and range in diameter from 0.10-0.55m and 0.09-0.14m and in depth from 0.04-0.55m and 0.12-0.22m respectively. At least 12 linear features from seven sites have contained Beaker pottery. These typically represent short narrow linear features best described as gullies or slot trenches, though the use of either term here is not intended to depict their function. The longest example is 5.6m, widths vary from 1.10m to 0.16m and depths range from 0.65m to 0.08m. There is so much diversity in their shapes and sizes that it is difficult to detect typical characteristics.

In the case of the three Beaker-associated stakeholes from Graigueshoneen, Co. Waterford, which clearly formed part of a coherent structure, it is obvious that these were interrelated to the other features of the house (see Section 3.3). On most of these sites, however, there was only a single posthole, stakehole or linear feature that contained Beaker pottery, although these often occurred alongside other feature types, predominantly pits, that also contained Beakers (Table 3.1). Although similar postholes, stakeholes and linears are commonly discovered in spatial association with the features containing Beaker pottery, it is rarely possible to deduce whether they should be regarded as contemporary when they do not contain this ceramic or other diagnostic artefacts and are not selected for radiocarbon dating. Furthermore, it is not always clear that the Beaker-related materials within some of these features were in a secure context. All of this is exacerbated by their occurrence among a palimpsest of other features and the fact that they rarely appear to form part of a recognisable structure. As a result, we are left with a rather artificial scenario, where this study distinguishes between features that may have been associated with one another because of a lack of evidence to confirm or deny their relationship. As this is done based on the presence or absence of Beakers, it continues the reification of this pottery as the definitive component of Beaker-related activity.

Site name	Sherds	Vessels	Feature Type	Sherd: vessel
Graigueshoneen Field 3	2	1	stakehole	2:1
Graigueshoneen Field 3	3	1	stakehole	3:1
Graigueshoneen Field 3	8	1	stakehole	8:1
Rathwilladoon	11	?	stakehole	?
Barnagore 2	1	1	stakehole	1:1
Mell	1	?	slot trench	?
Newtownbalregan 5	2	1	slot trench	2:1
Ahanaglogh Field 2 A13	3	1	slot trench	3:1
Ross Island	3	?	slot trench	?
Rathmullan Site 10	4	?	slot trench	?
Haggardstown Site 13	5	3	slot trench	1.6:1
Mell	5	3	slot trench	1.6:1
Rathmullan Site 10	5	?	slot trench	?
Kilbride	6	1	slot trench	6:1
Mell	6	2	slot trench	3:1
Kilbride	8	?	slot trench	?
Kilgobbin	10	?	slot trench	?
Ross Island	14	?	slot trench	?
Caherabbey Upper (185)	1	1	posthole	1:1
Caherabbey Upper 103.1;	1	1	posthole	1:1
Skreen 3	1	1	posthole	1:1
Kilgobbin	1	1	posthole	1:1
Kilgobbin	1	1	posthole	1:1
Beaverstown	1	1	posthole	1:1
Kilgobbin	1	1	posthole	1:1
Kilgobbin	1	1	posthole	1:1
Laughanstown Site 35	1	1	posthole	1:1
Danesfort 8	2	2	posthole	1:1
Kilmainham 1C	1	1	posthole	1:1
Beaverstown	2	1	posthole	2:1
Dunboyne 3	2	1	posthole	2:1
Mell	2	1	posthole	2:1
Newtownlittle	2	1	posthole	2:1
Rathwilladoon	2	1	posthole	2:1
Curraheen 1	3	1	posthole	3:1
Mell	3	1	posthole	3:1
Kilgobbin	3	1	posthole	3:1
Moanduff 2	3	1	posthole	3:1
Rathwilladoon	3	1	posthole	3:1
Kilmainham 1C	3	1	posthole	3:1
Newtownbalregan 5	14	4	posthole	3.5:1
Kilgobbin	7	2	posthole	3.5:1
Newtownbalregan 5	36	9	posthole	4:1
Newtownbalregan 5	15	3	posthole	5:1
Ballydrehid Site 185.5	10	2	posthole	5:1
Newtownbalregan 5	10	1	posthole	10:1

Table 3.2: The number of sherds and vessels found in each stakehole, slot trench, or posthole and their ratio.

The 12 Beaker-associated linear features have produced a total of 72 sherds from a minimum of 18 vessels. Most linears (8 of 12) contained five sherds or less and only two slot trenches produced ten sherds or more. One of these occurred at Ross Island, which contained 14 sherds representing the highest number recorded in any linear feature. Beaker-associated stakeholes have only produced a total of 24 small and worn sherds, 11 of which occurred within a stakehole at Rathwilladoon, Co. Galway, and 12 came from the three different stakeholes forming the Graigueshoneen structure (see Section 3.3; Table 3.2). Due to their small number and size, it is not possible to relate these sherds to specific vessels. The 34 postholes that contained Beaker pottery produced a total of 132 sherds from 31 vessels. Most postholes (22 of 34) contained three sherds or less with single sherds occurring in ten of these. Only five postholes produced ten sherds or more, four of which were at Newtownbalregan 5, Co Louth. Slightly more than half (19 out of 34) of the postholes contained the remains of a single vessel, while only three postholes contained the remains of two vessels.

A higher number of pots have only been retrieved from postholes at Newtownbalregan 5, where three of these features each produced a total of three, four and nine Beakers (Table 3.2). All Beaker-producing postholes displayed a sherd/vessel ratio that was less than or equal to 5:1 (11 of these had a ratio of 1:1), except for one such feature at Newtownbalregan 5, which contained ten sherds from one pot. Apart from Newtownbalregan 5, most of the sherds from postholes are small and worn. Based on the available information, most of these structural features tend to only contain a few sherds from one or two pots and display quite low sherd/vessel ratios. The sparse number of sherds and their small, worn and fragmentary nature all combine to suggest that the sherds have experienced considerable life-histories after their breakage and prior to their eventual deposition.

While cattle bones were discovered within the slot trenches at Ross Island and carbonised grains occurred at Graigueshoneen, the only other recurrent finds from stakeholes postholes and linear features are lithics. These occurred within 11 postholes on five sites and consisted almost entirely of flint debitage with only one formal tool, a scraper, being discovered in a posthole at Newtownbalregan 5 (Bayley 2009a). In the case of stakeholes, only a few pieces of debitage were recorded from two stakeholes at Graigueshoneen. Similarly, the lithics from linears mainly comprise flint debitage, which occur in five of these features, alongside a scraper from Haggardstown, Co. Louth, and a hollow-based arrowhead from Ross Island (Table 3.3). A high number of stone macro-tools – two anvils and 12 hammer-stones – also occur in slot trenches, but these are all from the 'camp' beside the copper mine at Ross Island (O'Brien 2004).

Akin to the stakeholes from Graigueshoneen, or the linears from Ross Island, the postholes from Newtownbalregan 5 represent something quite different from the other postholes. They are much wider and deeper than all the others and contained a much greater amount of artefactual material. In terms of their size, shape and contents, they most resemble the postholes forming timber circles and are further considered alongside other such monuments in more detail in Chapter Six. Overall, it is clear from this analysis that Beakers or other artefactual material were rarely deposited in postholes, stakeholes or linear features. There is very little obvious evidence for any formal or deliberate aspect to the deposition of the material within them. While these features were structural and may have originally represented a crucial element of a structure, how they functioned in relation to many of the sites under discussion is generally unclear.

Clearly, there are far fewer convincing Beaker 'houses' than has been alleged and no distinct architectural form of Beaker-associated dwelling is recognisable in Ireland. It seems that people must have lived in structures that did not leave a substantial trace within the archaeological record. The absence of identifiable structures from most excavations, many of which produced copious amounts of Beaker-associated occupational debris within pits, spreads and other features, certainly does not indicate that such sites were short-term temporary settlements. The paucity of evidence for houses is not reflective of contemporary settlement practices or levels of settlement stability. Instead, it directly reflects the kinds of architectural technologies that were employed in the construction of homes at this time and happen to leave little or no lasting footprint in the ground in most situations (see Gibson, A. 1996, 138).

Doubtlessly, the people who used Beaker pottery in Ireland symbolically expressed their worldview through the architecture of their structures, but the ways in which they did this has not entered the archaeological record, as is the case in many other parts of Europe (see Section 4.7). This scenario is typical of Irish prehistory, whereby highly recognisable houses are mainly known from the Early Neolithic (Smyth 2014) and the later Bronze Age (Cleary, K. 2007; Ginn 2016; Grogan 2017). Any of the more ephemeral prehistoric structures that have been discovered in Ireland and Britain owe their survival to the differential levels of preservation afforded to them by certain forms of land-usage and/or by the protection created by the construction of nearby upstanding monuments (for discussion and examples see Darvill 1996, 81; Gibson, A. 1996, 137).

What then does this assessment tell us about the evidence for Beaker-associated settlement activity; is there as much as had been thought? We have seen that understandings of Beaker-associated habitation in Ireland have been quite misinformed. Many of the features from

Finds	No. of artefacts	No. of slots
Unburnt animal bone	cow	3
Scrapers	1	1
Hammer-stone	12	3
Anvil	2	1
Arrowhead	1	1
Debitage	13	5

Table 3.3: The range and quantity of finds from Beaker slot trenches

historic landmark excavations that were deemed as archetypal examples of Beaker-associated habitation either pre-date or post-date the currency of Beakers. In the few cases where these investigations uncovered Beaker pottery within its original context of deposition, the relationship between these deposits and settlement activity is unclear. This lack of clarity seems to encapsulate what we have established thus far about the nature of the activity that has been regarded as Beaker-associated settlement. To date, much of this has focused upon what this evidence does not tell us and so it is necessary to address what it might contribute to our knowledge of this period. To do this, we need to turn our attention towards the pits and spreads that have been excavated within in a range of monumental and non-monumental settings across much of the island. These are explored in the next chapter.

4

Remembering everyday life

4.1 Introduction

Pits and spreads are often (very unfairly) seen as mundane; they are much underappreciated in terms of what they can tell us about the archaeology of the Beaker complex in Ireland. Over 177 Beaker-associated pits have been excavated across 91 of the 219 sites yielding Beakers in Ireland. Undoubtedly this represents the context in which this ceramic is most commonly found (see Chapter Nine). As we have also seen, these pits, as well as a range of features including spreads, stakeholes, postholes, linear features and *fulachtaí fia,* have been uncovered across much of Ireland, particularly during development-led excavations over the last 20 years (see Chapters One and Three). Yet, these rich repositories have never been studied in detail and are often interpreted from a functionalist perspective as the remains of Beaker-associated settlements (see Chapters Two and Three). This is exemplified by the way that the pits have been characterised as containers for storage or refuse. A key aim here is to gain insights into the deposition of Beaker material culture and the nature of the sites and features in which it occurs. This is essential to achieving a better understanding of the uses and social significance of this ceramic and the associated artefacts.

In the last chapter we examined the structural component of this evidence for Beaker houses, but here we explore the other features; pits, spreads and middens, and *fulachtaí fia*. This chapter comprises an assessment of the defining characteristics of each of these feature-types, as well as the range, frequency and manner of deposition of their associated Beaker-related artefacts, which are also contrasted with one another in terms of the type, quantity and condition of the objects, especially the pottery. This includes an appraisal of the total number of Beaker pots and sherds in each context and the number of sherds per vessel (see Section 1.4). Case studies from a few sites are used to examine some features in more detail. The aim is to identify patterning in these deposits from which to infer past social practices. As explained in the earlier chapters, only features containing Beaker-related objects are included, which problematically results in aceramic features being excluded. This is discussed further below.

4.2 Beaker-associated pits

All 177 pits are characterised, but detailed analysis is only presented on the 83 sites for a suitable level of information was available. Beaker-associated pits display a variety of different shapes in plan, ranging from linear to sub-rectangular to amorphous, but the majority (120 out of 177 pits; 68%) are shallow sub-circular or oval features with a bowl-shape in section (Fig. 4.1). While there is considerable variation in sizes, most of these display lengths and widths ranging between 0.25m and 1m and depths of less than 0.50m (Fig. 4.2). When considering the depth of these features, it is important to be cognisant that the uppermost parts of these pits may have been truncated during modern agricultural activities such as ploughing.

Just over half of these pits were filled in a single event by just one deposit and only a small number exhibit multiple deposits (Fig. 4.3). A select group (24 pits from 22 sites)

Fig. 4.1: A stereotypical pit, before and after excavation at Ballinaspig More 5, Co Cork (after Danaher 2005).

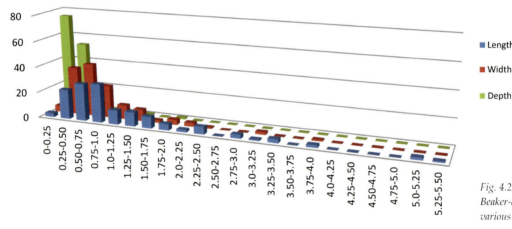

Fig. 4.2: The quantities of Beaker-associated pits of various sizes in cms.

display evidence for a stone-lining or stone deposit (Fig. 4.4). Almost all the pits in the study appear to have been backfilled with occupational debris from another context quite soon after they were dug. Only three of the 177 pits displayed any archaeological evidence for previous use or of being left open for an extended duration such as cumulative infilling or eroded sides or base. Pits containing more than one fill also appear to have received separate deposits of material over a short timeframe, as suggested by the common occurrence of sherds from the same vessels within each different layer. Based on this, it seems likely that these pits were created specifically to receive their deposits.

At least 4436 Beaker sherds from 472 vessels have been found in these 177 pits, representing roughly 20% of the 21772 Beaker sherds found in Ireland. This appears quite a low proportion compared to the 75% found in spreads and middens at settlement and ceremonial sites. If we exclude all the pottery from those contexts, however, then 76% of the remaining Beakers in Ireland come from pits. Other rare forms of Beaker ceramics, including the remains of (at least) three polypod bowls, have been found in pits on three sites; Newtownbalregan 2 in County Louth, Newtownlittle in County Dublin and Rathmullan 12 in County Meath, while two dishes were discovered within pits at Paulstown in County Kilkenny and Kilgobbin in County Dublin (Grogan and Roche 2005a; 2005b; 2009a; 2011; Grogan 2005c). Pieces of burnt or fired clay have been found in six pits

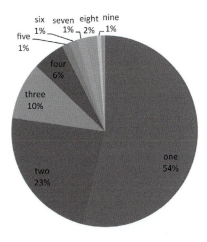

Fig. 4.3: The frequency of the number of fills within each pit.

Fig. 4.5: The lithics from the Beaker-associated pit at Gortore (photo by John Sutherland, after O'Donoghue 2010, courtesy of Eachtra).

Fig. 4.4: Beaker pits containing stones at Danesfort 8, Co. Kilkenny and Gortore, Co. Cork (after Jennings 2009 and after O'Donoghue 2010, courtesy of IAC and Eachtra).

and some of these appear to be wasters from the production of ceramics.

Leaving aside the ceramic content of these pits for now, let us turn attention to the other materials found in these features. The most common artefacts associated with Beakers in these pits are related to the manufacture and use of stone tools. Lithic debitage is recovered more frequently than any other material; split pebbles, chunks, cores, flakes, microflakes and micro debitage from flint, quartz and chert have been found in 46 Beaker-associated pits from 29 sites (Fig. 4.5). Unworked abraded lumps of flint have also been found in eight pits on five sites, occasionally occurring in large quantities such as the 29 natural pieces found with Beaker pottery in a pit at Ballymoyle, Co. Wicklow (Whitty 2006).

Formal retouched lithics, particularly flakes and blades, are less common than debitage; eight of these have been found in four pits. Small convex scrapers, which have the same breadth and length (20-30mm) and are often referred to as 'thumbnail', represent the artefact most frequently associated with Beaker pottery in pits. At least 80 of these scrapers have been recorded in 21 Beaker-associated pits on 15 sites and occasionally these occur in large enough quantities to be regarded as a cache (Table 4.1). For example, at Rathdown, Co. Wicklow, sherds from seven Beaker pots, hazelnut shells, barley and wheat grains, and an assemblage of 300 flints that included 11 thumbnail scrapers, were all found within the charcoal-rich fills of a pit dated to 2470-2210 BC (Beta-202304; 3870±40 BP; Eogan and O'Brien 2005). While as many as 16 of these scrapers were found with Beaker pottery in pits at Kilgobbin and Coldwinters, both in County Dublin.

Only seven arrowheads have been found within six pits on five sites, all of which were barbed and tanged (Table 4.1). For example, a pit at Hill of Rath, Co. Louth, contained 127 sherds representing at least 30 Beaker pots (two of which were Maritime Beakers),

Artefact Type	Arefact Total	Pit Total
Convex scrapers	80	21
Barbed and tanged arrowhead	7	6
Polypod bowls	3	3
Disc beads	23	1
Quern stones	2	2
Hammer-stones	9	7
Polished stone axes	6	6

Table 4.1: The numbers of artefacts found in Beaker pits.

Fig. 4.6: The large pit at Paulstown, Co, Kilkenny containing 23 disc-beads and 172 sherds from at least 23 Beakers (courtesy of IAC).

73 pieces of flint (including blades, scrapers, one partial and one complete barbed and tanged arrowhead) and fragments of burnt bone (species unidentifiable), all within a charcoal-rich matrix (Brindley, A.L. 2000; Duffy 2002).

Complete or fragmented polished stone axes were found with Beakers in a pit on at least six different sites: Cloghers, Dunmoon, Gortatlea, Monadreela 13, Burtonhall Demesnse and Gortore. Significantly, at Cloghers, Co. Kerry, one of these Beaker-associated pits contained a complete polished sandstone axe, two Beaker sherds, 11 flint flakes and 534 barley grains, as well as a hammer-stone and a grinding stone thought to represent a stone axe production kit (Kiely and Dunne 2005). Other stone macro-tools include nine hammer-stones from seven Beaker-associated pits, two grinding stones and three anvils. A quernstone came from a Beaker-associated pit on three sites (Ross Island, Barnagore 2 and Monadreela Site 13). At Barnagore, this pit also contained two rubbing stones which were probably used with the quern (see below)

The only discovery of obvious 'personal ornaments' in a Beaker-associated pit was made at the unusual site of Paulstown, Co. Kilkenny (Figs. 4.6-4.7; Elliot 2009), where 23 shale disc-beads, thought to have formed a necklace, were found in a large pit containing a total of 172 sherds from at least 23 Beakers charred hazelnut shell and cereal remains, as well as flint debitage (Grogan and Roche 2009a). Hazel charcoal from the primary fill of the pit, which also contained one of these beads, returned a radiocarbon date of 2430-2147 BC (UBA-15435; 3821±26 BP) (Elliott 2009). Significantly, this represents the only instance of disc-beads being found in secure and direct association with Beaker pottery in any context in Ireland (see Chapter Nine). Their presence in this pit serves to highlight the wide range of objects that are completely absent from these pits, including wrist-bracers, copper daggers, axes, halberds, gold ornaments and V-perforated buttons. While it may be the case that none of these objects were used in the type of setting represented by these pits, this can also be seen as evidence for selectivity regarding what was included and excluded in these features.

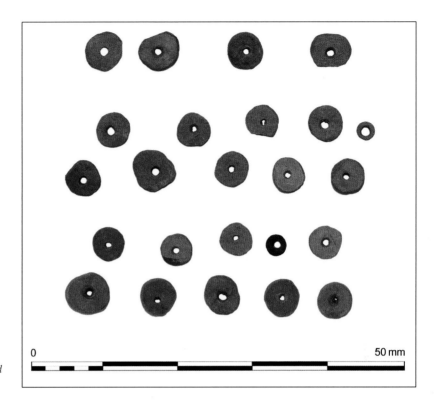

Fig. 4.7: The Paulstown Beaker-associated disc-beads (courtesy of IAC).

As we have seen, burnt and unburnt animal bone and the charred remains of cereals and fruits also occur in Beaker-associated pits, while seashells have only been found in one such pit, at Aughinish in County Limerick (Cleary, R. 2006). Unburnt animal bone representing cattle, pig and sheep/goat has been positively identified from 11 pits on eight sites. Burnt bone has been found with Beaker pottery in 26 pits on 20 sites; however, these mostly occur (16 pits from 14 sites) as fragments that are too small to be identified as either human or animal. For example, at Corbally, Co. Kildare, a pit produced 18 sherds from two Beakers, unidentifiable burnt bone and a barbed and tanged arrowhead (Purcell 2002). This site is considered in more detail in Chapter Five in terms of its relationship to Beaker-associated mortuary practices. Cereal grains, identified as barley, wheat, emmer wheat and bread wheat, which usually occur together, have been found with Beaker pottery in 14 pits on 13 sites. In some cases, such as the example mentioned above from Cloghers, these cereals occur in unusually high numbers and may represent deliberate deposits. At Mell, Co. Louth, a sub-rectangular pit contained 74 barley grains, 86 indeterminate cereals, a wheat grain and three sherds of Beaker pottery (McQuade 2005). Hazelnut shells have also been recovered from at least 15 pits on different sites, like those at Rathdown and Paulstown. The remains of fruit, including crab apples, blackberries, sloes and apples in the form of pips, seeds, stones and endocarps, have been found within four pits on four sites including Cloghers, Kilgobbin and Gortore.

There is no evidence to suggest any correlation between the size or shape of a pit and the quantity of sherds or vessels or other artefacts within it. Neither does there seem to be any link between the numbers of fills in a pit and the size of its Beaker assemblage (Table 4.2). In fact, pits filled with a single deposit occasionally contain the remains of more vessels than those with two or three fills. In many cases, pits containing multiple fills comprise a single artefact-rich deposit in combination with a few layers of clean artefact-free materials that probably represent some of the earthen spoil from the initial digging of the pit (see Garrow 2006, 44). An unusual pit found during Ines Hagen's excavations at Kilgobbin represents a unique discovery that will be discussed further below. This feature comprised six fills, each of which produced multiple sherds and contained the largest Beaker assemblage found in any single feature in Ireland (Grogan 2005c).

What about the overall number of Beaker-associated pits on each site? Is there any correlation between this and the quantity of sherds or vessels or other artefacts within these features? Typically, only one Beaker-associated pit occurs per site (58%: 48 of 83), though pairs of such pits are also relatively common (20%: 17 of 83). The discovery of three or four Beaker-associated pits on a site is a less frequent occurrence and greater numbers are rare (Fig. 4.8). However, at Paulstown, Co. Kilkenny – an exceptional site where, as we saw earlier, the 23 disc beads were found – as many as 11 such pits were found in association with three Late Neolithic timber circles

REMEMBERING EVERYDAY LIFE | 69

No. of vessels	One fill	%	Two fills	%	Three fills	%	Four fills	%
1-5	46	92	21	75	5	62	11	73
6-10	1	2	7	25	3	38	0	0
11-15	1	2	0	0	0	0	3	20
16-20	0	0	0	0	0	0	0	0
21-25	1	2	0	0	0	0	0	0
26-30	1	2	0	0	0	0	1	7

Table 4.2: Comparison of the number of Beakers found in pits containing various numbers of fills e.g. eleven pits containing four separate deposits produced between one and five vessels.

Artefact type	Isolated pit			Cluster of pits		
	No. of artefacts	No. of pits	% of pits	No. of artefacts	No. of pits	% of pits
Cremated human bone	n/a	0	0	n/a	4	3
Burnt animal bone or unidentifiable bone	n/a	1	3	n/a	19	16
Charcoal	n/a	8	26	n/a	21	18
Cereals	n/a	2	6	n/a	10	8
Fruit	n/a	1	3	n/a	1	1
Nuts	n/a	3	10	n/a	10	8
Scrapers	25	5	16	44	14	12
Hammer-stone	5	2	6	4	4	3
Anvil	3	1	3	0	0	0
Quernstone	0	0	0	2	2	2
Polished stone axes	1	1	3	4	4	3
Arrowhead	0	0	0	6	5	4
Grinding Stone	0	0	0	2	2	2
Disc-Beads	0	0	0	24	2	2

Table 4.3: Comparison of the occurrence of finds in isolated pits and groups of pits.

Site name	No. of pits	No. of sherds	No. of vessels
Kilgobbin	7	560	45
Hill of Rath	3	123	32
Dunmoon	2	210	30
Newtownbalregan 5	4	166	15
Cloghers II	2	256	13
Kilmainham 1C	4	121	12
Templerainey	3	273	12
Newtownbalregan 2	4	133	11
Rathwilladoon	2	62	10
Faughart 6	2	23	7
Haggardstown Site 13	4	62	7
Beaverstown	2	22	6
Graigueshoneen Field 3	2	43	6
Ballydrehid Site 185.5	2	21	5
Gortybrigane 1	4	37	5
Donaghmore 1	2	8	3
Kilbane II, Fd 1	2	200	0

Table 4.4: The number of Beaker sherds and vessels found in clusters of pits.

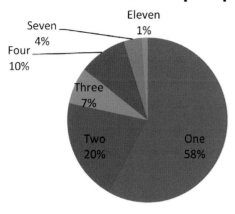

Fig. 4.8: The number of Beaker-associated pits per site.

Site name	Sherd Count	Vessel Count
Gortmakellis	418	16
Monadreela Site13	135	12
Lisnasallagh 2	14	7
Aughinish	43	5
Frankfort	204	3
Gortore	75	3
Carrigrohane 4	65	2
Coldwinters	75	2
Collinstown Site 16/17	5	2
Kilmurry	3	2
Ballinure	1	1
Ballymoyle	1	1
Boherard 2	6	1
Broomfield	3	1
Carnmore 5	7	1
Carranstown Site 3	1	1
Carrignanonshagh	1	1
Charlesland RMP Site,	1	1
Charlesland Site1B	3	1
Coolbeg Site 73	1	1
Curragh More	3	1
Derver 1	19	1
Farrandreg	3	1
Kilfinnane	8	1
Kilmainham 1B	15	1
Milltown North	1	1
Ardagh	4	?

Table 4.5: The number of Beaker sherds and vessels occurring in 30 isolated pits.

(see Chapter Six). On most (89%: 74 of 83) of the sites where Beaker-associated pits are excavated, no other features are found to contain Beaker pottery. Consequentially, on 38 of these sites, a single pit has proved to be the only feature containing Beakers. It is common, however, to find aceramic pits alongside their Beaker-associated counterparts that display many similarities in terms of shape, size and fill. Some of which have been proven to be of broadly contemporary date (see below).

The fact that these ubiquitous pits are generally the only identifiable Beaker-associated feature on each site raises the question of whether these directly represent settlement activity in that location? Before this is discussed, it may be instructive to consider whether there is any correlation between the number of Beaker-associated pits occurring together and their artefactual content? The solitary pits often contain very similar artefactual or ecofactual material to the pits occurring in clusters, such as scrapers, hammer-stones, a polished stone axe, as well as the remains of fruits, nuts and cereals. However, a much greater number and range of artefacts occur in pit groups than in isolated pits (Table 4.3). For example, rare finds like arrowheads and disc-beads have been found in pits that occur as a cluster, but never in solitary pits, perhaps suggesting that there is a connection between the quantity of Beaker-associated pits and the range of activities conducted in association with them. Yet this is not always the case.

Much larger ceramic assemblages are generally recovered from sites with clusters of Beaker-associated pits than from isolated or solitary pits (Table 4.4). Although there is considerable variation in the quantities of pottery in the latter category, most produce relatively lesser amounts and over half contain 20 sherds or less from of a single vessel (Table 4.5). These solitary Beaker-associated pits are often dismissed as the remnants of very short term-activities, but yet they occasionally produce greater quantities of Beakers than have been cumulatively produced by some pit groups. For example, at Gortybrigane, Co. Tipperary, only 37 sherds from five Beakers were retrieved from three pits that occurred within a larger group of aceramic pits (Long and O'Malley 2008). While in contrast, a solitary pit at Gortmakellis, also in County Tipperary, produced 418 sherds from 16 vessels (Roche and Grogan 2008). Solitary pits like this suggests that the key factor underlying the differences between the contents of pits is depositional choice, rather than settlement practices. No simple correlation can be observed between the number of features or even the number of pits per site and the amount of pottery deposited within them. This does not make it any easier to explain the discovery of such content-rich pits in apparent isolation from any other evidence for Beaker-associated activity. Is it likely that very few other traces of the activities conducted in those locations survived or were materials brought there from elsewhere for deposition in these pits? This issue is returned to below (see Section 4.5).

A closer examination of the numbers of Beaker sherds and vessels in pits reveals several significant patterns. Most of these pits (86%: 119 of 139) contain less than 50 sherds, indeed many (62%: 86 of 139) produced ten sherds or less and a sizeable proportion (20%: 29 of 139) have produced a single sherd (Fig. 4.9). Just 33 pits contained more than 50 sherds, but five of these contained more than 200 sherds; Kilgobbin, Co. Dublin, Lismullin,

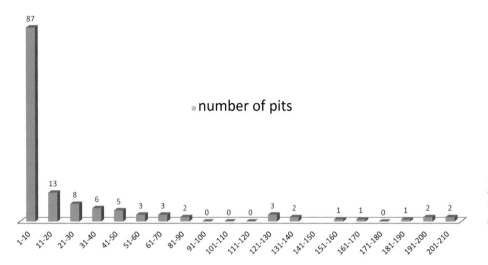

Fig. 4.9: The frequency of pits containing various amounts (in multiples of 10) of Beaker sherds up to 210 sherds.

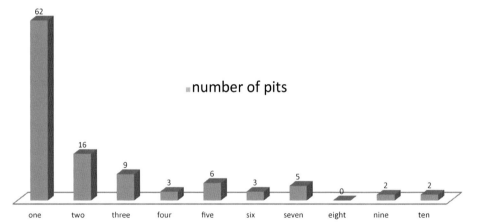

Fig. 4.10: The quantity of pits containing various amounts of Beaker vessels per pit where the pit only contains ten pots or less e.g. 62 pits contain the remains of a single vessel.

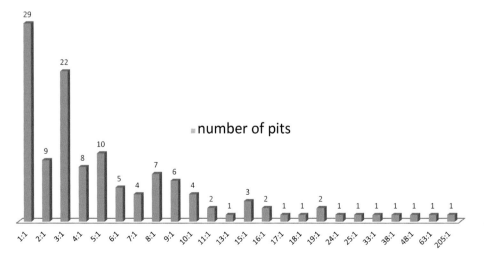

Fig. 4.11: Sherd/vessel ratios for 116 pits from 65 sites.

Co. Meath, and Dunmoon, Windmill Site 36bii and Gortmakellis, all in County Tipperary (Table 4.6). As alluded to above, the unusual pit at Kilgobbin contained the largest assemblage; as many as 696 sherds from a minimum of 38 vessels.

Similarly, most pits (82%: 96 of 118) contained the partial remains of five vessels or less and a single vessel is represented in just over half (52%: 61 of 118) of all these features (Fig. 4.10). Multiple pots are seldom found within individual pits, although 17 pits from 17 sites each contained between six and 15 vessels. The remains of more than 15 vessels have only been recovered from five exceptional pits, including the examples at Kilgobbin, Hill of Rath, Paulstown and Dunmoon (Table 4.6).

From 118 pits, an examination of the sherd/vessel ratio per pit (regardless of the number of pots) revealed that the vessels in most are only represented by a few sherds; 49 (42%) pits displayed sherd/vessel ratios ranging from 2:1 up to 5:1 and half that number (22%) displayed ratios between 6:1 and 10:1 (Fig. 4.11). The low sherd/vessel ratios are true of all these pits, regardless of how many or how few vessels are represented within them. This observation is confirmed by analysis of the sherd/vessel ratio for the 62 pits that contained the remains of just one vessel. Most of these pits (89%: 55 of 62) display a sherd/vessel ratio of 8:1 or less, though there are some extreme outliers such as a vessel comprising 205 sherds from a pit at Lismullin, which are explored further below as evidence for structured deposition.

Focusing now on the 29 pits where only a single Beaker sherd was retrieved, we see that these single-sherd pits generally occur alongside other Beaker-associated features just like the postholes or stakeholes discussed in Section 3.4. Consistent with the pits containing larger quantities of pottery, the artefacts found accompanying these single sherds are usually lithics; these include scrapers but predominantly consist of debitage (Table 4.7). For example, in another pit at Kilgobbin, over 200m from the artefactually-rich pit, a barbed and tanged arrowhead was found along with a flint flake and a single Beaker sherd. While it is tempting to dismiss the discovery of a single sherd as meaningless, incidental, or the product of various post-depositional factors, this fails to account for many of the recurrent characteristics of the artefacts within these or other Beaker-associated pits, such as are highlighted below. Similar fragmentary and highly partial assemblages have been uncovered within pits located in protected contexts, such as those buried under a barrow at Upper Ninepence in the Walton Basin, Wales, indicating that these pits have not been radically altered and that the partial nature of their assemblages accurately reflects the originally deposit (Gibson, A. 1999; Garrow 2006). The key implication here is that the placement of single Beaker sherds in pits formed part of a spectrum of depositional practices.

It is clear by now that the Beakers in these pits generally comprise the highly incomplete and fragmented remains of one or more vessels. Most of which are represented by just a few sherds, which cannot be

Site name	Total sherds from site	Total vessels from site	No. of sherds from pit	No. of vessels from pit
Kilgobbin	696	45	560	38
Gortmakellis	418	16	385	16
Paulstown	424	60	165	26
Paulstown	424	60	137	14
Windmill Site 36bii	332	27	258	19
Lismullin	234	6	205	1
Dunmoon	210	30	210	23
Frankfort	204	3	190	3
Cloghers II	256	13	140	11
Hill of Rath	123	32	156	30
Kilbane II, Fd 1	200	0	155	unknown
Templerainey	273	12	63	5
Newtownbalregan 2	133	11	133	11
Barnagore 2	125	10	126	7
Monadreela Site 13	135	12	84	10
Kilmainham 1C	121	12	82	10
Danesfort 8	47	11	44	9
Newtownbalregan 5	166	15	69	9

Table 4.6: Details of sites with a pit containing high numbers of Beaker sherds or vessels.

Site name	Finds
Ballinure	1 x blade
Ballycuddy More 1	1 x arrowhead, 2 x Early Neolithic pot-sherds
Ballymoyle	1 x scraper, 1 x retouched flake, 32 x debitage pieces, 29 x natural pieces
Carranstown Site 3	burnt bone
Carranstown Site 3	3 x debitage
Caherabbey Upper	a cache of cereal grain
Coolbeg Site 73	3 x debitage
Gortcobies pit	cremated human bone, 3 sherds of an Irish Bowl
Ballinaspig More 5	1 x grinding stone, 1 x nut, 2 x debitage
Charlesland Site A	6 x debitage
Haggardstown Site 13	5 x debitage, 1 x scraper
Kilgobbin	1 x debitage, 1 x arrowhead
paulstown	1 x debitage, 1 x scraper
Rathwilladoon	1 x debitage

Table 4.7: The finds from pits containing a single sherd of Beaker pottery.

refitted to forms a 'whole' vessel. This suggests that the pottery was probably not deposited until sometime after its breakage and that during this interval, between their fragmentation and final deposition, these vessels experienced considerable wear and movement. Unmistakable evidence for this is provided by the occurrence of burnt and unburnt, as well as abraded and unabraded sherd surfaces and edges deriving from the same vessels in pits that display no evidence for *in situ* burning. This kind of contrasting sherd damage has been noted at several sites such as Windmill 6BII, Co. Tipperary, where a Beaker (Vessel No. 5) from a pit at was represented by conjoining sherds, some of which were very well-preserved and others that had an abraded exterior (Grogan, E. and Roche, H. 2006). Similarly, at Carrigrohane, Co. Cork, 65 sherds from two Beakers were found within a pit containing a single fill that had been rapidly formed. One of these vessels was represented by a burnt portion, with reasonably fresh edges and surfaces, and an unburnt portion displaying worn surfaces and edges (Grogan and Roche 2005c).

Significantly, while the extent of the edge or surface damage displayed by the sherds varies, it is generally less than one might expect to occur, given the levels of fragmentation displayed by the vessels within these pits. Many of the sherds exhibiting signs of weathering have worn surfaces but very little edge-wear. This indicates that the Beaker ceramics found in pits were predominantly re-deposited from a far greater accumulation of pottery and other materials that had afforded them varying degrees of protection from the elements. Pot-sherds (often from the same vessels) tend to be distributed throughout the fill or fills of each pit, indicating that these sherds were deposited into the feature within a soil matrix. This is supported by the presence of tiny pieces of worked flint within many of these Beaker-pits, suggesting that materials were not being obtained for deposition on a piece by piece basis (see Garrow 2006, 43). The obvious conclusion to draw here is that most of the materials found within Beaker-associated pits were derived from larger aggregations of settlement debris such as a rubbish pile or midden, as has been suggested by various British studies (*e.g.* Case 1995b, 10-11; Pollard 2000, 365; Garrow 2006; Brudenell and Cooper 2008). This can be illustrated by the previously referred to pit at Kilgobbin that contained over 1400 artefacts including nearly 700 sherds from at least 38 Beakers (Hagen 2005). Eoin Grogan's (2005c) analysis of the sherds revealed that many of these displayed unabraded edges in combination with surface-damage on only one side, some of which was localised to just a portion of that surface. This is entirely consistent with the idea that these sherds had previously been on and in a much larger aggregation where only parts of their bodies were exposed to the elements. Sherds from the same pots were repeatedly found in both fills of the pit, suggesting that the deposits had been obtained from the same accumulation of occupational debris. The presence of unusually large quantities of lithics in the pit, including micro-flakes and tiny fragments, almost none of which could be refitted, suggests that the pit contents represents the deposition of scoops taken from a collection of occupational detritus (Milliken 2005).

Clearly, there was a complex range of depositional practices associated with these pits that is difficult to characterise using quantitative methods. By looking in more detail at two sites, Newtownbalregan 2 (Bayley 2009b) and Faughart Lower 6 (Hayes 2007), both in County Louth, we can better understand the complexity of this activity. These sites are situated 5kms from each other within a low-lying undulating landscape (c. 20-40m O.D.) to the west of Dundalk Bay and south of the Carlingford Mountains. They were excavated in 2005 in advance of the construction of the Dundalk Western

Fig. 4.12: Plan of features at Newtownbalregan 2, Co. Louth showing cluster of two Beaker pits in combination with aceramic pits and postholes (after Bailey 2010).

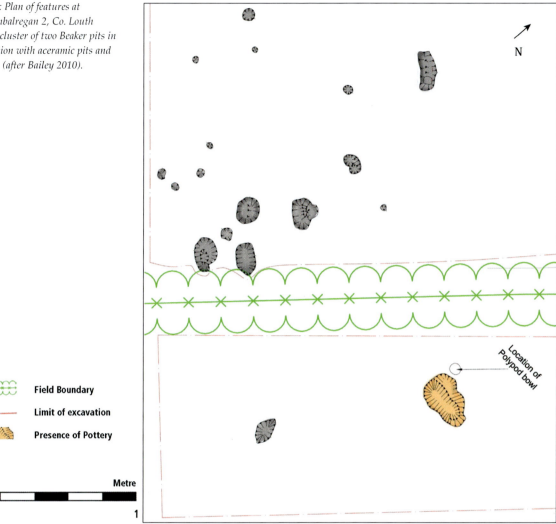

Bypass and form part of a wider cohort of Beaker-associated sites in this area, indicating that the north-western extent of the central plain of County Louth was clearly a focus of intense activity from 2400-2000 BC.

At Newtownbalregan 2, a Beaker-associated pit was excavated in combination with aceramic pits and postholes (Fig. 4.12). A near complete polypod bowl, that had been intact when deposited, was found in an upright position within a shallow pit (Fig. 4.13). Right beside this was an oval pit containing 133 sherds derived from at least 11 Beaker pots (Grogan and Roche 2005a) that was filled with four separate deposits and had large stones located at its base (Fig. 4.14). Numerous artefacts were recovered from the charcoal-rich basal layer; 126 sherds representing the partial remains of at least ten Beakers and 30 lithics, including a considerable number of unworked pieces, as well as two 'thumbnail' scrapers, a small cutting tool and a small number of burnt bone fragments (Nelis 2009). One of the overlying deposits contained three sherds and two pieces of flint debitage. Only four Beaker sherds were found in the uppermost fill. Alder charcoal from the primary deposit produced a radiocarbon date of 2190-1890 BC (WK-18558; 3649±49 BP), which partially overlaps with the end of the date-range for the pottery in this pit (see Fig. 8.2).

The presence of unburnt pottery and lithics in deposits that also contain charcoal and burnt bone, all within a pit displaying no evidence of burning, indicates that these materials were found in a derived position. The condition of the lithics in the pit ranges from heavily abraded or patinated to fresh and some of the worn flints suffered from post-use damage (Nelis 2009. This indicates that they had been exposed to the elements for some time before they were deposited. Only a small number of sherds from each of the 11 Beakers were present within the pit, similarly suggesting that these have been redeposited from another context. Yet many of the sherds could be rejoined, and they did not display any edge-wear abrasions indicative of pre- or post-depositional disturbance (Grogan and Roche 2005a). This implies that they were completely protected

REMEMBERING EVERYDAY LIFE | 75

Fig. 4.13: Almost complete polypod bowl that was found in an upright position within a pit at Newtownbalregan 2, Co. Louth (Photo by Eoin Grogan, courtesy of IAC).

Fig. 4.14: The Newtownbalregan polypod bowl in-situ beside the pit containing 133 sherds derived from at least 11 Beaker pots before excavation (after Bayley 2010).

from post-breakage weathering within the pre-pit context from which they were obtained prior to deposition. A midden seems to represent the most likely type of context from which these were derived.

The horizontal and vertical distribution of artefacts throughout the fills of the pit and the occurrence of tiny pieces of worked flint strongly suggests that these were deposited within a soil matrix. Furthermore, sherds from the same vessels occurred within the different pit-fills (Grogan and Roche 2005a). A flint scraper and a bipolar flake, which were almost certainly derived from the same core, were also found within the pit (Nelis 2009. All of this suggests that these layers were rapidly formed and may have been derived from the same source. The pit itself displayed no evidence for previous use, such as erosion to the sides and base. Instead it appears to have been dug and subsequently backfilled over a very short timescale. This points towards the conclusion that this pit may have been created specifically to receive the deposits that filled it.

At Faughart Lower 6, excavations revealed seven pits of similar form that each contained quite a uniform fill (Figs. 4.15-4.16); Four of the pits were radiocarbon dated and these returned determinations ranging from 2800-2400 BC, indicating that the various features were broadly contemporary (Hayes 2007). Two of these were situated only 0.1m apart and both produced Beaker pottery comprising 36 sherds representing seven 'fine' and 'domestic' Beaker pots (Roche and Grogan 2006). The five other pits were aceramic and were located at least 5m away. One contained a flint flake and two of the others yielded small quantities of burnt animal bone (species unidentifiable).

One of the Beaker-associated pits was filled by a single charcoal-rich deposit with occasional flecks of burnt animal bone (species unidentifiable), hazelnut shells, and 27 sherds derived from six Beakers (Roche and Grogan 2006). Hazel charcoal returned a radiocarbon date of 2850-2460 BC (Beta-217946; 4030±50 BP). One of these vessels was an AOC Beaker – one of the earliest styles of Beaker in Ireland (see Section 3.1) – represented by one sherd and three fragments (Fig. 4.17). The other Beaker-associated pit contained a dark charcoal-rich deposit with occasional flecks of burnt animal bone (species unidentifiable), and nine sherds derived from three vessels.

The ceramic assemblage from both of these pits was fragmented with only a few weathered and abraded sherds representing each vessel. All of this suggests that these Beakers had been exposed in an intermediate context such as a midden before their ultimate deposition within these pits (Roche and Grogan 2006). Sherds from the same vessel were found in both pits and this material connection between the features may indicate that the debris was obtained from the same source. Like the pits at Newtownbalregan, the relationship between these pits and the activities conducted in this location, including the deliberate re-deposition of occupational debris, remains unclear. If all seven pits were indeed broadly contemporary, this might imply that the placement of Beaker pottery in pits was quite selective and that the empty aceramic pits were part of the spectrum of Beaker-associated depositional activities on these sites. We do not, however, have the level of chronological resolution required to be certain of this.

Although many Beaker-pits clearly contain deposits of material derived from another context, the deposi-

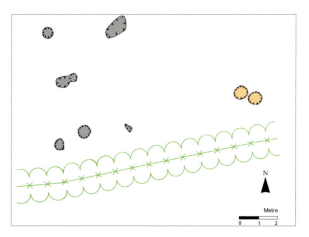

Fig. 4.16: Plan of seven pits at Faughart 6, Co. Louth, two of which were Beaker-associated (after Hayes 2007).

Fig. 4.15: The two Beaker-associated pits at Faughart 6, Co. Louth, before and after excavation (after Hayes 2007).

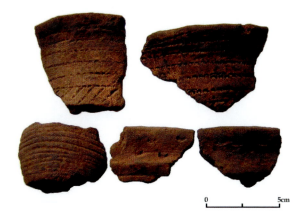

Fig. 4.17: A large sherd from an AOC Beaker and other sherds from two other vessels found in one of the Beaker pits at Faughart 6 (after Hayes 2007).

tion of an intact polypod bowl in an upright position within what seems to be a purpose-dug pit at Newtownbalregan 2 highlights that certain objects were certainly selected for deposition in a very careful manner. There are other instances of exactly the kind of 'formalised' or structured deposition described by Richards and Thomas (1984, 192), involving the deliberate selection and/or arrangement of artefacts within a feature. For example, at Doonmoon, Co. Tipperary, a pit contained 200 sherds representing the remains of up to 23 mainly incomplete Beaker pots, as well as three heat-shattered pieces of flint with a small mixture of silty clay. Few of the vessels were complete on deposition but some of the larger pots appeared to have been set inside one another with the outermost example inverted over the entire deposit. A greenstone axe was found among the sherds near the base of the pit (Gowen 1988, 53-4). Likewise, at Barnagore, Co. Cork, two water-rolled bolster-shaped stones that had been used for grinding or rubbing appear to have been deliberately placed in an upright position within a Beaker-associated pit along with a quern (Danaher 2003).

Similarly, at Rathmullan 12, Co. Meath, the primary fill of a large pit produced 33 sherds representing ten Beakers (Grogan and Roche 2011). Within this deposit, a distinct lens of black charcoal-rich clay was identified that yielded a large amount of burnt pig bone, two small worn Beaker sherds and 31 well-preserved conjoining sherds from a comparatively intact Grooved Ware vessel. A sample of the burnt pig bone returned a radiocarbon date of 2470-2200 BC (SUERC-31908; 3855±35 BP). The presence of so many sherds from the Grooved Ware vessel indicates that this pot was specially selected for deposition and may have been relatively undamaged at this time. Its appearance within a distinct localised layer suggests that it was deliberately placed into this Beaker-associated pit. The Grooved Ware pot was almost certainly not contemporary with these Beakers (see dating of the demise of Grooved Ware in Chapter Eight) and appears to represent an anachronistic object taken from elsewhere to be deposited within this pit.

The presence within pits of special or socially significant objects, such as polished stone axes, polypod bowls, barbed and tanged arrowheads and caches of scrapers, also suggests that materials were not simply being dumped into these pits, but in fact were placed there during a more complex set of activities. An example of this is provided by one of a pair of Beaker-associated pits excavated at Monadreela 13, Co. Tipperary (O'Brien, R. 2014). The base of the pit in question showed evidence for *in situ* burning and the materials within it included red ash, burnt clay, 110 sherds from at least ten Beakers, many fragments of burnt animal bone (15.3g), a large quantity of hazelnut shells and acorns, hazel, alder, oak and ash charcoal, four barley grains, 33 crab-apple fragments, flint debitage, quartz, a hammer-stone, and a small polished stone axe (Figs. 4.18-4.19). Peter Woodman suggested that the 'squarish' shape of this axe resembled that of early copper axes. A sample of the hazel charcoal produced a radiocarbon date of 2457-2204 BC (UBA-13903). Some of the sherds from one Beaker vessel were burnt but these conjoined with unburnt sherds from the same pot, suggesting that some at least were exposed to the fire that had been lit in the pit. Heavily abraded sherds from another vessel refitted with unworn fresh sherds indicating that there had been an interval in between their fragmentation and their deposition where they experienced different histories (Grogan and Roche 2006). While many of these objects seem to have been acquired from a larger accumulation of occupational debris, some of the artefacts such as the stone axe seem to have been specially selected for inclusion.

Other similar discoveries on other sites seem to represent objects that were also specially selected for deposition. These include the polished stone axe manufacturing kit in a Beaker-pit at Cloghers or the 23 disc beads from another Beaker-pit at Paulstown. Similarly, pits containing high numbers of flint tools but very little debitage,

Fig. 4.18: The pit at Monadreela 13, Co. Tipperary, during excavation (reproduced courtesy of Richard O'Brien and TII).

Fig. 4.19: The assemblage from a Beaker pit at Monadreela 13, Co. Tipperary (photographed by Stellar Photography on behalf of South Tipperary County Council, reproduced courtesy of Richard O'Brien and TII).

Site	Find Type	Sherd Count	Vessel Count	Ratio	Pot Detail
Lismullin	incomplete pot	205	1	205:1	decorated Rockbarton
Russellstown	sherds	48	1	48:1	n/a
Derver 1	sherds	19	1	19:1	decorated Rockbarton
Skreen 3	sherds	17	1	17:1	decorated Rockbarton
Graigueshoneen Field 3	sherds	15	1	15:1	decorated
Kilmainham 1B	incomplete pot	15	1	15:1	decorated Rockbarton

Table 4.8: Details of Beaker pits with high sherd/vessel ratio.

such as that at Rathdown, or caches of cereal grains, may also indicate the careful deposition of particular materials within pits. The repeated discovery of numerous adjoining sherds forming substantial portions of a specific kind of Beaker may also represent a similar type of depositional practice (Fig. 4.20). As we saw above, there are a small number of pits (23) containing between one and three pots that display unusually high sherd/vessel ratios (Table 4.8). Significantly, seven of these pits contain remnants from large bucket-shaped Beakers with cordons below the rim, often referred to (in an Irish context) as Rockbarton pots (Case 1961; Grogan and Roche 2010). Similar Beakers are also found in Britain and the Netherlands, usually in 'domestic' contexts, where they are known as a 'potbekers' or 'pot beakers' (Lehmann 1965; Gibson 1980; Sheridan 2008a, 63-4; Fokkens 2012b, 121).

The condition and quantity of these sherds from pits cannot be explained solely by the size of these vessels and must reflect a very deliberate and selective depositional treatment that differs from that of other Beakers. For example, at Lismullin, Co. Meath, a pit contained 205 sherds derived from a large Rockbarton pot that displayed evidence for repair (Grogan and Roche 2009b; O'Connell 2009). Forty-six sherds from the upper portion of a Rockbarton pot were also retrieved from the unusual pit at Kilgobbin (Grogan 2005c). At Kilmainham 1B, Co. Meath, a near complete Rockbarton pot was found in a pit with half of the vessel occurring *in situ* in the centre of the pit (Fig. 4.21); Grogan and Roche 2009c; Bayley 2010). Another Rockbarton pot was discovered at Cluntyganny, Co. Tyrone, as an almost complete inverted vessel within a stone-lined pit (Brennan *et al.* 1978, fig. 3). This vessel is very similar to a further such pot that was found during Emma Devine's (2006) excavations at Frankfort, Co. Wexford.

The Frankfort Rockbarton pot comprised 160 sherds, many of which conjoined. They were recovered from a pit containing several big stones, a large quantity of charred cereal grain and hazelnut shells, as well as 30 sherds from two other Beakers. Although this pit displayed evidence for *in situ* burning, none of the sherds had been burnt and most of the pottery only displayed a moderate amount of wear, although a few sherds from the Rockbarton pot were

Fig. 4.20: Conjoining sherds from Rockbarton pots found in a pit at Kilmainham1C, Co. Meath (after Walsh 2009) and a pit at Kilgobbin (courtesy of Ines Hagen).

Fig. 4.21: A near-complete Rockbarton pot in-situ in the centre of a pit at Kilmainham 1B, Co. Meath (courtesy of Fintan Walsh and IAC).

REMEMBERING EVERYDAY LIFE

quite abraded (Grogan and Roche 2008). This suggests that the Rockbarton pot had been broken for some time, during which some of its sherds were subjected to abrasion, while others enjoyed partial protection from the elements. While the presence of multiple and often conjoining sherds from a single pot might suggest that these were deposited very soon after breakage, the evidence from Frankfort indicates that this was certainly not always the case. One possibility here is that parts of specific pots may have been specially selected for deposition from a larger assemblage of Beakers. Yet this is complicated by the evidence detailed above, whereby one or a few sherds were placed in many pits. In those instances, the focus of the depositional activity was on just one or two sherds rather than on substantial portions of a vessel, suggesting that the part may have served to represent the whole.

While there is much that we remain uncertain about regarding these pits, the long-standing reductionist and functionalist interpretations of these features as mere storage or refuse pits are incorrect and grossly misrepresent the socio-cultural practices of people in the past. The quantity and character of the materials within these pits, as well as the pits themselves, suggest that these deposits were not just ad-hoc events (Pollard 1999, 89). These represent the outcome of highly meaningful and deliberate actions. This is an aspect that is returned to below, alongside other considerations like the function of these pits, the meanings behind the deposition of materials within them and their relationship to settlement. Before that, we need to consider the character of spreads, a related type of feature containing similar kinds of occupational materials that may reflect similar practices.

4.3 Spreads and middens

As we saw in Chapter Three, spreads comprising occupational debris and large volumes of Beaker pottery, such as those outside the passage tombs at *Brú na Bóinne*, represent a recurrent but poorly understood feature of the Irish archaeological record; they have traditionally been considered as Beaker settlement contexts in Ireland. Due to recent discoveries, at least 39 Beaker spreads or deposits have been excavated at 30 sites. The curious occurrence of some of these spreads at such places like Knowth and Newgrange raises the question of whether these deposits are comparable to those from non-monumental settings? This, and their relationship to settlement, is investigated here by considering 27 of these various surface deposits together.

As an initial challenge, it is difficult to know whether the examples that have survived within the archaeological record are representative of a wider set of Chalcolithic practices that have left little trace. The many occurrences of Beaker pottery in disturbed or residual contexts in Ireland suggest that above-surface deposition was recurrently practiced. Upstanding features such as spreads are by their nature particularly vulnerable to destruction or alteration. Most of the Beaker spreads that have been found seem to owe their survival to mitigating factors such as the construction of later features over or around them, or their occurrence in locations unsuitable for modern ploughing (see below). Yet, it is likely that even these features were once much higher but have been truncated through the millennia of activity conducted at each of those locations. It may be significant to note that most spreads in this study were excavated before 1997 rather than after it, when the amount of development-led archaeological activity occurring in advance of road building and other construction activity greatly increased (see Chapter One). The use of plant machinery (under archaeological supervision) to strip topsoil on most of these projects may be a factor here, but equally, these developments have mainly focused upon lower-lying areas that have generally been subject to extensive ploughing or land-improvements, rather than upland locations where upstanding deposits are more likely to survive.

The fact that 14 of the 39 sites were excavated before 1990, with a further five being excavated prior to the year 2000, is significant because approaches to excavation, recording, analysis and presentation of material from archaeological sites have changed radically in recent decades. This means that relevant detailed information is often lacking to enable in-depth analysis of these features' formation processes. In some cases, such as Newgrange and Monknewtown, it has not been possible to disentangle the Beaker element from the admixture of multi-period evidence (see Chapter Three). Despite the questionable chronological integrity of some of these deposits (see Section 3.2), they are included here because it is believed that they genuinely represent the above-surface deposition of Beaker artefacts.

The majority (20 out of 27) of these Beaker occupational deposits revealed only one spread per site, though an exceptional five spreads occurred at Knowth (Table 4.9). Spreads are generally associated with a range of other Beaker-associated features including postholes, slot trenches and gullies, though they are most often found with Beaker-associated pits (12 sites). Spreads also occur as isolated features. On at least nine sites, spreads were the only feature containing Beaker pottery (Table 4.9).

Most spreads display an amorphous shape that often owes much to the factors that have enabled its preservation, such as the occurrence of a hollow or depression. They range greatly in length from the longest examples of 25m at Kilgobbin and 21m at Knowth Concentration D (Fig. 3.11) to the smallest at Kilmainham 1C, Co. Meath (Walsh 2009), which was just 1m long. These survive to varying heights above ground level, with the

Site name	Year of excavation	No. of Spreads	No. of Beaker features	Other Beaker-associated features
Knowth	1990	5	?	pits and postholes
Kilmainham 1C	2006	3	14	9 pits, 2 postholes
Roughan Hill	1996	3	1	possible structures
Lough Gur 1977-78	1977	2	2	none
Ross Island	1995	2	5	2 slot trenches, 1 pit
Rathmullan Site 10	2001	2	8	4 pits, 2 linear gullies
Mell	2005	1	8	2 pits, a slot trench and postholes
Rockbarton Bog Site 1	1942	1	1	none
Rockbarton Bog Site 2	1942	1	2	hearth
Rockbarton Bog Site 3	1942	1	1	none
Moneen	1952	1	2	cist and cairn
Lough Gur Site D	1954	1	1	none
Downpatrick	1962	1	1	none
Longstone Cullen	1973	1	1	none
Monknewtown	1976	1	2	large pit
Newgrange Pit circle	1984	1	1	none
Kilbride	1997	1	3	2 linear gullies
Laughanstown Site 35	2000	1	12	4 pits, a hearth, a stone surface, a posthole
Kilgobbin	2003	1	18	6 pits, a slot trench, 6 postholes
Cornagleragh	2004	1	1	none
Newtownlittle	2005	1	10	7 pits, a stakehole, a posthole
Oldbridge 3	2005	1	1	none
Haggardstown Site 13	2006	1	10	8 pits, slot trench,
Gardenrath 2	2006	1	3	pit and spread
Moanduff 2	2007	1	2	posthole
Lismullin	2007	1	6	pits
Newgrange	1980	1	?	none
Lough Gur Site 10	1952	1	1	none
Lough Gur Circle K	1952	1	1	none

Table 4.9: The number of Beaker spreads per site and the types of other Beaker-associated features occurring on each site.

Site name	Length	Width	Height
Mell	9.5	5	0.40
Rathmullan Site 10	5.1	2.05	0.25
Oldbridge 3	10	3.5	0.20
Newtownlittle	7.3	3.4	0.16
Gardenrath 2	8.95	3.2	0.15
Kilgobbin	26	9	0.10
Knowth Concentration D	21	12.5	0.10
Haggardstown Site 13	7	4.6	0.10
Kilmainham 1C	5.7	3.1	0.10
Kilmainham 1C	5.5	5.5	0.08
Moanduff 2	1.25	1	0.08
Knowth Concentration B	17	15	0.07
Lismullin	3.44	1.68	0.05
Rathmullan Site 10	1.76	1.3	0.05
Kilmainham 1C	1.1	0.8	0.04

Table 4.10: The size of Beaker spreads (in metres).

Site name	Sherd count	Vessel count	Sherd/vessel ratio
Moneen	?	?	
Lough Gur 1977-78	3	?	?
Newgrange 1984 Pit circle	4	0	?
Laughanstown Site 35	5	?	?
Lough Gur 1977-78	5	?	?
Haggardstown Site 13	9	?	?
Kilmainham 1C	9	?	?
Kilbride	12	?	?
Rockbarton Bog Site1	20	?	?
Kilgobbin	37	?	?
Rockbarton Bog Site2	40	?	?
Roughan Hill	178	?	?
Lough Gur Circle K	394	?	?
Monknewtown	5000	?	?
Cornagleragh	1	1	1:1
Kilmainham 1C	1	1	1:1
Rockbarton Bog Site3	1	1	1:1
Moanduff 2	6	2	3:1
Lismullin	4	1	4:1
Ross Island mining spoil layer	50	12	4:1
Kilmainham 1C	5	1	5:1
Oldbridge 3	26	5	5:1
Knowth E	341	45	7:1
Gardenrath 2	9	1	9:1
Knowth A	446	46	9:1
Ross Island occupation layer	182	18	10:1
Knowth B	300	30	10:1
Mell	471	37	12:1
Knowth C	1043	75	14:1
Newtownlittle	362	23	16:1
Newgrange 'Beaker layers'	3600	200	18:1
Lough Gur Site10	570	29	19:1
Knowth D	2072	104	19:1

Table 4.11: The numbers of Beaker sherds and vessels found in each spread.

highest example of 0.4m occurring at Mell, Co. Louth (McQuade 2005; Table 4.10). Though as discussed above, this probably reflects the poorly preserved nature of these types of features.

At least 9721 sherds from a minimum of 567 Beaker vessels have been found in 39 spreads on 30 sites in Ireland. Spreads from 13 of these sites contained more than 200 sherds; however, the amount of Beaker pottery in each spread varies greatly (Table 4.11). Large quantities were recorded in the deposits in monumental settings, such as the 'Beaker layers' at Newgrange (5000 sherds), Concentration D (2072 sherds deriving from at least 104 Beakers) and Concentration C (1043 sherds) at Knowth. The closest comparisons from non-passage tomb contexts are provided by the sites of Mell and Newtownlittle, which produced as many as 471 and 362 sherds respectively. These sites stand out in contrast to the much smaller quantities from other spreads, only 11 of which produced more than ten vessels, while 14 yielded ten sherds or less. The sherd/vessel ratios (for the 19 spreads with sufficient details for this analysis) show a similar contrast; higher ratios of up to 19:1 occurred at six spreads including the Newgrange 'Beaker layers' (18:1), Knowth Concentration D (19:1) and Lough Gur site 10 (19:1), while eight spreads displayed a low ratio of less than or equal to 5:1.

Artefact type	No. of sites	No. of objects
Beaker pottery	28	-
Convex scrapers	7	152
Polypod bowls	4	5
Hollow-based arrowhead	3	3
B and T arrowhead	2	5
Plate	2	2
Lead rod	1	1
Wrist-bracer	1	1
Gold disc	1	1
Lough Ravel axe	1	1
Killaha bronze flat axe	1	1

Table 4.12: The numbers of sites where spreads produce each of these artefacts.

The remains of five polypod bowls were discovered within a spread on four sites; Mell, Co. Louth (McQuade 2005), Newgrange (Cleary, R. 1983, 74, fig. 25, group 15) and Rathmullan, Site 10 (Bolger 2012), both in County Meath and Newtownlittle, Co. Dublin (Grogan and Roche 2005b). At Newtownlittle, the spread was relatively small (7.30m by 3.40m by 0.16m) and contained 350 sherds derived from at least 20 Beaker pots, including a Beaker dish, a polypod bowl and five pieces of flint debitage (Ward 2006). A pit that was dug into the top of this spread also produced sherds and a foot from another polypod bowl. At Mell, the polypod sherds came from a series of overlying Beaker-associated deposits (see below).

Other forms of pottery of earlier or later date have been found in six Beaker spreads. For example, both Concentrations A and C at Knowth contained Grooved Ware. In Concentration A, Grooved Ware and Beaker came from the same horizon; however, the Beakers were mainly found within the north-western extent, while the Grooved Ware was only found in the north-eastern part (Roche and Eogan 2001, 129). A small number of sherds (six sherds from two vessels) from Irish Bowls of the Food Vessel tradition have been found in spreads with Beaker pottery at Roughan Hill (Jones, C. 1996; Roche 1999) and Ross Island (Brindley, A.L. 2004). Vases were discovered with Beakers in a spread at Laughanstown, Site 78, Co. Dublin, within a deposit (2.8m by 3.0m by 0.2m) of dark black brown sandy silt with frequent flecks of charcoal, occasional flecks of burnt bone and animal teeth, all of which filled a shallow irregular hollow (Seaver 2004a and b; 2005). It produced 33 Beaker sherds, 85 sherds of Vase and Cordoned Urn pottery, as well as 122 flint pieces, including burnt and unburnt split pebbles, bipolar cores, scrapers and other retouched lithics. A radiocarbon date of 1690-1520 BC (OxA-12751; 3341±31 BP) was obtained from charcoal (species unidentified) within the midden deposit. This may suggest that deposition continued episodically (at what would have been a visible feature) over an extended duration, akin to the way people continued to deposit materials at the Knowth and Newgrange spreads.

Fig. 4.22: A fragmented wrist-bracer (Type A2 -2TPC) found with 250 Beaker sherds in a spread at Rathmullan Site 10, Co. Meath (courtesy of IAC).

Only a very small amount of ecofactual material has been recovered from these deposits of occupational debris. Barley cereal grains were identified within the Beaker spread at Mell. Unburnt faunal remains in the form of cattle bones were recorded at Ross Island. These were also present within the midden deposits at Roughan Hill where they occurred alongside pig and sheep or goat bones, while unidentifiable burnt bone occurred within the spread at Mell. The only human remains from any of the spreads were found within a Beaker-associated surface deposit under the cairn at Moneen, Co. Cork, but as discussed in Chapter Five, these seem to have been displaced from the large central cist that was also sealed by the cairn.

Lithics have only been found in 13 spreads on 11 sites and the most common retouched artefacts within these assemblages are small convex scrapers; 152 of which have been found within nine spreads on seven sites. Most of

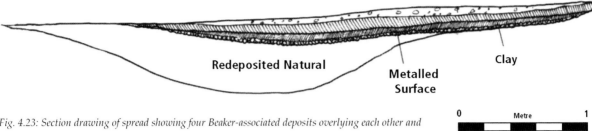

Fig. 4.23: Section drawing of spread showing four Beaker-associated deposits overlying each other and situated within a depression (after McQuade 2005).

these tools (94 in total), however, were found within the Beaker-associated midden deposits at Roughan Hill (Jones, C. 1998b; O'Hare 2005). Although 29 examples were found in the spread forming Concentration C at Knowth and another nine were recovered from the deposits at Mell, such large volumes of scrapers did not occur elsewhere.

Spreads have produced at least nine arrowheads; this includes two barbed and tanged and one hollow-based example from the concentrations at Knowth (Eogan 1984, 274, Fig. 99, 273; Dillon 1997, 251) and three barbed and tanged projectiles from the 'Beaker layers' at Newgrange (Lehane 1983, fig. 64, nos E56: 781, 675 and 1025). Excavations of the Roughan Hill midden (Jones, C. 1996) and the spreads of Beaker-associated habitation debris at Lough Gur, Circle K and Site 10 (Grogan and Eogan 1987, fig. 63: 14a, fig. 70:1112), also each produced a single hollow-based arrowhead (Table 4.12). Two flint knives came from the spreads at Haggardstown (McLoughlin, G. 2009) and Mell (McQuade 2005). A single polished stone axe was found within the spread of occupational debris and ore processing spoil at Ross Island, along with other stone macro-tools including two quernstones, a honestone and large numbers of hammer-stones. Over 38 shale stone axe flakes also came from the midden at Roughan Hill (O'Hare 2005; Jones, C. 2008).

A small number of additional items have been discovered in this group of occupational spreads that are rarely found in association with Beaker pottery in Ireland and certainly not in apparently 'domestic' contexts; they are also rarely discovered during archaeological excavations (see Chapters Five and Six). At Rathmullan, Site 10 (Bolger 2012), a fragmented wrist-bracer (Type A2-2TPC) occurred within a deposit along with 250 Beaker sherds, the foot of a polypod bowl and lithics (Fig. 4.22). An enigmatic lead rod was present in the spread at Mell (McQuade 2005). A gold sun-disc, part of a copper chisel and a Lough Ravel type copper flat axe were discovered within the spread of Beaker-associated habitation debris that lay under a later Bronze Age terrace wall at Site D, Lough Gur (Ó Ríordáin, S.P. 1954, 410-12) and a Killaha type bronze flat axe (O'Kelly and Shell 1979) was found in close proximity to a putative metalworking area in the

'Beaker layers' at Newgrange. Even though the chronological integrity of the Newgrange and Lough Gur deposits is highly questionable (see Chapter Three), it does seem to be the case that some of these features were suitable contexts for the deposition of artefacts like wrist-bracers, which are not usually found with Beaker pottery in Ireland (see Chapter Nine). While each of these spreads undoubtedly comprise occupational debris, as indicated by the presence of carbonised residues and sooting on the interior of the sherds, food remains, stone tools and other occupational by-products, discerning the extent to which the excavated characteristics of these spread's accurately reflects their original nature is complicated, as is deciphering whether these spreads represent trampled habitation layers or deliberate deposits of material.

To try to address these issues, we now consider in greater detail the surface deposits at Mell, Knowth Concentration E and Newtownlittle, including the condition of the Beaker pottery within these spreads and what this tells us about its deposition. Excavations during 2005, near the base of a sloping hill at Mell, Waterunder, Co. Louth, in the Boyne Valley, uncovered a multi-period site dating from the Early Neolithic to the post-medieval period, including Chalcolithic and Late Bronze Age activity (McQuade 2005). Definite Beaker-associated features included a spread, two pits and a posthole. An aceramic inhumation that was broadly contemporary with the Beaker activity and resembles aspects of classic Beaker burials was also excavated on this site (see Chapter Five).

The spread comprised four extensive (10m by 5m) deposits that overlay each other to a height of 0.4m (Fig. 4.23). Ash charcoal from one of the deposits produced a radiocarbon date of 2470-2290 BC (WK-17457; 3906±33 BP). These deposits sealed a metalled surface that occurred within a deep hollow, which had previously been in-filled with a deposit of sterile boulder clay. A slight depression remained, however, and seems to have assisted the survival of the overlying deposits in this location. A discontinuous arc of four curvilinear gullies defined the northern and eastern extents of the spread but the chronological and stratigraphic relationship between these features is not clear.

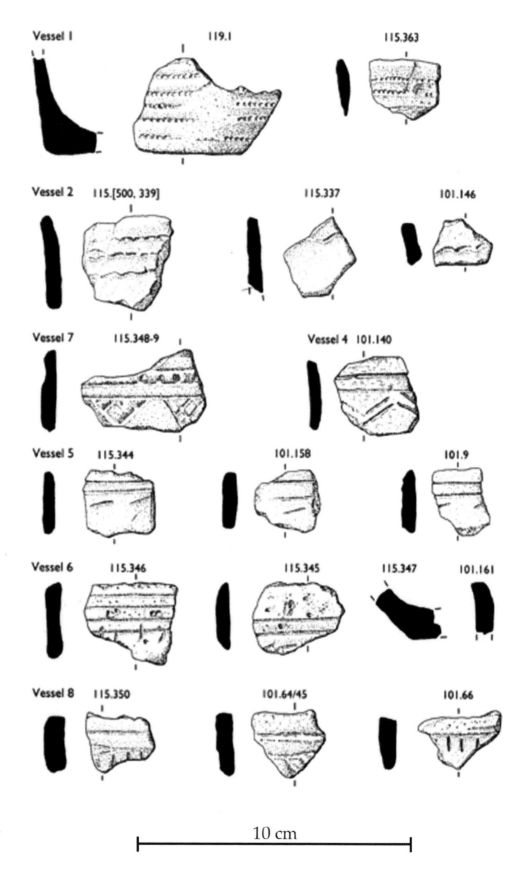

Fig. 4.24: Highly fragmentary Beaker sherds from the deposits at Mell (after McQuade 2005).

REMEMBERING EVERYDAY LIFE | 85

Fig. 4.25: Excavation of the Beaker deposits at Newtownlittle, Co. Dublin (courtesy of Kara Ward).

Fig. 4.26: The numerous deposits forming the Beaker spread at Newtownlittle (after Ward 2006).

The four deposits forming the spread produced 471 sherds from a minimum of 38 Beakers, seven sherds from a polypod bowl, as well as a lead rod, fired clay wasters, burnt bone (species unidentifiable) and carbonised barley grains. A total of 38 lithics were found, including a core, 26 flakes, eight convex scrapers and a flint knife. Most (26 examples) of the vessels in the spread are highly fragmentary and are predominantly represented by fewer than ten sherds (Fig. 4.24). As well as this low sherd/vessel ratio, there are many fragments (89) and sherds (113) that were too small to assign to any specific vessels, although six vessels are represented by more than 20 sherds each, with a further three comprised more than 30 sherds each.

This seems noteworthy in comparison with the Beaker pottery from pits (65%) that generally display a ratio of less than 10:1 (see above). The highly partial and fragmentary nature of most of the Mell pottery suggests that a period elapsed during which it was exposed to weathering after the vessels' breakage, but before its deposition into this context. This is borne out by Helen Roche and Eoin Grogan's (2005) observation that a substantial proportion of the sherds from this spread displayed worn edges and surfaces and very few of the sherds could be refitted. Sherds from the same vessels were present within each of the deposits, suggesting that the spread was created over a short duration through the deposition of materials derived from the same source. All of this indicates that post-breakage, this assemblage was in an exposed location for some time, where it was subject to a considerable level of damage, before being gathered for deposition within the spread, which provided protection to most of the pottery. Yet, the nature of the activities that generated all this occupational debris or resulted in its deposition here are unclear. The large quantity of pottery and modified tools may indicate occupational activity in this locale with a considerable level of intensity and duration (see Schofield 1991; Hill 1995), though very few other features containing Beakers were found on the site.

Excavations of a gentle slope at the foot of Three Rock Mountain at Newtownlittle, Co. Dublin, revealed multi-period activity dating from the Middle Neolithic, Early, Middle and Late Bronze Age (Ward 2006). Beaker-associated features consisted of eight pits, two of which were sealed under a surface deposit containing a large assemblage of Beaker pottery (Fig. 4.25). The spread was relatively small (7.30m by 3.40m by 0.16m) and comprised several separate deposits (Fig. 4.26). Similar to Mell, these were situated within a slight depression that facilitated its survival in this location. Large granite boulders were also very prevalent across the site and these seem to have deterred damaging agricultural activities such as modern ploughing.

This spread contained 362 sherds derived from at least 23 Beaker pots, including a Beaker dish, two plain

Beaker bowls and a polypod bowl, as well as five pieces of flint debitage (Ward 2006). Similarly to Mell, sherds from many of the pots occurred throughout the deposits, suggesting that these accumulated rapidly over a short amount of time. Eoin Grogan and Helen Roche (2005b) observed that although this pottery is well-preserved and unabraded, some wear was present on the surfaces and edges on many of the sherds. The presence of the edge-wear resulted in a very small number of refitting sherds and there were also many small fragments (204) and sherds (200) that could not be assigned to any vessel. Fewer than five sherds (16 examples) represent most of the vessels, with only four vessels represented by ten sherds. Akin to Mell, a very small proportion of the Newtownlittle pottery displayed higher sherd/vessel ratios of 22:1, but the fragmentary and partial nature of this assemblage indicates that these sherds were exposed in another context for some time before being accumulated here, within the protective environment of the spread.

At Knowth, Concentration E was a rectangular-shaped deposit (16.5m by 10m by 0.14m) of black organic earth that overlay the boulder clay on the south-eastern part of the hill (see Chapter Three; Eogan and Roche 1997, 241). It was located directly opposite the entrance to Tomb 2 and extended right up to the base of the kerbstones of the main mound (Fig. 3.11). This spread contained 341 sherds from 45 Beaker pots and 100 lithics composed of flint cores, debitage, seven unmodified tools and 30 modified tools including eight 'thumbnail' scrapers and one barbed and tanged arrowhead (ibid., 241-60). Fewer than five sherds represented most of the pots (27 examples), while more than ten sherds represented 11 vessels and the highest number of sherds from a pot within the assemblage was 16. Although the condition of the Knowth pottery is not explicitly stated (Eogan and Roche 1997), there were very few refitting sherds in the assemblage and this may suggest that the edges of most of the sherds had experienced some wear. Like the spreads at Mell and Newtownlittle, many fragments (165) occurred at Knowth (ibid.), but it's assemblage displays lower sherd/vessel ratios than at Newtownlittle or Mell.

The substantial amounts of highly fragmented pottery present within some Beaker spreads has led to the impression that these deposits represent habitation surfaces or trample zones, where pottery and other debris accumulated over an extended duration due to the conduct of occupational activities in that location. The sherd surfaces of the pottery from the three spreads examined in detail here do not, however, display the considerable levels of abrasion usually found on ceramics from floor surfaces. Each of these three spreads contained multiple Beakers, most often represented by a few sherds, though a small number of these pots consist of a greater number of sherds. The fragmentary and highly partial nature of this pottery indicates that these spreads do not represent primary (*in situ*) refuse that built up slowly over the course of an occupation. Instead, these spreads are aggregations of material that were deliberately brought together. The sherds appeared to have been collected from where ever they had been exposed to weathering before being gathered together in piles that protected most of the pottery from further wear.

The sizable quantities of pottery present within some of these spreads suggest that they may have functioned as repositories of occupational debris akin to middens. Needham and Spence (1996, 80) critiqued the uncritical application of the term 'midden' to refuse spreads that were not the product of the deliberate and sequential accumulation of refuse at one location. In the case of these spreads, it is unclear whether they represent the sequential deposition of materials. This is largely due to taphonomic factors and in many cases it is plausible that episodic dumping occurred at these places but that only the bottom-most layers of these features survived. But no matter what label we assign these deposits, their relationship to settlement activity remains opaque. Despite the presence of occupational debris within them, the inclusion of unusual materials, like the wrist-bracer from Rathmullan, that are rarely found in other 'settlement' contexts like pits adds to the confusion. These features do, however, indicate a considerable attachment to place in the mid-third millennium BC. These repositories served as visible reminders of past events and activities at particular locations and in doing so, physically demarcated these as meaningful places. The above-surface nature of these deposits also enabled ongoing engagement with them. This included the addition and subtraction of materials to or from these features to fulfil various practical and social functions. These are all aspects that are considered in more detail below when we examine pits and spreads in relation to each other, both of which seem concerned with the gathering and depositing of materials from settlements.

4.4 Fulachtaí fia

Fulachtaí fia, also known as burnt mounds, are the most common prehistoric monument in Ireland with over 7000 examples identified throughout the country (Ó Néill 2009; Hawkes 2015). Recent investigations in Ireland have revealed an exponential increase in their use during the Chalcolithic (Hawkes 2013, 26). Examples include the results of excavations in advance of the M4 motorway (Carlin *et al.* 2008), the Gas Pipeline to the West (Grogan *et al.* 2007) and the Sligo Inner Relief Road (Danaher 2007). These sites generally comprise a ploughed-down mound of burnt stone and charcoal overlying several consistently present features; a trough, traces of fires that are sometimes represented by a formal hearth and pits. These mounds consist of the debris formed using hot-stone technology to boil water and provide indirect heat (Ó Néill 2009; Hawkes 2015).

Although *fulachtaí fia* were often located in low-lying, poorly-drained, boggy or marshy places in marginal areas, and may only have been used seasonally, evidence from recent investigations confirms that they formed an integral part of the contemporary inhabited landscape, with many *fulachtaí fia* being placed on the interface between wet and dry land in spatial proximity to settlement sites, albeit at a slight remove (Cooney and Grogan 1999, 141; Grogan 2005b, 41; Danaher 2007, 39-41). These types of places were considered appropriate for the use of hot-stone technology and many were episodically revisited and re-used for these purposes over the course of millennia (Danaher 2007; Carlin *et al.* 2008). Significantly, the construction and use of these open-air monuments was the product of group activity that required substantial investments of energy and time. Experimental work by O'Kelly (1952) demonstrated that these could represent cooking places. More recently, Alan Hawkes (2013; 2015) has marshalled the supporting evidence from newer excavations to convincingly argue that these were almost certainly communal places associated with gatherings for outdoor feasting or related activities.

Despite hundreds of these sites dating from the Chalcolithic, Beaker artefacts are rarely found during their excavation, thereby suggesting that *fulachtaí fia* were rarely a focus for Beaker-associated deposition. This is not wholly surprising given the marked scarcity of finds of any date from *fulachtaí fia* (Cherry 1990; but see Hawkes 2013; 2015). Beaker pottery has, however, been found during excavations at six of these sites; Cherrywood (Ó Néill 2000) and Carmanshall (Delaney 2001), both in County Dublin, Charlesland Site 1C (Phelan 2004) and Ballyclogh (Carlin 2006), both in County Wicklow, Ballyvollane II, Co. Limerick (Coyne 2002), and Aghanagloch, Co. Waterford (Johnston *et al.* 2008). These six *fulachtaí fia* have produced at least 155 sherds from at least 11 Beaker vessels. It is possible that more examples have been found since this research was conducted.

Artefacts other than lithics are rarely discovered in association with Beakers within *fulachtaí fia*. At Cherrywood, a spread (24m by 9m by 0.4m deep) of burnt stone and charcoal consisted of two layers that produced 42 sherds from a Beaker pot, 33 lithics including a convex scraper, two hammer-stones and an unburnt animal tooth (species indeterminable) (Ó Néill 2000). The tooth returned a radiocarbon date of 2400-2100 BC (GrA-23011; 3800±40 BP). Sealed under the mound were eight troughs, one of which contained sherds from a Grooved Ware pot as well as heat-shattered stone debris. The Beaker-associated burnt mound at Carmanshall also contained Bowls and Vases of the Food Vessel tradition, although it is not known if all of these were contextually associated. At Charlesland, Site 1C, a few pieces of lithic debitage were present in the same burnt mound layers that contained Beakers (see below; Phelan 2004). At Ballyvollane, a burnt spread sealed an oval pit that was filled with a black deposit of firing debris containing one Beaker sherd. This pit had been cut by another pit that contained a broken wooden shovel. A hollow-based arrowhead was found in the excavation of a burnt mound at Rathbane South, Co Limerick, dating to 2140-2040 BC, though no pottery was recovered (O'Donovan 2002).

The amount of pottery present within each of the Beaker-associated *fulachtaí fia* is quite small. The remains of a single pot were retrieved from four *fulachtaí fia* and these were often represented by a single sherd. For example, at Ahanaglogh, Co. Waterford, a burnt mound consisted of an oval trough and a very shallow spread of burnt stone containing a small worn Beaker sherd (Johnston *et al.* 2008). Charcoal (species undetermined) from the trough produced a radiocarbon date of 2300-2040 BC (Beta-170159; 3790±40 BP). Comparatively higher sherds from the same vessels were only recovered at three sites; Cherrywood, Ballyclogh and Charlesland, Site 1C. As we have already seen, 42 sherds were derived from a single Beaker at the former, so we will now look at the latter two sites in more detail as they also produced the largest quantity of Beaker vessels.

Sealed beneath the mound at Ballyclogh was a pit filled by a charcoal-enriched, black silty sand deposit with heat-shattered stones that contained an unretouched flint flake as well as a worn sherd from one Beaker and 37 sherds from another (Grogan and Roche 2007a). These 37 sherds were in good condition with little evidence for surface or edge wear and a relatively high percentage could be refitted (ibid.). This suggests that this pot suffered very little pre- or post-depositional disturbance and that it was almost complete when deposited. A comparatively large quantity of Beakers – 72 sherds from five vessels – were discovered within the mound at Charlesland, Site 1C, located on low-lying wet poorly-drained land at the base of a low hill (Roche and Grogan 2004). Most of these sherds (59) occurred within the primary layer, which comprised grey silty clay that was lacking heat-fractured stones, and all were derived from the same vessel. Sealing this was a main deposit of burnt stone debris containing 13 other Beaker sherds (Phelan 2004).

Unlike Ballyclogh, the surfaces and edge breaks of most of the sherds at Charlesland were very worn. This latter scenario typifies the highly fragmented and worn condition of the Beaker sherds from the other *fulachtaí fia*, suggesting that these ceramics experienced extensive life-histories after their breakage. Their poor preservation is consistent with the types of activities that would have been conducted at these sites, such as the heating of water and the discard of large volumes of shattered stone. While the presence of single sherds in some of the mounds might be considered incidental, the rare occurrence of multiple sherds from pots, particularly the well-preserved vessel from Ballyclogh, suggests that some of this pottery was deliberately deposited. This seems particularly noteworthy given the scarcity of finds from *fulachtaí fia* of any date.

4.5 Connecting spreads and pits

Bringing Chapters Three and Four together, we see that most of the evidence for Beaker-associated settlement comprise pits and to a lesser extent spreads. Pits represent the most commonly found Beaker-associated feature (71% of 250 features) in a settlement context (Fig. 4.27). They appear to be one of the few unitary aspects of Beaker settlement evidence, occurring where ever Beaker sherds are found in postholes, stakeholes or slot trenches, though they are also often the only Beaker-associated feature on many excavations. Both pits and spreads provide broad insights into aspects of settlement practices such as routinely-used artefacts, diet and economy. The sherds that they contain often have carbonised residues and sooting on their interior, indicating that they were most probably used for cooking and serving foodstuffs. The burnt and unburnt animal bone from cattle, pigs, sheep/goats, as well as the charred remains of cereals (especially barley), provides evidence for animal husbandry and cultivation. The wild foods, particularly hazelnut shells and fruits, found regularly in these deposits provide further evidence for food preparation and consumption.

Determining whether Beaker-associated pits and spreads represent the remains of a permanent settlement, a seasonal occupation or some other form of short-term activity, for example where people came together for celebrations, or even if these features relate directly to occupational activity in the vicinity, is very problematic. This is exacerbated by the paucity of archaeologically recognisable Chalcolithic houses and it is possible that materials were specifically brought from elsewhere to certain locations to be deposited (see Thomas 1999, 68). Little concrete evidence is available to confirm or deny this, however, and so the simplest approach may be to assume that these pits were filled with occupational debris that was generated on-site unless there is unambiguous evidence to suggest otherwise (see Garrow 2006, 35).

In this regard, the discovery of so many Beaker-associated pits and related features in places that were historically favoured as settlement locations – as demonstrated by their co-location with both Early Neolithic and Late Bronze Age houses (see Chapter Three) – suggests that at least some of these reflect on-site occupation. In some cases, it certainly seems likely that these features do represent the only surviving element of what must have been long-term or repeated habitations; groups of contemporary features, including Beaker-associated pits and spreads, have been found to contain a wide range of tools that form a high proportion of the total chipped stone assemblage, as well as evidence for cereal cultivation in the form of carbonised cereal grains and quernstones (Carlin 2005a; 2005b). Although the relationship

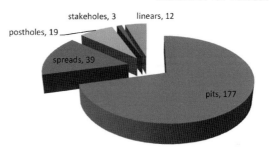

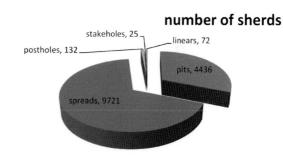

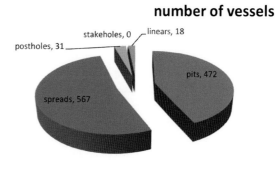

Fig. 4.27: The percentage of each type of 'settlement' feature containing Beaker pottery, as well as the percentage of Beaker sherds and vessels found in each category.

between the quantity of artefacts in a feature and the duration of occupation is not necessarily a straightforward one, pits and spreads containing the remains of multiple vessels suggest that activity in that location had been of sufficiently significant extent or duration to provide such a large supply of pottery (Hill 1995). Conversely, the repeated discovery of a small number of pits and/or small surface deposits containing smaller numbers of artefacts may also represent short-term, task-specific or episodic activity, perhaps even feasting.

In some cases, the aggregated materials within spreads may have derived from everyday habitation activities in their vicinity, but in others such as at Knowth, Newgrange and Monknewtown within *Brú na Bóinne* (see Section 3.2), this may have been created through large-scale acts of consumption, including social feasting. This could explain the very large amounts of pottery that survive at these locations and seem to reflect events of considerable intensity and/or duration. Indeed, given that these locations fulfilled important ceremonial roles for people in the Middle and Late Neolithic, it would be unsurprising if people continued to aggregate there for various social functions (see Chapters Three and Six).

There does not seem to be a simple straightforward relationship between the sub-surface deposition of settlement materials and actual occupational activity. Clearly, pits were key features for the deposition of Beakers and seem to have been specially created to receive exactly these kinds of deposits, but yet a far greater number of sherds have been found in spreads (9721 sherds or 68%) than pits (4436 sherds or 31%). Only in a few exceptional cases does the combined number of vessels from all the Beaker-associated pits in a cluster, such as at Kilgobbin, match the number of pots present within some spreads. The same applies to the discovery of 80 scrapers from a total of 21 Beaker-associated pits on 15 sites compared to the sum of 152 scrapers from nine spreads. While these larger quantities are reflective of the far greater volume of spreads than pits, these quantitative differences tell us that many more Beakers were deposited above rather than in the ground (Fig. 4.27).

While the pits themselves were rapidly formed, their contents were certainly not. We know this because the pottery found in these features was very incomplete and fragmentary and had been accumulated elsewhere as part of a larger aggregation of occupational debris prior to its deposition (see above). The existence of material connections (*e.g.* sherds from the same vessel) between different pits, such as those discovered at Faughart Lower 6, or between different contexts in the same pit, implies that these deposits were obtained from the same source. We also know from the differential post-breakage biographies of sherds deriving from the same vessels that the pottery within these pits had previously been stored in an intermediate context that offered various levels of protection from the elements, depending on whether the sherds were located near the outermost or innermost parts of this repository. It is highly plausible that the spreads featured in this study represent the intermediate contexts from which debris was obtained for deposition within pits. If so, the depositional treatment of Beaker pottery involved a highly complex and lengthy chain of events before its burial within a pit or some other feature, one stage of which seems to be represented by the provisional or ultimate deposition of the pottery within these spreads. As discussed below, the complicated post-breakage life-histories of these pots echo the treatment of human remains during the Chalcolithic and beyond (Brück 2009; see Chapter Five).

Like the treatment of human bone, it seems that a certain level of selectivity was exercised regarding how, what and where things could or could not be deposited. Some of these selections, such as the preference for depositing Beakers in pits rather than postholes, are obvious and seem to indicate a widely shared set of rules (see Barrett and Needham 1988, 130). Similarly, we see that items such as a wrist-bracer, stone arrowheads, a gold sun-disc and metal axes seem to have been deposited in spreads, but not in pits. Conversely, six polished stone axes have been found within pits, but only one is known from a spread. This seems related to the way that we see the deposition of near complete Rockbarton pots within certain pits, but in the spreads at Mell and Newtownlittle, each of these pots were only represented by a few sherds that had clearly been broken and then exposed in another context for some time before being gathered and placed into the spread (see above). This indicates that people chose to follow a diverse range of depositional processes for various kinds of Beaker pots as well as other types of objects (see Brudenell and Cooper 2008 for discussion of this complexity of practice in a British later Bronze Age context).

The implication of all this is that spreads and pits reflect a diverse range of selective and circumscribed depositional practices that often involved a very complex and lengthy chain of events and the movement of materials between different contexts at various stages. The highly partial nature of the assemblages found in spreads, pits or related contexts indicates that a very large proportion of the materials that were generated by occupation were probably not deposited in these spreads and certainly not in pits. In other words, the deposits in pits and spreads predominantly represent the end-product of the selective and strategic deposition of occupational debris from a settlement (Hill 1995; Thomas 1999, 73; Pollard 2001, 316; 2002). The survival of these materials within the archaeological record owes much to the culturally prescribed and highly formalised way these depositional activities were routinely conducted (Bradley 2003, 6-12; 2005a, 208-9). So, while the creation of Beaker-associated pits and spreads was probably inherently associated with the process of occupation and these features prove to be among the only surviving aspect of occupation in many locations, these features and their contents are only an indirect and carefully crafted representation of settlement (Thomas 1999, 7; Harding, J. 2006, 123).

4.6 Ideologically significant depositions

Leaving aside the issue of establishing a direct link between these Beaker deposits and settlement activity, it is important to consider what these deposits represent and what they tell us about the people behind their creation. Our understanding of rubbish is culturally specific (see Moore, H.L. 1982; 1986), and from our present-day dispositions it is easy to dismiss settlement debris as refuse without giving it further consideration (see Pollard 2002, 23). It is clear from the complex treatment of Beaker-associated occupational debris that it was considered a highly significant and meaningful cultural material that fulfilled numerous important social roles. Indeed, as discussed below, the fragmentation of the pottery served important social functions (see Chapman 2000a; 2000b).

Pottery was probably regarded as an object that both possessed and created meaning and therefore played a key role in the social lives of people. After all, it was used in a range of routine activities and it is through people's everyday material engagement with the world in which they are temporally and spatially located that they construct and negotiate their relationships, identities and worldview. It was not just the vessels that were ideologically or socially significant, the depositional treatment of the fragmentary remains of these pots, including that of single sherds, indicates that these took on a life of their own that was independent of the vessels to which they once belonged (see Appadurai 1986; Kopytoff 1986). Refuse such as fragmented sherds are generated during daily activities and, consequentially, social relationships become enmeshed in these material remains to the extent that these sherds come to signify these interactions (Moore, H.L. 1986; Brück 2006a, 298). In other words, these sherds gained biographies and symbolic meanings over the course of their use-lives, through which they became metaphorical representations of connections across time and space between people, places and things (see Pollard 2001, 327; Woodward 2002, 1040-41). This made these sherds a social resource that people used to construct and maintain their relationships and identities, as well as to negotiate and understand changes to their world, such as transitions in life-stages (Chapman 2000a; 2000b; Brück 2004b, 326; 2006b).

It was probably because of these valuable social characteristics, gained during their life history, that some sherds had to be treated in such culturally-prescribed ways, including their collection, curation and deposition in middens or pits (see Chapman 2000a; 2000b; Brück 2006a, 303). From this perspective, we can understand the deposition of Beaker-associated occupational debris in pits and spreads as a conscious practice whereby people used the meanings that had been acquired through an object's life to negotiate and reproduce cultural values and social relations (Needham 1988; Pollard 2001, 325; 2002, 22; Fontijn 2002). The process of digging and immediately backfilling pits with occupational debris served to presence the material being deposited and to physically locate a particular time and place in people's minds (see Pryor 1995, 105). The removal of these fragments of everyday life through their burial resulted in the meanings associated with these artefacts being recalled and reproduced (Rowlands 1993, 146; Fontijn 2007, 76-7). These remembrance practices enabled people to maintain a continuous link between themselves and the past events or people represented by this debris (Chapman 2000a, 64; Pollard 2001, 323-8). The burying of these mementoes of sociality in specially dug pits within specific locations inscribed meaning and memories onto places in a way that was not easily forgotten (Thomas 1996, 197; 1999, 87; Pollard 1999). This served to create and sustain their sense of belonging to a group and place and demarcated that locale as an important location within the landscape (Pryor 1992, 519; 1995, 105).

In other words, the physical transformation of these quotidian items enabled people to think about their place in the world, the passing of time and the cyclicality of life (see Brück 2006a, 297-303; 2006b, 86). Given the inherent connection of these artefacts with the preparation and consumption of food, these may have symbolized the vitality and productivity of the social group (Brück 1999b, 155; 2006a, 304). Indeed, there may have been a close relationship between the life-cycle of occupational debris and the people who produced it, whereby the fragmentation and sequential burial of Beaker sherds in different contexts may have deliberately mirrored the life-cycles of the people associated with them, particularly the transformative journey of human bodies into the after-life (Brück 1999b, 155; 2006a, 299; 2006b; see Chapter Five). This is illustrated by the way that the life of a Beaker did not always end upon breakage. Instead, its form changed from a vessel into sherds, some of which were gathered and stored before being placed in another context, while others were recycled as grog during the creation of new pots. As the sherds went through these various stages, they would have gained new characteristics and meanings, but it may not have been forgotten that this was once part of a Beaker that had been used for particular purposes (see Brück 2006a, 303). As suggested by Joshua Pollard (2002, 23): *"the process of transformation of refuse, involving primary discard (the death of objects), its incorporation in middens (essentially a liminal state), then deliberate reburial in a pit (reincorporation), perhaps stressed metaphoric connections between the transformation of the material world and that of the human dead'*. This close connection between the life cycle of potsherds, pots and human remains is also indicated by Rose Cleary's (1984) identification of a bone tempered Beaker sherd from Grange, Co. Limerick. Furthermore, Neil Curtis and Neil Wilkin (2017; in press) recently discovered that the white paste used to decorate the inlay of many Beaker pots in north-eastern Scotland was also made from crushed bone. Although in both cases, it is unknown whether this was from animals or humans.

Ideologically significant acts involving the placement of occupation debris into pits may also have been conducted at important occasions or stages in the lifecycle of a settlement, such as the transition from childhood to adulthood or the marriage of some of the inhabitants (Brück 1999b, 154; 2001, 153; 2006a, 299-303). Given that Beaker-associated pit deposition occurred at the end of a long and complex chain of events, it can be speculated that most Beaker-associated pits were dug and then filled with the ceramic residues of the inhabitation of that spot to mark or commemorate the end of an occupation (Pollard 1999, 89; Thomas 1999; Harding, J. 2006, 123). These depositional acts may have represented an important occasion for local groups, during which the life stories of the people and the places associated with these settlement deposits may have been remembered and celebrated (Thomas 1996, 197; 1999; Pollard 1999; Fontijn 2008, 102). Returning to the example given above of the transformation of the Beaker pot, we can see that the burial of these ceramics and other occupational debris enacted a belief that death, fertility, renewal, and regeneration were interconnected aspects of the cycles of natural and human life (Pollard 2000; Brück 2006a, 297-303). The deposition of pot-sherds and other debris into or onto the ground returned them to the source of the material from which they had been made and in doing so they may have been considered to fertilise and regenerate it, thereby ensuring a positive future or at least maintaining a cosmological equilibrium (Case 1973).

Bringing some of these different points together, it has not proved possible to tell whether these features and their contents were created during or after on-site settlement activity or something entirely different. Yet, in some ways, this question seems less important now, because these features seem to have been formed through activities that deliberately emphasised the routines of everyday life within a specific spatio-temporal context (see Bradley 2005a, 32-36; Cooney 2005, 25). The deposition of fragments of inhabitation acted as metaphorical representations of communal endeavours, such as the preparation and consumption of food, which symbolised the sociality of the household. The activities associated with their deposition created memories of these and the various social ties that bound people, places and their ancestors together as members of an imagined 'domestic' community (see Lévi-Strauss 1983; Carsten and Hugh-Jones 1995; Waterson 1995; Thomas 2010). This point is of key significance for understanding the Beaker phenomenon in Ireland and we will return to it in the concluding chapter.

4.7 Beaker settlement in Ireland in its wider context

Overall then, it seems that Beaker pottery was used for a wide range of different occupational activities. It is commonly found in settlement debris within pits and spreads and there is no evidence that this was a special-purpose vessel whose use was restricted. Most of the evidence for Beaker-associated settlement activity reflects the lack of a clear division between 'domestic' and ritual spheres at this time (see Brück 1999a, 319-26). Beaker-associated settlement debris was a highly significant symbolic resource that was treated in a complex and circumscribed fashion. People constructed their identities, values and relationships through the collection and deposition of refuse from occupations. As we saw in Chapter Three, very few Beaker-associated 'domestic' structures are known, but this scenario is a consistent feature of the Middle and Late Neolithic as well as the Early Bronze Age (Smyth 2007, 2010; Carlin and Brück 2012). Indeed, the character of Beaker-associated settlement sites is highly comparable to those from these periods, each of which displays evidence for a strong emphasis upon the deposition of 'domestic' materials in pits and to a lesser extent in spreads (Carlin and Brück 2012; Carlin and Cooney 2017). There is little evidence, however, to support the traditional depiction of the Beaker phenomenon in Ireland as being settlement-rich with much direct evidence for houses and occupations (see Chapters Two and Three).

In opposition to these traditional views, we now see that the best comparison to the Irish settlement-related evidence is to be found in Britain, where settlement sites mainly consists of ephemeral remains such as pits, artefact scatters and spreads. Direct evidence for Beaker occupation such as houses is rarely found (Case 1995b; Needham 1996; Thomas 1999, 64-74; Allen 2005; Garrow 2006; Bradley 2007, 150); outside of exceptional locations like the Western Isles (Parker Pearson *et al.* 2004a). Indeed, the Irish evidence is matched almost exactly by the character of Beaker-associated pits and spreads in Britain (see Thomas 1999, 64-74; Woodward 2002; Garrow 2006). Just like in Ireland, large amounts of Beaker occupational debris were generated but mostly placed above surface, and so Beaker sherds remained in circulation for an extended duration after breakage but before deposition (Brück 1999c, 376; Bradley 2000a, 128; Woodward 2002; Garrow 2006, 130-36).

At a wider scale, there is a diverse body of evidence for Beaker-associated settlement sites, and houses from some parts of Europe, but this remains scarce in others (Turek 1997; Guilaine *et al.* 2001; Vander Linden 2015, 612-13; Salanova 2016). None of these regions, however, provide evidence that is comparable to that from Ireland. Although in each case, whether it is Atlantic France or southern France, Denmark or the Netherlands, or elsewhere, Beaker pottery occurs in occupational contexts that reflect the pre-Beaker settlement practices of that region, as is the case in Ireland (Guilaine *et al.* 2001; Sarauw 2007a; Bradley *et al.* 2016, 135; Salanova 2016).

5

Fragments of the Dead?

5.1 Introduction

Throughout Europe, Beaker pottery is stereotypically found as part of funerary assemblages in association with other artefacts accompanying single burials (Vander Linden 2006a). In contrast, the classic crouched inhumation with Beaker-associated grave-gifts is often thought to be completely absent from Ireland and the Irish Beaker complex is viewed as having a much smaller funerary component comprising collective burials in primary and secondary contexts in megalithic tombs (Case 1995a, 19; Needham 1996, 128; Brindley, A.L. 2007, 250). This scenario has contributed to the view that the use of Beaker ceramics and many of the objects forming part of the associated 'package' in Ireland was radically different from elsewhere in Europe (*e.g.* Clarke 1976, 472-3; Burgess 1979, 213). Little effort, however, has been made to investigate or understand these apparent differences. Detailed study of the occurrence of Beaker artefacts in funerary settings in Ireland has been lacking and these generalisations may have masked the complexity and richness of Beaker-associated deposition in these contexts.

To remedy that, this chapter examines the deposition of Beaker pottery and other artefacts in megalithic and funerary contexts in Ireland including earlier Neolithic megalithic tombs and a distinctive form of megalithic monument known as wedge tombs, which were newly constructed during the Chalcolithic, as well as cists, cairns and pits. We also consider the relationship in these settings between the use of Beakers and another Irish and British style of ceramic, Bowls and Vases of the Food Vessel tradition whose currency overlapped slightly with that of Beakers. These Food Vessels began to be made at the start of the full Early Bronze Age (c. 2200 BC) in tandem with a sharp increase in evidence for formal burials (Brindley, A.L. 2007; Wilkin 2014).

The aim of this chapter is to characterise Beaker-associated mortuary customs on this island and identify the different forms of social practices that produced these deposits. This analysis enables these to be appropriately considered within their wider European context, as is done here, so that an improved understanding of the relationship between Beaker-associated practices in Ireland and elsewhere can be attained. The frequency and manner of occurrence of Beaker materials, particularly the pottery, in these various contexts are examined in terms of the type, quantity and condition of the objects. This includes an appraisal of the total number of Beaker pots and sherds in each context as well as the condition of these pots, and where possible, the number of sherds per vessel. This level of quantification is necessary to identify patterning in the deposits within the various types of contexts, which may be reflective of varying social practices (see Chapter One).

Particular attention is paid to identifying and interpreting Beaker-associated deposits of human remains. This includes an assessment of whether these were deposited in conjunction with Beaker pottery and represent funerary practices or some other kind of activity. Clear-cut divisions between funerary and ceremonial or settlement activity probably did not exist at this time (see Brück 1999a; Bradley 2005a) and correspondingly not all deposits of human remains constitute burials. These may reflect some other form of ritual practice, cf. skull fragments in later Bronze Age settlement contexts (Brück 1995; Cleary, K. 2017). Focusing on those deposits from megalithic monuments, many of these have been disturbed or poorly preserved. As exemplified by an Iron Age pit within the wedge tomb at Altar, Co. Cork (O'Brien 2002, 167), many megaliths remained open and continued to be re-used for millennia after their construction. Secure closed deposits are very rare and the achievement of complete certainty of association between objects and human remains is just not possible. Where a burial from a tomb containing Beaker pottery has returned a radiocarbon date consistent with the currency of that ceramic and there is no other ceramic with a similar currency present in the tomb, we can assume that these depositions were indeed directly linked. Similarly, where the excavator observed a particularly strong association between a specific pot and a burial, we can accept that they were deposited contemporaneously. In the absence of radiocarbon dates, it can be very difficult to identify the 'Beaker component' of the funerary remains present in these monuments, particularly when multi-period activity has occurred in conjunction with multiple burials. Even when radiocarbon dates have been obtained, there are question marks about the strength of association between the dated sample and the materials with which it was found. There may also be problems with some of the dates themselves. For example, where direct dates have been obtained on cremated bones, there is the possibility of an 'old carbon' effect whereby the radiocarbon date of the bone may occasionally have been influenced by carbon from 'old wood', if it were used in the cremation pyre (Snoeck et al. 2014). Thus, human remains from many megaliths cannot be definitively associated with the deposition of Beaker-related objects in these contexts and so it is unknown if the rituals enacted at these places were sepulchral in any sense.

To conduct this study, it was essential to collate all the known occurrences of Beaker material in funerary contexts. All available information from various reports was examined, including site photos, plans and section drawings to ensure that recorded associations between objects and or burials are genuine and not just the chance juxtaposition of different residual or intrusive artefacts. Most of these sites were excavated prior to 1950 when archaeologists' methods of excavation and recording, as well as their understanding of chronologies, was very different to today (see Chapter One). Accordingly, some of these excavations suffer from problems associated with their age and many of the human remains are poorly dated. It was necessary to incorporate all new information or interpretations relating to the older investigations, particularly concerning the identification and reassessment of the Beaker pottery (e.g. Case 1961; Herity 1982; 1987; see Chapter One). While efforts have been made to integrate the artefacts and ecofacts from older excavations for contextual analysis, much of the information is highly ambiguous and so it is difficult to argue for associations between various artefacts and/or particular burials. It remains the case that the pottery, lithics and bone also need to be re-examined at many sites, as has recently been done at Largantea, Co. Derry (Schulting et al. 2008).

A total of 697 sherds representing 92 Beakers have been recovered from a total of 38 funerary and/or megalithic contexts. Thirty of these 38 Beaker-associated ceremonial and funerary sites are megaliths, 13 represent wedge tombs, where the Beaker pottery has been recovered from an apparently primary position and the remainder (17 examples) comprise earlier Neolithic monuments that have produced Beaker-associated deposits from secondary contexts. Court tombs represent by far the most common of these (14 examples), with Beaker pottery only being recovered from two passage tombs and one portal tomb. Beaker pottery has also been recovered from six cists and two ring-ditches. Post-depositional activities in megalithic monuments may also have resulted in the destruction or removal of Beakers, but it is not possible to quantify which sites have been more disturbed than others. The results of this comparative analysis of the number of sherds per vessel in each context is therefore limited. Nevertheless, the patterns identified in these examinations are quite consistent and there are no wild variations to suggest that these results are anomalous.

5.2 Beaker deposition in wedge tombs

There are at least 560 monuments in Ireland known as wedge tombs, comprising stone-built chambers of wedge-shape or trapezoidal plan that are wider and higher at the front, where occasionally a straight orthostatic façade occurs. In many cases a second wall within a trapezoidal or round cairn, often delimited by a kerb, encloses the chambers (Fig. 5.1). These chambers vary from simpler small rectangles to longer more complex arrangements with a short antechamber to the front and/or a small subsidiary chamber at the rear, all of which were roofed with large lintels or capstones (O'Brien 1999; Jones et al. 2015). The more elaborate tombs display various forms of segmentation including jamb and sill stones. Some of these architectural differences appear to reflect regional variations (Walsh 1995, 121-3). Although some wedge tombs occur in the east, they are predominantly distributed in the west and north of Ireland and display a more Atlantic and southerly distribution than any other megalith on the island (ibid.). These megaliths mainly occur as single monuments, but some clusters of two or three tombs also occur in places such as the Burren in County Clare. They are sited at a range of locations with some preference for slightly higher elevations, but in many

Fig. 5.1: Ballyedmonduff wedge tomb with the remains of an orthostatic façade occurring in the foreground at the front of the tomb. The chamber is enclosed by a U-shaped cairn which is delimited by a kerb (courtesy of Muiris O'Sullivan).

Site name	Sherds	Vessel count
Aughrim	?	5
Ballybriest	all near complete	6
Ballyedmonduff	140	8
Baurnadomeeny	33	1
Carriglong	18	?
Cashelbane cairn	a near complete pot and 48 sherds	10
Giants Grave (Loughash)	three near complete pots	4
Kilhoyle	48	4
Kilnagarns	1	1
Labbacallee	12	1
Largantea	two near complete vessels and 15 sherds from three other Beakers	5
Lough Gur wedge tomb	250	?
Moytirra	7	4

Table 5.1: The numbers of Beaker sherds and vessels in wedge tombs.

regards, these echo the location of the Early Neolithic court and portal tombs with which they sometimes occur (Cooney and Grogan 1999, 85; O'Brien 1999). One of the most consistent characteristics of wedge tombs is the alignment of the chamber so that its front faces the west or south-west, towards the setting sun in winter months; a place/direction that may have been strongly associated with death and darkness (O'Brien 1999; 2002). In referencing the motion of the sun, however, there may also have been a concern with ideas relating to transformation and rebirth. This is a point to which we will return below.

While these are the most numerous form of Irish megalith, just over 40 of these monuments have been excavated. Most of these excavations were conducted over 50 years ago and so the quality of recording, particularly of the context of artefacts, is highly variable. Further-more, many of these tombs suffered a considerable level of re-use and later disturbance, accordingly very few have been found to contain what could be regarded as secure closed deposits. While Billy O'Brien (1999) excavated two wedge tombs in the southwest County Cork during the early 90s, neither of these produced any clear evidence for Chalcolithic activity. Thankfully, much needed work to further clarify the character of deposits within wedge tombs is currently being conducted by Ros Ó Maoldúin in the Burren. Brindley and Lanting (1991/2) dated charcoal and bone from seven wedge tombs and more recently, dates have been obtained from wedge tombs at Ballybriest (Hurl 2001) and Largantea (Schulting *et al.* 2008), both in County Derry and Loughash and Cashelbane (Cleary, K. 2016), both in County Tyrone, to produce a grand total of 33 radiocarbon determinations. These are not of

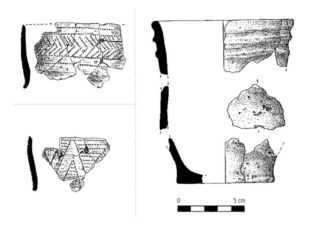

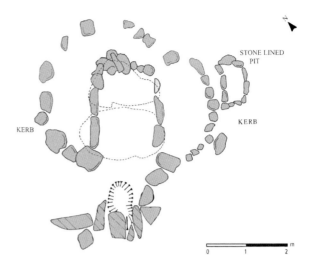

Fig. 5.2: Pot A and B from Ballyedmonduff wedge tomb, Co. Dublin (after Ó Ríordáin and de Valera 1952, 73, Fig. 1) and a Rockbarton style pot from Aughrim wedge tomb, Co. Cavan (courtesy of John Channing).

Fig. 5.3: The wedge tomb at Ballybriest, Co. Derry containing the remains of six near complete Beaker vessels (after Hurl 2001).

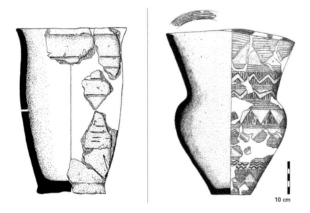

Fig. 5.4: Pot E and the large Beaker from Ballybriest wedge tomb with a height of 50cms and rim diameter of 36cms which is one of the largest Beakers in Europe (after Hurl 2001, fig. 13 and 15).

universally high quality, nor are they all securely associated with deposits of Beaker pottery (see Table 5.4). Nevertheless, Bayesian modelling of some of the early radiocarbon dates from wedge tombs indicates that these began to be built quite suddenly c. 2450 BC and that their primary use dates to the period 2400-2050 BC (Schulting *et al.* 2008, 13). There is no evidence to suggest that they were built pre-2500 BC, but their construction probably continued until the end of the third millennium BC and maybe even beyond.

While it is not currently possible to state the total amount of Beaker pottery or number of sherds per vessel found in wedge tombs (without a complete reassessment of the ceramics), based upon available information, 13 wedge tombs have produced at least 509 sherds from 51 vessels. The majority of these (six) contained a minimum of four

to six Beaker vessels with single pots occurring in only three tombs (Table 5.1). The greatest number was discovered during the excavation of the Cashelbane tomb (Davies and Mullin 1940), which produced the remains of ten Beakers.

Many Beakers are represented by multiple large conjoining sherds, such as Pot A and B from Ballyedmonduff, Co. Dublin (Fig. 5.2; Table 5.2); suggesting that these may have been deposited in a much more intact state (Ó Ríordáin and De Valera 1952, 73, fig. 1) and this is supported by the discovery of almost complete pots within at least three tombs (Table 5.1). For example, the wedge tomb at Ballybriest contained the remains of six near complete Beaker vessels (Figs. 5.3-5.4). The high number of sherds present from each pot led the excavator, Declan Hurl (2001, 16), to suggest that these may have been broken *in situ* – "where they stood within the burial chamber". Although it is equally possible that they may have been whole when deposited and subsequently became broken during the repeated use of the tomb or subsequent post-depositional disturbance.

Not all Beakers from these monuments are so well represented. A total of 24 Beakers (from six tombs) were represented by ten sherds or less and eight of those vessels consisted of a single sherd. Beakers represented by only a small number of sherds, regularly occurred alongside almost-whole examples or Beakers comprising multiple conjoining sherds. This was the case at Largantea, where a stone cist-like structure within the tomb contained two near-complete Late-style Beakers including a Long-Necked example and sherds of an earlier-style Beaker (see below; Fig. 5.5). In contrast to these two pots, the chamber deposits produced an additional four Beakers, three of which were represented by only two sherds each. There may originally have been more of those pots in the

Site name	Vessel	No. of sherds	Comments
Ballyedmonduff	A	18	most of these were conjoined
Ballyedmonduff	B	16	at least 7 of these are conjoined
Ballyedmonduff	2	2	
Ballyedmonduff	3	1	
Ballyedmonduff	4	4	
Ballyedmonduff	5	16	
Ballyedmonduff	6	9	
Ballyedmonduff	7	6	
Ballyedmonduff	8	15	
Ballyedmonduff	9	2	
Ballybriest	?	near complete	six near complete Beaker vessels
Baurnadomeeny	?	33	all from the same pot
Cashelbane	A	6	
Cashelbane	B	11	
Cashelbane	c	3	
Cashelbane	D	9	
Cashelbane	E	near complete	
Cashelbane	F	2	weathered sherds
Cashelbane	G	1	
Cashelbane	L	1	
Cashelbane	M	1	
Cashelbane	O	near complete	
Largantea	B1	near complete	
Largantea	B2	near complete	
Largantea	A1	2	
Largantea	A2	9	many conjoined
Largantea	A3	2	
Largantea	D1	2	
Loughash	A	near complete	entire base, nearly all the body and neck
Loughash	B	1	
Loughash	C	5	
Loughash	D	near complete	
Lough Gur	?	?	very fragmented
Kilhoyle	1	18	
Kilhoyle	2	1	
Kilhoyle	4	11	
Kilhoyle	7	18	small sherds found throughout the tomb
Moytirra	A	6	
Moytirra	B	1	
Moytirra	C	1	
Moytirra	D	2	

Table 5.2: *The number of sherds per Beaker in wedge tombs.*

Site	Cremations	Inhumations
Ballybriest	8	0
Ballyedmonduff	?	0
Cashelbane	5	0
Kilhoyle	1	0
Labbacallee	0	3
Baurnadomeeny	1	0
Largantea	3	0
Lough Gur	1?	5
Moytirra	0	6
Totals	18	14

Table 5.3: The number of Beaker-associated inhumations and cremations in wedge tombs.

chamber at Largantea but these could easily have become damaged and dispersed in the course of the ongoing re-use of the tomb throughout the Bronze Age. This is suggested by the fact that the pots in the protected environment of the cist are far more complete. The largest amount of Beaker sherds found in any megalith came from the Lough Gur wedge tomb (Ó Ríordáin and Ó h-Iceadha 1955), where 250 sherds were recorded, but these were quite small, making it impossible to reconstruct any vessels (Tables 5.1-5.2). It remains unclear whether the variety in the fragmentation of Beakers in this and other wedge tombs represents diversity in depositional practices or is largely due to the high levels of disturbance caused by their long history of re-use.

Human remains representing at least 73 burnt and unburnt individuals, mostly comprising multiple cremations, have been recorded in 24 wedge tombs (Cooney and Grogan 1999, 86; O'Brien 1999); however, many of these were not Beaker-associated, and have either not been dated or post-date the currency of Irish Beakers. Beaker sherds have only been found in association with burnt or unburnt human bone in apparently primary positions in nine wedge tombs; Moytirra, Co. Sligo (Cremin Madden 1969, 157-9, fig. 2), Aughrim, Co. Cavan (Channing 1993), Labbacallee, Co. Cork (Leask and Price 1936; Brindley et al. 1987/8), Baurnadomeeny, Co. Tipperary (O'Kelly 1960), Lough Gur, Co. Limerick (Ó Ríordáin and Ó h-Iceadha 1955), Cashelbane, Co. Tyrone (Davies and Mullin 1940) and Kilhoyle (Herring and May 1937), Largantea (Herring 1938; Schulting et al. 2008) and Ballybriest (Hurl 2001), all in County Derry Table 5.2).

Cremated bones representing at least 18 different individuals have been found with Beaker pottery in six wedge tombs (Table 5.3), but only a few exceptional examples from Ballybriest; Largantea, Loughash; Cashelbane have been directly radiocarbon dated (Hurl 2001; Schulting et al. 2008; Cleary, K. 2016). This makes it difficult to conclusively identify these as Beaker burials, especially where there is also evidence for multi-period activity (Table 5.4). For example, although three near complete Beakers and the cremated remains of at least four individuals were found in the chamber of the Loughash wedge tomb, these were recovered from mixed deposits that included a Vase Urn, Encrusted Urn and Late Bronze Age pottery (Davies 1939). In the absence of radiocarbon dates of multiple bones from these four cremations, it is currently impossible to identify any connection between these and the Beakers in the monument.[4]

The wedge tomb at Largantea provides an excellent illustration of how difficult it is to conclusively demonstrate a connection between the deposition of Beakers and burials, even when radiocarbon dates are obtained. Beaker pottery and the cremated remains of at least eight individuals representing six adults (male and female), a child and an infant were found in the tomb (Herring 1938, 174-5). In the main chamber, a primary layer contained black charcoal-rich soil and a large quantity of cremated human bone. Radiocarbon dating of three separate cremations returned determinations clustering around 2455-2208 BC and oak charcoal from the same deposit produced a date of 2468-2211 BC (Schulting et al. 2008). Overlying this black layer was a deposit containing artefacts dating from later in the Bronze Age, including a bronze razor, sherds from a Food Vessel, a Cordoned Urn, and Late Bronze Age pottery, as well as cremated bone dating to the Middle Bronze Age (Herring 1938, 172-3). In the entrance chamber, nine sherds from four Beakers and a small amount of undated cremated human remains (thought to have been disturbed from the burials in the main chamber) were found on the floor surface. Overlying this was a yellow brown deposit that contained other sherds from a tripartite Irish Bowl, two other Food Vessels and a Cordoned Urn. Immediately inside the entrance chamber, a stone cist-like structure contained the two near-complete late-style Beakers (mentioned above) and conjoining sherds of an early-style Beaker, as well as a convex scraper (Herring 1938, 171). Thus, neither these Beakers nor those inside the entrance were contextually associated with any of the dated cremated human bone. Furthermore, the deposition of the late-style Beakers is likely to have post-dated the interment of the human remains because the inception of this form of pot post-dates 2250 BC (see Chapter Eight). However, the charcoal and three cremation burials within the primary black aceramic layer all produced dates clustering around 2455-2208 BC strongly suggesting that they were deposited at the same time as the earlier-style Beaker pottery and therefore can be considered as Beaker burials.

---

4   K. Cleary's (2016) attempt to radiocarbon date a cremated human femur from the wedge tomb chamber failed.

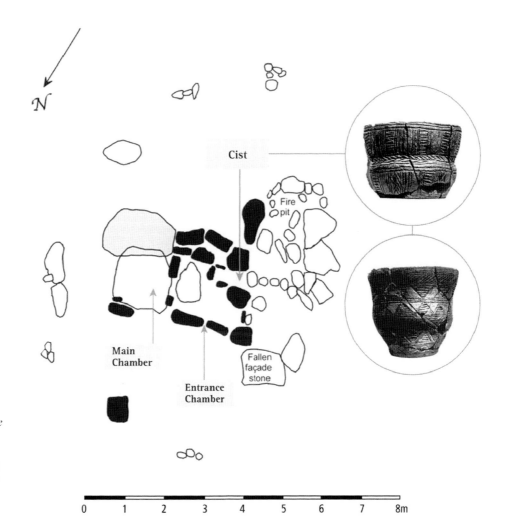

Fig. 5.5: Largantea wedge tomb with the stone cist-like structure highlighted and photos of the two near-complete Beaker vessels (B1 and B2) from the cist (after Herring 1938).

The greatest number of individuals deposited in definite association with Beaker pottery in a wedge tomb was recorded at Ballybriest (Hurl 2001). Here, a large quantity of highly fragmented cremated bone representing the remains of at least seven people including an adult male, an adult female, a 2-5-year-old child and an infant was found in a sealed primary deposit in the main chamber (Murphy 2001), which also contained multiple sherds deriving from four late-style Beakers, charcoal and a few flint flakes. A sample of burnt human bone from the deposit returned a radiocarbon date of 2139-1830 BC (GrA-13273; 3630±50 BP). Interestingly, one pot from this deposit displays a volume of about 9.5 litres, which appears to be among the largest Beakers in Europe (see Fig. 5.4; ibid.).

A high number of cremation burials (representing at least five individuals) were discovered inside the Cashelbane wedge tomb, which also contained higher quantities of Beaker pottery than usual (see above). These were closely associated with one another in primary stratigraphic positions (Davies and Mullin 1940, 150-51). Sherds from ten Beakers were discovered in the forecourt, antechamber, main chamber and two cists (see Fig. 5.7). Most of these were found in a primary deposit in the main chamber, along with two barbed and tanged arrowheads (Sutton and Green Low) and cremated bone from at least four individuals (a juvenile, two adult females and an adult male). Two Bowls were also found at quite a high level within this deposit, in apparently secondary positions. A femur fragment from one of the four individuals was recently dated to 2470-2286 BC (UBA-29665; 3888±31 BP; Cleary, K. 2016). This confirms that the internment of at least some of the human remains was associated with the deposition of Beakers and pre-dated the currency of the Bowls. At least one more cremated individual occurred in one of the two subsidiary cist-like chambers at the rear of the tomb (see below).

In other tombs, fewer cremated individuals could be identified as occurring with Beakers. For example, at Kilhoyle, Co. Derry, it was observed that the cremated remains of an adult female were very closely associated

FRAGMENTS OF THE DEAD? | 101

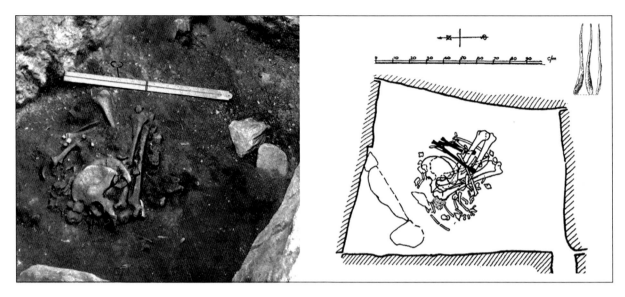

Fig. 5.6: Photo and plan of the disarticulated adult female inhumation in cist-like terminal chamber at the rear of the wedge tomb at Labbacallee, Co Cork and bone pin that accompanied the Labbacallee inhumation (after Leask 1936, figs. 2 and 15).

Site name	Lab code	Year BP	±	Cal BC	Sample material	Beaker associated?	Comments
Cashelbane	UBA-29665	3888	31	2470-2286	burnt human femur	unequivocal	closely associated with Beakers in primary stratigraphic positions
Largantea	UB-7024	3877	34	2468-2211	charcoal: oak	insecure	charcoal not contextually associated with Beaker pots but likely to have been deposited at same time
Largantea	UB-6977	3871	37	2467-2209	burnt human bone	insecure	dated cremated bone not contextually associated with Beaker pots but likely to have been deposited at same time
Largantea	UB-6974	3837	35	2459-2200	burnt human bone	reasonable	dated cremated bone not contextually associated with Beaker pots but likely to have been deposited at same time
Lough Gur	OxA-3274	3830	80	2481-2126	inhumation	insecure	Skeleton no. 18 – infant
Largantea	UB-6976	3828	37	2458-2147	burnt human bone	reasonable	dated cremated bone not contextually associated with Beaker pots but likely to have been deposited at same time
Labbacallee	GrN-11359	3805	45	2458-2062	inhumation	reasonable	the single inhumation not directly associated with the Beaker, but its skull was associated in the adjoining chamber.
Lough Gur	OxA-3270	3780	70	2459-2031	inhumation	insecure	Skeleton no. 9 – adult
Labbacallee	OxA-2759	3780	70	2459-2031	inhumation	reasonable	Skeleton B directly associated with Beaker sherds
Lough Gur	OxA-3269	3740	100	2464-1911	inhumation	insecure	Skeleton no. 8 – adult
Lough Gur	OxA-3272	3720	70	2341-1921	inhumation	insecure	Skeleton no. 14 – child
Lough Gur	OxA-3267	3710	70	2333-1901	inhumation	insecure	Skeleton no. 6 – adult
Labbacallee	OxA-2760	3630	70	2201-1775	inhumation	reasonable	bone may have been in a secondary position or disturbed by later activity
Ballybriest	GrA-13273	3630	50	2139-1830	burnt human bone	unequivocal	
Ballybriest	GrA-13254	3580	50	2114-1769	burnt human bone	reasonable	date from pit cutting into late Beaker associated burial deposit so acts as a *taq*

Table 5.4: Details of the 15 Beaker – associated radiocarbon dates from wedge tombs obtained from high quality single entity short-life materials (except for the charcoal sample from Largantea). However, the strength of association between the Beaker pottery and the actual sample is not strong for all these burials.

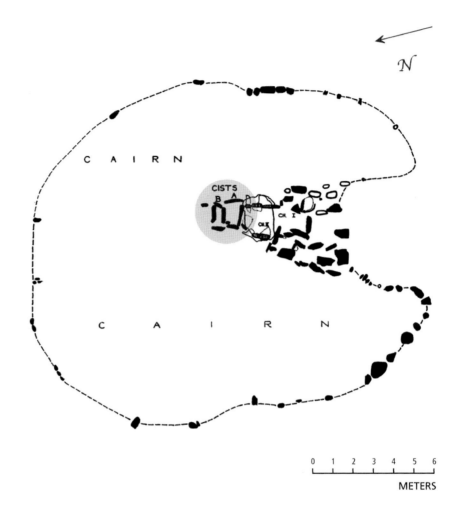

Fig. 5.7: The two small cists (in highlighted area) at the rear of the main chamber of the wedge tomb at Cashelbane, Co. Tyrone (after Herring 1938).

with Beaker sherds on the floor of the main chamber (Herring and May 1937, 45-6). Two other cremated individuals were also excavated, but the absence of radiocarbon dates from their bones prevents them being regarded as Beaker-associated.

At least 14 Beaker-associated inhumations have been discovered within a total of three wedge tombs. It is possible that a greater number of these burials may have been deposited alongside Beakers but may have been either removed during later phases of activity or destroyed by the acidic soil conditions common across much of Ireland. The greatest quantity of Beaker-associated inhumations in a single tomb, representing six individuals (5 adults and 1 child), were found at Moytirra, Co. Sligo, during two separate antiquarian investigations of this monument. Accurate details of these burials or of the relationship between these and the Beaker pottery in the tomb are not known (Cremin Madden 1969). One skeleton was described in an antiquarian report as being "in a crouching posture … the skull and bones in a heap" (ibid., 157). The other skeletons appear to have been found in two separate groups within one of the chambers; one group consisting of the bones of two adults and a child that were associated with three Beaker vessels, while the other group comprised the bones of two adults along with sherds of a fourth Beaker.

At Lough Gur, Co. Limerick, nine separate skeletons could be identified from the bones that were found scattered in highly disturbed deposits throughout the main chamber (Ó Ríordáin and Ó h-Iceadha 1955, 47). Five of these returned radiocarbon dates that overlap with the currency of Beakers, while four returned determinations post-dating these, two of which were probably deposited with two Bowls that were also found in the tomb. It is impossible, however, to associate any of the pottery with any particular inhumation because the contents of this tomb were extensively scattered and the exact location of any artefact from the tomb is not documented. While a stratigraphic association between the Beakers and the five contemporary inhumations cannot be demonstrated, most of the artefacts from the tomb were early-style Beakers and these seem to form the most significant association with the burials (Brindley and Lanting 1991/2, 24; Brindley, A.L. 2004, 335).

Site name	MNI cremations	MNI inhumations	Adult	Adult male	Adult female	Juvenile	Infant
Ballybriest	8	0	2	1	1	1	1
Ballyedmonduff	?	0	0	0	0	0	0
Cashelbane	5	0	3	1	2	1	0
Kilhoyle	1	0	1	0	1	0	0
Labbacallee	0	3	2	1	1	1	0
Loughash	?	0	0	0	0	0	0
Baurnadomeeny	1	0	0	0	0	0	0
Largantea	3	0	3	?	?	?	?
Lough Gur	1?	5	3	?	?	1	1
Moytirra	0	6	5	?	?	1	0
Totals	18	14	0	0	0	0	0

Table 5.5: The age and sex of Beaker burials in wedge tombs.

Site name	Cremations	Inhumations	Early/mid Beakers	Late Beakers	Irish Bowl	Irish Vase	Vase Urn
Cashelbane	5	0	yes	no	yes		
Kilhoyle	?	0	yes	no	yes	yes	
Largantea	3	0	yes	yes	yes		
Lough Gur	1?	5	yes	no	yes	yes	
Loughash			yes	yes	yes		yes
Ballybriest	8	0	yes	yes			
Ballyedmonduff	?	0	yes	yes			
Moytirra	0	6	yes	no			
Labbacallee	0	3	yes	no			

Table 5.6: Details of different burial types in wedge tombs with different ceramics.

The primary deposits within the wedge tomb at Labbacallee, Co Cork (Leask and Price 1936), were found to contain sherds from a Beaker pot and the unburnt remains of three individuals (an adult female, an adult male and a child). The adult female inhumation was found on the floor of its terminal cist-like chamber in a strangely disarticulated and partially disordered state (Fig. 5.6). The skeleton lay on its right-hand side with the legs pulled behind the body, but with the left arm (rather than the right) under the body in an articulated position and the skull and neckbones were missing (though see below). The excavators suggested that the body had been reburied after the flesh had become decomposed, but while some of the tendons still remained holding the bones together (Leask and Price 1936, 88). The disarticulated skeleton was accompanied by burnt animal bone (pig, cattle and sheep) and a bone pin strongly resembling a boar's tusk (Fig. 5.6). A longbone from this individual was radiocarbon dated to 2458-2062 BC (GrN-11359; 3805±45 BP; Brindley et al. 1987/8, 16).

An adult female skull that almost certainly belongs to this skeleton was found within the main chamber in direct association with 12 sherds from a 'domestic' Beaker (Leask and Price 1936, 93). Also in the main chamber, unburnt fragments of two other skeletons, a male adult and a child, were found mixed with animal bones and more sherds of the same 'domestic' Beaker found in the terminal chamber. A longbone from the male adult was radiocarbon dated to 2459-2031 BC (OxA-2759; 3780±70 BP), while a longbone from the child returned a date of 2201-1775 BC (OxA-2760; 3630±70 BP; Brindley and Lanting 1991/2).

In most cases, the successive placing of bodies in the same tombs obscures our ability to identify instances of single burial or to distinguish groupings of grave-gifts that may have been associated with specific individuals. Some evidence for these practices can, however, be found in compartmentalised locations such as the cist-like chambers located at the termini or inside the entrances of some wedge tombs. The Beaker-associated adult female inhumation from Labbacallee (described above) is one such example of this. Perhaps another example of this was excavated at the rear of the main chamber at Cashelbane (Davies and Mullin 1940, 150-51), where two small cists contained large quantities of cremated bone (Fig. 5.7). Each consisted of an upper deposit of dark earth and a primary layer of grey clay that overlay a paved floor. In one of the cists, the upper deposit produced a probable Beaker sherd and burnt bone, while the primary layer contained another probable Beaker sherd, a flint flake and the cremated remains of an adult male. From the upper horizon of the other cist came burnt bone and a convex scraper. Underneath this, the primary layer contained a small Beaker sherd and "a great deal" of burnt bone which may be human, but could not be identified as such" (ibid., 151). The creation of these cist-like compartments within tombs may represent an attempt to visibly individualise a particular deposit. This may also apply to the cist inside the entrance of the Largantea tomb (Herring 1938), containing two near complete Beakers and a scraper, though no human bone was identified within this compartment (Fig. 5.5).

There are no detectable demographic patterns in the Beaker-associated burial practices within wedge tombs (Table 5.5). There are 11 adult inhumations representing two females, one male, and eight individuals of unknown sex, while there are ten adult cremations comprising two males, four females and four individuals of unknown sex. This suggests that adults of both sexes were being cremated and inhumed in wedge tombs and there is no evidence to indicate that sex was a factor that influenced the form of burial rite chosen. Similarly, juveniles were deposited both as cremations (total=2) and inhumations (total=3). So, although fewer children than adults were being buried in wedge tombs in association with Beakers, there is nothing that indicates age affected the treatment of the body.

The most commonly associated artefacts found with Beakers in wedge tombs are lithics and these assemblages are dominated by debitage including split pebbles and chunks, but mainly flakes. This was the case at Ballybriest (described above) where the only grave-gifts other than pottery were a few flint flakes. Similarly, inside the badly disturbed tomb at Ballyedmonduff, where 140 sherds from eight Beakers were recovered, the only other artefacts were a few flint flakes and split pebbles that were found in a primary deposit along with 46 Beaker sherds in the terminal chamber (Ó Ríordáin and De Valera 1952, 69).

A total of 14 convex scrapers have been recorded in association with Beakers in three wedge tombs; Cashelbane, Kilhoyle and Largantea. At the latter, one such scraper was found in a primary deposit inside a stone cist alongside sherds from three Beakers (see above). Six scrapers came from the tomb at Cashelbane where Beaker was the main ceramic; however, the only contextual details available for five of these are that they were found in the burial area. Presumably this means they were found in the chamber deposit, which contained the cremated remains of at least four people associated with Beaker pottery (see above), but this is not certain. As detailed above, the sixth scraper was found in the cist-like structure, in a layer overlying a Beaker-associated deposit and possible human bone. At Kilhoyle, four convex scrapers were found in a deposit within the main chamber that contained Beakers and burials but also displayed evidence for multi-period activity, thereby preventing any definitive identification of these as Beaker-associated lithics. Overall, the strength of association between these 14 scrapers and Beaker pottery or Beaker burials is questionable.

Seven barbed and tanged arrowheads have been recovered from five wedge tombs; Cashelbane (Sutton and Green Low) and Clogherny (type unknown), both in County Tyrone, Kilhoyle (Green Low) and Boviel (Sutton Type B), both in County Derry, and Harristown, Co. Waterford (Green Low). It is, however, difficult to identify a strong association between the deposition of these objects and Beaker pottery. At Cashelbane, two of these projectiles were found in the main chamber with Beaker pottery and the cremated remains of at least four individuals (Fig. 5.8). At Kilhoyle, the arrowhead was found under the septal slab (Herring and May 1937, 45-6), perhaps suggesting that it was deposited during construction. Despite the lack of evidence for a direct association, all of these projectiles can still be regarded as indicators of Beaker depositional activity as barbed and tanged arrowheads have never been found associated with Irish Bowls or Vases, and the few that are found with Collared and Cordoned Urns are quite different, *e.g.* Ballyclare type arrowheads (Woodman *et al.* 2006, 138).

Polished stone axes have also been found in wedge tombs, such as Boviel and Lough Gur, Co. Limerick (Herring and May 1940; Ó Ríordáin and Ó h-Iceadha 1955). At the former, the axe occurred outside the chamber, but inside the area defined by the monument's orthostatic kerb, while at the latter, an axe fragment was discovered in the chamber. However, it is not possible to determine whether these represent Beaker-associated depositions or to date them on typological grounds alone. Objects other than stone tools and production waste are rarely found with Beakers in these monuments. Two very notable exceptions are the wedge tombs at Labbacallee and Moytirra. A bone pin/ spatula resembling a boar's tusk was discovered with the Beaker-associated disarticulated skeleton of an adult female at Labbacallee, Co. Cork (Fig. 5.6). A long thin bronze or gold object was reportedly found during the antiquarian investigations at Moytirra, Co. Sligo, but details are vague and there is every chance that it reflects a later phase of activity (Cremin Madden 1968, 157).

Overall, few typical Beaker object types are found in wedge tombs other than pottery, arrowheads and scrapers. There is a lack of evidence for a close associ-

Loughash Cashelbane Flints

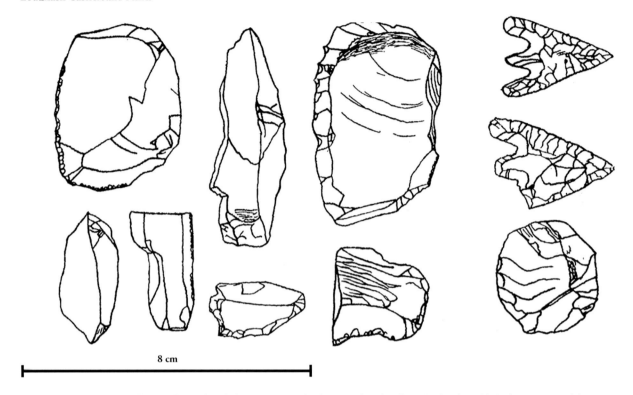

Fig. 5.8: Lithics from Cashelbane wedge tomb including two projectiles that were found in the main chamber with Beaker pottery and the cremated remains of at least four individuals (after Davies and Mullin 1940).

ation between these artefacts and either Beaker pottery or any of the human remains of Beaker date. With the exception of the pottery, obvious Beaker grave-gifts are very rare and, in many cases, the connection between the deposition of the burials and the pottery in these tombs is slightly ambiguous. In some cases, the paucity of aceramic grave-gifts may be attributed to the degree to which these monuments remained open to re-use over millennia. The consistency of the evidence, including that from better preserved tombs sealed beneath peat for millennia such as at Ballybriest (Hurl 2001, 12), suggests that this is genuinely reflective of Beaker-associated depositional practices.

Returning to chronological matters, to focus on the dating of Beaker-associated deposits within wedge tombs, we see that early styles of Beakers were found in the wedge tombs at Moytirra, Largantea, Lough Gur and Cashelbane (Table 5.6). This is consistent with the Bayesian modelling of early wedge tomb use as pre-dating c. 2450 BC. Later styles occurred at Ballyedmonduff, Largantea, Loughash, Ballybriest and Carriglong indicating that Beaker pottery was still being deposited in those tombs after 2250 BC (Table 5.6; see Chapters Three and Eight for further details and dating of pottery types). The occurrence of both forms in some wedge tombs suggests that Beakers continued to be deposited in these monuments for several hundred years, probably from 2450 to 2050 BC. This date range is also supported by 15 of the 33 existing radiocarbon determinations (seven from cremated human bone and eight from unburnt human bone) that were contextually associated with Beaker pottery (Fig. 5.9; Table 5.4). In combination, these dates and the pottery chronologies also point towards some chronological patterning in the practices associated with these monuments.

Early-style Beakers dating from c. 2450-2200 BC have been found in wedge tombs containing either inhumations or cremations or both. In contrast, stylistically late Beakers, dating from 2200-2050 BC (see Chapter Eight), have only been found in tombs containing cremations. Notwithstanding the often-questionable strength of association between this pottery and the human remains, this broad-scale patterning suggests that Beaker pottery was deposited in these monuments with cremations and inhumations until c. 2200 BC, but only with cremations thereafter. The current evidence is, however, insufficient to unequivocally confirm this or to fully reveal the extent of changes in wedge tomb practices across time and space. Further investigation is needed, particularly the radiocarbon dating of more cremations, including those found alongside unburnt bone such as at Lough Gur wedge tomb.

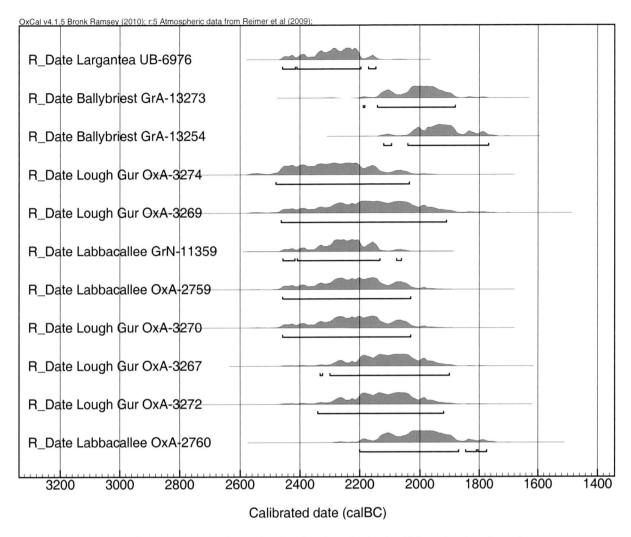

Fig. 5.9: Radiocarbon dates from Beaker associated cremations (top three determinations) and inhumations in wedge tombs.

5.3 Beaker deposition in court tombs

Just 36 out of 394 Early Neolithic court tombs have been excavated in Ireland. A complete reassessment of the ceramics from these chamber tombs is required to state the total amount of Beaker pottery and the exact number of sherds per vessel. While that is outside the scope of this research, it can be stated that at least 103 sherds from 19 Beakers have been discovered in 14 (39%) of these monuments; Creevykeel, Co. Sligo, Ballyglass, Co. Mayo, Clontygora Large, Co. Armagh, Aghanaglack and Ballyreagh, Co. Fermanagh, Barnes Lower and Legland, Co. Tyrone, Tamnyrankin, Ballybriest and Carrick East, Co. Derry, and Ballyalton, Ballyedmond, Ballynichol and Goward, Co. Down. None of these Beakers, however, were found in secure closed contexts; they predominantly occurred in disturbed deposits alongside artefacts ranging from the Early Neolithic to the Late Bronze Age.

The remains of only one Beaker was present in nine of these court tombs, but three pots, representing the highest number in any example, were excavated at Carrick East and Ballynichol (Table 5.7). At the former, the southern chamber contained a layer of soft yellow earth that yielded the remains of three Beaker pots. Overlying this was a black layer containing sherds from two of the same Beakers, as well as multiple sherds of a Middle Neolithic globular bowl, flint scrapers and human bone (Mullin and Davies 1938; Herity 1982, 285, 332; 1987, 194). Two of the Beakers were represented by at least three sherds each, while the third was represented by eight sherds found "in all parts of the south chamber and at very divergent levels" (Mullin and Davies 1938, 103). All of these Beaker sherds were so widely scattered throughout the chamber that it was impossible to identify any associations between these and any other materials in the tomb. From the above discussion of wedge tombs, we have already become familiar with the difficulties of identifying associations between Beaker pottery and the contents of chamber tombs (including human bone) and the limits to what can be known about Beaker-associated practices in these tombs.

Another example of these interpretative challenges comes from the court tomb at Ballyglass, Co. Mayo, which produced the largest number of Beaker sherds recovered from one of these monuments; 56 sherds representing two vessels (Roche forthcoming). These were found inside the front chamber of the eastern gallery within a layer that included human bone, Middle Neolithic and Late Bronze Age pottery (Ó Nualláin *et al.* forthcoming). Interestingly, one of these pots had an estimated height of only 9.2cm and appears to be the smallest Beaker ever recorded in Ireland or Britain (Fig. 5.10). The presence of numerous conjoining sherds from both vessels suggests these were deposited as complete pots. No other evidence for this form of depositional practice was detected at any of the other court tombs. Instead, most Beakers were represented by a few small sherds. For example, at Barnes Lower, Co. Tyrone, an "undisturbed deposit" within one of the chambers consisted of a concentration of cremated bone in black soil along with a Middle Neolithic bipartite bowl, two burnt flakes, and four sherds of a Beaker (pot 2; Collins 1966, fig 8:1-3; Herity 1987, 233). It is impossible, however, to decipher whether this is because of later re-use/disturbance of the tombs or if the low sherd/vessel ratios are an accurate reflection of past depositional activity.

Although human bone and Beaker pottery have been found in the same deposits in court tombs, there is currently no definite evidence for Beaker-associated burials within their chambers. Cremated and unburnt human bone with radiocarbon dates ranging from 2300-2000 BC are known from the court tombs at Aghanaglack, Ballyalton and Audleystown (Schulting *et al.* 2012,). None, however, have clear Beaker-associations or unequivocally date from 2450-2200 BC. All fall within the post-2200 BC date range of Early Bronze Age Food Vessels and seem more likely to reflect part of the increased burial activity that we see at that time. For example, one of the chambers at Aghanaglack contained a few sherds from a Beaker and what was described in the original publication as a flint javelin. This javelin may be a flint dagger or a foliate knife, though only one example of the former is known in Ireland (see Frieman 2014). Two barbed-and-tanged arrowheads (Green Low types) were also found in another chamber in a layer that also produced an Early

Site	Vessel Quantity	Sherd Quantity
Carrick East	3	?
Ballynichol	3	5
Ballyglass	2	56
Goward	2	3
Clontygora Large	1	3
Creevykeel	1	4?
Aghanaglack	1	?
Ballyalton	1	4
Ballybriest	1	8
Ballyedmond	1	3
Ballyreagh	1	3
Legland	1	6
Tamnyrankin	1	8

Table 5.7: The number of Beaker vessels and sherds per court tomb.

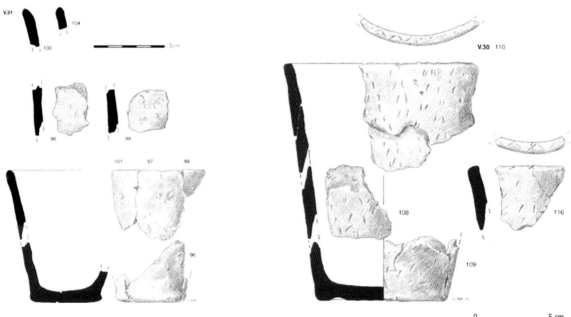

Fig. 5.10: The two Beaker vessels from the Ballyglass court tomb, Co. Mayo (after Ó Nualláin et al. forthcoming).

Neolithic Carinated bowl (Davies 1938; Herity 1987, 154). A date of 2128-1881 BC (UB-7188; 3608±38 BP) was obtained from a cremated human longbone from one of the chambers (Schulting *et al.* 2012, 34).

Similarly, at Audleystown, Co. Down, cremated bone fragments from one chamber produced dates of 2333-2041 BC (UB-7190; 3774±36 BP) and 2205-1985 BC (UB-7189; 3719±33 BP), while unburnt bone from another chamber returned a date of 2277-2029 BC (UB-7593; 3732±35 BP) (Collins 1954; Schulting *et al.* 2012, 34-5). Sherds from Bowls rather than Beakers were, however, recovered from this monument, suggesting that these deposits post-date the Chalcolithic. Perhaps the best evidence for Beaker burial in a court tomb context comes from the exterior of the monument at Ballybriest, Co. Derry (Evans 1939), where a stone-lined pit or cist that had been dug into the cairn of the court tomb contained the cremated remains of an adult male and at least eight sherds from a 'domestic' Beaker (Fig. 5.11). In the absence of radiocarbon dating, however, it remains possible that like at Knowth (see Section 5.4), the Beaker pottery may have been deposited later than the burial.

Further evidence for Beaker-associated deposition within court tombs is provided by the discovery of stereotypically Beaker-related objects within these monuments. Six barbed and tanged arrowheads have been retrieved from deposits within the interior as well as the cairns of four court tombs, including the

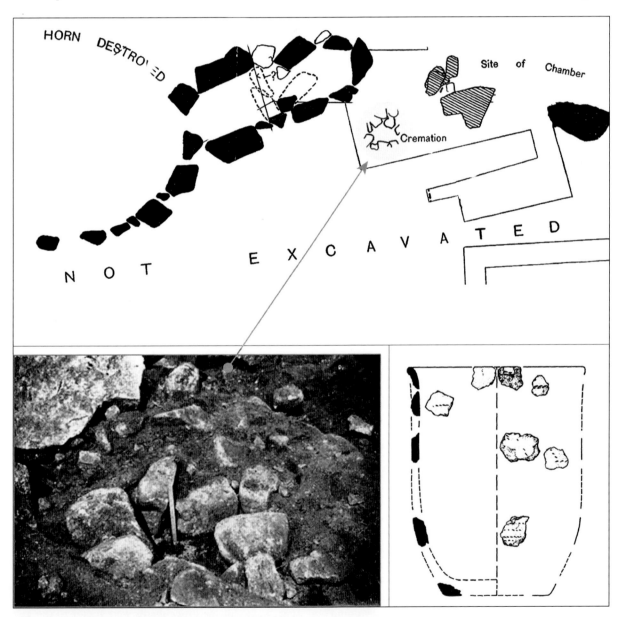

Fig. 5.11: Cremation burial within a stone-lined pit or cist at Ballybriest court tomb, Co. Derry (after Evans 1939 and Herity 1987, Fig. 28).

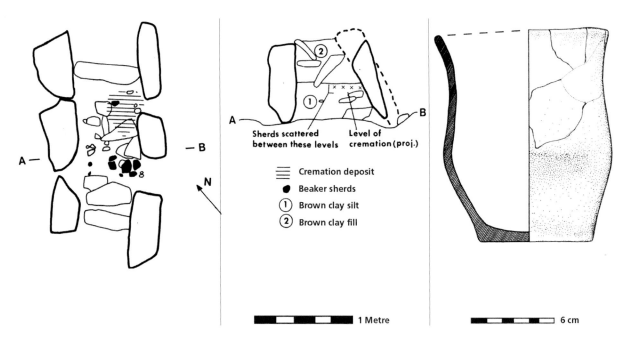

Fig. 5.12: Plan and section of the passage into Tomb 15 at Knowth showing the occurrence of Beaker pottery beside the Late Neolithic cremation burials within a cist-like stone compartment and a drawing of the almost complete undecorated fine Beaker (after Eogan 1984, fig. 117).

aforementioned examples from a chamber at Aghanaglack. Two Conygar Hill types were found in the cairn of the Ballyglass court tomb which contained Beaker pottery (Ó Nualláin *et al.* forthcoming), while another barbed and tanged example (of unknown type) and a hollow-based arrowhead were recovered from a 'much disturbed fill' in the front chamber of another smaller court tomb at Ballyglass (Ó Nualláin 1998). Another barbed and tanged arrowhead was found in the Creggandevesky court tomb, Co. Tyrone, but its contextual details are unknown (Herity 1987, 132). Significantly, a probable wrist-bracer was found in one of the chambers of a court tomb at Ballywholan, also in County Tyrone (Kelly, D. 1985). Although this stone object is now lost, its description as being red in colour with a perforation at either end and a plano-convex section certainly suggests that this is a Type A wrist-bracer, however, as we will see in Chapter Nine, this represents a very unusual context in which to find one of these objects.

In the main, only Beaker sherds and projectiles seem to have been placed in court tombs. This suggests that the Beaker-associated deposition was quite circumscribed and type-specific in these contexts. While these artefacts may have been deposited in tombs as grave-gifts and may reflect the former location of Beaker burials, there is no definitive evidence for this. It is possible that these artefacts represent some other form of ceremonial depositional practice that served to mark ancestral places and maintain social relationships between local communities and their ancestors (see Section 5.10).

5.4 Beaker deposition in passage tombs

Although the best-known Beaker-associated activity in Ireland has been found in what has usually been interpreted as settlements outside the monuments at Newgrange and Knowth, Co. Meath (see Chapter Three), Beaker pottery has only been discovered within three passage tombs in Ireland, all of which are at Knowth; Tombs 2, 15 and 17 (Fig. 3.11). A single sherd was found above the old ground surface within the passage of Tomb 2 and a further two sherds occurred immediately opposite its entrance (Eogan, G. 1984, 308). Beaker pottery was loosely associated with the poorly preserved Tomb 17; one of the kerbstones (no. 8) had been removed in antiquity and the depression created by its removal contained six sherds from two vessels (ibid., 307).

What has traditionally been regarded as a Beaker burial was found inside the passage of Tomb 15 at Knowth (Eogan, G.1984, Roche and Eogan 2001). A cist-like stone compartment, two sides of which were formed by a sillstone and two orthostats, contained the cremated remains of an adult female and a child. Recent radiocarbon dating of a longbone fragment from the adult, however, yielded a Late Neolithic date of 2912-2877 BC (UBA-12683; 4265±24 BP; Schulting *et al.* 2017). Sherds forming a near-complete 'fine' undecorated Beaker were found close to the burial; some were stratigraphically associated with the bones, others were in the fill above it, but most of the sherds were just outside the compartment (Fig. 5.12). All the lower sherds were found to the east and all the upper sherds were found to the west, suggest-

Fig. 5.13: The three V-perforated buttons, bronze awl and disc bead necklace that were found with Early Bronze Age burials in the chamber of the Mound of the Hostages passage tomb and a crouched inhumation (burial 18) within a pit dug into the chamber that was accompanied by an anthracite button, a bronze awl and an Irish Bowl (after O'Sullivan 2005).

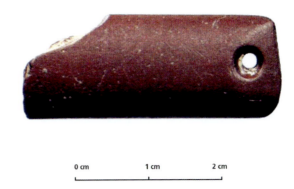

Fig. 5.14: A (type A) wrist-bracer found in topsoil during excavations 500m east of the Fourknocks passage tomb, Co. Meath (after King 1997).

ing that this pot was inserted as a complete vessel and was subsequently broken during the tomb's destruction (Eogan, G. 1984, 311-2). Its deposition with an earlier burial of Late Neolithic date, just inside the entrance of the tomb, seems to fulfil a referential or commemorative function (see Carlin 2017).

Despite the paucity of Beaker pottery and complete lack of evidence for associated burials from passage tombs, a relatively large number of Beaker-related objects including arrowheads, wrist-bracers and V-perforated buttons have been found in and around these monuments. As we will see, however, in the case of the buttons there is every chance that these represent Food Vessel-associated deposits rather than Beaker-associated activity. In a British context, most of these buttons occur in burials post-dating 2200 BC (Needham 2005; Woodward and Hunter 2015, 148). In Ireland, six of these buttons have occurred in association with four passage tombs; Carrowmore Site 49, Co. Sligo, Dowth, Mound of the Hostages and Loughcrew Cairn R2, all in County Meath (Harbison 1976, 14). Another was found on the mountainside near the probable passage tomb known as *Miosgán Meadhbha* at Knocknarea, Co. Sligo, although no further details about its provenance are known (Harbison 1976, 35). Monument no. 49 in the Carrowmore passage tomb cemetery comprised a central chamber that was surrounded by a boulder circle. This contained two burials (one cremated and one unburnt) that were associated with oyster shells, a V-perforated button and three sherds of "reddish pottery" (Wood-Martin 1888, 68; Harbison 1976, 14). A star-shaped V-perforated button made from jasper was found "in the sepulchral caverns during the excavations of the tumulus" at Dowth, Co. Meath (Wilde 1857, 122), while an unperforated jet button came from Cairn R2 of the passage grave cemetery at Loughcrew (Harbison 1976, 14).

The remaining three V-perforated buttons were discovered within the chamber of the Mound of the Hostages passage tomb (Fig. 5.13). The exact context and associations of two of these are slightly ambiguous, but one example seems to have accompanied an Early Bronze Age Bowl (Food Vessel) burial (O'Sullivan, M. 2005, 104-9). This anthracite button was found with a crouched inhumation (Burial 18; sex unknown) at the base of a pit dug into the original fill of the chamber where it rested on its left-hand side with its head to the southwest. This burial was also accompanied by a bronze awl and a Bowl positioned beside its head (ibid., 107-10.). A.L. Brindley (2007, 249) observed that this Bowl is of a late type, dating from around 1980-1920 BC, although cremated human bone from the base of the pit produced a radiocarbon date of 2393-1983 BC (GrA-17719; 3760±50 BP). Interestingly, this represents the earliest date for an Early Bronze Age burial from the Mound of the Hostages (see Brindley *et al.* 2005, 290; Bayliss and O'Sullivan 2013, 38).

Also in this pit, a second anthracite V-perforated button was found in the uppermost levels of a layer of "clean yellow clay" that overlay Burial 18. This yellow

FRAGMENTS OF THE DEAD? | 111

layer was sealed by a stone paving upon which lay the disarticulated remains of another crouched inhumation (Burial 19; adult, sex unknown) as well as unburnt bones from an adolescent, children's teeth and two skulls, one of which was full of cremated bone. A Bowl was also found in the corner of the pit beside the skulls and the upper half of another Bowl was found within the pit at the same level as the inhumation burial. The location of the second button, within the yellow clay over Burial 18 but separated from Burial 19 by the stone paving, suggests that this ornament had not accompanied Burial 19. It may originally have been deposited with Burial 18 and then disturbed at a later stage, perhaps during the deposition of the yellow layer, which may have been laid in preparation for the Burial 19 inhumation. The original associations of this button are, however, unclear due to post-depositional disturbance, including the displacement of some human bones, and the methods of excavation employed in the 1950s. It is possible that the buttons originally accompanied the cremation burial, whose date range of 2393-1983 BC overlaps with the main currency of Irish Beakers, but became displaced during the insertion of the inhumations. Given the post-2200 BC date range of most V-perforated buttons the balance of evidence suggests that these were part of the earlier Bowl-associated crouched inhumation.

Wrist-bracers have been found in topsoil in proximity to three passage tombs. A (Type B2) wrist-bracer was found within 400m of Cairn K at Loughcrew, Co. Meath (Cooney 1987). Another example (Type A) was found in close proximity to the Carrowkeel passage tomb complex in County Sligo, where it lay near the base of the peat that also covered some of the tombs (Harbison 1976, 24) and yet another (Type A); (Fig. 5.14) was discovered in topsoil 500m east of the passage tombs at Fourknocks, Co. Meath, along with a barbed and tanged arrowhead (Sutton A type) (King 1999). Arrowheads have occurred within three passage tombs. A hollow-based form was sealed by slip from the cairn of Site Z, the destroyed satellite passage tomb at Newgrange (O'Kelly *et al.* 1978, 333), while two barbed and tanged types were on chamber floors; one (Green Low or Conygar) was found in the Slieve Gullion passage tomb, Co. Armagh, while another (Sutton Type A) came from Cairn R2 at Loughcrew (Green 1980, 226). Although the deposition of the archery items found in proximity to passage tombs cannot be shown to be directly related to these monuments, the spatial associations shared by several of these suggests that this was not simply fortuitous and that these deposits were focused on the vicinity of these megaliths (see Section 9.5).

Overall, the nature of Beaker deposition associated with these monuments seems to have fulfilled a ceremonial function. It was highly restricted and did not include the internment of human remains. This resembles what we observed from court tombs, but in contrast, Beaker sherds were largely deposited outside rather than inside passage tombs. This, and the greater quantities of artefacts from the exterior and environs of passage tombs, suggests that these monuments were more of a locus than a focus for Beaker deposition. As discussed in Chapter Three, culturally-rich occupational debris seems to have been deliberately deposited at Knowth and Newgrange to emphasise particular aspects of these megaliths, particularly the entrance areas. Much of the Beaker deposition at passage tombs seems to have served to establish or maintain material connections between the users of the Beaker pottery and the history of these important monuments (see Carlin 2017). This activity appears to represent non-sepulchral commemorative interactions between the community of the living and the community of ancestors. The Killaha type bronze flat axe discovered in a Beaker horizon sealed by collapse from the cairn of the tomb at Newgrange (O'Kelly and Shell 1979) can be considered as a continuation of this tradition (but see Section 3.2.2).

5.5 Beaker deposition in portal tombs

Beaker-associated deposits in pits and occupation spreads like those outside the passage tombs at Newgrange and Knowth, were found outside and around a portal tomb at Taylorsgrange, Co. Dublin (Keeley 1989; Lynch, R. 1998). Like passage tombs, Beakers and other associated objects are rarely found in Earlier Neolithic portal tombs and their identification as funerary deposits is also problematic; most have come from disturbed deposits within the interior. Beaker pottery has only been recovered from a portal tomb at Poulnabrone, Co. Clare (Lynch, A. 2014). This tomb's chamber contained the remains of at least 35 individuals dating from the first six centuries of the fourth millennium BC, Early and Middle Neolithic pottery, as well as two 'domestic' Beaker sherds, a hollow-based arrowhead and debitage of comparable date. None of the 30 radiocarbon determinations from human bone (including at least 16 distinctly dated individuals) overlap with the currency of Beaker pottery. This suggests that while Beaker pottery and other materials were certainly deposited in small quantities within the chamber, human remains were not placed inside the monument at this time. Instead, this seems to have occurred outside, as indicated by an unburnt human cranium fragment dating from 2457-2142 BC (UBA-23505; 3822±37 BP), which was found with an unburnt longbone under the edge of the tomb's cairn (ibid., 44-6, 51-2). This indicates that at least some kind of Chalcolithic depositional activity involving human bone was occurring at this monument. Rick Schulting (2014, 109) has suggested that the cairn may not have been added to this Early Neolithic monument until sometime around 2400-2200 BC, but this remains unclear.

Cremated human bone from two tombs – Ballyrenan, Co. Tyrone (Davies 1937), and Drumanone, Co. Roscommon (Topp 1962) – has produced radiocarbon dates indicating burial activity concurrent with the use of Beakers. Cremated human skull bone from the distal chamber at Ballyrenan returned a date of 2281-2033 BC (UB-6706: 3743±36 BP) (Kytmannow 2008). The only finds with which the cremated bone was physically associated was an Early Neolithic Carinated bowl (Davies 1937). Six disc and two fusiform stone beads of a type dating from 2450-1900 BC were, however, found within a different chamber of the tomb. A cremated human skull fragment from a disturbed position within the chamber at Drumanone produced a radiocarbon date of 2134-1905 BC (UB-6696; 3639±37 BP; Kytmannow 2008, 107). No Beaker pottery was found in either tomb. It seems probable that these deposits reflect the increased evidence for burials that we see occurring from 2200-1900 BC in association with Food Vessels.

As well as the Poulnabrone example, hollow-based arrowheads have also been discovered at two other portal tombs; Melkagh, Co Longford (Cooney 1997b), and Kiltiernan Domain, Co. Dublin (Ó Eochaidhe 1957). The Melkagh projectile was found during excavations conducted after the tomb had been badly damaged by land improvement works. This arrowhead was discovered in a spread of flat stones thought to represent the base of the cairn (Cooney 1997b, 219). How exactly it ended up in this context is unknown, but it may be speculated that it was deliberately inserted into the cairn. Partial excavation of the chamber at Kiltiernan Domain produced another hollow-based arrowhead, along with three concave scrapers, one convex end scraper and at least two pots of Middle Neolithic Impressed Ware (Ó Eochaidhe 1957).

5.6 Beaker deposition in cists

Cists provide a highly divergent and complex set of evidence for Breaker-associated activity that defy precise interpretations. A small quantity of Beaker pottery (minimum of 11 vessels) has been discovered within six cists in association with burials, including those with or without associated cairns; Poulawack, Co. Clare, Gortcobies, Co. Derry, Knockmullin, Co. Sligo, Longstone Furness, Co. Kildare, Cappydonnell, Co. Offaly and Lyles Hill, Co. Antrim. Except for Gortcobies, where seven Beakers were found, these monuments usually contained the remains of only one Beaker, each of which was represented by a few small sherds. This raises the possibility that there may have been a custom of depositing a few Beaker sherds rather than entire vessels into cists. Most of these sites, however, were excavated before 1950 and suffer from many of the problems associated with the interpretation of older excavations as discussed above. While both cremations and inhumations have been found in contextual association with Beaker pottery in cists, details about the nature of these burials is often lacking and concrete evidence for a Beaker association is absent. In keeping with the small quantity of Beaker pottery recovered from cists, the number of associated grave-gifts from this context is also quite low. In some cases, such as detailed below at Kinkit, Co. Tyrone, there is no direct association between Beaker pottery and the burial itself.

More recent excavations also present similar interpretative challenges; more forensic analysis and radiocarbon dating have revealed the complexities of the practices that were undertaken. The excavation of a multi-period site at Ballynacarriga, Co. Cork, for example, uncovered two pits containing Beaker pottery and occupational debris in an area that had been the focus of activity in the Late Neolithic, as indicated by the presence of a series of Grooved Ware-associated timber circle-like structures that probably fulfilled a range of residential and ritual functions (Johnston and Kiely, forthcoming; Johnston and Carlin, forthcoming). Uncovered just 50m south of this area was an Early Bronze Age funerary complex, comprising two ring-ditches and a group of cists and pits containing cremation burials with Food Vessels and Encrusted Urns (Fig. 5.15). While these features mainly dated from 1900-1600 BC, two cists provided indications of an earlier phase of burial activity dating from 2400-2200 BC and therefore contemporary with the nearby Beaker pits. Both cists took the form of stone-lined pits and did not include Beaker pottery or any other artefacts (Johnston and Kiely, forthcoming). One contained 154g of cremated human bone from an infant and a juvenile, the latter returning a date of 2460-2206 BC (UBA-14777; 3852±34 BP). The other cist did not contain any human remains, but pomoideae charcoal from it produced a similar date of 2461-2211 BC (UB-13165; 3861±23 BP). It is likely that it may once have, but that these bones were not preserved or were subsequently removed, resulting in an apparently 'empty' cist.

Supporting evidence, albeit circumstantial, for the latter scenario is provided by a pit-burial that was centrally located within one of the ring-ditches (Fig. 5.15). Inside this pit was a Vase and an incomplete Encrusted Urn, both of which had been deposited inverted. The Encrusted Urn contained cremated human bone (1539g) from at least three individuals: a young adult female, a foetus representing an in-utero burial as well as a fragment of a left clavicle belonging to a second, older adult (ibid.). A longbone from the adult female returned a radiocarbon date of 2344-2060 BC (UBA-14778; 3793±34 BP), but this is strangely early for an Encrusted Urn or Vase, which have firmly es-

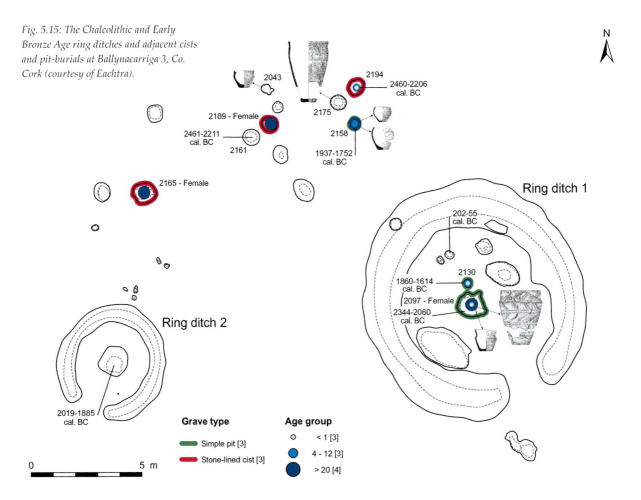

Fig. 5.15: The Chalcolithic and Early Bronze Age ring ditches and adjacent cists and pit-burials at Ballynacarriga 3, Co. Cork (courtesy of Eachtra).

tablished date ranges of c. 2020-1800 BC (Brindley, A.L. 2007, 266-274). Significantly, radiocarbon dates from human remains and charcoal corresponding directly with the expected currency of this pottery were obtained from two other pit burials associated with this ring-ditch, one of which contained two Vases. This chronological discrepancy may be due to an 'old wood effect' where the radiocarbon date of the cremated bone has been unduly influenced by carbon from 'old wood' during the cremation process (see Snoeck et al. 2014). However, the presence of the clavicle from another adult in the burial pit suggests that this anomaly is more likely to reflect the complexity of depositional practices at this site. One potential explanation is that the pregnant adult female dating from the third millennium BC was originally deposited within the 'empty' cist, which contained charcoal of comparable date. Subsequently these bones were removed from the cist and redeposited within the Encrusted Urn, along with bone from another person. While this remains uncertain, the key point here is that two of the cists indicate that burial activity was being conducted at broadly the same time Beaker pottery was current on this site, potentially by the same group of people.

A similar interpretative challenge is provided by a partially excavated central cist within a kerb cairn at Coolnatullagh, Co. Clare. This contained the remains of three individuals; an adult inhumation dating from 2460-2140 BC (OxA-10530; 3835±45 BP), a child's scapula and a cremation deposit representing adult long and cranial bones (Eogan, J. 2002, 124). Two tiny sherds of probable Beaker pottery were found in the cairn, but there was no certain evidence to indicate that these were directly associated with the partially excavated cist burials, even though the radiocarbon date from one individual overlaps with the main currency of Beaker pottery and pre-dates the widespread use of Food Vessels.

Another example of the complications of identifying Beaker-related burials is illustrated by the nearby site of Poulawack, where Hencken (1935) excavated a multi-phase monument containing eight cists and the remains of 16 men, women and children, all within a kerbed cairn (Fig. 5.16). Radiocarbon dating suggests that there were three main phases of burials spanning almost 2000 years, each of which saw changes to the appearance of this monument, the last of which was the insertion of cists into the cairn c. 1600 BC (Brindley and Lanting 1991/2). Activity here began with the dep-

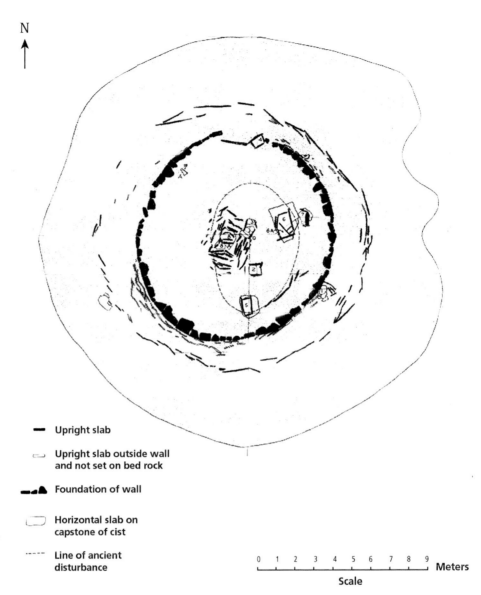

Fig. 5.16: The kerbed cairn at Poulawack, Co. Clare (after Hencken 1935).

- Upright slab
- Upright slab outside wall and not set on bed rock
- Foundation of wall
- Horizontal slab on capstone of cist
- Line of ancient disturbance

osition of human remains c. 3600-3300 BC within a Neolithic Linkardstown-type megalithic cist (Graves 8 and 8A) that was surrounded by a low cairn and kerbstones (Ryan 1981; Brindley and Lanting 1991/2, 13). This formed a focus for the later construction of three cists (Graves 4, 5 and 6) towards the end of the third millennium BC, all of which were subsequently sealed beneath an enlarged cairn (see Henken 1935, 202). One of these was a large cist (Graves 6 and 6a; 1m long by 1m wide) that had been divided in two (Fig. 5.17). One part (Grave 6A) contained a Beaker sherd, cremated bone and unburnt bones from an adolescent and an adult male, the latter of which was disarticulated. Bone from the adult male and from the adolescent produced radiocarbon dates of 2020-1686 BC (OxA-3262; 3520±60 BP) and 2185-1772 BC (OxA-3263; 3600±65 BP) respectively (Brindley and Lanting 1991/2, 16). The other part

(Grave 6) of the cist also contained bones belonging to the adult male and the adolescent, in addition to the unburnt remains of a child and an adult male cremation deposit. Another cist (Grave 4) located along the outer limits of the cairn contained unburnt bones from an adult and a child, with the adult returning a date of 2560-2040 BC (OxA-3260; 3830±90 BP; ibid.).

Jessica Beckett (2011) observed that the unburnt burials at Poulawack had largely been interred in an intact state and subsequently been disturbed. Given the complex history of the site and associated levels of disturbance, as well as the fact that only a single Beaker sherd was identified, and the date ranges overlap with the currency of Food Vessels, we should be hesitant to conclude that these represent Beaker-associated burials. Additional radiocarbon determinations, particularly from the cremated bone in Grave 6 are needed to clarify

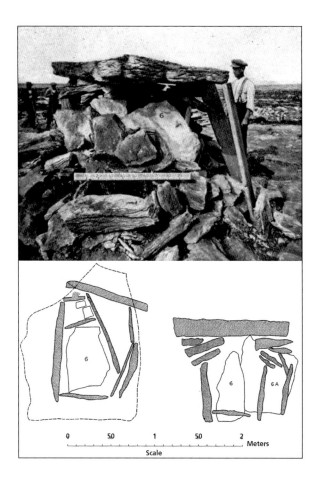

Fig. 5.17: Cist 6 at Poulawack containing a sherd of Beaker pottery as well as the cremated remains of an adult male, the unburnt bones of an adolescent, a child and an adult male (after Hencken 1935).

this. It may be more appropriate to see the Beaker sherds as either the surviving remains of earlier deposits that were disturbed by repeated activity in the same locale or as the deliberate deposition of curated heirlooms. This is a topic to which we will return below (Section 5.9), after considering some other examples of this phenomenon.

Similar issues arise regarding the burial found with Beaker pottery in a centrally located cist grave within a kerbed cairn at Lyles Hill, Co. Antrim, which sealed earlier Neolithic activity (Evans 1953). Outside the kerb of the cairn were three Early Bronze Age burials associated with Food Vessels (two Vases and a Bowl) and an Encrusted Urn. The central cist had a paved floor and two fills. The primary layer contained the cremated remains of an adolescent as well as sherds of Early and Middle Neolithic pottery, a hollow scraper, a leaf-shaped arrowhead or foliate knife, a quartz core and two rim sherds of a pot originally identified as an unusual Food Vessel (Evans 1953, 10, fig. 18, vessel no. 90) but subsequently recognised as a Beaker (Case 1961, 224; Apsimon 1969; Eoin Grogan, pers. comm).

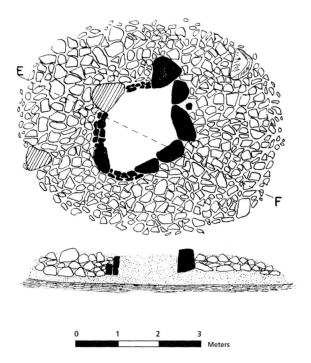

Fig. 5.18: Plan and Section of the Beaker associated cairn and chamber at Gortcobies, Co. Derry (after May 1947, fig. 5).

Cremated human and red deer bone and another Beaker sherd were found within the cairn beside the central cist and are thought to have been disturbed from that grave. Recently, however, Kerri Cleary (2016) radiocarbon dated a cremated human femur from the central cist to 1877-1644 BC (UBA-29666; 3431±31 BP), which indicates that this burial was probably contemporary with those in the other cists that contained Early Bronze Age ceramics whose accepted date range overlaps with this radiocarbon date.[5] This raises the question of whether the Beaker sherds here were residual, just like the Neolithic pottery and lithics also occurring in the central cist.

Likewise, a disturbed cist excavated on a multi-period site at Cappydonnell, Co. Offaly, was found to contain four fragments from a Beaker and fragments of cremated human bone radiocarbon dated to 2029-1887 BC (UBA-10189; 3589±30 BP) within its primary deposit (Coughlan 2010; Tim Coughlan, pers. comm.). This was sealed by another deposit containing three sherds and three fragments from a Vase of the Food Vessel Tradition, whose date range more closely matches with the burial. It is difficult to discern whether the

---

5   Kerri Cleary (2016, 157) expressed uncertainty about the exact context of the sample she dated because of incomplete information regarding the labelling of the bone and its context.

Fig. 5.19: Plan and section of the cist burial at Furness, Co. Kildare (after Macalister et al 1913).

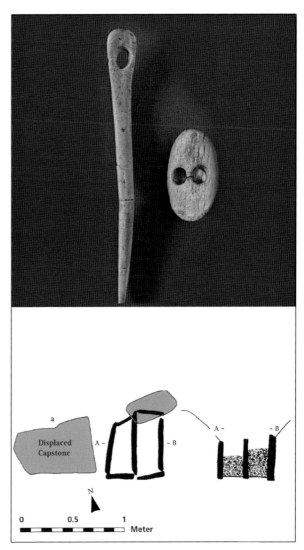

Fig. 5.20: A bone pin and v-perforated button that were found with the cremated remains of a young adult of indeterminate sex in a cist at Kinkit, Co. Tyrone (after Ryan 1994 and Glover 1975).

small Beaker fragments represent a deliberate deposit or something more random.

By comparison, the large sub-megalithic rectangular cist within a cairn at Gortcobies, Co. Derry, is less ambiguous and does not seem to have suffered from post-depositional disturbance (Fig. 5.18). It contained a deposit yielding the remains of at least seven Beaker vessels including two almost-complete examples, a pygmy Bowl, convex scrapers and undated cremated human bone (May 1947). No further information is known about the burial(s), but some of the Beakers here are stylistically-late, dating from 2200-2050 BC, which would have been contemporary with the pygmy Bowl. Given the volume of pottery, it can be assumed that this does represent a Beaker-associated burial. Furthermore, the character of these deposits and the resemblances of the Gortcobies cist and cairn to the Ballybriest wedge tomb suggest that it may represent a small wedge tomb (see Figs 5.3 and 5.18).

Another above ground, large sub-megalithic cist (c. 2.5m long) was found beside a tall monolith at Furness, Co. Kildare, at the centre of a circular embanked enclosure with external ditch (external diameter c. 90m) and two opposing entrances (Macalister *et al.* 1913). The cist was constructed on an old ground surface that had been buried under 0.6m of earth (Fig. 5.19). Although it is unclear when that occurred, it may be significant to note that no covering slab was present on top of the cist, the contents of which seemed to resemble a "confused mess" suggesting that the cist had been disturbed before the ground level was raised. This cist contained a flint flake, three fragments of a wrist-bracer, a possible disc

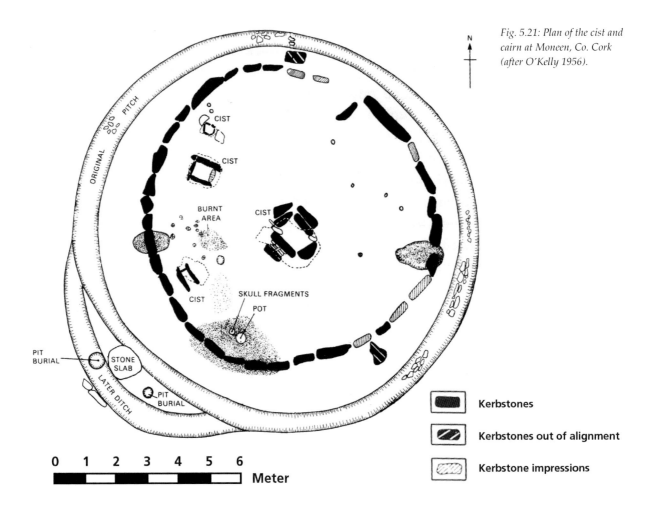

Fig. 5.21: Plan of the cist and cairn at Moneen, Co. Cork (after O'Kelly 1956).

bead, three sherds of 'domestic' Beaker pottery and the cremated remains of two adults, a male and a possible female (Eoin Grogan, pers. comm; see Carlin 2011a). Very few artefacts have been found with Beaker pottery in cists, so the discovery of these objects, particularly a wrist-bracer, is very unusual. The only other ostensibly comparable stereotypically Beaker aceramic object from a cist is a bone V-perforated button that was found with the cremated remains of two young adults of indeterminate sex and a bone pin at Kinkit, Co. Tyrone (Fig. 5.20; Glover 1975). Unlike the stone versions of these ornaments, which post-date 2200 BC, examples made from bone are considered to pre-date these by a few centuries based upon their early appearance in Central Europe and Iberia (Schuhmacher *et al.* 2013; Woodward and Hunter 2015, 155). Antiquarian accounts claim that a pair of gold discs from Ballyshannon, Co. Donegal, were found with an inhumation burial in a cist, but in the absence of further information it is difficult to assess its authenticity (Case 1977b; Eogan, G. 1994, 21).

Similar to Kinkit, there are other aceramic cists displaying particular traits that suggest they may also form part of the Irish Beaker complex. For example, ex-cavation of the cairn at Moneen, Co. Cork, revealed a centrally located sub-megalithic cist containing the very partial remains of two adult inhumations (a male and possibly a female) and cremated human bone (subadult) which was considered to be a much later insertion (O'Kelly 1952, 124-6). None of these were unaccompanied by any artefacts and O'Kelly considered the inhumations to have been considerably disturbed by the deposition of the cremation. However, the character of the inhumations may reflect the manipulation of these bones at this site, before and after their deposition (see Section 5.10 below; Waddell 1990, 20, 30). Bone from either of these unburnt burials was radiocarbon dated to 2260-2140 BC (GrN-11904; 3755±30 BP; Brindley *et al.* 1987/8).

The cist had been constructed over an 'old turf layer', which apparently sealed a charcoal-rich spread of Beaker occupational materials that had been preserved under the cairn (Figs. 5.21-22; O'Kelly 1952, 141). This spread contained sherds from two or three early Beaker pots, as well as unburnt human skull fragments and oak charcoal that produced a radiocarbon date (GrN-10629; 3960±60 BP) of 2560-2390 BC (Case 1961, 228;

118 | THE BEAKER PHENOMENON

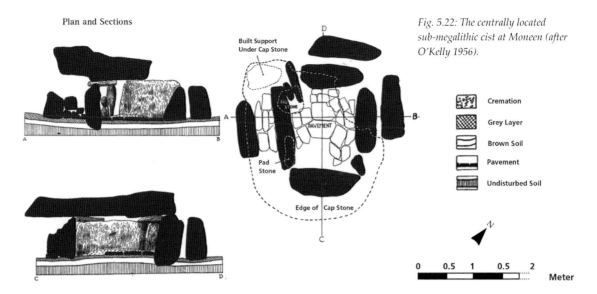

Fig. 5.22: The centrally located sub-megalithic cist at Moneen (after O'Kelly 1956).

ApSimon 1986, 11; Brindley *et al.* 1987/8; Brindley, A.L. 2007, 373). Despite the apparent stratigraphic relationships, it seems quite possible that like at Labbacallee, the skull belongs to one of the two individuals found within the cist. Twelve sherds of a late-style Beaker and sherds from two Food Vessels (probably Bowls) from the lower levels of the cairn, are thought to have been deliberately deposited during its construction (O'Kelly 1952, 128). However, given the date-ranges of this pottery, this means that either the entire monument was not created until post-2200 BC or that the cairn was only added to the cist after this date. The latter scenario would fit with the evidence that the cist was repeatedly accessed. It also supports the possibility that it was created and used during the Chalcolithic in association with the Beaker pottery found under the cairn.

Potentially similar activity may have been conducted at one of the cists (No. 4) forming the Early Bronze Age cemetery within the mound of the passage tomb at Fourknocks II, Co. Meath (Hartnett 1971, 64-74). This cist contained a poorly preserved of a crouched inhumation (adult) with a Bowl beside its skull, as well as some bones from another skeleton and the cremated remains of another adult. A femur fragment from one of the inhumations and the cremation were recently radiocarbon dated (Cleary, K. 2016, 150-1). These respectively produced determinations (UBA-29676: 3848±34 BP and UBA-29674: 3518±30 BP) dating from 2458-2206 BC and 1926-1751 BC (ibid.). This implies that one of the inhumations may have been deposited by people who used Beaker pottery before the advent of Bowls (c.2160 BC) and that this burial was subsequently added to and subtracted from.

Some of the cists that have been detailed here, such as Gortcobies, Moneen, and Furness, display some recurrent characteristics that differentiate them from the typically small sub-surface cists of the full Early Bronze Age. These comprise sub-megalithic cists with external lengths of c. 2m that were built above ground from large slabs of rock and more closely resemble the chamber of small simpler wedge tombs, like the well-known examples that commonly occur in regions like the Burren, Co. Clare, and south-west Cork (Jones *et al.* 1996; O'Brien 1999, 84). The similarities between these box-like structures has long-been recognised (de Valera and Ó Nualláin 1961, 101-2; Cremin Madden 1968, 13; Jones *et al.* 2015, 5), but other common features include the use of double-walling in the construction of the cist/chamber, like at Moneen, or the occurrence of a kerbed cairn around the cist/chamber, as exemplified by both the Gortcobies cist and cairn and the Ballybriest wedge tomb (Figs. 5.3 and 5.18). It is also noteworthy that sub-megalithic cist-like structures occur within or at the termini of larger more complex wedge tombs, such as at Largantea, Ballyedmonduff, Lough Gur, Baurnadomeeny, Moytirra and Labbacallee (see Figs 5.1, 5.5 and 5.7). All of this combines with the evidence for Beaker-associated deposition within sub-megalithic cists to suggests that these form part of a wider range of architectural elements including cists, cairns and defining kerbs that were used in the construction of wedge tombs in Ireland, but represent the smaller end of its structural spectrum. It has been suggested that sub-megalithic cists were constructed from 2500-2300 BC (*e.g.* Cooney and Grogan 1999, 86), but they are more likely to have been constructed over a similarly broad timeframe as wedge tombs. Other similar sub-megalithic cists have been found to contain burials at sites like Ballynagallagh, Lough Gur, Co. Limerick (Cleary and Jones 1980) and Longstone Cullen, Co. Tipperary (Raleigh 1985), but these lack any grave-gifts and have not been radiocarbon dated.

5.7 Beaker deposition in ring-ditches and ring-barrows

Beaker pottery has been discovered within ring-ditches on at least three sites[6]; Kerlogue, Co. Wexford (McLoughlin, C. 2002), Gortcobies, Co. Derry (May 1947) and Harlockstown, Co. Meath (O'Connor, D. 2005; Fitzgerald 2006). The deposition of this pottery does not, however, seem to be strongly linked to funerary activity at any of these monuments.

At Kerlogue, 60 Beaker sherds from six vessels (five 'domestic' and one 'fine'), two 'thumbnail' scrapers and a fragment of a chert bead were found in the fill of a penannular enclosure (8.8m in diameter) defined by a ditch with a southern entrance. Beside the ring-ditch was a sub-rectangular pit resembling a grave-cut and containing the fragmented remains of an almost complete Bowl, although its upper portion was missing (McLoughlin, C. 2002). Although no human remains were found within this feature, it may have contained an inhumation that has not survived due to the acidic nature of the local soils. The single 'fine' Beaker is represented by two conjoining rimsherds, while the five 'domestic' Beakers are represented by 52 sherds (Roche 2004). The sherd/vessel ratio for these pots is quite low, with the highest number being the 15 sherds deriving from a large Rockbarton pot (Vessel 11). While it is not possible to establish the level of truncation that has occurred on this site prior to excavation, there is no evidence to suggest that the Beaker pottery was deposited as complete or near complete vessels. Indeed, Helen Roche (ibid.) observed that some of the Beaker sherds are worn. Combined with the presence of a few sherds from multiple pots, this suggests that the Beaker sherds were probably obtained prior to deposition from an intermediate context comprising an aggregation of habitation debris (see Chapter Four). The nature of their deposition within this monument seems more like the depositional practices exhibited within Beaker pits and contrasts sharply with the multiple sherds from the single, almost complete Food Vessel in the pit. In the absence of corroborating evidence such as radiocarbon dates, it remains possible that these Beaker sherds represent activity pre-dating the monument that were incorporated into it at a later date.

The security of the association of the Beaker pottery with the monuments at Harlockstown and Gortcobies is a lot less certain. At a multi-period site at Harlockstown, a ring-ditch (25m in diameter) enclosed two crouched inhumations in stone-lined graves with almost intact Bowls. One of these skeletons was radiocarbon-dated to 2120-1870 BC (Wk-16290: 3599±36 BP), while alder charcoal from the primary fill of the enclosure was radiocarbon-dated to 1960-1690 BC (Wk-16288: 3515±45 BP) (O'Connor, D. 2005; Fitzgerald 2006). The upper fill of the ring-ditch contained a single sherd of Beaker pottery and a 'thumbnail' scraper. However, this upper deposit is thought to have formed long after the primary use of the monument, which would make the Beaker sherd residual. Also found in the vicinity was a Beaker-associated pit and other features containing a total of seven Beaker sherds from six vessels (but no other associated artefacts), at least some of which seem to have been disturbed from another context during later phases of activity on the site.

Excavation of the mound of a ring-barrow at Gortcobies (May 1947) revealed a pit sealed beneath. This contained cremated bone, sherds from a Bowl and a single Beaker sherd, but the contents had been disturbed by the later insertion of a Collared Urn. Given the presence of just a single Beaker sherd in this context, it is unclear how it related it to the original deposition of this cremated bone or the construction of the ring-barrow. The most likely scenario is that the remains of some earlier form of activity involving Beaker and Food Vessel pottery was disturbed near the end of the Early Bronze Age, when a Collared Urn and a burial were deposited, and the ring-barrow was probably constructed.

Clearly, there is little evidence to directly link Beaker deposition with the construction or use of earthen-burial monuments in Ireland. In each case, particularly at Kerlogue, the Beaker deposits resemble those found in pits and seem to consist of occupational debris. However, it is notable that the Beaker pottery was associated with Bowls on all three of these sites and the relationship between these different ceramics is examined in more detail below.

5.8 Beaker deposition in pit graves

There are no typical examples of Beaker pit graves in Ireland, but a small number of pits have been found to contain both Beaker pottery and human bone, some of which were detailed in Chapter Four.[7] The strength of association between the Beaker sherds and the bone is often unconvincing, however, and this uncertainty is exacerbated in situations where the human remains have not been directly dated. Similarly challenging are the examples where human bone with a date range matching that of Beaker pottery has been found in an aceramic feature. In many of the former cases, the identification of these

---

6   This excludes two enclosures at Ballingoola (MacDermott 1949) and Rathjordan (Ó Ríordáin 1948), both in County Limerick, that were spatially associated with Beaker pits and spreads but considerably post-date them.

7   This excludes an early medieval cemetery at Gortnacargy, Co. Cavan, which was cut into a Beaker and Bowl-associated surface deposit. As a result, sherds of both were accidentally incorporated into graves (Ó Ríordáin, B. 1967; O'Brien. E. 1984).

deposits as Beaker burials is highly problematic because they either contained cremated fragments that were too small to be positively identified as human or the quantity of human bone is so small that it is not obvious that its deposition had an exclusively funerary purpose. These interpretative challenges are best illustrated by two proximal pits at Corbally and Brownstown, both in County Kildare (Purcell 2002, 33). The latter produced two sherds from a Beaker pot, a 'thumbnail' scraper and burnt bone, some of which was definitely from an animal, but most of which was too fragmented to be identifiable as human or animal. The former contained 18 sherds from two Beakers, a barbed and tanged arrowhead, and 23g of burnt bone that included both animal and human remains (Buckley 2001). Neither represents a convincing Beaker burial (contra Mount 2012), although it is tempting to interpret the arrowhead as a grave-gift.

Similarly, Beaker pottery and human bone was found together in a pit forming part of a larger series of intercutting pits at Lismullin, Co. Meath (O'Connell 2013), containing artefacts of widely varying date indicating that the contents of these features are not chronologically secure (contra Mount 2012). The stratigraphically earliest pit contained Early and Middle Neolithic pottery as well as undated cremated human bone. The stratigraphically latest of these pits contained cremated bone (242g), some of which was identifiably human (88g). It also included two Early Neolithic sherds, 19 sherds from two Beaker vessels, hazel charcoal dating from 2470-2290 BC (SUERC-23489; 3905±30 BP) and a broken Bush Barrow macehead, of a type that was current from 1825-1700 BC and certainly post-dates the use of the Beaker pottery (Simpson 1988; 1989; Lanting and Van der Plicht 2001). This pit seems to have incorporated dislocated materials from the earlier pits it was dug into, thereby raising the question of whether the Beaker pottery and/or the human bone were in a disturbed context. None of the human bones from any of these pits was directly dated and a recent attempt to radiocarbon date a longbone from the pit with Beaker pottery failed (Cleary, K. 2016).

Enigmatically, the upper part of an inverted Beaker vessel apparently containing the cremated remains of a minimum of one individual of indeterminate age and sex was found in a highly truncated stone-lined pit at Treanbaun 3, Co. Galway (McKeon and O'Sullivan 2014, 132). Apart from the almost complete Rockbarton pot found in a pit at Cluntyganny, Co. Tyrone (see Section 4.2), inverted Beakers had not previously been found in Ireland and this burial epitomizes a classic Bronze Age burial practice. A recently obtained radiocarbon date of 1886-1667 BC (UBA-29698; 3455±38 BP) from a fragment of this bone (Cleary, K. 2016), suggests that the Beaker pot may well have been an antique when it was deposited. It is also worth highlighting that this Early Bronze Age date is contemporary with that from a cremation burial in a stratigraphically later position within the same group of features. It seems that there was considerable complexity to the past activities at this site that we may not fully grasp without further radiocarbon dating and reanalysis of the site archive.

A much more convincing Beaker burial that has been directly dated to the Chalcolithic was discovered in a truncated grave at Mell, Co. Louth, in proximity (60m) to a Beaker-associated occupation spread (Fig. 5.23; Section 4.3; McQuade 2005). This partly stone-lined sub-rectangular grave contained a prone west–east inhumation of a female adult (head to the west) dating from 2490-2200 BC (Wk-17463; 3894±50 BP). Animal bone (species unknown) and two convex scrapers were also recovered from the grave. The position of the skeleton, with its head to the west, is partially consistent with that of female Beaker burials in Scotland and Yorkshire, where these were placed on their right sides and orientated to the west (Tuckwell 1975; Shepherd, A.N 1989, 79; 2012). This suggests that the burial at Mell was conducted by Beaker users aware of Beaker-associated burial practices in northern Britain, but whom still chose not to include a pot in the grave. Significantly, this aceramic burial represents an early example of the formal burial of inhumations in single-graves that would briefly become prominent between 2200 and 1900 BC. This is an important point to which we will return below.

In some instances, a few Beaker sherds have been found in association with Early Bronze Age cemeteries containing burials of the Bowl tradition. At Carn More 5, Co. Louth, the poorly preserved remains of a cairn sealed a large rectangular pit containing an intact Bowl and unidentifiable cremated bone (Bayley 2005). This may also once have contained an inhumation, although no trace of this has survived. Seven highly fragmented and poorly preserved sherds from a Beaker were found in an upper fill of this pit and two small sherds from a possible Beaker/Bowl hybrid were discovered in the cairn material (Grogan and Roche 2005d). Eight cist burials surrounded the cairn, four of which produced Bowls and cremated human bone. Similarly, at Moone, Co. Kildare, a single Beaker sherd was found in the fill of a grave containing a Bowl, a chert scraper, a flint blade and a crouched inhumation dating from 2200-1960 BC (SUERC-24981; 3685±30 BP) closely matching the accepted date range of the Bowl (Hackettt 2010). Another Beaker sherd was found in a pit cutting the grave of an aceramic crouched inhumation dating from 2280-2030 BC (SUERC-24984; 3745±30 BP). A further two Beaker sherds from two separate vessels were found to be associated with an inverted Vase Urn containing a single cremation burial dating from

Fig. 5.23: Female inhumation burial at Mell (after McQuade 2005, courtesy of Melanie McQuade).

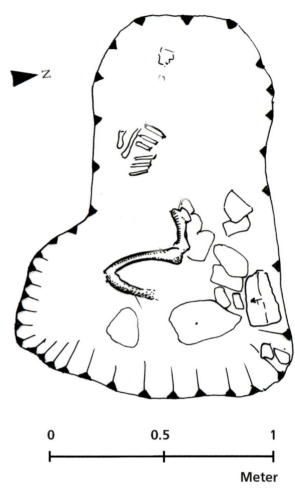

1940-1680 BC (SUERC-25364; 3480±50 BP). In each of these examples, the Beaker sherds occurred in a funerary setting, but the location and condition of these sherds might suggest that they represent residual materials that were accidentally incorporated into these burials. Yet no evidence for any other Beaker-associated activity was discovered on either site, however, thereby suggesting that these sherds could also have been deliberately deposited, perhaps as heirlooms (see Chapter Four). This suggestion may be supported by the recurring discovery of a few Beaker sherds with Bowls in funerary contexts (see Section 5.9). Either way, the presence of the Beaker sherds in association with Bowls of the Food Vessel tradition suggests that the use of these different ceramics was related in some way.

Overall, there is very little substantial evidence for Beaker-associated pit graves in Ireland and certainly there are no examples of the Beaker graves commonly found in southern England. While Beaker pottery has been found in association with definite and possible human bone, the character of these deposits suggests that they did not serve an ostensibly sepulchral purpose and may represent the remains of ceremonial activities.

5.9 Understanding deposition in mortuary and megalithic contexts

A broad spectrum of activity involving diverse ways of depositing typical Beaker artefacts has been uncovered within all these funerary and/or megalithic contexts. The highest quantities of Beaker pottery (509 sherds from 51 vessels) were found in wedge tombs. This far exceeds the few Beaker vessels that were represented within passage and portal tombs or the 103 sherds from a minimum of 19 Beaker pots from court tombs (Table 5.8). These quantitative differences are directly reflective of the distinctive depositional practices associated with each of these settings. Although a near complete Beaker was placed in Ballyglass court tomb and one of the Knowth passage tombs, the majority of Beaker pottery recovered from Neolithic megaliths is represented by a few fragmentary and worn sherds, indicating that it was generally deposited as sherds rather than as complete pots (Table 5.9). In contrast, the number of sherds per Beaker in wedge tombs is much higher signifying that some of this pottery appears to have been deposited as complete or near complete pots and may have been made especially for this purpose.

	Court tomb	Wedge tomb	Portal tomb	Passage tomb	Cists	Ring ditch	Total
No. of sites with Beaker pot	14	13	1	2	6	2	38
Total Beaker sherds	103	509	2	21	?	62	697
Total Beaker pots	19	51	1	2	11	8	92
No. of sites with arrowheads	4	5	3	3	0	0	15
Barbed and tanged arrowhead	6	7	0	3	0	0	16
Hollow-based arrowhead	0	0	3	1	0	0	4
No. of sites with buttons	0	0	0	4	2	0	6
No. of v-perforated buttons	0	0	0	6	3	0	9
Bone pin	0	1	0	0	1	0	2
No. of sites with wrist-bracer	1	0	0	*	1	0	2
Wrist-bracer	1	0	0	3	1	0	5
Bead	0	0	0	0	0	1	1
Scrapers	?	14	0	0	0	0	0

Table 5.8: Comparison of the number of Beaker pots, burials and artefacts from each type of megalithic or funerary site.

Table 5.9: The average sherd/vessel ratio for Beakers in each context type. This is a very crude indicator and the results are quite skewed. For example, the average number of sherds per Beaker from passage tombs is 10.5, but this is not particularly representative of the fact that only two Beakers were found in this context, one of which was almost complete.

Context	Sherds	Vessels	Ratio
Court tomb	103	19	5.42:1
Wedge tomb	509	51	9.9:1
Portal tomb	2	1	02:1
Passage tomb	21	2	10.5:1
Cists	?	11	2:1
Ring ditch	62	9	6.8:1

Lithic debitage is most commonly found in direct association with Beaker pottery in wedge tombs. Seven barbed and tanged arrowheads have also been found in wedge tombs containing Beakers, but it is less clear if these were deposited in association with the pottery (see Section 5.2). Other typical Beaker-related objects such as wrist-bracers are completely absent from wedge tombs, but a few have been found in the vicinity of passage tombs (Table 5.8). Although Beaker sherds occur comparatively frequently in court tombs, six barbed and tanged arrowheads and a probable wrist-bracer represent the only other Beaker-related objects from these megaliths (see Section 5.3). Very few Beaker-related objects have been found in cists, but the wrist-bracer from Furness and bone V-perforated button from Kinkit are particularly noteworthy; they represent very rare examples of such objects being deposited in association with Beaker pottery and/or human remains in a funerary context in Ireland. Indeed, the paucity of classic Beaker aceramic artefacts from either a funerary or megalithic setting provides one of the few common threads between these different contexts.

It should be apparent by now that the disturbed nature of many of the sites and the way some were excavated makes it unclear whether the deposited human remains represent Beaker-associated burials. This is further complicated by the lack of a clear distinction between sepulchral and ceremonial deposits in the Chalcolithic. As a result, detailed quantitative discussion of patterning in burial practices is impossible and only the broadest of trends can be discerned and discussed with any conviction. One of the most obvious of these trends is the fact that Beaker-associated activity at wedge tombs seems to have included the deposition of human remains, whereas that at earlier Neolithic tombs rarely did. No definitive examples of Beaker-associated human remains have been recovered from passage tombs, portal tombs or court tombs (although one Beaker-associated cremation burial was found in a cist-like pit dug into the cairn of one court tomb) and it is doubtful whether any of the activity within these monuments was related to contemporary mortuary practices between 2500-2150 BC. Thereafter, we do see burials in these contexts, but these are associated with the use of Bowls and Vases of the Food Vessel tradition (see 5.10 below).

Yet, that is not to say we are simply looking at Beaker-associated closing or blocking deposits at these various tombs. There is no evidence to support such a reductive position and instead we seem to be looking at something much more complex. There appears to have been a widely shared set of broad understandings about which practices could be conducted at these places, including what things could be deposited and the correct ways of doing so. The highly selective nature of Beaker-associated depositional activity within and around these older monuments is illustrated by the way that the Beaker deposits within Neolithic megaliths mainly comprised sherds of pottery similar to those found in pits in settlement contexts (see Chapter Four). These sherds do not seem to have been broken *in situ* within these tombs. Instead, it seems that they may have been specially acquired from an intermediate context such as an aggregation of occupational debris, where these ceramics had already been fractured for quite some time. These deposits parallel those found immediately outside the passage tombs at Knowth and Newgrange (see Chapter Three). Remarkably, despite the extent of those external deposits, the Beaker placed beside a Late Neolithic burial in a passage tomb at Knowth represents the only Beaker from within one of these types of monuments. This shows an awareness of a pre-existing tradition of depositing materials, including Late Neolithic Grooved Ware, outside rather than inside the tomb to emphasise the exterior of these monuments (Carlin 2017).

What this illustrates is the extent to which these and the various Beaker deposits within all the other Neolithic monuments have a very referential character that portrays a strong concern with past traditions (Carlin and Brück 2012). Significantly, while the Beaker deposits at passage tombs seem to echo the Middle and Late Neolithic activities conducted there, those at court tombs appear to establish a link to a more distant past. Very few Late Neolithic objects have been found in those tombs (Carlin 2017; Carlin and Cooney 2017, 49), so the deposition of Beaker sherds within them represents a rebirth of earlier Neolithic traditions of depositing occupational debris in court tombs (see Case 1969; 1973). This heightened interest in earlier Neolithic tombs amongst Beaker-using communities may represent a concern to redefine and assert their local identity in the context of the wider inter-regional interactions occurring in the second half of the third millennium BC (see Chapter Ten). Alternatively, it might reflect a deliberate attempt to mask radical social transformations by appealing to aspects of the past that people were familiar with. However, the strong evidence for continuity and the lack of indicators of widespread social changes in Ireland at this time militate against this (Carlin and Brück 2012; see Chapter Ten).

Each of the deposits in or around these ancient communal monuments seems to have fulfilled a sacrificial, ceremonial and/or commemorative function. Beaker pottery may have been deposited in these tombs as gift exchanges between the communities of the living and the ancestors, or as offerings to ensure the positive well-being of the community (see Fokkens 1999, 38-41; Bradley 2007, 60). It may be that these megaliths were viewed as ancestral burial places containing the remains of the original representatives or founders of that group (Fokkens 1999). The depositional ceremonies at these collective burial monuments would have served to highlight people's enduring membership of a local community through their familial bonds (whether real or imagined) to one another, to the place they inhabited and to their ancestors. The physical act of deposition at monuments that were already ancient may even have given them a timeless quality (Fokkens and Arnoldussen 2008, 9; Fontijn 2008, 94). Perhaps the Beaker-associated deposits at the earlier Neolithic Linkardstown-type cist burial at Poulawack – which seems to have a very similar character to those at other Neolithic megaliths – also represents this kind of activity.

5.10 Wedge tombs and cists as Beaker burials?

Wedge tombs were used very differently to other contexts and have produced the most convincing evidence for Beaker burials in Ireland, as represented by the 14 cremations and 18 inhumations from nine of these megaliths (Table 5.3). Their chambers seem to represent one of the only spaces in which it was occasionally acceptable to deposit Beaker pottery with burials. While near-complete pots have been found in association with these, accompanying grave-gifts are rare. Some Beaker-associated human remains also seem to have been deposited in cists and pits, but this is more tenuous. The burial practices associated with certain sub-megalithic cists are very similar to those in wedge tombs and it has been argued above that these two types of monument form different aspects of the same tradition (see Section 5.6). Collective burial predominates in both wedge tombs and sub-megalithic cists, though there is some evidence for successive individual burials and for single burials within cist-like chambers within wedge tombs. There seems to be almost equal numbers of males and females and there are more adults than juveniles or infants, but no clear age or sex-related aspects can be conclusively identified.

The available evidence suggests that formal burials such as those found in wedge tombs were restricted to a very small proportion of the overall population. The treatment of the dead accorded to most of the population during the Chalcolithic rarely left an archaeologically recognisable trace (Fokkens 2012b; Fowler 2013). This brings us back to the point made in Chapter Four that the archaeological record is a direct reflection of cultural intent (Bradley 2003, 6-12; 2005a, 208-9). The small numbers of Beaker burials that we do find are archaeologically detectable solely because they were the product of unusual, highly selective and intentional acts of deposition (see Needham 1988; Fontijn 2002; Pollard 2002, 22).

Indeed, this exploration of Beaker-associated mortuary practices in Ireland has revealed that human remains were treated in a wider and more complex range of ways than previously appreciated. While detailed consideration of this topic is beyond the limits of this study and more detailed analysis and increased levels of radiocarbon dating are required to further reveal the nature of this, it is appropriate to highlight some aspects here. Many of the burnt and unburnt Beaker-associated human remains seem to have undergone a series of transformative treatments after death, as well as before and after their final deposition. This is exemplified by the Labbacallee inhumation that was buried after excarnation, as well as evidence for the manipulation of human remains, including the skull at Moneen and the disarticulated bones within the cist at Poulawack. Furthermore, these multi-stage treatments included the burning, fragmentation, retention, dispersal and deposition of human bone. Multiple burials were not confined to wedge tombs but also occurred in cists. In some cases, there is good evidence for the reopening of cists and removal of particular bones, perhaps for retention as ancestral relics or for deposition elsewhere at a much later stage, as indicated at Ballynacarriga. Similar types of activities have been recognised from Chalcolithic burials in Britain, including the Amesbury Archer (Gibson, A. 2004; Brück 2006a; Fitzpatrick 2015). Of relevance here is the fact that in an Irish context, many of these bones were deposited in wedge tombs, whose very design facilitated access to deposits of human remains. This also suggests that the transformation of the dead within these tombs through the ongoing manipulation and perhaps fragmentation of the bodies may have been one of the principal functions of these monuments (Thomas 2000). This is something that is also borne out by the western orientation of the entrances to most of these tombs, which seems to reflect a cosmological concern with the transformative life-cycle of the sun.

The inclusion of only a small section of the population within wedge tombs and cists indicates that these were not household or family burial places (see Fontijn 2008, 94). The community who conducted this activity presumably selected those whom they considered important for this special treatment. These people had been chosen by the community of the living to become ancestors, or to interact with the ancestors on their behalf, and in so doing, to maintain social relationships between them and their ancestral dead (Thomas 1999, 162). Like most of the Beaker burials from across Europe at this time, the internment of human remains within wedge tombs seem to have provided a way for people to establish and maintain a shared identity, as well as to negotiate and reproduce social relations and cultural ideals. The ceremonies associated with the deposition of these selected bodies alongside fragments of other human remains in these communal monuments suggests that particular forms of social relationships were being portrayed and enacted between the collective dead and the local corporate group (Fokkens 1997, 369; van der Beek and Fokkens 2001, 307). These probably involved the construction of a particular form of idealised identity for the dead that emphasised the mutual identity and values of the local group (Fontijn 2008, 94-102).

Contra O'Brien (2012, 217, 220), there is little to suggest that the deposition of burials within wedge tombs represent powerful individuals. Indeed, such is the transformative nature of the burial treatments within these monuments, that in many cases, it is hard to see how that kind of social identity could have been maintained (see Chapter Ten). Similarly, there is little to suggest that the construction of these tombs represent displays of wealth relating to elites. Both the creation of these monuments, as well as the deposition of materials (human or otherwise) within them implies a strong concern with the communal expression of shared values and beliefs (Cooney and Grogan 1999, 93; Thomas 1999, 162). For example, the large size of many of the stones that people chose to use in the construction of wedge tombs indicates that a group of people were involved in this activity. This issue is returned to in the concluding chapter, but the key point here is that neither the construction nor use of these monuments seems to relate primarily to social differentiation in the ways that have been suggested.

None of this accords with O'Brien's (1994; 1999; 2012; 2016, 295-7) view of these monuments as territorial markers, which served to legitimize one group's claims over another's to ownership of land and associated resources by reference to descent from the ancestors. This type of approach, which borrows heavily from the social evolutionary work of Renfrew (1976), has been extensively and convincingly critiqued for various reasons, including the way in which it imposes modern western economics onto the past (Hodder 1982, 218-28; Hughes 1988; Holtorf 1996, 130; Brück and Goodman 1999; Hodder and Hutson 2003, 28-9). O'Brien's interpretation does not account for the diverse character of wedge tombs in terms of their architecture, location and distribution within the landscape, nor the deposits found within them or the people who created and curated them.

Unlike the other types of megalithic tomb in Ireland, which were created exclusively during the fourth millennium BC, wedge tombs began to be built and used quite suddenly c. 2450 BC (see Schulting *et al.* 2008, 13). The abrupt beginning of this new form of monument after a 500 year-long hiatus in megalithic construction seems to have been intimately linked with the adoption and use of Beaker pottery and associated objects, as well as whatever social changes were occurring at this time. These wedge tombs were once assumed to be a Beaker-associated introduction from north-western France, where it's supposed proto-types, *allées couvertes*, were located (see Chapter Two). While there are some architectural similarities such as double walling (de Valera and Ó Nualláin

1961; Ó Maoldúin 2014), there are also many clear differences in chronology, architecture, alignment and use (*e.g.* Waddell 1978). For example, these Armorican tombs were built at the start of the third millennium BC and have parallel-sided rectangular chambers within which Beakers only occur in non-funerary secondary deposits; in relatively small numbers compared to the much greater quantities of Beaker deposits from passage tombs in the same region (Briard 1984; Scarre 2002; Salanova 2003a, 385-6; 2007, 214).

While it remains possible that wedge tombs were an indigenous response to the re-use of *allées couvertes* and their equivalents on mainland Europe (see below), convincing inspirations for wedge tombs are to be found among the pre-existing megaliths of Ireland including court, passage and Linkardstown-type tombs. Wedge tombs were built in the same types of locations as these earlier monuments, particularly court and portal tombs, and often occur in association with pre-existing tomb types, as is the case in the Burren. Indeed, there is a particularly strong spatial relationship between wedge and court tombs in the northern part of the island (Cooney and Grogan 1999, 84-5; Cooney 2000a, 148-51). As exemplified by the wedge tomb at Largantea (Herring 1938, 173), some of these megaliths, particularly the northern examples, share architectural features with court tombs, including jamb stones, sillstones, frontal façades and trapezoidal-shaped cairns (De Valera 1960, 70). Other wedge tombs seem to copy structural details from the Irish passage tomb tradition, which includes Linkardstown-type monuments, such as a trapezoidal chamber set within a circular kerb and cairn. Such is the morphological similarities between wedge tombs and undifferentiated passage tombs that some of the former have consistently been wrongly identified as the latter, for example, Carriglong and Harristown, both in County Waterford (Powell 1941; Ó Nualláin and Walsh 1986; Moore, M. 1999). Furthermore, the concern with the setting sun evidenced by the orientation of wedge tombs seems to echo the way that a small proportion of developed passage tombs were aligned on the midwinter sunrise and sunset (Prendergast 2011).

All of this suggests that wedge tombs represent a Beaker-associated reinvention of an essentially Neolithic tradition of megalithic tomb construction in Ireland. From this perspective, similarities with *allées couvertes* can be explained by the fact that both were influenced by passage tombs, which were a widely shared architectural tradition across much of north-western Europe. Despite being influenced by older tombs wedge tombs also seem to represent a new category of place that was formed to enable the expression of particular social relationships between the living and the dead in tandem with the adoption of Beaker pottery. It may be the case that the length of time that had elapsed since the final burials in earlier megaliths necessitated the creation of new ancestors and ancestral spaces, which took the form of wedge tombs in many parts of Ireland c. 2450 BC. It is also likely, however, that the creation of these new monuments and the deposition of human remains and Beaker pottery within them is directly related to the wider array of changes in practices and material culture that seem to be happening at this time (see below).

As detailed above, there are a small number of inhumations and cremations in cists and pits with radiocarbon dates that fall within the date range of 2500-2200 BC, as exemplified at Mell, Co. Louth. However, these rarely contain Beaker pottery or other Beaker-related objects and when they do, the range and quantity of these artefacts is much less than found in stereotypical Beaker burials in other regions. While Beakers have been excluded from the burial in most cases, it is no longer possible to maintain the traditional position that there is no evidence for single inhumations before 2150 BC (contra Brindley *et al.* 1987/8, 16; Brindley, A.L. 2007, 373). Significantly, there are over 27 examples of crouched inhumations in cists without grave-gifts in Ireland (Grogan 2004, 62). Many of these occur in cemeteries alongside Bowl burials and hence are presumed (perhaps incorrectly) to be contemporary. Radiocarbon determinations are generally only obtained for aceramic inhumations when they occur in isolated graves, rather than in cemeteries.[8] Thus, the small number of inhumation burials known to date from 2500-2200 BC may also be partially due to the dating strategies routinely employed by archaeologists. While inhumation was most certainly performed before the advent of Bowls, c. 2160 BC, a better understanding of the extent and development of this practice requires further investigation through increased radiocarbon dating of burials.

This need for greater dating is highlighted by two aceramic burials presumed to be Chalcolithic or Early Bronze Age but recently radiocarbon dated to the Late Neolithic. Excavation of a cairn circle (Site K) at Piperstown, Co. Dublin, revealed a centrally located pit containing a token deposit of a cremated adult male and a flint flake underneath the cairn (Rynne and Ó hÉailidhe 1965). Oak charcoal from this pit was radiocarbon dated to 2537-2343 BC (UB-7825; 3958±37 BP) by Kim Rice (2006), but more recently, Kerri Cleary (2016) obtained a date from the bone of 2832-2457 BC (UBA-29699; 4004±40 BP). K. Cleary (2016, 162) also

---

8   Often, budgetary constraints prevent more than a few radiocarbon dates being obtained for an Early Bronze Age cemetery. To achieve best value for money, dates are usually only obtained for those burials with associated grave-goods because these will improve/build our typo-chronologies for these artefacts.

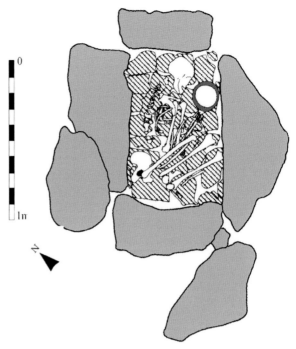

Fig. 5.24: Crouched single inhumations in cist graves with Irish Bowls placed beside the head: (right) an east–west orientated (adult female) burial in Grave 6 at Keenoge, Co. Meath (after Mount 1997b, fig. 11) and (left) a north–south orientated (adult male) burial at Glassamucky, Co. Dublin (after Kelly 1998 and Ryan 1994).

radiocarbon dated the bone of an adult female inhumation from a cist within a cairn at Killarah, Co. Cavan, to 2620-2470 BC (UBA-29681; 4019±32 BP). While the Late Neolithic date for the inhumation is exceptionally unusual, both burials seem to form part of a wider, albeit restricted, practice of depositing human bone without pottery throughout the entire third millennium BC (see Carlin 2017, 12; Carlin and Cooney 2017, 49). Problematically, this highlights that the recognition of either Chalcolithic or Late Neolithic burial activity in Ireland has relied far too narrowly upon the identification of accompanying ceramics. The current study is also guilty of that.

Humphrey Case (2004b, 200) previously suggested that aceramic burials represent an aspect of Beaker-associated funerary practices in Ireland. The details presented here certainly provide increased evidence for the deposition of human remains c. 2450-2150 BC, when Beakers were the only pottery current on the island and were widely used for daily activities (see Chapters Four and Nine). The absence of accompanying ceramics and/or typical Beaker-related objects, however, raises the complex issue of whether we should regard these as Beaker burials. What we can say is that the burial of stereotypical crouched single inhumations accompanied by Beakers and a restricted set of other grave-gifts within earth-cut graves was not a feature of mortuary practices in Ireland. This highly uniform burial type which dates from 2500-2300 BC was a very specific and rarely occurring phenomenon with a very patchy distribution in Britain and elsewhere in Europe (see Needham 2005; Fokkens 2012b; Garwood 2012); it seems that a deliberate choice was made not to adopt this custom in Ireland.

It is not until the full Early Bronze Age, c. 2160-1920 BC, that a form of burial resembling this was practised in Ireland, when a sudden short-lived increase in single inhumations occurred, but these were accompanied by Bowls rather than Beakers (Brindley, A.L. 2007, 250, 373). We see these Bowl-associated inhumations occurring in small rectangular cist or pit graves as well as in Neolithic court tombs and passage tombs. Bowls were a novel type of pottery, which along with Vases (2020-1740 BC), form part of the Food Vessel tradition that replaced Beakers. The early use of Food Vessels occurred in tandem with the emergence of much more coherent and archaeologically visible mortuary traditions (Waddell 1990; Brindley, A.L. 2007, 249). These burials often occur within small groups of between ten and 15 burials in cists or pits, either in flat cemeteries (Mount 1997a) or placed under round barrows and cairns, or into natural and manmade mounds (Eogan, J. 2004).

Bowls appear to have been a distinctly Irish innovation that were adopted in western and northern parts of Britain towards the end of the third millennium BC (Apsimon 1969, 37; Harbison 1975, 112; 1976, 20; Waddell 1976, 286; Case 2004a, 375; Brindley, A.L. 2007; Wilkin 2014). Their currency in Ireland (2160-1920 BC) was broadly contemporary with the widespread expansion and marked increase of Beaker burials in Britain. Beaker burials had been quite limited in extent until this point, c. 2250-2150 BC – Needham's (2005; 2012) 'fission horizon' – when there was a considerable regional diversification in mortuary practices and a wide range of new insular Beaker styles began to be made and deposited with burials. While these various late-style Beakers proliferated across many different parts of Britain, very few late-style Beakers are known from Ireland (see Chapter Eight). This seems to be because Bowls and Bowl-burials formed the Irish equivalent of these British regionally divergent ceramics and associated mortuary traditions. Certainly, these Bowl burials show far greater affinities to British Beaker burial customs than to those previously employed in wedge tombs.

Although Bowls were made using very different ceramic-technologies, there are some overlaps in the decorative motifs, such as the 'bar chevron' used in Bowls and late-style Beakers, for example, Needham's (2005, 188) Weak-Carinated Beaker and Case's (2001) Group B (see Wilkin 2014). Further evidence for the interrelatedness of Beakers and Bowls is provided by the occurrence on the base of Bowls of cross-in-circle and/or other concentric decorations. Exactly the same kind of motifs have been identified on Chalcolithic gold sun-discs, and on a small number of Beakers in Ireland, Britain and other parts of Europe (Cahill 2015, 2016; see Chapter Nine). Marked resemblances can be observed between single graves containing inhumations and Bowls in Ireland and those containing Beakers in northern Britain (Waddell 1974, 35). Both traditions share the practice of east–west oriented inhumation, often placed within a sub-surface cist, with the pot deposited by the head (Fig. 5.24). Similarities can also be noted in accompanying grave-gifts, which include boars' tusks, bronze knives, awls and bangles, and jet-like beads and buttons. In northern Britain, these mainly occur in burials with late-style Beakers (Case 2004c, 195-7, fig. 4). In Ireland, most of these items have rarely if ever been found with Beaker pottery but they occur in Bowl burials instead. Indeed, the only ceramic association shared by V-perforated buttons and the earliest form (flat and riveted) of bronze dagger (Type Corkey a.k.a. Buttterwick) is with Bowls.

Bowls appear to have been a completely new ceramic form designed by Beaker-users specifically to accompany inhumation burials and function as the Irish version of British funerary Beakers. Unlike Beaker pottery, which is commonly found in settlement and non-funerary contexts (see Chapters Four and Nine), Bowls, are rarely found in 'domestic' contexts or in association with other contemporary pottery types (Brindley, A.L. 2007, 52). This suggests that Bowls, unlike Irish Beakers, were considered special purpose funerary vessels whose use was restricted outside of the mortuary context. There also seems to have been categorical differences between Bowls and Vases, even though both belonged to the Food Vessel tradition. Unlike Bowls, Vases are found more regularly on 'domestic' sites, where they are often associated with Beaker ceramics (Carlin 2005a) and seem to have performed both 'domestic' and funerary roles, more akin to Beakers in an Irish context.

We have already seen various instances of Beaker sherds occurring in association with Bowls in funerary and megalithic settings at sites like Carn More 5 or Moone, which hinted that the use of Beakers and Bowls was strongly inter-related (see Figs 5.6 and 5.8; Section 5.8). The recurrent association of often just one or two Beaker sherds with complete Bowls and burials suggests that these were deposited as part of a broader suite of deliberate and selective choices. In Chapter Four, we saw how Beaker sherds were seen as highly meaningful and socially active objects whose (real or imagined) biographies provided physical links to past people, places and experiences. Such was the potency of these fragments of past times, that in most Beaker-associated depositional practices in Ireland, a small part of the pot often seems to have been just as suitable as a complete vessel, if not more so. Each occurrence of a Beaker sherd with a Bowl reflects activity post-dating 2160 BC, but the Beaker sherds all seem to pre-date this, suggesting that they were being deposited as heirlooms or relics, as has also been observed in a British context (Woodward 2000). The same interpretation can be applied to the Beaker sherds found with a Vase burial at Cappydonnell.

Beakers and Bowls are also found together in apparently primary contexts within the wedge tombs (Brindley, A.L. 2007, 51), for instance at Aughrim, Co. Cavan (Channing 1993). Both ceramic types have been recovered from the chambers of Loughash, Cashelbane, Kilhoyle, Largantea, and Lough Gur. Much has been made of the fact that cists containing Bowl burials are concentrated in the eastern-half of Ireland while wedge tombs are predominantly found in the west (*e.g.* Bradley *et al.* 2016, 145). While there is a contrast, it is important to realise that their distributions are not mutually exclusive. There are many areas of considerable overlap, most obviously in the northern parts of the island, and viewing these as oppositional is unhelpfully reductive (see Brindley, A.L. 2007, 53) The possibility that there is something meaningful lying behind these patterns is, however, suggested by the fact that Bowls have occasionally accompanied cremations in wedge tombs, but Bowl-associated inhumations have never been found in these monuments. This is remarkable because Bowls are intrinsically connected with a dramatic increase in inhumation burials in a range of other contexts, including earlier Neolithic tombs. It suggests that the inception of Bowl-burials in Ireland was connected to the apparent decline of interring Beaker-associated inhumations in wedge tombs (see Section 5.2). Above, it was suggested that the treatment of inhumations in wedge tombs was concerned with representing/establishing a collective form of social relationship between the communities of the living and the dead. The switch away from this to deposition of single inhumations in closed contexts reflects a greater desire to maintain the bodily integrity of the interred. If the human body symbolises the body politic (*e.g.* Douglas 1966; Fowler 2005), this suggests that defining and maintaining the boundaries of kin groups may have grown in importance c. 2200 BC. This is, however, complicated by the extensive evidence for the continuation of cremations at the same time. An alternative way of understanding these changes is simply as diverse ways of creating social memories.

The invention of Bowls and the contrasting manner of its deposition compared to Beakers suggests that a widely shared set of conventions must have prevented people from depositing Beaker artefacts, especially pottery, with human remains. This highlights the highly codified nature of depositional practices in funerary and megalithic contexts. Those wedge tombs containing Beaker-associated burials represent the exception to this, but typical Beaker non-ceramic objects are just as lacking from these monuments. It may be the case that Beaker pottery and/or other Beaker-related objects were used in funerary rituals, but these were only deposited with human remains in certain circumstances. Whether this was because it was not permitted or was not necessary for a successful ritual to be conducted is open to interpretation.

As we have already seen above, Beaker-associated deposition in older megaliths was also similarly selective. This patterning appears even more pronounced when we consider the considerable number of objects, such as wrist-bracers, which have been found in other contexts in Ireland (see Chapters Seven and Nine). All of this indicates that there were widely shared traditions of practice regarding how and where objects could be deposited, which were largely adhered to by people across Ireland who used Beaker pottery. Despite the apparently island-wide character of these shared 'set of rules', there is also convincing evidence for the existence of distinct regional traditions in funerary and megalithic contexts, as evidenced by the provincially-distinctive architecture of wedge tombs and the apparent paucity of these monuments in eastern parts of the country

5.11 A wider European context?

It is useful at this stage to compare the Irish evidence for Beaker-associated depositional practices in funerary and megalithic settings, with that known from Britain and Europe. This helps us to more fully understand these practices in Ireland, as well as the extent to which they might represent either the introduction of novel approaches to death and ancestry from elsewhere in tandem with Beaker pottery or a local response to the arrival of such innovations. Due to the absence from Ireland of the single crouched Beaker inhumation that is so typical of central and northern European mortuary activity (*e.g.* Strahm 1995; Turek 1998; Müller 2004 Czebreszuk 2003; Vander Linden 2004), we will focus on funerary practices in other regions that are more directly comparable, especially along the Atlantic façade and Britain.

There is a general consensus that Beaker-using communities along the Atlantic façade exerted a stronger influence upon the development of the Beaker phenomenon in Ireland (*e.g.* Herity and Eogan 1977, 117-22; Mercer 1977; Burgess 1979; Needham 1996, 128; Case 2004a; O'Brien 2004, 565; see Chapter Two). There were certainly links between Ireland and other Atlantic coastal regions, as is evidenced by the stylistic similarities of various objects including Beaker pottery (see discussion in Chapter Nine). As we will see, however, the similarities between the diverse range of highly complex practices from these different areas has been overstated. Indeed, the longstanding view that the Irish Beaker phenomenon had an Atlantic character was based mainly upon the occurrence of Beaker-associated deposits in earlier megalithic tombs. This perception was strongly influenced by the tendency in Beaker studies to reductively contrast single burials (often in flat graves or under barrows) and collective burials as if they represented very different practices.

Like Ireland, Beakers have been discovered in megalithic tombs in other parts of the Atlantic façade, such as northern Portugal, western Spain, and north-western France, where Beaker-associated single graves are also very rare. These Beakers were deposited with collective burials in these monuments, along with arrowheads and palmella points, though at least some of the human remains were interred individually in association with some of these objects, including Beakers (Salanova 1998a; 2004, 71; 2007; Guilaine *et al.* 2001; L' Helgouach 2001; Gibson, C. 2013; Vander Linden 2013; Bradley *et al.* 2016). Although these enabled access to deposited bones in a similar manner to wedge tombs, the Beaker-associated burials in the Irish megaliths only occur in primary contexts in newly built wedge tombs and comprise both burnt and unburnt human remains. Whereas, these other burials are exclusively inhumations that occur in secondary contexts within earlier Neolithic megaliths; there is no evidence for the construction of new megaliths on mainland Atlantic Europe at this time (Salanova 2007, 214). For example, as we already saw above in the case of *allées couvertes*, where collective burials were deposited in megaliths in France, these all occur in pre-existing monuments that include passage tombs and gallery graves (Salanova 2003b; 2007; in press). This differs significantly from the apparently non-funerary nature of Beaker deposition in Irish Neolithic megaliths. Indeed, this issue is further complicated by the fact that deposits of Beaker pottery are also known from earlier megalithic tombs beyond the Atlantic façade, in the Netherlands, Denmark and northern Germany (Vander Linden 2006a, 46; Bradley et al. 2016). Of course, it remains possible that the depositional practices in some of these Neolithic tombs in continental Europe influenced the ways in which Beakers were deposited in both primary and secondary contexts within various types of megaliths in Ireland, but this is not obvious, and the character of the Irish deposits are significantly different from elsewhere.

Furthermore, in Atlantic coastal regions, Beaker pottery, arrowheads and other items are almost exclusively recovered from funerary contexts and were regularly found together with burials in megaliths. For example, over half of all French Beakers were found in earlier Neolithic megalithic tombs located in the western half of France (Salanova 2003a). In Brittany, there are 121 Beaker sites, most of which are burial contexts within earlier Neolithic megalithic tombs (Salanova 2004, 66; Vander Linden 2006a, 85). Particular kinds of aceramic Beaker-related objects such as tanged copper daggers and wrist-bracers are rarely found in burial contexts along the Atlantic façade, including southern Portugal and northern France, but this is reflective of their paucity in these regions (Salanova 2004; Harrison and Heyd 2007, 203-5). This scenario contrasts strongly with Ireland, where large quantities of Beaker pottery, wrist-bracers, daggers and arrowheads are known across much of the island, but were deliberately kept apart and excluded from certain contexts including burial settings (see Chapter Nine). At first glance, it might appear that the Atlantic regions provide parallels for the aceramic burials that we see in Ireland. In areas such as the Paris Basin in north-eastern France, hundreds of contemporary individual and collective burials have been found in graves with objects that rarely included Beaker pottery (Chambon and Salanova 1996; Salanova 2004, 66-69, fig. 4; 2007, 213-7). The same is true of the burials found in megaliths in Alentejo, Portugal, which often lack any grave-gifts and have been radiocarbon dated between 2500-2000 BC (Salanova 2007). Unlike Ireland, these burials occur in areas where very few Beakers are known, leading Laure Salanova (2007, 217) to hypothesise that the Beaker ceramic was rejected in these regions.

Perhaps the greatest similarity between the mortuary practices of the Atlantic façade and Ireland is the contemporary development of regionally distinctive traditions of single inhumation with accompanying grave-gifts after 2200 BC. Like Irish Food Vessel burials, these also echoed the customs of the classic Beaker burial (Salanova 2004, 73). For example, in Brittany, Early Bronze Age graves comprise cists containing individual burials that were succeeded by Armorican Tumulus culture burials. These graves comprised a barrow that covered a wooden structure containing single burials accompanied by items from the Beaker package such as tanged copper daggers and wrist-bracers made from amber or gold (Needham 2000; Salanova 2004, 73). Similarly, at the same time in Alentejo, Portugal, single graves containing wrist-bracers, daggers and undecorated vessels also start to appear at the beginning of the Bronze Age (Salanova 2004, 74).

The Irish manifestation of the Beaker phenomenon has traditionally been juxtaposed with that in Britain, much of this attention has focused on the dissimilarities in mortuary practices on both islands (see Chapter Two). In contrast to the Irish evidence detailed above, Beaker pottery and associated objects are often found in funerary contexts in Britain, stereotypically accompanying crouched inhumations within single pit graves. Frequently, these occur under barrows like those associated with Beaker burials in the Netherlands and Belgium (Bradley et al. 2016), no contemporary examples of which are known in Ireland. Despite these significant divergences, it seems that the differences in practices have been exaggerated. Key here is the fact that it has only been recently recognised that British Beaker-associated mortuary practices are far more diverse and complex than previously assumed, and that these changed considerable across both time and space (Gibson, A. 2004; Needham 2005).

It is now known that in Britain there are very few burials dating to the earlier phase of Beaker usage (c. 2450-2250 BC). These rare forms of early Beaker burials display a striking level of uniformity of grave-type, orientation, burial position and the restricted range of associated objects, including wrist-bracers and particular types of Beakers (Needham 2005; 2012; Garwood 2012, 299-300). These have a very thin and uneven distribution; no examples of these early stage Beaker burials have been identified from many British regions including the west midlands, south-east or south-west England, East Anglia, Wales, the Peak District and the Isle of Man, as well as the east-central and the Moray Firth regions of Scotland (Curtis and Wilkin 2012; Garwood 2012; Crellin 2014). The highly standardised character and sparse distribution of these is reflective of Beaker practices across other parts of Europe during this timeframe (Fitzpatrick 2011, 208-34; Garwood 2012).

As mentioned above, a marked diversification in burial practices occurred between c. 2250-2150 BC, which saw various new burial traditions develop in association with different Beaker pot types (Needham 2005; 2012). The importance of the Beaker to the burial rite also seems to have faded at this time and in some regions they began to be replaced by Food Vessels. It was in tandem with the development of these hybridised Beaker funerary practices, that burials became widespread across Britain. These occurred in large numbers across the island, including those areas where Beaker burial in its classic form had been lacking. For example, in Cornwall, Beaker burials only appear after 2200 BC and mainly comprise cremations (Jones, A.M. 2005, 31; Jones and Quinnell 2006). Similarly, in east-central Scotland where very few Beaker graves are known, single burials start to occur at this time, but in association with Food Vessels (see Wilkin 2009; Curtis and Wilkin 2012; Fowler and Wilkin 2016).

It is important to highlight that despite the increased evidence for Beaker mortuary activity post-2200 BC, the deposition of complete inhumations in single graves with associated artefacts remained an exceptional rarity and highly atypical (Gibson, A. 2004; Garwood 2012, 300). As in Ireland, normal mortuary practice in Britain during the second half of the third millennium BC left little trace (Fowler 2013), but formal treatment of human remains comprised a highly diverse mixture of collective, individual and token burial, as well as excarnation, inhumation and cremation within a wide range of contexts, including secondary deposits in long barrow ditches and megalithic tombs (Gibson, A. 2004). Because these more diverse kinds of burials have received little attention and often contain no accompanying artefacts (Harrison 1980, 85; Gibson, A. 2004), their chronology is much less clear-cut, and it remains possible that some may date to the first few centuries of Beaker use in Britain.

The re-use of Neolithic tombs in Britain for a variety of depositional practices, including Beaker-associated burials, is of interest here given that we have already seen how earlier Neolithic monuments provided a focus for Beaker-associated deposits in Ireland and continental Europe (Woodham and Woodham 1957; Henshall and Wallace 1964; Burl 1984; Bradley 2000b, 221-4; Case 2004c, 196; Gibson, A. 2004, 183). Numerous Neolithic chambered tombs in northern and western Scotland have been found to contain Beaker pottery and their deposition has recently been analysed by Neil Wilkin (2016). Like in Ireland, only very limited evidence for Beaker burials has been recovered from these older megaliths, with all the less ambiguous examples post-dating 2200 BC (ibid.). In another direct parallel, Wilkin identified that there was also a formalised 'sets of rules' regarding how Beakers should be deposited in various funerary and megalithic contexts in Scotland. Just like in Irish court tombs, he observed that already fragmentary Beaker sherds were being deposited rather than complete pots. Significantly, these sherds were from different varieties of Beaker to those occurring with burials in Scotland, thereby emphasising the non-funerary nature of these deposits (ibid.).

In other parts of western Britain, which had strong links with communities across the Irish Sea in the fourth and third millennium BC, there are echoes of the sort of practices that we saw in Early Neolithic tombs in Ireland. For example, sherds of Beaker pottery have been recovered from portal tombs at Dyffryn Ardudwy (Powell 1973) and Carreg Coetan Arthur (Barker 1992) in Wales; a monument type which has produced very few Beakers in Ireland. Fragments of a wrist-bracer were also found inside the chamber at Dyffryn Ardudwy (Powell 1973). Unlike British examples, which are generally four-holed and found in single graves, this was a two-holed wrist-bracer like those commonly found in Ireland, which were also often fractured (Roe and Woodward 2009; Woodward and Hunter 2011). A similarly fragmented two-holed wrist-bracer was found on the sea-shore at Broadford Bay, Isle of Skye, western Scotland, in proximity to a Hebridean chambered cairn. It is thought that this may originally have been placed within the tomb but was subsequently moved outside at a later date (Henshall 1972, 484-5; Woodward and Hunter 2011, 112). Both of these atypical British discoveries parallel the occurrence of wrist-bracers in a court tomb and within the vicinity of passage tombs in Ireland, yet aspects of these practices also seem distinctly local.

We also see the construction of a broad group of new megalithic monuments in coastal areas of Britain during the second half of the third millennium BC, some of which are directly analogous to Irish wedge tombs and contained Beaker-associated burial deposits (Case 2004c; Bradley 2007, 174-5). In each case, their construction and use responded to the introduction of new ideas, things and people, including Beaker pottery. Like wedge tombs, these new tomb types seem to deliberately reference aspects of the architecture of Neolithic passage tombs and their construction continued into the Early Bronze Age (Jones and Thomas 2010; Bradley et al. 2016, 129). These include Clava cairns near Inverness in northern Scotland (Bradley 2005b) and probably also the Bargrennan Group, in south-west Scotland (Darvill 2010, 179), as well as entrance graves in south-western Britain (Jones and Thomas 2010). Furthermore, Richard Bradley (2009) has also highlighted the existence of a few wedge tombs in the Outer Hebrides, north-western Scotland. Bradley's (2000b; 2005b) investigations of Clava cairns and another monument type known as recumbent stone circles in north-east Scotland, have demonstrated that these contain Beaker-associated cremation burials and their architecture displays the same north-east to south-west alignment as wedge tombs.

As mentioned in relation to wedge tombs, this orientation seems to share a concern with certain Middle Neolithic Irish and British passage tombs regarding cosmological beliefs about death and regeneration that were linked to the movements of the sun. It is also possible that this alignment was equally influenced by the cosmological principles relating to the sun's diurnal journey across the sky, which is evident in the recurrent alignments (east–west, facing south or north–south, facing east) of many Beaker graves across Europe (Harrison and Heyd 2007; Shepherd 2012). Either way, these various newly built Irish and British monuments reflect a wider set of practices that were shared across the Irish Sea, including the re-use of older tombs. Contrary to traditional views, the evidence from funerary and megalithic contexts in many parts of western and northern Britain is very similar to that from Ireland, particularly in those regions that were strongly linked to this island during the Neolithic. These interconnections are indicative of the continuation of pre-existing interaction networks that included parts of Britain and Ireland in association with the use of Beaker pottery (Wilkin 2016, 280-81). We will revisit these issues and their implications in Chapter Ten.

This brief review of European mortuary practices shows how Beaker-associated funerary and megalithic practices varied greatly from region to region across Europe and changed considerably over time. While there is a widespread veneer of incredible uniformity formed by classic Beakers burials, these are quite rare, and their distribution is very uneven. Indeed, the extent and significance of these burials and their common aspects has been greatly overstated, while the heterogeneity of the wider funerary evidence has been understated. As discussed in Chapters One and Two, the tendency to overly focus upon these apparently common aspects has had a disproportionate effect on how this phenomenon has been viewed (Vander Linden 2012, 20-1). This approach is exemplified by the notion of a coherent global Beaker funerary assemblage, often referred to as the 'Beaker package' (*e.g.* Shennan 1976; 1986), whose identification was based upon the repeated co-occurrence of objects such as wrist-bracers, arrowheads and copper tanged daggers with Beaker pots in certain graves in specific parts of central Europe. This assemblage, however, is rarely found together in the same grave elsewhere in Europe and many components are commonly absent from burial contexts (Salanova 2007). For example, only four graves in western Europe have contained a dagger, wrist-bracer and arrowhead; Arenberg-Wallers (France), Lunterne (Holland), Fuente Olmedo (Spain) and Amesbury (England) (ibid., 218).

In Ireland, there is a very distinct lack of Beakers and other objects in the funerary sphere and they are rarely found in association like elsewhere in Europe. Apart from this, there is nothing particularly unusual about the scarcity of early Beaker burials, the complete lack of stereotypical examples and the diversity of practices that we see in megalithic tombs on this island. The surviving evidence for mortuary rites conducted by Beaker users in Ireland reflects diverse interactions with communities in other regions and comprised the adoption of some new elements, as well as the adaptation and rejection of others. This is entirely characteristic of the Beaker complex's enigmatic mix of highly diverse regional (mortuary) customs involving homogenous culture materials over a wide geographical area (see Vander Linden 2007a, 185-6).

This study shows us that there is a greater body of evidence for Irish Beaker-associated activity in funerary and megalithic contexts than has previously been recognised. This reveals that considerable changes were made to practices in these spheres during and after the introduction of Beaker pottery. While the quantity of burials is far less than that from subsequent stages of the Early Bronze Age, an increase in evidence for funerary deposition certainly occurred, including the numbers of inhumation burials and cremations (Carlin and Brück 2012). Other related changes include a renewed emphasis upon non-funerary deposition in megalithic contexts and the construction and use of a new type of monument, wedge tombs, which represent the main context where Beakers and human remains were deposited together. A notable characteristic of all this activity is its highly codified nature as illustrated by the selective nature of depositional practises. There were clear ideas about how and where Beaker pottery could be used and deposited, and these seem to have been strongly influenced by older customs. In this way, we can see much of the character of these practices as reflecting a local response to the ideas associated with the Beaker phenomenon. People on this island were probably aware that Beaker pottery and other objects were being deposited in specific ways in funerary contexts elsewhere, but a conscious choice was made not to directly replicate these. Instead, they adopted those aspects that fitted with their pre-existing cosmology in a manner that was strongly influenced by traditional practices.

Significantly, some of these traditions had not been practiced since around c. 3000 BC (though see Carlin 2017) and so as well as the continuation of some indigenous practices, we also see the reinvention of others. The long-standing custom of depositing occupational materials in various megalithic tombs was reborn and the Neolithic practice of building these megalithic monuments was re-imagined with the construction of wedge tombs. While some Beaker-associated unburnt human remains were deposited as individuals within wedge tombs, and a small number of contemporary inhumations that were unaccompanied by ceramics are known, there appears to have been resistance to adopting aspects of the practice of depositing Beakers and other objects with inhumations. That reluctance may have been influenced by this adherence to long-standing cultural traditions. For example, cremation was the dominant mortuary practice in the Irish Neolithic and continued to be so in the Early Bronze Age and beyond, despite the brief florescence of inhumations between 2200-1900 BC (see Mount 1995, 107; Cooney 2014; 2017). An indigenous solution to this is represented by the development of Irish Bowls c. 2200 BC, which seem to have enabled the much more widespread adoption of the practice of single inhumation in pits or cists. This is indicated by the sudden increase in inhumation burials after 2200 BC with accompanying Irish Bowls, which represent the Irish version of the British later Beaker mortuary tradition and fit within the context of the upsurge, diversification and regionalisation in Beaker funerary practices across Britain.

The nature of these various indigenous responses to contact with the Beaker phenomenon means that there is little evidence (except for Bowl burials or the infrequent occurrence of Beaker pots with human remains in compartments within wedge tombs) to directly link particular Beaker-related objects with specific individuals or for any form of accentuation of individuals in the funerary realm (see Chapter Ten). Beaker-associated deposition of collective settlement debris within Neolithic court tombs and collective burials within newly built megalithic contexts indicates the continuation of a strong concern with the expression of communal identities. The divergent ways in which Beakers and other objects were deposited across Ireland suggests that either these assemblages had meanings that were different to those typically ascribed to them, or that the value system of those who were using them was different to elsewhere. Certainly, their treatment does not seem to fit with the generally accepted doctrine that the spread of the Beaker phenomenon represents the emergence of an ideology of the individual and the development of Europe's first hierarchical societies, in which status was attained and represented by the competitive exchange and display of exotic goods (see Chapter Two). This raises important questions about understandings of this complex in Ireland and beyond, which will be returned to at various different points throughout the book, but particularly in Chapter Ten.

6

Commemorations of Ceremonies Past?

6.1 Introduction

One of the aims of this book is to develop an enhanced understanding of Beaker-associated ceremonial practices in Ireland. A far greater level of evidence exists for this than previously recognised, some of which has only recently been excavated, but much of it comes from poorly understood older discoveries that have traditionally been regarded as either settlement or funerary activity (*e.g.* Case 1995a, 19; Needham 1996, 128). As we have already seen and contra to what was previously believed, distinct domestic and ritual spheres did not exist during this period (*e.g.* Brück 1999a, 325-7; Carlin and Brück 2012). Activities that had a strongly ceremonial element but involved what seems to have been habitation debris were conducted in a very wide range of contexts. This includes deposition in pits, spreads and court tombs. In many cases, this activity was focussed on a variety of pre-existing ceremonial foci. This is exemplified by the well-known Beaker-associated deposits outside the passage tombs at Knowth and Newgrange that seem to have resulted from the continuation of ceremonial activities in those locations. As detailed in Chapter Three, these have traditionally been misinterpreted as the remains of settlements, but actually form part of a spectrum of interlinked social practices that are best understood in relation to one another. This is a point to which we will return towards the end of this chapter.

This chapter primarily examines the deposition of Beaker pottery and other typical Beaker-related objects within a restricted selection of contexts comprising wooden and earthen circular enclosures. The latter are large embanked earthen enclosures or henges, which are very poorly dated. The former comprise the remains of Late Neolithic sub-circular timber-built structures typified by the well-known examples at Knowth (Eogan and Roche 1997, 220-21), Newgrange (Sweetman 1985) and Ballynahatty, Co. Down (Hartwell 1998). These structures occur at a range of scales, but most of the recent discoveries are less than 7m in diameter (Carlin 2017; Carlin and Cooney 2017). There appears to have been a spectrum ranging from substantial to much less tangible constructions. Many share the features of Late Neolithic houses and may once have been inhabited, while others seem to represent monumentalised representations of those homes (Bradley 2005a, 53-6; Thomas 2007). These structures are referred to as timber circles, but attempting to distinguish which were houses or ceremonial structures is highly problematic and it is likely that many fulfilled a range of residential and ritual functions during the course of their use-lives (Thomas 2010).

For all the sites detailed here, it was necessary to re-evaluate the findings from the original excavations and to propose new interpretation of these sites. Attention is paid to the nature of Beaker deposits in terms of their frequency, location and manner of occurrence within earthen enclosures and timber circles. The relationship of these deposits to the previous activity at each site is also considered. In the case of timber circles, the taphonomy of the features and deposits containing Beaker pottery are studied to discern

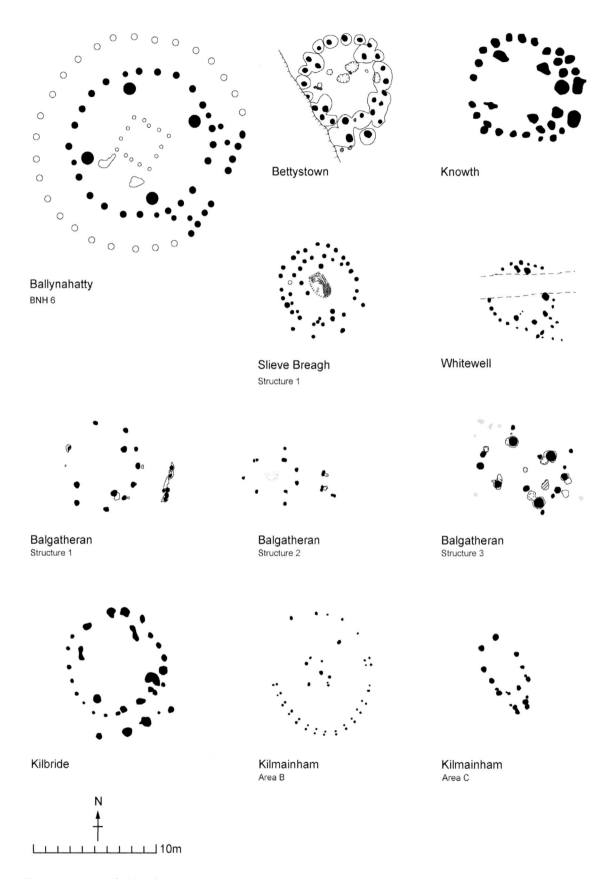

Fig. 6.1: A selection of Irish timber circles (after Smyth 2014, courtesy of Jessica Smyth).

136 | THE BEAKER PHENOMENON

the stage at which Beaker materials were deposited in the use-life of these monuments. A detailed analysis of the deposition of the pottery is conducted to reveal as much information as possible about the events and meanings associated with its final use. Where possible, this includes an assessment of the total number of Beaker pots and sherds and sherds per vessel, as well as their condition in each context. In the case of Paulstown, Co. Kilkenny, Newtownbalregan 5, Co. Louth, and Armalughey, Co. Tyrone, this is based upon original ceramic analysis by Eoin Grogan and Helen Roche (2005b; 2009a), as well as Julie Lochrie and Alison Sheridan (2010).

6.2 Beaker deposition in timber circles

Beaker pottery has been found in secondary contexts within the postholes of at least two Late Neolithic timber circles; Paulstown, Co. Kilkenny (Elliot 2009), and Armalughey, Co. Tyrone (Dingwall 2010). To this may be added two other probable examples of this phenomenon, excavated at Newgrange, Co. Meath (Sweetman 1987) and Newtownbalregan 5, Co. Louth (Bayley 2009a). Beaker pottery was also spatially associated with three timber circles at Knowth and Newgrange in County Meath and Ballynahatty in County Down (see Section 6.3). This informs us that deposition persisted at some Late Neolithic timber circles in association with the use of Beaker pottery in Ireland, after it had replaced Grooved Ware; the ceramic used by those who had originally built and used these timber structures. While Grooved Ware was in use in Ireland from c. 3000/2900-2450 BC, these structures were mainly built and used between 2700-2450 BC (Carlin and Cooney 2017).

These Late Neolithic timber circles display a high level of uniformity that aids our understanding of the Beaker activity at these sites. Typically, they comprise a sub-circular ring of postholes that enclosed a central square setting of four larger postholes symmetrically orientated with respect to a well-defined south-east-facing entrance (Fig. 6.1). These features often contain deliberate deposits of occupational debris that were focused on important locations, including the four-post setting, the posts to the right-hand side, the entrance area and the corresponding back posts. These deposits are predominantly found within pit-like voids created in the upper part of the postholes, post-dating their construction and primary

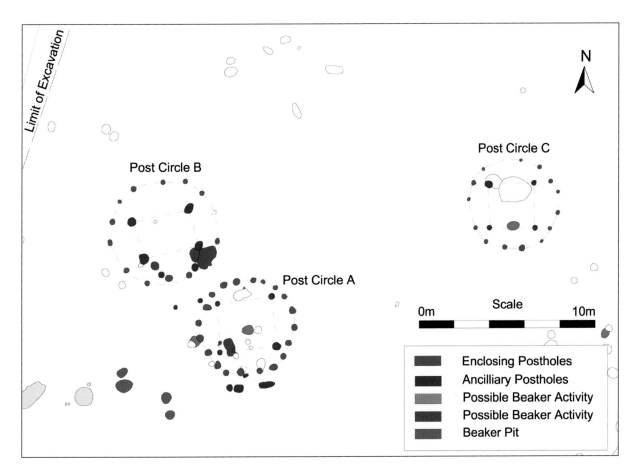

Fig. 6.2: Post-ex plan of Paulstown showing three timber circles (courtesy of IAC).

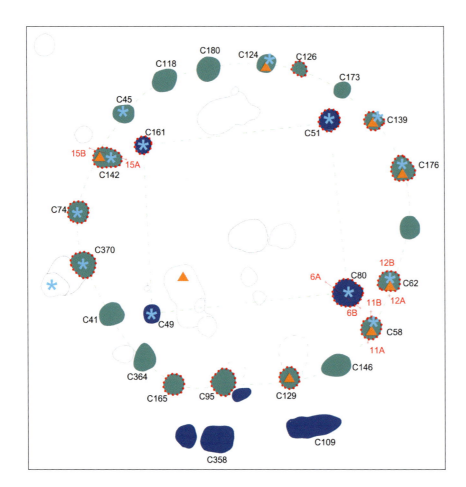

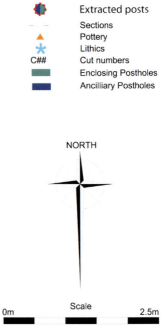

Fig. 6.3: Schematic plan of Post circle A at Paulstown (based on original image supplied by IAC).

use. These voids seem to have been created and backfilled during the dismantling of these structures, often after the timbers had rotted or burnt (see Carlin and Cooney 2017; Carlin, O'Connell *et al.* 2015; Johnston and Carlin, forthcoming). This suggests that people often returned to the site of these timber circles after they had entered a state of decay, to make deposits within the former structural features of these buildings. As we will see, the materials they deposited were fragments of everyday life; potsherds, knapping debris and charcoal that they obtained from repositories where this kind of material was stored.

At Paulstown, Co. Kilkenny, a total of 424 sherds from at least 62 Beakers were discovered during excavations that revealed a cluster of three separate timber circles (A, B and C) and a scattering of pits (Elliot 2009). Timber circle A was situated 1m to the south-east of Timber circle B and 10m south-west of Timber circle C (Fig. 6.2). Each of the structures comprised a ring of posts, approximately 5m in diameter, surrounding rectangular post settings. Although no Grooved Ware was recovered from Paulstown, radiocarbon dating indicates that the construction of the three timber circles was contemporary with other Late Neolithic examples. Most of the Beakers were found in 11 of the nearby pits (see Section 4.2), but 69 sherds representing 11 Beaker vessels came from the features forming Timber circle A (Grogan and Roche 2009a). Timber circles B and C also produced a few sherds that were too small and worn to be definitively identified as Beaker.

Timber circle A comprised a ring of 20 evenly spaced postholes that encircled a rectangular arrangement of four internal postholes and displayed evidence for a southern entrance that may have been flanked by a façade (Fig. 6.3). The postholes were quite substantial in size, averaging 0.3m in diameter and 0.4-0.5m in depth. Post-pipes indicating the former location of timber posts, as well as packing material that would have supported these posts, were recorded within many of these features. The regular, straight sides of some of the post-pipes suggest that their posts decayed *in situ*; while the irregular-shapes of the post-pipes within six of the postholes forming the outer ring indicates that their timber uprights were deliberately extracted (Fig. 6.4). No packing material or post-pipes were detected in some postholes, including two of those forming the internal square arrangement. This indicates that the remains of their posts had been dug out, probably after their decay. In total, the posts appear to have been deliberately extracted from at least ten of the 20 postholes forming the external ring and three of the four postholes forming the internal square arrangement. The voids created within the postholes by both pulling

138   THE BEAKER PHENOMENON

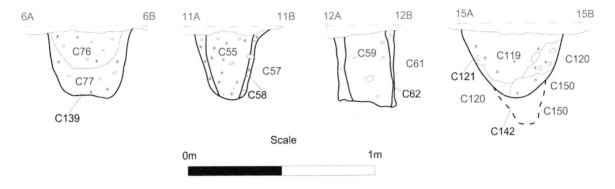

Fig. 6.4: Sections through postholes (C139 aka C80), (C58), (C62) and (C142) from Post circle A at Paulstown (based on original image supplied by IAC).

out some posts and digging out the rotted remains of others were then deliberately backfilled with new deposits.

A total of 64 lithics (both flint and chert) were recovered from nine postholes in the external ring and all four postholes of the square setting. These comprised six natural chunks, two cores, 28 pieces of debitage, 17 flakes, seven blades, two convex end scrapers, a knife, a quernstone and a rubbing stone. Carbonised plant remains, including hazelnut shells and seeds, were recovered from four of the postholes, three in the external ring and one in the square setting, while also recovered from two separate postholes in the external ring were a small amount of unidentifiable burnt bone and a human rib fragment (see Table 6.1).

A total of 69 abraded sherds representing 11 Beakers (Nos. 3-4 and Groups II – X) came from the fills of eight postholes in the external ring (Grogan and Roche 2009a). Two of these postholes contained a single Beaker sherd each. Small amounts of between three and six sherds (representing the remains of single vessels) were each recovered from three of the postholes. Larger quantities – 19 sherds representing two vessels and 14 sherds from three different vessels – were found within two of the postholes, while the highest number, 31 sherds derived from four Beakers was discovered in another posthole.

Most of the Beaker vessels from the timber circle are represented by only a few sherds, none of which refit, indicating that these ceramics are exceptionally incomplete and very fragmented (Grogan and Roche 2009a). Some sherds are heavily abraded, while others are lightly worn. Sherds displaying these different levels of wear, as well as burnt and unburnt knapping debris and carbonised plant remains were found in the same contexts within features that show no evidence for burning (see Table 6.1). All of this indicates that the contents of the postholes represent partial assemblages that were obtained from a greater accumulation of habitation debris, where the pot fragments had been stored for some time in between their original breakage and final deposition.

Significantly, most of the Beakers (seven of 11 vessels) and the lithics (54 out of 61) occurred in postholes where the posts had been removed and subsequently backfilled (Table 6.1). No artefacts were recovered from the packing fills of any of the postholes; this suggests that the detritus did not enter these features during construction. If cultural debris had been in the vicinity during the timber circle's erection and became accidentally incorporated into the postholes, then these artefacts would almost certainly have also entered into the packing contexts, rather than just into the fills of the post-pipes. Most of the postholes that show no evidence for secondary alterations produced no finds, conversely almost all of those that had been obviously modified were found to contain artefacts. Thus, it appears that the Beaker pottery and the lithics from the timber circle were all found within secondary contexts that were deposited either during the extraction of the post or the removal of its decaying stump. Radiocarbon dates from these contexts suggest that these deposits post-date the original use of the building, which was probably constructed sometime before the appearance of Beakers in Ireland.

Six radiocarbon dates were obtained from a range of construction and abandonment contexts within four of the postholes (C180, C364, C176, C124) forming the external ring of Timber circle A. Three samples were analysed from three separate contexts within one posthole (C180) that displayed a well-defined narrow vertical post-pipe, suggesting that its post had rotted *in situ*. Oak charcoal from the clay packing material at the base and sides returned a date of 2862-2579 BC (UBA-15438; 4115±24 BP). Ash charcoal from the lower fill of the post-pipe was radiocarbon dated to 2577-2474 BC (UBA-15431; 4015±24 BP), while hazel charcoal from the upper post-pipe fill produced a date of 2855-2501 BC (UBA-15436; 4087±25 BP). These three determinations indicate that this posthole was dug before 2474 BC at the latest, but probably prior to 2501 BC. Elm charcoal

Context No.	Location	Pipe Present	Packing Present	Extracted	Backfill?	Quadrant	Lithics Count	Sherd Count	Vessel Count	Sherd Condition	Tool	Other Finds
C41	ring	yes	yes	no	no	sw	0	0	0	n/a		
C45	ring	yes	yes	no	no	nw	1	0	0	n/a		
C49	four-post	yes	yes	no	no	sw	3	0	0	n/a		
C51	four-post	yes	yes	yes	yes	ne	6	0	0	n/a		charred seeds and hazelnuts
C74	ring	yes	yes	yes	yes	nw	1	0	0	n/a	scraper	
C80	four-post	no	no	yes	yes	se	2	0	0	n/a		
C118	ring	yes	yes	no	no	nw	0	0	0	n/a		
C126	ring	no	no	yes	yes	ne	0	0	0	n/a		
C137	ring	yes	yes	no	no	ne	0	0	0	n/a		
C146	ring	yes	yes	no	no	se	0	0	0	n/a		
C161	four-post	no	no	yes	yes	nw	5	0	0	n/a	knife, quern, rubbing stone	
C165	ring	yes	yes	yes?	yes	sw	0	0	0	n/a		
C173	ring	yes	yes	no	no	ne	0	0	0	n/a		
C180	ring	yes	yes	no	yes?	nw	0	0	0	n/a		charred seeds
C194	ring	no	no	yes	yes	sw	0	0	0	n/a		
C364	ring	yes	yes	yes	yes	sw	0	0	0	n/a		burnt clay
C370	ring	yes	yes	yes	yes	sw	2	0	0	n/a		hazelnuts
C58	ring	yes	yes	yes	yes	se	7	1	1	abraded		
C62	ring	yes	yes	yes	yes	se	1	3	1	heavily abraded		
C124	ring	yes	yes	no	yes?	ne	3	31	4	heavily abraded	scraper	clay daub, charred seeds, hazelnuts
C129	ring	no	no	yes	yes	se	0	6	1	abraded		
C139	ring	no	no	yes	yes	ne	8	14	3	heavily abraded		burnt bone
C142	ring	no	yes	yes	yes	nw	17	1	1			
C176	ring	no	no	yes	yes	ne	5	19	2	heavily abraded: V. 4		
C361	ring	yes	yes	yes	yes	sw	0	3	1	n/a		

Table 6.1: The depositional biography of each posthole forming Timber circle A at Paulstown, Co. Kilkenny.

produced a radiocarbon date of 2465-2286 BC (UBA-15433; 3875±24 BP) from a deposit containing pieces of burnt clay/daub, which backfilled the void created by the extraction of the post from one of the postholes (C364). This suggests that this material was deposited in the posthole sometime after 2465 BC and that the timber circle was being deconstructed by this stage. Another posthole (C176), which been re-dug towards the latter stages of the timber circle's use-life was backfilled with a single Beaker-associated deposit that yielded five pieces of flint debitage, 19 Beaker sherds and ash charcoal dating from 2573-2467 BC (UBA-15437; 3989±27 BP). If this charcoal is genuinely associated with the Beaker activity rather than being residual from the Late Neolithic, then it represents quite an early date for the deposition of Beaker pottery in Ireland (see Chapter Eight). The deposit within the top of another posthole (C124) contained 31 sherds from four Beakers, a flint blade, a piece of debitage, a convex end scraper, carbonised seeds and hazelnut shells, as well as a cremated human rib fragment that returned a radiocarbon date of 2617-2471 BC (UBA-15430; 4017±28 BP). Like the dated charcoal, however, it is impossible to decipher whether this bone was old when deposited and whether its date is more reflective of Late Neolithic or Beaker-associated activity.

There may have been an east–west or right–left division of space within the structure. This is suggested by the fact that the structural postholes on the eastern side produced a far greater quantity of artefacts (74 sherds and 24 lithics) than the western side (four sherds and

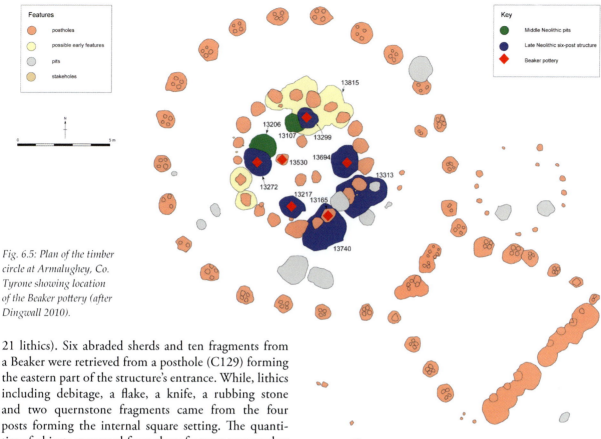

Fig. 6.5: Plan of the timber circle at Armalughey, Co. Tyrone showing location of the Beaker pottery (after Dingwall 2010).

21 lithics). Six abraded sherds and ten fragments from a Beaker were retrieved from a posthole (C129) forming the eastern part of the structure's entrance. While, lithics including debitage, a flake, a knife, a rubbing stone and two quernstone fragments came from the four posts forming the internal square setting. The quantities of objects recovered from these features suggest that the postholes forming the entrance and the internal four-post element formed the main focus of deposition within the structure. The greatest quantity of artefacts – 64 Beaker sherds and 16 lithics – was discovered in the postholes forming the north-eastern sector of the post-ring (Table 6.1; Fig. 6.3). Three postholes (C139, 124 and 176) in this area each contained far more pottery than any other structural features. The posthole (C124) containing the greatest number and range of artefacts (see above) was located directly opposite the entrance. Another posthole (C126) right beside it contained absolutely no finds, this suggests that the occurrence of such a culturally-rich deposit in the posthole (C124) opposing the circle's entry point was not the result of a random or natural process. A much smaller number of artefacts were found in the other sectors; ten sherds and eight lithics in the south-eastern quadrant, one sherd and 19 lithics in the north-western quadrant and three sherds and two lithics in the south-western quadrant. Significantly, the Beaker activity here certainly replicates the Grooved Ware-associated depositional patterns observed at many other timber circles (Carlin and Cooney 2017).

At Armalughey, Co. Tyrone, 50 sherds from at least 12 Beakers were discovered during the excavation of a Late Neolithic timber circle resembling that at Paulstown (Carlin 2010; 2016; Dingwall 2010). This was a multi-phase structure, however, with a more complex layout and history of use, as indicated by the presence of both Middle Neolithic Carrowkeel Ware and Late Neolithic Grooved Ware. It comprised two concentric post circles; an inner ring (8.5m in diameter) of 21 evenly spaced large postholes and an outer ring (15m in diameter) of 24 large shallow pits. Each of the pits in the outer ring contained the post-pipes of four posts (Fig. 6.5). Attached to the outermost circle was an elaborate south-eastern entrance defined by two radiating lines of similar postpits that were joined at their termini by a line of large intercutting postholes to form an outer façade. The innermost ring of posts encircled an internal square setting of four very large and deep pits, each of which had once contained a post that had been removed. These displayed evidence for a complex sequence of backfilling and recutting representing several phases of activity and appear to embody the most enduring structural aspect of the site (Fig. 6.6).

There appears to have been a complex sequence of development at the Armalughey monument involving the repeated recutting and/or replacement of postholes, as well as the addition of the inner and outer ring. While ra-

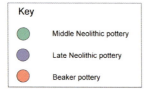

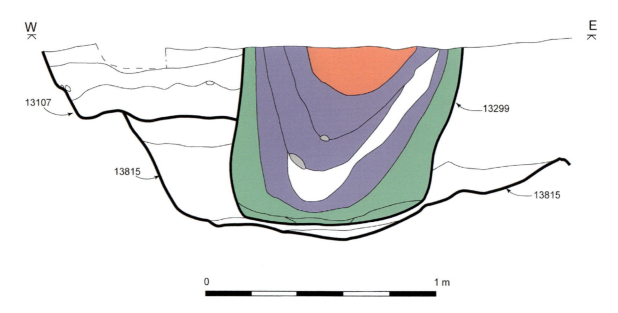

Fig. 6.6: Section drawing showing recutting of pits 13107, 13815 and the large pit 13299 which forms part of the internal four post arrangement at Armalughey (after Dingwall 2010). A Beaker sherd was found in the uppermost fill of the large pit and Grooved Ware was found in the underlying fills. It is clear from this illustration that the formation of the deposits within this pit could not have resulted from a natural sequence of events. The fills of this pit are clearly the product of a long and complex sequence of backfilling and recutting.

diocarbon dating is not suitably accurate to reveal precise details of the chronological sequence of this activity, such as whether the two concentric rings of posts were built at the same time, at least three distinct phases of the structure can be identified. The earliest activity is represented by shallow pits containing Middle Neolithic Carrowkeel Ware (Fig. 6.5). These were truncated by the rear pair of large pits forming the internal four-post setting. This square arrangement of four large pits formed part of the earliest timber structure at the site, along with two other large sub-rectangular pits that all share the same axial symmetry. In combination, these six features represent the only surviving elements of a timber monument comprising a four-post structure with a pit-defined entrance way. At a later stage, this earlier six-post structure was transformed by the construction of the inner and outer rings of posts representing the second phase of the monument. By this time, the two original entrance pits (C13313 and C13740) had been backfilled and these were truncated by some of the posts forming the inner circle. This was probably when the square arrangement comprising the other four pits of the original structure were re-dug to form part of the new monument.

Significantly, the various different architectural aspects of the monument received different treatments throughout the use of this structure, particularly towards the end of its life-cycle. The presence of distinct and undisturbed post-pipes in the outer ring indicates that the outer circle was left to rot *in situ* (Dingwall 2010). Similar evidence suggests that some of the posts forming the inner circle were also left to decay, while others were clearly dug out. In contrast, each of the posts within the four large pits forming the internal central square arrangement had been extracted and then backfilled.

A few sherds of Carrowkeel Ware were retrieved from features forming the inner and outer rings, while Late Neolithic Grooved Ware pottery occurred in the inner and outer ring as well as the entrance façade of the timber circle and the most north-eastern of the four large pits forming the internal square setting at the centre of the timber circle. Beaker pottery also came from each of these four large pits, as well as an entrance posthole (CI3165) from the inner ring and a small posthole (C13530) near the centre of the circle (Fig. 6.5).

The posthole forming the entrance to the inner ring produced a single Beaker sherd. This came from an upper fill that seems to have been deposited after the post had decayed or been extracted. The posthole within the central interior of the inner ring contained five sherds (and 19 fragments) from at least two Beaker vessels, many of which were quite abraded. These were all found in the void (post-pipe) formed by either the decay or the removal of the post, along with a sherd of Middle Neolithic Carrowkeel Ware and three sherds of Late Neolithic Grooved Ware. A fragment of burnt pig bone from this deposit produced a radiocarbon date of 2760-2570 BC (SUERC-

Fig. 6.7: Large conjoining sherds from Rockbarton Vessels 37 (left) from Armalughey timber circle (courtesy of Julie Lochrie and Headland U.K Ltd).

2078; 4105±30 BP) that seems to relate to the Grooved Ware-associated activity in this location.

Most of the Beaker pottery (44 sherds derived from ten vessels) occurred within the internal square arrangement of four large pits. Each of these features has been re-dug at least once. Each appears to have contained a large post that had been removed before the pit was subsequently backfilled and then recut at a later stage to receive Beaker-associated deposits. This indicates that the deposition of Beaker pottery at the Armalughey timber circle occurred during later phases of activity, post-dating the main phases of use of the respective parts of the monument. In many ways, this mirrors the context of the Grooved Ware at this site, which also appears to have been deposited at a late stage in the use-life of the building. This is an important point to which we will return.

The north-western pit of the internal square arrangement contained four sherds from two Beakers within an upper deposit that had clearly been deliberately backfilled after the removal of its post. Sherds from a Middle Neolithic pot were also found in this feature. A single Beaker sherd also occurred in a backfilled upper deposit of the south-eastern pit. The north-eastern pit had been recut and then filled in on several occasions (see Fig. 6.6). A single Beaker sherd, as well as five sherds from a Grooved Ware vessel, were found in the uppermost deposit of this pit, along with burnt bone fragments (species indeterminable) that returned a radiocarbon date of 2660-2470 BC (SUERC-20796; 4045±25 BP). The majority of the Beaker pottery came from the south-western pit, near the entrance. The final deposit consisted of a dark charcoal-rich fill that produced 34 Beaker sherds from at least five different vessels. Oak charcoal from this produced a radiocarbon date of 2290-2030 BC (SUERC-20768; 3750±30 BP). Although two of the Beaker pots were only represented by two sherds each, the other three vessels (nos 36-38) were large 'domestic' Beakers represented by ten sherds each, many of which conjoined (Fig. 6.7).

The sherds from these three pots are far larger and represent a greater vessel percentage – as much as 15-20% of each vessel – than those from any of the other Armalughey Beakers (see Table 6.2). The sherds from these vessels conjoined, their edges and surfaces are uniformly well preserved, the breaks are clean and do not display any edge wear (Julie Lochrie, pers. comm.). All of these sherds were exclusively from one side of each pot and included parts from the rim, neck and body but not the base (ibid.). These appear to have placed into the top of the pit as much larger pieces of pottery very soon after their breakage and only broke into smaller pieces after deposition (ibid.). It may even be the case that these Beakers were smashed, specifically to be deposited within a hole that had been dug to receive them as part of a single sequence of acts. In contrast, the other nine Beaker vessels are represented by only a few small, worn (and in some cases quite abraded), highly fragmented non-conjoining sherds, with clearly different depositional histories (Table 6.2). The amount of pottery deposited at Armalughey represents a very small proportion of the vessel assemblage that these sherds once formed, before breakage. The highly incomplete and fragmented condition of the pottery suggests that it was obtained from a larger aggregation of occupational debris where it was subject to abrasion, indicating that a substantial period of time elapsed between its fracture and final deposition

Beaker deposition at Armalughey was largely focused upon the four large pits that represent its oldest element (see above), while the outer ring of posts appears to have been left untouched to rot *in situ*. The longevity of this four-poster arrangement of features and the pre-existing tradition of depositing material within these (as indicated by the inclusion of Grooved Ware) may account for the decision to choose these features as the main focus for Beaker deposition. One might argue that the sheer size of the four post-pits would have made them the most visible surviving component of the monument, but this misses the point. Similar occurrences have been noticed at other Grooved Ware-associated timber circles, such as Ballynahatty (Hartwell 1998) and Dunragit in Scotland (Thomas 2004b). At the former, the outer ring of posts was left to decay, while the inner ring and the central four-posts were burnt down, dug up and then backfilled

Vessel #	No. of sherds	Feature	Location	Description
34	1	C13299	four-post	Beaker: thin, fine, abraded body sherd
35	1	C13694	four-post	Beaker; Small undiagnostic body sherd
45	1	C13694	four-post	small body sherd, possibly Beaker
39	2	C13217	four-post	neck and body sherd of large domestic Beaker.
40	1	C13217	four-post	featureless, thick body sherd
36	10	C13217	four-post	Beaker: 10-15% of a large, fairly slender undecorated 'domestic' Beaker with an upright rim (estimated rim diameter c 170 mm) with two low cordons below it on the exterior, and a sinuous profile.
37	10	C13217	four-post	Beaker: 15% of a large decorated 'domestic' Beaker, with a sinuous profile, with incised diagonal lines on its neck framed top and bottom by horizontal lines; below it the lines extend down to the upper body
38	10	C13217	four-post	Beaker: 15-20% of a Beaker, estimated rim diameter 160 mm, estimated body diameter 140 mm, estimated height 166, with incised decoration on the exterior from just below the rim to the lower body
42	3	C13272	four-post	Beaker-body sherd with horizontal incised lines. 2 sherds and 3 frags
41	1	C13272	four-post	Beaker; Small thin, fine abraded body sherd.
43	5	C13530	internal posthole	Beaker; comb impressed
44	1	?	inner ring	Beaker body sherd; decorated with incised linear pattern

Table 6.2: The number of sherds per Beaker in relation to its context at the Armalughey timber circle, Co. Tyrone (based on information supplied by Julie Lochrie).

Posthole	Sherd Totals	Vessel Totals	Vessel I.D
C154	63	6	Vessels: 2, 3, 4, 5, 6, 7
C162	34	3	Vessels: 2, 3, 6
C174	59	5	Vessels: 3, 4, 6, 7, 10
C160	39	6	Vessels: 2, 3, 4, 6, 8, 9
C181	13	3	Vessels: 4, 6, 8
C166	11	1	Vessel: 10
C156	20	4	Vessels: 2, 4, 6, 10

Table 6.3: The number of Beaker sherds and vessels in each posthole forming the probable timber circle at Newtownbalregan. Note that sherds from vessel 2 and 4 occur in nearly every posthole.

before being marked by low cairns of stones (Hartwell 1998, 41; 2002, 529).

A cluster of pits and postholes producing 166 sherds from 15 Beaker vessels were excavated on a multi-period site at Newtownbalregan 5 (Grogan and Roche 2005e; Bayley 2009a). It is rare to find more than a few Beaker sherds from a single vessel in a posthole (see Chapter Four), unless it is part of a timber circle. The quantity of sherds found in as many as five of the postholes at Newtownbalregan is similar to that seen at timber circles. For example, one posthole contained 63 sherds from six different vessels, while another produced 59 sherds from five vessels (Table 6.3). As well as their contents, the postholes at Newtownbalregan had straight vertical sides and flat bases with an average depth of 0.5m and diameter of 0.5m, like those seen at timber circles. Re-examination of the site plans revealed a square arrangement of four large posts, set 4m apart, which resembles the four-post settings commonly found within Irish Late Neolithic timber circles (Fig. 6.8). Three of these posts all produced quantities of Beaker pottery ranging from 11 to 59 sherds. An additional two features that also contained multiple sherds may well represent the rearmost postholes of a timber circle that occur directly opposite the entrance. Though no clear entrance features were recorded at Newtownbalregan, the orientation of the axis of the four-post setting combined with the two aforementioned postholes suggest that this structure may have had a south-eastern entrance like most Irish timber circles. It seems quite probable that the postholes at Newtownbalregan represent the poorly preserved partial remains of a timber circle. The full extent of this structure may not have survived or been recognised at the time of excavation (see Carlin, O'Connell *et al.* 2015; Carlin and Cooney 2017; Johnston and Carlin, forthcoming).

Grogan and Roche (2005e) observed that the Newtownbalregan pottery was of an unusually fine quality and in good condition with little evidence for heavy wear, yet the assemblage was heavily fragmented with few refitting sherds. This suggests that these sherds had been obtained for deposition from an intermediate context such as a midden that offered protection from the elements (see Section 4.3). This is supported by the presence of several sherds from multiple different fragmented pots within many of the features. Sherds deriving from the same vessels were also found in different postholes suggesting that their contents

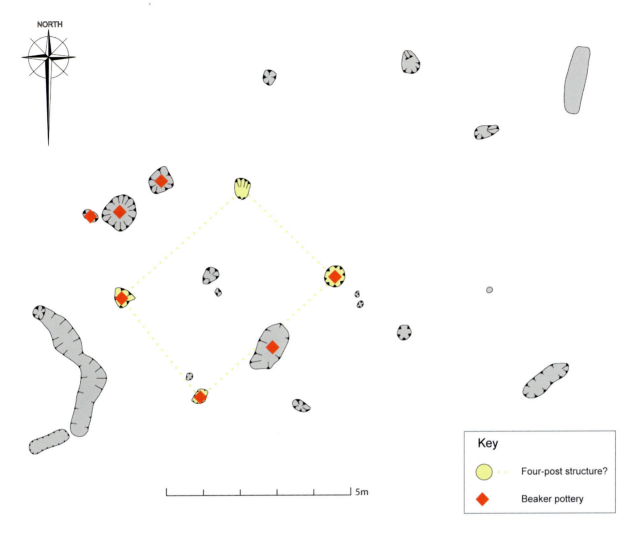

Fig. 6.8: Plan of the pits and postholes containing Beaker pottery at Newtownbalregan 5, Co. Louth (after Bayley 2010). The four postholes coloured yellow seem to represent the internal four poster element of a timber circle.

were obtained from the same source (Table 6.3). Similarly, burnt and unburnt, fresh and abraded lithics occur within the same contexts. Some of the worn flints suffered from post-use damage, indicating that they had been exposed to the elements for some time before they were deposited, but this did not apply to all the lithics, thereby indicating that the wear occurred before deposition.

No post-pipes or any evidence for packing material were detected within any of the postholes, most of which contained a single homogenous fill. This suggests that the entire original contents of the postholes were removed during extraction of the posts, and then rapidly backfilled. Although confirmatory evidence is not available, the most plausible interpretation of these features is that a timber circle or similar structure was constructed here and then demolished at the end of its use-life by removing the posts, redigging the postholes and deliberately filling these voids with occupational debris.

Investigation of a small area 30m west of the main passage tomb mound at Newgrange revealed two almost concentric arcs of pits that have been interpreted as a partially excavated Beaker-associated pit/timber circle approximately 20m in diameter (Fig. 3.8; Sweetman 1987). Eighteen sherds deriving from at least six Beakers and other finds including convex scrapers, *petit tranchet*-derivative arrowheads, a portion of a decorated stone bowl and burnt cattle and pig bone were found within seven of these pits (Fig. 6.9). Although the features excavated may indeed form a structure such as a timber circle, the area of investigation was too restricted to be definitive about this. While some pits certainly pre-date the use of Beakers at this site and returned radiocarbon dates that match with the known date ranges for Late Neolithic timber circles, it remains possible that some of the other features represent unrelated phases of activity dating from other periods, including the Neolithic, Bronze and Iron Age. Perhaps a

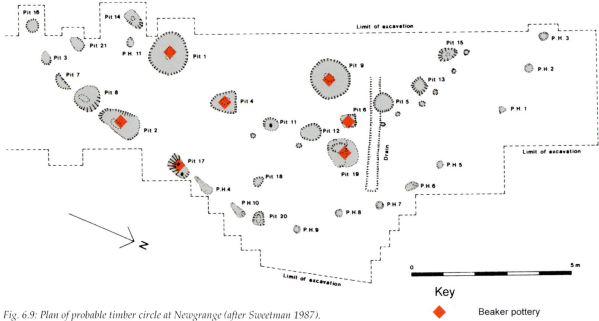

Fig. 6.9: Plan of probable timber circle at Newgrange (after Sweetman 1987).

more convincing interpretation of this excavation may be that four of the large deep features (Pits 1, 2, 4 and 17), which contained Beaker pottery, formed a square arrangement of posts like that seen within other Late Neolithic timber circles, but it is difficult to confirm this.

David Sweetman (1987, 283) identified five large pits (Pits 1, 2, 8, 9, and 19) that each contained charcoal-rich basal deposits, which had been backfilled with sterile clay after their primary use. These pits were then re-dug to contain what Sweetman interpreted as posts. One of these pits (1) produced a Beaker sherd (no. 85), a round scraper, some "utilised flints", some burnt bone and charcoal (species not determined) from its uppermost fill that returned a radiocarbon date of 2577-2468 BC (GrN-12828; 4000±30 BP; Sweetman 1987, 286). A single Beaker sherd (no. 87) was found in another of the large pits (2). Close to the central part of the base of another pit (19), a "mass of charcoal and burnt bone", representing cattle and pig, produced nine small sherds of very fragmented Beaker pottery (ibid., 287).

Sweetman (1987, 287) also grouped the smaller pits (Pits 3, 4, 5, 6, 7, 12, 13, 16, 17 and 18) together, some of which (including pits 4 and 17) seem to have been filled with debris and then re-used as postholes. For example, one of these pits (4) contained five large sherds from a Beaker (vessel 90, Sweetman 1987, fig. 4) that were found at varying depths along with burnt bone (species unidentifiable), burnt clay and numerous stones that appeared to have been packing for a post. A Beaker sherd (no. 98) was also discovered near the top of pit 17, while another pit (6) contained Middle Neolithic pottery (no. 92; Helen Roche, pers. comm.), a stone bowl, two *petit tranchet*-derivative arrowheads (of a type that are found in association with Grooved Ware in Ireland) and charcoal (species unidentified) that produced a radiocarbon date of 2565-2320 BC (GrN-12829; 3930±35 BP). This could relate to either the Late Neolithic or Beaker deposits in this area.

The six Beaker vessels from these features (Pits 1, 2, 6, 9, 17 and 19) at Newgrange were highly fragmented and each was only represented by one or more sherds. The partial nature of the assemblage suggests that these ceramics may have been obtained from an intermediate context for deposition within these features; however, in such a scenario, sherds from multiple different vessels would usually be present rather than just one vessel being represented in each feature, as was the case here.

Although the exact contexts of the Beakers within these features is not entirely clear, the available evidence suggests that these sherds were recovered from secondary deposits within the pits. Most, if not all of the Beaker pottery occurred within conical recuts that were dug into pre-existing pits that the excavator interpreted as the remains of former posts (Sweetman 1987, 286). This begs the question of how the Beakers came to be present within these putative postholes. Sweetman (1987) did not attempt any interpretation of how and when the Beaker materials became incorporated into these features. It is most probable that the artefacts represent deposits that were deliberately placed into the voids created by the *in situ* rotting or the removal of the posts. Alternatively, these conical recuts may represent the redigging of the pits for depositional purposes. Either way, the important point is that the Beakers were deposited in secondary contexts that post-date the primary phases

Site	Total sherds	Total vessels
Newtownbalregan 5	166	15
Armalughey	50	12
Paulstown	69	11
Newgrange	18	6

Table 6.4: The numbers of Beaker sherds and vessels found in each timber circle.

and most likely represent the final stages in the use-life of this probable monument, in whatever form it took.

Overall, 303 sherds from 50 Beakers have been recovered from two definite and two probable timber circles in Ireland (see Table 6.4). Other artefacts occurring in these deposits include convex end scrapers, a quernstone, a rubbing stone and a hammer-stone, but lithic debitage is by far the most common aceramic find. The amount of Beaker pottery from individual postholes forming each of these structures varied greatly at each site. This ranged from postholes containing a single sherd to those that contained more than 31 sherds. Similarly, although some postholes only contained the remains of one vessel, at least one posthole per structure produced multiple sherds deriving from between four and six vessels. For example, at Armalughey, a post-pit produced 34 sherds from five vessels and at Paulstown, a posthole yielded 31 sherds from four vessels. A common aspect of the pottery from these timber circles is that many of the vessels are very incomplete and represented by only a small number of highly fragmented and/or worn sherds, very few of which conjoin. Their condition (see above) suggests that they represent partial assemblages that were obtained for deposition from a larger aggregation of cultural materials where they had been stored for a considerable duration after their original breakage. The presence of knapping debris, charcoal and carbonised plant remains along with the fragmentary ceramics suggests that in many cases, these repositories were formed from occupational debris.

The deposition of Beaker material in timber circles seems strongly related to pit deposition. The pits dug into the tops of the postholes often resemble the shape and size of the typical Beaker pits found on what appear to be settlements (see Chapter Four). Both practices involved the selection and deposition of habitation debris that has been obtained from an intermediate context such as a midden and formed part of a complex sequence of events involving digging, backfilling and recutting of holes. Despite these similarities, pit deposition appears to have been considered as a distinct practice that followed a different set of rules, which permitted the deposition of a much greater range and quantity of artefacts such as arrowheads, wrist-bracers, polypod bowls and polished stone axes, all of which were excluded from Beaker deposits at timber circle (see Chapter Nine).

A striking aspect of Beaker activity at timber circles is the extent to which they parallel Grooved Ware practices at these types of site. This is demonstrated by the way Beaker deposits do not just maintain the practice of depositing collective debris in timber circles, they also replicate the spatial patterning of Grooved Ware deposits. Both were selectively focused upon the same particular parts of the structure such as the entrance or rear of the structure, as well as the central four posts (Carlin and Cooney 2017). As is typical of Late Neolithic practices, the original structural features that formed the monuments seem to have been deliberately modified at a late stage in their lifecycle to receive deposits of occupational debris during the Chalcolithic. This seems to have occurred during or after the dismantling of these structures and can be seen as ritualised acts of abandonment and/or commemoration of the past history of these monuments (ibid.). All of this resonates with the observation made in a British context by Julian Thomas (1996, 212-22), that Beaker and Grooved Ware pottery were both used according to the same set of rules at the Mount Pleasant timber circle.

6.3 Beaker deposition at timber circles

A different form of Beaker-associated commemorative activity seems to be represented by the deposits of Beakers that were spatially associated with three Late Neolithic timber circles at Knowth (Eogan and Roche 1997), Ballynahatty (Hartwell 1998) and a second, larger example at Newgrange (O'Kelly *et al.* 1983; Sweetman 1985). At Ballynahatty, part of a Beaker pot was recovered during excavations of the Grooved Ware-associated timber circle complex, but details of its exact context remain uncertain (Hartwell 2002, 526).

To the south-east of the main passage tomb at Newgrange, a large timber circle (70m in external diameter) consisting of three concentric rows of post-pits enclosed the small passage tomb, Site Z (see Fig. 3.2; O'Kelly *et al.* 1983, 16-21; Sweetman 1985). Only the western circuit and part of the interior have been excavated, but geophysical surveys have revealed the full extent of this enclosure (Smyth 2009, fig. 1.35). Radiocarbon dates ranging between 2865-2450 BC were obtained from charcoal (species unidentified) within the post-pits (Grogan 1991, 131). Pottery described by O'Kelly *et al.* (1983, 18, 21) as "undecorated Beaker-associated bowls" were found in at least three of the post-pits, but this has subsequently been recognised as Grooved Ware (Roche 1995). No Beaker pottery was found within any of the features forming the monument, but five sherds of Beaker pottery and flint flakes were recovered from a spread within the interior of the enclosure (Sweetman 1985, 200-218). Some of the features forming this timber circle were sealed beneath a series of spreads representing multi-period deposits containing Grooved Ware and Beaker pottery, which flanked the front of the main passage tomb (see Chapter Three).

A Grooved Ware-associated timber circle was also discovered at the Knowth passage tomb complex, just in front of the entrance to the eastern passage tomb of the main mound (Eogan and Roche 1997; see Fig. 3.11). Radiocarbon dating indicates that the Grooved Ware materials had been deposited in the postholes of this timber circle between 2700-2450 BC (ibid.; Whitehouse *et al.* 2014). It was directly overlain by an extensive spread of culturally-rich occupational debris known as Concentration D, which contained 2072 sherds deriving from at least 104 Beakers (see Section 4.3; Roche and Eogan 2001, 137). No Beakers were found within the underlying features forming timber circle, however, nor was any Grooved Ware discovered within this spread, unlike two of the other spreads, Concentrations A and C (Eogan and Roche 1997, 223-60; Roche and Eogan 2001, 131). The lack of Beaker deposits within the features and the lack of association between Grooved Ware and Beaker at this timber circle stand out in comparison to those within other timber circles. This may be reflective of a considerable time-lapse between the Grooved Ware and Beaker phases of activity at Knowth, but this seems unlikely given the other evidence for Beaker-associated deposition at this monument complex.

Instead, the decision to place deposits over, rather than in, the features forming the remains of this timber circle at Knowth seems to have been deliberate. This also seems to be true of the Beaker deposits overlying the western extent of the large timber circle at Newgrange. This form of depositional practice may have been regarded as more appropriate at these passage tomb complexes. It formed part of the Beaker-associated continuation of the pre-Neolithic tradition of placing deposits outside of passage tombs entrances to emphasise their exteriors (see Carlin 2017). Yet, it also seems to have achieved the same commemorative effect as the smaller Beaker-associated depositional acts at Armalughey or Paulstown. Both involved the deliberate deposition of materials with connections to particular people or places and maybe also to specific events at these Late Neolithic structures. An intriguing aspect of all this is whether these timber structures were still standing or in a state of decay. Given that some may have been constructed c. 2500 BC, there is every reason to believe that they were still standing, particularly in the case of those structures where their timber posts were extracted before deposition. This suggests that what we are seeing here are contrasting ways of remembering and making connections with Late Neolithic activities during the Chalcolithic; one relied upon a visible above-surface presence, while the other seems to have involved dismantling the structures and burying materials so that they were remembered through their absence (see Rowlands 1993).

6.4 Beaker deposition in earthen enclosures

Only a few open-air earthen embanked or ditched circular monuments have been investigated in Ireland and each of these has only been partly excavated and very poorly dated (Stout 1991; Cooney and Grogan 1994, 87-91; Condit and Simpson 1998; Carlin and Cooney 2017). The confusion about their chronology stems partially from the fact that various forms of these enclosures were constructed throughout later prehistory in Ireland and Britain, often at locations with evidence for pre-existing Neolithic and Chalcolithic activity (Roche 2004; Gibson, A. 2010; Carlin and Cooney 2017). In Ireland, Beakers have been found in the interiors of two such monuments; the embanked enclosure at Monknewtown, Co. Meath, and the embanked stone circle at Grange, Co. Limerick (Ó Ríordáin, S.P. 1951), but there is no evidence to suggest a direct association between the construction or primary use of any large-scale earthen monuments and the use of Beakers in Ireland. Furthermore, the absence of definitive dating evidence for the construction of these monuments means that it is presently impossible to discern whether many of these monuments had even been built by the Chalcolithic period.

The embanked enclosure at Monknewtown, Co. Meath (Sweetman 1976), was assumed to be Late Neolithic (Stout 1991; Condit and Simpson 1998; Cooney and Grogan 1999, 87-91), but no evidence relating to the dating of its construction was found during excavation (see Section 3.2.4). Investigations of this site resulted in the discovery of multi-period activity ranging from the Middle Neolithic to the Late Bronze Age, though no evidence for Late Neolithic Grooved Ware-associated activity has yet been identified, apart perhaps from a few *petit tranchet*-derivative arrowheads (Roche and Eogan 2001, 135). Five thousand sherds of Beaker pottery were recovered from the excavation, mainly from an extensive surface deposit of occupational debris (Sweetman 1976). This deposit also contained a mix of Early Neolithic, Middle Neolithic and Middle Bronze Age pottery spanning three millennia and the Beaker pottery may well have been found in a residual context.

A total of 1231 Beaker sherds, two Sutton type barbed and tanged arrowheads and two hollow-based arrowheads (Ó Ríordáin, S.P. 1951, figs 3:1 3:2 and 3:6) were discovered during the excavation by Seán P. Ó Ríordáin of the embanked stone circle at Grange, Lough Gur, Co. Limerick. Other finds included Early Neolithic Carinated bowls, Middle Neolithic globular bowls, Late Neolithic Grooved Ware, Early Bronze Age Food Vessels, Cordoned Urns and Late Bronze Age coarse ware (Brindley, A.L. 1999, 32; Roche 2004, 115), though see R. Cleary (2015). At the time of excavation, the Grooved

Ware, Cordoned Urns and Late Bronze Age coarseware were all considered to be an Irish reaction to Beaker pottery called Lough Gur Class II (see Chapter Two; Section 3.2.1) and both components of the monument, the earthen bank and the stone circle, were considered to have been constructed in the Late Neolithic/Early Bronze Age (Ó Ríordáin, S.P. 1951). As the site and its pottery have subsequently been revisited, however, there have been conflicting interpretations of the chronology of events and it is uncertain when either enclosing element was erected and whether these occurred at the same time (see Roche 2004; Cleary, R. 2015).

Helen Roche (2004) argued that the stone circle and bank were actually built in the Late Bronze Age, based on her observation that the most recent of the Class II pottery within the bank of the enclosure was later Bronze Age. More recently, Rose Cleary (2015) has conducted investigations to clarify when the monument was constructed. As part of this, she has re-examined the ceramics from the site, as well as their condition and contexts. She has confirmed the categorisation of some of the Class II pottery as Grooved Ware, which was also previously identified as such by both Helen Roche (1995; 2004) and A.L. Brindley (1999). Radiocarbon dating of charred residues on three pots that were previously identified by Roche as Grooved Ware returned determinations ranging between 3020-2680 BC (Cleary, R. 2015). These three dated pots were recovered from the old ground surface that occurred under the bank and within the interior of the enclosure. Based on the dates from these three vessels and the methods used to manufacture some of the pottery, R. Cleary (ibid., 65) contends that all the Class II pottery at Grange is in fact Late Neolithic Grooved Ware. Cleary did not, however, date residue on any of the pots from within the bank that Roche (2004) identified as Bronze Age, and it therefore remains to be determined that none of the Class II pottery is of Late Bronze Age date.

In 2012, Cleary also excavated a small part of the bank and surrounding area to clarify the date of its construction. She obtained radiocarbon dates ranging from 3000-2574 BC from animal bones and ash charcoal within the old ground surface in the interior and under the bank, as well as redeposited material within the bank. The redeposited material within the bank is explained by the fact that it was constructed from material scooped up from the interior of the area that it enclosed. This is significant for interpreting the relationship of the radiocarbon dates obtained by Cleary to the construction of the bank, all six of which, including those from residues on Grooved Ware, date to the Late Neolithic. These dates confirm that Late Neolithic activity occurred in this location and that some of the materials from that activity were both incorporated into the bank and preserved beneath it during its construction sometime after 3000 BC. It is, however, unknown how long after 3000 BC this happened. R. Cleary (2015, 63) has argued that the lack of greater levels of wear on the pottery in the bank, including the radiocarbon-dated vessels, indicates that these sherds had only recently been 'discarded' at the time the bank was built. There are two issues to be considered here, one is whether any of this pottery might be Late Bronze Age, as suggested by Roche (2004), and the other relates to whether the Grooved Ware sherds may originally have been deposited in a manner that protected them from attrition. As things stand, further work is required to conclusively resolve whether the bank was built in the Late Neolithic or the Late Bronze Age. The chronological relationship of the Beaker sherds to the monument also remains unclear. R. Cleary (2015) has contended that no Beaker pottery came from under or within the bank, whereas Roche (2004, 113-5) observed that the Beaker pottery was recovered from the old ground surface under the bank as well as within the interior of the enclosure (ibid., fig 3, 32). Roche (ibid., 115) also commented that most of the Beaker sherds are tiny fragments that represent "protracted activity" and were largely recovered as residual artefacts within secondary contexts.

While the exact relationship of the Beaker pottery to the construction of the enclosures at both Monknewtown and Grange remains unknown, the evidence for other kinds of earlier activity at both locations indicates that these were already important places which held particular meanings for people by the time that Beakers were placed there. It is very likely that significant quantities of this ceramic were deposited above ground along with other contemporary materials and these were amassed in large artefact-rich accumulations, such as the well-known examples from Knowth and Newgrange (see Chapters Three and Four). These may well represent the remains of deliberately curated debris produced through large-scale episodic social gatherings and feasts. Given the long history of ceremonial activity at both Grange and Monknewtown, these seem to have been suitable locations for such assemblies and for the curation of the assemblages they created. The above surface nature of these deposits enabled ongoing engagements with the material contained within them and this would have fulfilled various practical, social and ceremonial functions (see Sections 4.5-6). These deposits served as physical reminders of past events and activities, whatever these may have been, and in doing so, may have further demarcated these locations as important spaces and meaningful places. The interest in places of historical importance that is indicated by Beaker deposition at these and other enduring ceremonial foci forms part of an emerging theme explored further below.

6.5 Understanding Beaker ceremonial deposition

Like in Ireland, Grooved Ware-associated and Beaker-associated deposits occur in secondary contexts in many British timber circles such as the Durrington Walls Southern Circle, Woodhenge, Mount Pleasant, Marden and North Mains (Richards and Thomas 1984; Gibson, A. 2005, 68, 75, 105-6; Parker Pearson *et al.* 2007, 631; Thomas 2007, 148-51). Small quantities of Beaker sherds have been retrieved from at least 15 examples, including North Mains in Perthshire (Barclay 1983), Balfarg in Fife (Mercer 1981) and the Durrington Walls Northern and Southern Circles (Wainwright with Longworth 1971, 71-3; Parker Pearson *et al.* 2007, 631; Cleal and Pollard 2012, 327). In contrast to Ireland, c. 2200 BC a few timber circles in Britain, such as Balfarg and North Mains, were re-used for Beaker-associated burials or were replaced by Beaker-associated cairns, as is the case for Oddendale in Cumbria (Gibson, A. 2005, 75). This seems to be related to the stronger association between Beaker pottery and mortuary practices in Britain compared to Ireland after 2300 BC (see Section 5.10).

Apart from timber circles, the deposition of Beaker pottery at older monuments or places with a long history of ceremonial activity is also paralleled in Britain. For example, Beaker sherds have been found in the ditches of the Late Neolithic henges at Durrington Walls, Mount Pleasant and Forteviot (Bradley 2000a, 128; Parker Pearson *et al.* 2004b; 2006; 2007, 635; Brophy and Noble 2012), as well as at Stonehenge and earlier Neolithic monuments like the Windmill Hill causewayed enclosure (Whittle *et al.* 1999) and the West Kennet long barrow (Case 1995b; Bayliss, Whittle *et al.* 2007; Cleal and Pollard 2012). In some cases, this has been interpreted as closing activity that represents a break away from the past (Bradley 2000a, 220-31; 2005a, 100-6). Though in the Wessex region, where many of these sites are located, this has more convincingly been argued to represent a continuation of pre-existing traditions and there is little evidence for change in ceremonial practices c. 2450-2200 BC (Cleal and Pollard 2012, 324-5).

Like Ireland, there is little firm evidence for changes in monument traditions and the construction of new ceremonial monuments in association with Beaker pottery during the first few centuries of its use (Needham 2012, 18-21; Pollard *et al.* 2017). The construction of large-scale monuments seems to have continued slightly beyond 2500 BC with the erection of Silbury Hill, the Stonehenge blue stones, the features defining the Stonehenge Avenue, the henges at Durrington Walls and Bluestonehenge, but these seem to represent the tail-end of Late Neolithic construction projects and there is nothing connecting this activity to early use of Beakers (Bayliss, McAvoy *et al.* 2007; Parker Pearson *et al.* 2007; Darvill *et al.* 2012; Pollard *et al.* 2017).

One of the striking things in both Britain and Ireland is the extent to which Beaker depositional and ceremonial practices seem to continue aspects of Grooved Ware-associated Late Neolithic traditions. Both Grooved Ware and Beaker ceramics occur in very similar contexts; mainly found in pit clusters filled with occupational debris or in spreads, and both deposited (albeit to a much lesser extent in the case of Beakers) as part of more formal ceremonial activities at timber circles (see Carlin 2017; Carlin and Cooney 2017). The similarities in their deposition are particularly obvious at timber circles, where Beaker pottery seems to have fulfilled the role of Grooved Ware, even at sites like Paulstown, where no Grooved Ware had been deposited. These Beaker deposits seem to represent a continuation of the Late Neolithic practice of emphasising and referencing the concept of the homeplace through the commemorative deposition of occupational debris (Carlin and Brück 2012; Carlin and Cooney 2017). This is especially evident when we consider the selective deposition of these materials within timber circles, which appear to have been formalised representations of people's homes (Bradley 2005, 53-6; Thomas 2007; 2010). The ceremonial deposition of collective occupational waste within the structural features of these communal wooden circles, long after their original construction, suggests that people were drawing upon the symbols of everyday 'domestic' life to emphasise a shared group identity. The ideological symbolism of these structures must have remained relevant for local communities after Beaker pottery replaced Grooved Ware.

Beaker deposition at these and other sites displayed a deep respect for later Neolithic traditions and seems to have been maintained to such an extent that non-ceramic novelties from the Beaker package, such as arrowheads, were deliberately excluded from deposition within the postholes of the timber circles. Significantly, these objects were included in the Beaker deposits placed over timber circles at Newgrange and Knowth, which again highlights that the above-surface deposits were somewhat different in character. The strongly referential aspect of Beaker-associated activity at Late Neolithic timber circles is well illustrated by the way in which the Beaker deposition at Armalughey focused almost exclusively on the large central arrangement of four post-pits representing the oldest and most enduring architectural elements of that monument (Carlin 2016). These Beaker deposits represent a very deliberate attempt to maintain a link back to the earlier use-life of this monument.

This concern for and awareness of the past histories and meanings of particular areas and monuments is also evident in the activities of people who used Beaker pottery at pre-existing ceremonial locales with a long history of ceremonial activity and monument complexes, as at Grange, Monknewtown and other sites at *Brú na*

Bóinne like Newgrange and Knowth. Not only do we see continuity of place, but we also see that the practices associated with these were also maintained. This is particularly obvious in the way that Beaker pottery was deposited (often in association with or in deposits overlying Grooved Ware) outside the entrances to passage tombs at Newgrange and Knowth. This depositional activity not only referenced the past activities that were conducted there but also maintained a longstanding practice of emphasising, enclosing and encircling the exterior of the passage tomb which had begun when these monuments were first built (Carlin 2017). Again, this highlights how the ceremonial practices associated with the use of Grooved Ware were continued after it was replaced by Beakers.

Despite the compelling evidence for the continuation of Late Neolithic depositional practices in tandem with the use of Beaker pottery, these two ceramics are rarely found in contextual association and there is almost no evidence to indicate much of an overlap in their use (see Chapter Eight). It seems that Beaker pottery rapidly replaced Grooved Ware and took on many of the roles previously associated with this Late Neolithic ceramic. In this regard, the adoption of Beaker materials in Ireland was strongly influenced by pre-existing Late Neolithic traditions, which we will explore further in Chapter Ten. Despite the introduction of a suite of novel aspects of material culture, a strong concern with the past in terms of places, people and practices is clearly visible. It may even be the case that new ceremonial monuments (apart from wedge tombs), or centres, were not developed in the Irish Final Neolithic because there was such interest in ancestral traditions and places at this time, although this is not to deny that change happened.

7

Transformational acts in transitional spaces

7.1 Introduction

Many of the apparently 'personal' non-ceramic ornaments and objects such as copper daggers, stone wrist-bracers and gold ornaments, found in graves alongside Beaker pottery in various parts of Europe, have also been discovered in Ireland. Although commonly viewed as a means of accentuating the individual, especially in the funerary realm, remarkably few of these have been found with burials on this island. As we have already seen, the same is true of Beaker pottery, which was mainly deposited in a very circumscribed fashion within a range of ceremonial and settlement contexts. In complete contrast, however, the classic aceramic Beaker-related objects have largely been recovered from places that are often referred to as 'natural', such as bogs, mountains, caves and rivers. In Ireland, 12 copper daggers, ten gold discs and 26 lunulae, at least four wrist-bracers and 38 V-perforated buttons have been found in so-called 'natural places'; bogs in at least 18 instances, in rivers in seven, dryland 'natural places' in 13, as well as in three caves and one lake. Significantly, the depositional treatment of these objects is very similar to that of copper axes and halberds c. 2450-2150 BC, or at least those that were not recycled.

While previous studies of these objects have been conducted (*e.g.* Harbison 1969a; 1976; Taylor 1980; Becker 2013), the implications of their depositional treatment for understanding Beaker practices and the Beaker complex have not been addressed in Ireland or beyond (see Chapter One). Although the deposition of some Beaker-related objects in these kinds of places have been considered as part of wider studies of metalwork deposition in northern European countries like the Netherlands and Scotland (*e.g.* Fontijn 2002; Cowie 1988; 2004), this has received very little attention in Beaker studies due to the extent to which these have focused on funerary contexts. Further research at a European level on this topic is required. This chapter examines the character of the deposition of these artefacts in 'natural places' in Ireland to better understand the nature of this activity, the reasons behind it and their implications for the wider Beaker complex. For this purpose, the range, quantity and manner of deposition of these artefacts, in each of these types of places, are examined and contrasted so that non-random patterning reflecting recurrent choices representative of social practices can be identified (Fontijn 2002; Pollard 2002).

We have already seen that people in the Chalcolithic or subsequently in the Bronze Age did not view their world in terms of strict dichotomies between ritual and domestic activities or between people and objects (Brück 1999a). The same is true of people and places and so, it seems equally unlikely that they maintained clear distinctions between nature and culture in the same way that modern western populations do, not least as the very concept of 'nature' is itself a cultural construct (see Bradley 2000a, 34-6; Insoll 2007). Furthermore, so-called 'natural places' in Ireland were clearly altered by the depositional activities that were conducted within them. In the case of boglands, we also see evidence for past human activities such as trackway construction (Raftery 1996, 71; Stanley 2003; O'Sullivan, A. 2007). So, while these places may not have been transformed quite as dramatically or in the same ways as other places, they were just as much a part of the culturally constructed social landscape (Brück 2011). Nevertheless, the fact that people chose to deposit specific objects almost exclusively in particular settings like bogs rather than in settlements, with burials or at ceremonial enclosures, suggests that these were regarded as a distinct and significantly meaningful set of spatial contexts. This is something we will consider further after examining deposition within these 'natural places' in more detail.

Traditional understandings of deposition in 'natural' contexts have also been criticised for reading the past in excessively utilitarian or economic terms (Fontijn 2002). Recent studies of deposition have moved beyond the simplistic idea that deposits from all wet contexts were permanent, and therefore, represent ritual activity, while objects from dry places were retrievable and so can be seen as purely functional (O'Flaherty 1995, 37; Needham 2001, 287-8). There is increasing recognition that not all wetland deposits were intended to be totally irretrievable (Becker 2013). In particular, bogs characteristically comprise a unique mixture of both wet and dry conditions and so any objects deposited at the edges of drier areas would have been readily retrievable (Yates and Bradley 2010), particularly to those who were familiar with the local terrain. Rivers and lakes seem to represent the most secure and enduring contexts in the archaeological record from which objects could not be recovered (Needham 2001, 287-8), although even this would have depended upon a range of factors such as how deep the various parts of any lake or how fast-flowing a particular part of a specific river may have been.

'Natural places' are not timeless and are liable to both natural (including animal) and human alterations, so the contexts in which objects have been found could be different from those in which they were originally deposited. For example, finds from wet, marshy or boggy contexts might have been placed in dry ground that subsequently became waterlogged or alternatively placed in lakes or pools that then became peat filled (Bradley 1990, 5). Conversely, finds from apparently dryland contexts might have been deposited in a wet environment that was later converted to dry land through drainage works (see Yates and Bradley 2010). Future research is required on this, including detailed palaeoenvironmental investigations of findspots to fully mitigate these issues and ensure a proper understanding of the original depositional context of each object (ibid.). Nevertheless, general patterning of the kind sought here can still be observed. Indeed, as we will see, the strong patterning present within the record in terms of the types of places in which certain kinds of artefacts occur suggests that the context of discovery for most objects in this study was very similar to their original context of deposition.

7.2 Beaker-related objects in bogs, rivers and lakes

The deposition of particular objects in a circumscribed manner within bogs seems to have been a feature of social practices in Ireland during the Chalcolithic. For example, 50% of all 400 contexted copper flat axes in Ireland have been recovered from bogs and similarly, more halberds have come from this context than any other (after O'Flaherty 1995; Becker 2006). Objects including copper tanged daggers, wrist-bracers, beads and gold ornaments that commonly occur with Beaker pottery elsewhere in Europe have been found in bogs, but evidence for the pottery itself is entirely absent from these places. This might reflect a choice on the part of the depositors or the survival rate of pottery within the highly acidic peatlands. This is discussed below.

Intact wooden versions of Beaker pottery have, however, been recovered from bogs in the form of polypod bowls. Six of these have been found during turf-cutting, including an example from Tirkernaghan, Co. Tyrone, that has been radiocarbon dated to 2870-2147 BC (OxA-3013; 3960±100 BP; Earwood 1991/2). At least four stone wrist-bracers have been recovered from bogs. These represent almost half of all nine examples for which contextual details are known, despite over 100 having been found in Ireland (see Chapter Nine). Two of these wrist-bracers were isolated single finds at Ironpool, Co. Galway (Costello 1944), and at Carrowkeel Mountain, Co. Sligo (Watts 1960, 115; Harbison 1976, 24), while the other two occurred together in a hoard at Corran bog, Co. Armagh, alongside two gold discs and several jet beads (Wilde 1857, 89; Case 1977b, 21). Other 'personal ornaments' such as V-perforated buttons also occur in bogs, both singly and in caches that may represent the deposition of necklaces. A single button was found in Lurgan bog, near Dromore, Co. Down (Munro 1902; Harbison 1976, 34). A cache of ten bone buttons was discovered 'on a flagstone pavement' in a bog/boghole at Skeagh, Co. Cavan, and another 14 stone examples were found in a bog at Drumeague, Co. Cavan (Harbison 1976, 15).

In addition to the pair of gold discs from the Corran hoard, another pair of these discs was found together with a lunula in a bog at Coggalbeg, Co. Roscommon (Kelly and Cahill 2010), which means that a minimum of four (40%) of the ten discs known from 'natural places' have been discovered in this context (Fig. 7.1). Another 13 lunulae have been found in bogs, both singly (six examples) and in a further three hoards, meaning that this also represents the main context in which lunulae occur (see Chapter Nine). For example, a lunula was found "under twenty feet of peat" near Enniskillen, Co. Fermanagh (Frazer 1897, 65), and a hoard of three folded lunulae was recovered from Banemore bog, Co. Kerry (Cahill 1983, 78-80). At least six of the

12 copper daggers from 'natural places' have been found in bogs, including five single finds from Blacklands Bog, Co. Tyrone (Harbison 1978, 333-5), Kilnagarnagh, Co. Offaly, Clontymore, Co. Fermanagh (Harbison 1969a, 7), Derrynamanagh, Co. Galway (Rynne 1972, 240-43) and Listack, Co. Donegal (Harbison 1969a, 8), as well as an example from the Knocknagur hoard. This hoard at Knocknagur, Co. Galway, comprised a copper tanged dagger, three copper Lough Ravel type thick-butted axes and three copper double pointed awls (Harbison 1969a, 10, 19). The association between the copper dagger and the copper axes is highly significant here because although over half of the contexted copper flat axes from Ireland have been found in bogs (after Becker 2006), this is the only known example of them occurring with a dagger in this context. The evidence from this and other hoards (see below), however, suggests that these objects may have been more connected in their use than is implied by the archaeological record.

Numerous hollow-based and barbed and tanged arrowheads have been recovered as stray finds in peaty contexts, suggesting that deposition of archery equipment in bogs was a distinct social practice at this time. For example, barbed and tanged arrowheads were discovered in bogs at Sorne, Co Donegal (Beatty and Collins 1955, 117), Leitra, Co. Offaly, Tobertynan, Co. Meath (Lucas 1966, 8), Tankardsgarden, Co. Kildare, Gortrea, Co. Galway (Green 1980, 410-12), and Ballykilleen bog,

Fig. 7.1: The gold lunula and discs found together within Coggalbeg bog, Co. Roscommon (photograph reproduced with the permission of the National Museum of Ireland ©).

TRANSFORMATIONAL ACTS IN TRANSITIONAL SPACES | 155

Co. Offaly (Wilde 1861). Hollow-based arrowheads were discovered from deep within the blanket bog on Divis Mountain, Co. Antrim (Collins 1957), in boglands at Botera Upper, Co. Tyrone (Collins 1959), and another was found with a portion of its shaft at Kanestown bog, Co. Antrim (Knowles 1885, 126-8). However, to establish the total numbers of each arrowhead type found in this context and the details of their deposition, requires further research beyond the scope of this study.

By comparison with bogs, very few classic Beaker items have been recovered from rivers or lakes. Five decorated gold bands, which have been considered to represent basket-shaped ornaments, were discovered in a stream-bed that formed a tributary of the River Erne at Belville, Co. Cavan (Cahill 2005a, 267; Needham 2011; Needham and Sheridan 2014). Four of the 12 known copper daggers were recovered from three rivers: River Shannon at Jamestown, Co. Leitrim and Shannonbridge, Co. Offaly; the Sillees River, at Ross, Co. Tyrone and the River Skene, near Dunshaughlin, Co. Meath (Case 1966; Harbison 1969, 18; Sheridan and Northover 1993), while two early stone battleaxes were found in the River Shannon (Simpson 1990). This pattern is consistent with the low proportion of contemporary metalwork, such as copper axes, found in rivers and lakes (Becker 2006), particularly the earlier Lough Ravel type, of which less than 10% were found in these contexts (Schmidt 1978, 319-20).

7.3 Beaker-related objects in dryland 'natural places'

Unlike wetland 'natural' contexts, Beaker pottery has been found in dryland 'natural places', all three of which are cave/rock shelter sites; Oonaglour Cave and Brother's Cave, both in County Waterford (Dowd 2004, 164; 2015, 125-31), and a natural rock-shelter at Caherguillamore, Co. Limerick (Hunt 1967). At Oonaglour Cave, four sherds from two Beaker vessels were recovered from disturbed strata within the cave (Dowd 2015; 131). At Brother's Cave, a sherd from a domestic Beaker vessel was found within a chronologically mixed deposit along with Early Bronze Age materials including human teeth (ibid., 129). At Caherguillamore, a deep deposit contained a mix of artefacts from different periods including sherds from two 'domestic' Beakers, as well as two Middle Neolithic vessels, a probable Late Bronze Age pot, the unburnt remains of 13 individuals and eight disc beads. It is not currently possible to discern any secure associations between the Beaker pottery and the burials or the beads. At least one of the skeletons, a crouched inhumation in a pit containing a Globular bowl, dates to the Middle Neolithic, but the other individuals remain undated. Some sherds from one of the two Beakers were also found with a convex scraper on a shelf in the cliff above the burials.

It was not just wetland natural locations that were regarded as suitable places to receive deposits of particular types of non-ceramic objects. People also seem to have chosen to place certain Beaker-type artefacts in topographically distinctive natural dryland contexts, albeit to a lesser extent than in wet places. Just 13 V-perforated buttons have been discovered in two apparently dryland natural locations, both of which were mountainsides. As mentioned in Section 5.4, a single stone specimen was discovered near the possible passage tomb known as *Miosgán Meadhbha* at Knocknarea, Co. Sligo (Harbison 1976, 35), while a cache of 12 stone buttons were found at Ballyboley Mountain, Co. Antrim (Wood-Martin 1895, 534). No further contextual details are available for the latter finds and it remains possible that they were deposited within blanket bog and not within a dry context at all. Three wrist-bracers have dryland findspots, yet these were all discovered as unstratified objects within topsoil, making it impossible to detect whether these originally had different depositional contexts that were subsequently disturbed by ploughing or other agricultural activities. The same problem affects stone arrowheads, of which there are many from unstratified dryland contexts.

At least 11 (42%) of the 26 lunulae deposited in 'natural places' have been found on dryland. Six of these occurred in two hoards; a group of four was recovered from a spread of gravel at Dunfierth, Co. Kildare (Eogan, G. 1994, 34), and another two were found together under a boulder at Rathroeen, Co Mayo (Taylor 1970, 70; Cahill 2005b, 57). Six lunulae were discovered as single finds; one came from a quarry, another three came from present day agricultural land and two examples were found on mountains (Becker 2006). The latter were found at Trillick, Co. Tyrone, and at Trenta, Co. Donegal; both of these, and another example from a field at Carrickmore, Co. Tyrone, were also found under boulders (Frazer 1897). At least six sun-discs have also been recovered from natural dryland contexts, all of which were found in pairs on present-day agricultural land at Cloyne, Co. Cork (Cahill 2005a, 329), Kilmuckridge, Co. Wexford (Cahill 1994), and Tedavnet, Co. Monaghan (Eogan, G. 1994). At least two (16%) of the 12 copper daggers from 'natural places' have been recovered from a dryland context. Both were found within a rock crevice at Whitespots, Co. Down, in a hoard that also included a copper thick-butted axe (Case 1966, 162; Harbison 1969a, 7, 18).

Again, the lower numbers of objects of different types occurring in non-watery 'natural' contexts fits with the general patterning evident in the deposition of Chalcolithic metalwork, particularly objects such as copper axes, only a small proportion of which was deposited in dryland settings (Becker 2006; 2013). Most of these were

	Beaker vessels	Wooden polypod bowls	Wrist-bracers	V-perforated buttons	Arrowheads	Copper daggers	Gold discs	Gold head Ornaments.	Lunulae
Bogs	0	6	4	25	yes	6	4	0	14
Rivers	0	0	0	0	0	4	0	5	0
Dryland	0	0	0	13	0	2	6	0	11
Lakes	0	0	0	0	0	0	0	0	1
Caves	4	0	0	0	0	0	0	0	0

Table 7.1: The quantity of different types of objects from various 'natural' contexts.

deposited as hoards, like that at Whitespots, rather than single finds. It may be the case that some of the objects in dryland places were deposited with the intention of retrieving them, but there is no reason to assume that this was more likely than would be the case in certain wetland settings such as bogs (see Becker 2013). This is a point to which we will return below.

7.4 Identifying depositional patterns and practices

So far, we have seen that the deposition of Beaker-related objects in 'natural' places was a feature of the Irish Chalcolithic. There are hints that these deposits reflect a selective set of practices that followed particular rules, in other words, deliberate and organised. For example, apart from three caves, Beaker pottery has not been found in any other 'natural' locations including bogs, rivers and lakes. While this may be partially a reflection of issues relating to taphonomy and modes of discovery, this scenario does seem to reflect a deliberate choice. The survival of Middle Neolithic pots in bogs at Bracklin, Co. Westmeath and Lisalea, Co. Monaghan suggests that prehistoric ceramics can survive in bogs (Ó Ríordáin, B. 1961; Herity 1974). While being aware that absence of evidence is not evidence of absence, it is hard to resist reaching the conclusion that during the Chalcolithic, wooden vessels were deposited in bogs, but ceramic ones were not.

Similarly, the latter locations, which can be considered as wet places, received a far greater quantity and range of objects than dryland places (Table 7.1). Gold discs, however, appear to represent a notable exception to this broader trend, as a greater number (60% of ten examples) occur in dryland 'natural places', although this interpretation is tentative as there are nine uncontexted examples, at least some of which were probably found during bog-cutting during the nineteenth or early twentieth century (see Chapter Nine).

Most of the deposition of Beaker-related objects in watery places occurred in bogs which received deposits of almost every kind of Beaker object except Beaker pottery and gold head ornaments (see Section 9.9). Compared to the other 'natural places', a far greater number of buttons, daggers and lunulae have been recovered from bogs and in the case of wrist-bracers, these represent the only known 'natural' setting where these have been found (see Table 7.1). Indeed, bogs represent the context in which most copper daggers, buttons and lunulae have been found in Ireland (see Chapter Nine). The same is true of copper halberds and axes, which were deposited in bogs in far greater quantities than any of the aforementioned objects.

Only a small number or range of objects, comprising four copper tanged and riveted daggers, two early stone battleaxes and five gold head ornaments have been recovered from rivers. An even more limited assemblage is represented by finds from lakes and caves (see above; Table 7.1). Significantly, only a small proportion of copper axes and halberds have been found in rivers (Becker 2013) and the deposition of daggers within this context only began to be practiced in Ireland as the use of Beaker pottery was waning. No early-style (Knocknagur) copper tanged daggers have been found in rivers at all. Apart from the Whitespots hoard, where the tanged dagger occurred with another slightly later (Type Listack), tanged and riveted example, bogs represent the only known contexts in which simple tanged blades occurred (see Chapter Nine). An increased emphasis on river deposition occurs in the Early Bronze Age, c. 2100 BC (Needham 1988, 230. 241; Becker 2006, 85; 2013), and the Listack daggers may well fit into that trend. Indeed, very large numbers of bronze objects dating from this period until the end of the Bronze Age have been retrieved from rivers as well as bogs (see Becker 2013, 9-12). This suggests that the much lesser quantity and range of Copper Age objects found in rivers compared to bogs directly reflects prehistoric reality, rather than resulting from any kind of recovery bias. This indicates that bogs must have been preferentially selected for the deposition of these objects.

Further patterning is evident in the way that some objects such as wooden polypods, stone wrist-bracers and copper tanged daggers were predominantly deposited singly, while others like V-perforated buttons and gold discs were mainly deposited within hoards. Significantly the hoards of buttons, discs, daggers and lunulae are predominantly one object-type only hoards (Table 7.2). The four hoards containing a mixture of items, such as those from Coggalbeg

	Wooden polypod bowls		Wrist-bracers			V-perforated buttons			Copper daggers			Gold discs			Gold head Ornaments.			Lunulae		
	S	H	S	H	N	S	H	N	S	H	N	S	H	N	S	H	N	S	H	N
Bogs	6	0	4	2	1	1	24	2	5	1	1	0	4	2	0	0	0	6	8	4
Rivers	0	0	0	0	0	0	0	0	4	0	0	0	0	0	0	5	1	0	0	0
Dryland	0	0	0	0	0	1	12	1	0	2	1	0	6	3	0	0	0	5	6	2
Lakes	0	0	0	0	0	0	0	0	0	0	0	0	0	0	0	0	0	1	0	0
Caves	0	0	0	0	0	0	0	0	0	0	0	0	0	0	0	0	0	0	0	0
TOTALS	6	0	4	2	1	2	36	3	9	3	2	0	10	5	0	5	1	12	14	6

Table 7.2: The numbers of different Beaker objects found in various natural contexts, as well as the quantities of these found as single finds, within hoards and the number of hoards from each context. KEY: S=number of single finds, H= number of objects in hoards, N=number of hoard.

bog or Corran bog, are exceptional rarities. In tandem with the single finds, this indicates that it was important to keep these various kinds of objects apart from one another during deposition by maintaining a contextual separation between them. Again, the high proportions of object types deposited singly matches with the depositional treatment of most copper axes, halberds and daggers, the vast majority of which have each been found as single finds (Becker 2013). Similarly, when these copper objects are found in hoards, these generally occur in axe-only or halberd-only hoards (O'Flaherty 1995; Becker 2006; 2013).

Clearly, the deposition of Beaker-related objects in 'natural places' followed particular rules. There were characteristic ways of depositing these artefacts, which were type-, context- and place-specific, thereby resulting in recurrent patterns of association. Significantly, the patterning present in the deposition of these objects is mirrored in the treatment of other contemporary copper metalwork. The consistency of this patterning indicates that these deposits represent the residue of a coherent set of highly structured depositional practices that were widely followed across much of Ireland. That is not to deny the clear evidence for regionality in depositional and other practices that is indicated by variations in the distributions of specific object types in particular areas of the country. This is explored in Chapter Nine.

7.5 Beaker-related objects in 'natural places' in Europe?

Like Ireland, large copper objects like axes and halberds were not placed with burials in most other European regions (Bradley 1990, 64-5; Vandkilde 1996; Needham 2016), but there is only limited evidence for the deposition of classic Beaker-associated objects in 'natural places' across Europe. In France, a few copper daggers have been discovered in rivers (Briard and Roussot-Larroque 2002) and a hoard comprising a palmella point and copper axes was discovered in the River Loire at Trentemoult (Harrison 1980, 112). Palmella points are the only Beaker object that are frequently recovered as single finds from 'natural places' (Laure Salanova, pers. comm.) and these are often found in caves, but as with other Beaker-related objects, have mainly been found in a mortuary setting. In the Netherlands, most early copper and bronze artefacts were deliberately deposited in rivers and swamps and only a small proportion occur in the few known Dutch 'rich graves' (Fontijn 2002; Butler and Fokkens 2005, 384). While this is an under-represented area in Beaker studies, it can be said that the placement of items of adornment does not appear to be have been a sustained social practice in continental Europe.

Flint daggers were items of exchange that form part of the Beaker complex and occur in graves with Beaker pottery in the Netherlands, Denmark Sweden and Britain (Butler and Fokkens 2005, 386; Sarauw 2008; Frieman 2014). Some of these have also been found in hoards, in both dry and wet 'natural places', including bogs near to the flint quarry from which they had been sourced in Denmark (Sarauw 2008). Also in Denmark, early Beaker gold sheet ornaments, such as lunulae, and copper flat axes were predominantly deposited in dry 'natural places', though some of the gold items have been found in bogs (Vandkilde 2005, 25-7). The deposition of early metalwork in hoards in 'natural places' is well known in Scotland, particularly in the north-east; but this was almost exclusively associated with axes and halberds (Henshall 1968; Cowie 1988, 13-19; Needham 2004, 234-9). In this region, however, the Midgale hoard, which was found in a dryland location within a weathered joint of rock on a hill, represents an exceptionally rare discovery of items of ornamental dress that are usually only found in a funerary context in Britain (Cowie 1988, 19; 2004, 251). This hoard contained ornaments such as jet V-perforated buttons, a bronze basket-shaped ornament and bronze tubular beads. As we will see further below, this resonates strongly with some of the depositional practices that we see in Ireland and provides a striking parallel to the similarly exceptional hoard from Corran bog in County Armagh. Indeed, given the strong links between Ireland and north-eastern Scotland at this time, the Migdale hoard could be seen as an adaptation of Irish practices. Apart from this, there is little evidence from elsewhere to match the highly structured ways in which a very wide range and high quantity of 'personal ornaments' were placed in bogs. This very much seems to have been an indigenous practice that was strongly influenced by past traditions of depositing supra-regional objects in 'natural places'. This is a point to which we will return to in Chapter Ten.

7.6 Understanding deposition in boglands in Ireland

When compared to other European regions, where many of these objects occur together with Beaker pottery and burials, the patterning identified in depositional practices in Ireland can be very be frustrating to study or explain. However, the highly structured ways in which these objects were deposited in 'natural places', particularly bogs, were strategically selective. Indeed, the recurrent character of this suggests that these depositional acts may have occurred during highly formal ceremonial activities. All of this means that these depositional treatments are the product of the meaningful choices made by people as part of a wider practical strategy for dealing with the world around them (see Needham 1988; 2007, 279; Brück 1999a; Fontijn 2002). Therefore, these reflect the ideological values of the time, as well as the values that were ascribed to these various object types (based on a range of factors including their style, type and biography) and to the types of places where they were being deposited. Whatever these values were, they seem to have largely prevented the deposition of Beaker-related objects in a wide range of other contexts, including with burials.

This leads us back to reconsider the character of the type of place where so many of these objects were deposited. We know that landscapes are culturally constructed through a complex web of symbiotic interactions between humans, animals, things and the physical environment. As part of this, the recurrent conduct of particular practices in specific places often results in these locales becoming dynamically imbued with various meanings (Knapp and Ashmore 1999; Fontijn 2007, 71). This means that the depositional practices outlined here that were conducted almost exclusively in bogs would have had a place-making effect, whereby these acts created, reproduced or transformed the special meanings that were attached to these places, as well as the objects themselves. The range and quantity of Beaker-related objects from bogs, many of which are rarely found in any other context, suggests that bogs were socially defined as uniquely suitable locales for these kinds of objects to be deposited. This is supported by the varying ways depositional practices were completed in a consistently rule-bound manner. That boglands were regarded as a special category of place is further indicated by the fact that at this time they were not altered in quite the same way as other drier parts of the landscape (O'Sullivan, A. 2007, 170). For example, Beaker-associated ceramics, settlements, megaliths or ceremonial monuments are almost totally absent from boggier areas such as the central lowlands of the island (see Chapter Nine). Evidence for funerary activity in these wetlands is also absent and no Chalcolithic bog burials are known yet from Ireland (Ó Floinn 1988; 1995).

This is not to deny that boglands may also have been engaged with routinely for everyday purposes (see Stanley 2003; O'Sullivan, A. 2007; Becker 2008). A closer study than is possible here, of the landscape context of Beaker deposits in bogs, including paleoecological analysis of their original receiving environment is required to gain a better understanding of how bogs were being used at this time. However, apart from the deposition of aceramic objects the main archaeological evidence for contemporary activity in bogs relates to the construction of Chalcolithic brushwood pathways, platforms and trackways such as the well-known example at Corlea 6, Co. Longford, which displayed metal axe marks (O'Sullivan, A. 1996, 307-313). These 'accessways' were physical links that connected people to these places (Raftery 1996, 71-7). The majority of these did not cross bogs, but rather were short tracks that led into the bog (McDermott 1998, 7; Stanley 2003, 65; O'Sullivan, A. 2007; 175).

Although, bogs were spaces for everyday activities, paradoxically they could also have been regarded as a kind of sacred symbolic place within the social landscape of the Irish Chalcolithic, one that existed at the edges of the more obviously and intensely humanly modified environment (Bradley 2000a; Fontijn 2002, 265; 2007, 76; Stanley 2003, 65; O'Sullivan, A. 2007; 184). It has been convincingly argued that supernatural properties may have been attributed to 'natural' features, especially those occurring at the edges of the more familiar landscapes, such as hilltops, rivers and bogs (see Bradley 2000a). Within the more tree-covered landscape of Chalcolithic Ireland, these open expanses of bogland would have formed spatially discrete liminal places that formed a threshold between drier and wetter places. As such, they may have been seen as otherworldly places that provided appropriate contexts for human interactions with the gods and ancestors and seem to have served both as barriers and/or openings between people and the underworld (Larsson 2001; Fontijn 2002, 265; Brück 2011). In this regard, it seems more fitting to understand 'natural places', especially bogs as sacred or supernatural places.

Becker (2008; 2013) has argued that bogs may have been chosen for deposition precisely because of the ways in which they facilitated the recovery of items. The very small amount of Beaker-related objects or other contemporary copper metalwork deposited in irretrievable contexts, like rivers or lakes, might be taken to support this view. As Becker highlights, some gold artefacts including discs, basket-shaped ornaments and lunulae show evidence for having been rolled and unrolled (see Fig. 9.13; Cahill 2005b). Lunulae such as those from Carrickmore, Co. Tyrone, may still have been rolled up when found (ibid.). It has been suggested that these objects had a long use-life and may have been repeatedly rolled and unrolled each time they were hidden and retrieved (Cahill 2005b; Becker 2008; see Chapter Nine). It is also plausible, however, that the use-wear on these objects was entirely pre-depositional and that once deposited, these were not retrieved.

Eamon P. Kelly (2006, 30) has argued that objects used during Iron Age kingly inauguration ceremonies were deposited at the physical boundaries forming the edges of tribal lands, both as a demonstration of the king's sovereignty and as gifts to the gods to ensure the future well-being of the people. He suggests that these boundaries changed little since the Neolithic and that the deposition of objects like lunulae in the same locations as Iron Age deposits indicates similar kinds of activity was being conducted in the third millennium BC (ibid.). Of course, Kelly's hypothesis is concerned with elites and their land ownership, which we do not have evidence for in the Chalcolithic and it remains unclear whether the physical features which served as Chalcolithic depositional locales were considered social boundaries c. 2400 BC. It must also be highlighted that few Beaker-related objects have been found in rivers compared to bogs, even though these would have represented both boundaries and routeways. Nevertheless, some insights are to be gained from this analogy with later Iron Age practices in sacred places, which may help to answer the question of why these objects were deposited in bogs, just like copper axes, rather than in graves as was the case in other parts of Europe. This idea that specific kinds of Iron Age objects, which had been used during a very particular set of ceremonies relating to the transformation of identity, were subsequently deposited in bogs as gifts to the gods seems to have much relevance. Interestingly, the deposited Beaker-related objects seem to refer to a sphere beyond the everyday (see Chapter Nine), many were made of specific materials such as Yorkshire jet or porcellanite from Antrim that referred to other people, places and values (Fontijn 2002, 218, 229; Fokkens 2012b). The strict and repetitive ways in which these were deposited in so many graves across Europe suggest that these objects symbolized what must have been widely shared cosmological values and beliefs (Fokkens 2012b, 123). This is echoed by their treatment in bogs in Ireland.

Many of the Beaker-related objects found in bogs in Ireland, but in burials elsewhere, represent a highly selective range of objects that transformed a person's physical appearance (see Fokkens 2012b, 120). David Fontijn (2002, 218) has suggested that the supra-regional styled body ornaments in these burials transformed the identity of the deceased by dressing them in internationality. If so, it may be the case that like in the Iron Age, these Beaker-related objects were also deposited in bogs during ceremonies associated with the transformation of identities. The particular values and ideas associated with them may even have necessitated that they be removed (either permanently or temporarily) in this manner. As supernatural places, bogs may well have represented very apt locales for this kind of identity transformation and for the deposition of the objects associated with it. These are issues that we will return to and consider in more detail in Chapters Nine and Ten, to address the issue of why this particular set of objects were deposited in very structured and deliberate ways within bogs.

8

A time for Beakers?

8.1 Introduction

To better understand the Beaker complex on this island, it is necessary to refine the chronology of the various Beaker-associated developments that occurred. This is also required to locate when such things happened in Ireland in relation to their wider European chronological context. There is a consensus that Beaker pottery was first made in Ireland c. 2450 BC and continued to be used until c. 2000 BC (Case 1995a; 2004a; Brindley, A.L. 2004, 334-5; 2007, 301). Yet there has been no concerted attempt to refine the chronology of the Beaker phenomenon in Ireland. This is in stark contrast to elsewhere, such as Britain, where extensive programmes of radiocarbon dating have been conducted, as well as the analysis of these dates and their associations (*e.g.* Kinnes *et al.* 1991; Needham 2005; Bayliss, McAvoy *et al.* 2007; Parker Pearson *et al.* 2007; 2016; Sheridan 2007a; Barclay and Marshall 2011). This is at least partially because the Irish manifestation of the Beaker phenomenon is less amenable to accurate radiocarbon dating than other parts of Europe where complete Beaker vessels regularly occur in closed short-life settings such as graves; contexts that are suitable for highly accurate radiocarbon dating.

By comparison, Beaker pottery generally occurs in Ireland as sherds in non-grave assemblages within pits or spreads containing materials derived from an accumulation of occupational debris. Many of these contexts do not represent secure well-defined short-life contexts (see Chapters Three and Seven). The taphonomy of the dateable materials found in these features is also seldom clear-cut and it is often impossible to conclusively demonstrate that the contents of these pits and spreads were freshly generated. Thus, it is difficult to achieve certainty regarding the strength of association between the datable materials and the pottery, even though they have been found together. Similarly, Beaker pottery has been found with burials in wedge tombs, where the degree of association between artefacts and human remains is highly equivocal because these represent open structures that were subject to extensive periods of re-use (see Chapter Five).

Rather than despairing at this situation, it is possible to use an evaluative approach to present an evidence-based interpretation of the chronology of the Beaker phenomenon in Ireland. This means primarily focusing on establishing a more precise understanding of the dating of the Irish version of the Beaker complex and examining the dating and duration of the various depositional practices that have been discussed in the other chapters. Beyond proposing date ranges for broadly earlier and later forms, the dating of specific types of Beaker pottery is not discussed here because that would also require a detailed examination of form and decoration, which is beyond the limits of this study.

8.2 Methodology and date selection criteria

A total of 78 radiocarbon determinations were collated from materials that were contextually associated with Beaker pottery. All radiocarbon determinations were calculated using the calibration curve of Reimer *et al.* (2004) and the computer program OxCal (v4.1.7) (Bronk Ramsey 1995; 1998; 2001; 2009). The calibrated date ranges cited in the text are presented at two sigma (95% confidence levels). Dates associated with other Beaker-related objects are not included here because few reliable examples of these exist. In recognition of potential problems with the dataset, it was necessary to assess each determination in terms of the quality of the dated sample and strength of association between the sample and the pottery (Waterbolk 1971; Brindley, A.L. 2007, 23).

Sample quality was determined to be 'excellent' if the dated material had a short own-life (*e.g.* hazelnut shells, cereals, bone or short-lived charcoal such as hazel, alder, willow, pomoideae); was a single-entity sample that

Selection	Quality	Materials	Contexts
High: 25 dates from 20 sites	short own-life, single-entity, samples reasonable strength of association	short-life charcoal; human bone; animal bone; hazelnut shells; carbonised residue from inside of Beaker	pits x 16; wedge tombs x 5; surface deposits x 2; burnt mound x 1; posthole x 1
Medium: 36 dates from 20 sites	Either the strength of association or the own-age of these samples is open to doubt	animal bone; human bone; mostly charcoal	pits x 14; wedge tombs x 8; spreads x 7; postholes x 2; burnt mound x 1; cist x 1; stakehole x 1

Table 8.1: Details of the assessment of 'High quality' and 'Medium quality' radiocarbon determinations in terms of sample quality and strength of association.

Name	Lab	Feature	Sample	Degree of association	Year BP	±	Cal BC
Faughart 6	Beta 217947	pit	hazel charcoal	reasonable	4070	50	2860-2470
Faughart 6	Beta 217946	pit	hazel charcoal	reasonable	4030	50	2850-2460
Dunboyne 3	Beta-241273	pit	ash charcoal	reasonable	3960	40	2570-2340
Curraheen 1	Beta-171422	pit	alder charcoal	reasonable	3920	70	2580-2200
Ballycuddy More 1	Beta-244831	pit	alder charcoal	reasonable	3910	40	2480-2290
Mell	WK-17459	spread	ash charcoal	reasonable	3906	33	2470-2290
Rathmullan 9	SUERC-31910	pit	hazel charcoal	reasonable	3905	30	2470-2290
Lismullin	SUERC-23489	pit	hazel charcoal	reasonable	3905	30	2470-2290
Rathmullan 12	SUERC-31907	pit	pig bone	reasonable	3890	30	2470-2280
Gortybrigane 1	UBA-11745	pit	hazelnut shells	reasonable	3858	26	2461-2209
Rathmullan 12	SUERC-31908	pit	vertebrate	reasonable	3855	35	2470-2200
Rathmullan 10	SUERC-31920	spread	pig limb	reasonable	3850	30	2460-2200
Laughanstown 35	OxA 12811	posthole	hazel charcoal	reasonable	3847	35	2460-2200
Danesfort 8	UBA – 11001	pit	nut	reasonable	3846	27	2457-2205
Rathmullan 2	SUERC-31897	pit	oak charcoal	reasonable	3840	30	2460-2200
Largantea	UB-6974	wedge chamber	cremation	reasonable	3837	35	2459-2200
Largantea	UB-6976	wedge chamber	cremation	reasonable	3828	37	2458-2147
Paulstown	UBA 15435	pit	hazel charcoal	reasonable	3821	26	2430-2147
Labbacallee wedge tomb	GrN-11359	wedge chamber	inhumation	reasonable	3805	45	2458-2062
Lismullin	SUERC-23551	pit	hazel charcoal	reasonable	3805	30	2350-2130
Cherrywood Area B	GrA-23011	burnt mound	animal tooth	reasonable	3800	40	2400-2100
Labbacallee	OxA-2759	wedge chamber	inhumation	reasonable	3780	70	2459-2031
Kilmainham 1C	UBA-14139	pit	carbonised residue	unequivocal	3766	28	2287-2051
Newtownbalregan 2	WK-18558	pit	alder charcoal	reasonable	3649	49	2190-1890
Ballybriest	GrA-13273	wedge chamber	cremation	unequivocal	3630	50	2139-1830

Table: 8.2 Details of high quality dates.

had been determined since the mid-1980s; displayed a standard deviation less than ±100 and was not noticeably contaminated (see Ashmore 1999; Sheridan 2007a, 93-4; McSparron 2008).

Determining the strength of association between the dated sample and Beaker pottery was less clear-cut and few samples were deemed to be indisputably closely associated. This reflects the fact that most of the radiocarbon dates in this study come from materials within pits. Their contents represent the closest approximation to short-term closed Beaker deposits in Ireland because most pits were dug and then immediately filled. This is complicated, however, by the fact that most of the artefacts within these deposits were derived from another context (see Chapter Four). As a result, the degree of association between the dated material and the pottery from pits is open to interpretation. Assessing this requires an appraisal of the mechanisms by which the sample and the object came to be in the same context. Where there was a reasonably good chance that the pottery and the dated material were genuinely contemporary, these were deemed to be 'reasonable'. For example, if the dated sample and the

Name	Lab	Feature	Sample	Life-span	Degree of association	Year BP	±	Cal BC
Broomfield	GrN-13879	pit	oak charcoal	unknown	reasonable	3880	30	2460-2310
Paulstown	UBA 15430	posthole of timber circle	burnt bone	short	reasonable	4017	28	2617-2471
Coldwinters	GrA-32116	pit	cremated bone	short	reasonable	4005	35	2620-2465
Largantea wedge tomb	UB-7024	chamber -primary layer	oak charcoal	unknown	insecure	3877	34	2468-2211
Kilmainham 1A	UB12101	spread	hazel charcoal	short	insecure	3989	25	2571-2468
Paulstown	UBA 15437	posthole of timber circle	ash charcoal	short	reasonable	3989	27	2573-2467
Haggardstown Site 13	UBA-9853	pit	hazel charcoal	short	insecure	3974	45	2618-2310
Rathdown	Beta 202304	pit	alder charcoal	unknown	reasonable	3870	40	2470-2210
Curraheen 1	Beta-171422	pit	alder charcoal	unknown	reasonable	3920	70	2580-2200
Caherabbey Upper	UB-7237	pit	oak charcoal	unknown	reasonable	3642	38	2135-1914
Newgrange	GU-1622	spread	charcoal	unknown	insecure	3905	70	2585-2140
Lisnasallagh 2	Beta-201077	pit	oak charcoal	unknown	reasonable	3890	60	2490-2190
Newgrange	GrN-6342	pit	charcoal	unknown	reasonable	3885	35	2471-2213
Ross Island	GrN 19628	spread	charcoal	unknown	insecure	3875	45	2470-2206
Largantea wedge tomb	UB-6977	chamber -primary layer	cremation	short	insecure	3871	37	2467-2209
Ross Island	GrN 19624	spread	charcoal	unknown	insecure	3845	40	2467-2147
Ross Island	GrN 19627	spread	charcoal	unknown	insecure	3820	35	2457-2142
Graigueshoneen	Beta 170161	stakehole	charcoal	unknown	reasonable	4110	40	2860-2490
Barnagore 2	Beta-171410	pit	oak charcoal	unknown	reasonable	3840	70	2480-2050
Gortore	UB-6768	pit	charcoal	unknown	reasonable	3832	36	2458-2152
Lough Gur wedge tomb	OxA-3274	chamber	inhumation	short	insecure	3830	80	2481-2126
Newgrange	GrN-12828	pit	charcoal	unknown	insecure	4000	30	2577-2468
Graigueshoneen	Beta 170160	pit	charcoal	unknown	reasonable	3860	40	2460-2200
Lough Gur wedge tomb	OxA-3270	chamber	inhumation	short	insecure	3780	70	2459-2031
Ross Island	GrA 7512	spread	cow	short	insecure	3760	50	2345-2025
Armalughey	SUERC-20768	post pit of timber circle	charcoal	unknown	reasonable	3750	30	2290-2030
Lough Gur wedge tomb	OxA-3272	chamber	inhumation	short	insecure	3720	70	2341-1921
Lough Gur wedge tomb	OxA-3267	chamber	inhumation	short	insecure	3710	70	2333-1901
Ross Island	GrA-7523	slot trench	cow	short	insecure	3690	50	2271-1937
Ahanaglogh	Beta 170159	burnt mound	charcoal	unknown	reasonable	3790	40	2300-2040
Labbacallee wedge tomb	OxA-2760	chamber	inhumation	short	unequivocal	3630	70	2201-1775
Ballybriest wedge tomb	GrA-13254	antechamber	cremation	short	insecure	3580	50	2114-1769
Nugentstown 3	UB 12068	pit	alder charcoal	short	insecure	3517	23	1915-1759
Cappydonnell	UBA 10189	cist	cremation	short	insecure?	3589	30	2029-1887

Table 8.3: Details of medium quality dates.

Beaker pottery were found in the same fill of an undisturbed pit and if no obviously earlier or later materials were also found in that pit, then it can be assumed that it represents a short-term deposit of broadly contemporary materials with a reasonable strength of association. Samples displaying an insufficiently close association with the pottery were considered 'insecure'.

After each radiocarbon determination had been assessed in terms of sample quality and strength of association, the dates were then qualitatively grouped into two categories in accordance with their compliance with the various selection criteria; 'Highest quality' and 'Medium quality' (Table 8.1). Dates that failed to meet the criteria because of poor sample quality or an insufficiently secure association with the pottery were excluded. The 'Medium quality' dates meet many of the same standards as the 'Highest quality' dates; however, there are doubts about either the strength of association or the own-age of these samples. Dates belonging to both the 'Highest quality' or 'Medium quality' categories exceed the minimum criteria required for these to be considered as reliable radiocarbon determinations (Tables 8.2-8.3).

The existence of several plateaux in the relevant parts of the calibration curve around 4000 BP and 3700 BP means that calibrated radiocarbon dates from the latter half of the third millennium BC display falsely long ranges of probability and tend to bunch together, thereby making it difficult to accurately date archaeological events or detect short-term chronological changes (see Müller and van Willigen 2004, fig 2; Bayliss, Bronk Ramsey *et al*. 2007, 5). To lessen the impact of this imprecision, a Bayesian statistical approach is employed here in the analysis of both the 'Highest quality' or 'Medium quality' sets of Beaker-associated radiocarbon dates (see Bayliss, Bronk Ramsey *et al*. 2007, 8-9). Bayesian analysis takes account of the statistical scatter caused by the error margins inherent in radiocarbon dates in a rigorous manner that utilises an explicit statistical methodology (ibid.). It is used here to model the 'Highest quality' dates and also a combination of all the 'Highest quality' and 'Medium quality' dates. Combining these together provides a larger dataset for modelling, the results of which can be compared with those from the smaller but higher quality category.

Bayesian analysis in this study operates on the assumption that all the radiocarbon determinations in each dataset randomly reflects the complete distribution of dates from a single coherent phase of activity in Irish prehistory, whose exact chronological sequence is unknown. Using the 'phase' tool in OxCal (v4.1.7), the mathematical distribution of these dates is analysed in relation to the calibration curve to constrain their probability ranges and provide estimates of the span of activity represented by the dates within the model (Bronk Ramsey 1995; 1998; 2001; 2009). Other tools like 'span' and 'duration' are used to query how long a phase of activity may have lasted and when it began. These date estimates are referred to in italics to distinguish them from unmodelled calibrated radiocarbon dates.

The application of Bayesian statistical analysis does have some potential pitfalls because the results are influenced by the subjective assumptions that are made about sets of dates, especially those relating to the uncertainties represented by the start and end of a given phenomenon (Sheridan 2007a, 96-8; 2008a, 62). Such postulations can be problematic because of the many known and unknown archaeological uncertainties about the development, duration and distribution of any cultural trend, including whether these were uniform across the entire study area. Therefore, it is important to state that the results of this analysis are only interpretative estimates, which are based upon what we currently know and upon the assumption that the selected samples are representative. As such, these estimates are liable to change as more dates are obtained and added to the model (see Bayliss, Bronk Ramsey *et al*. 2007, 9). Notwithstanding this note of caution, it can be assumed that the date ranges from the modelling of either datasets are indeed representative of the duration of use of Beaker pottery in Ireland. Although the quantities of dates selected for inclusion in either category are not high, they each come from features that are genuinely representative of the wider body of evidence for Beaker pottery deposition.

8.3 The dating of the Irish Beaker phenomenon

The Bayesian model of the 'Highest quality' dataset estimates that the deposition of Beaker pottery in Ireland began sometime between *2604-2473 BC* (*95% probability*) and ceased between *2196-2022 BC* (*95% probability*) (Figs. 8.1-8.4). Very similar start and end dates of *2595-2496 BC* and *2183-2047 BC* (*95% probability*) are also estimated for the model of both the 'Highest quality' and 'Medium quality' dates together (Fig. 8.2). Use of the 'First' and 'Last' tools in OxCal for the 'Highest quality' dataset estimates that the very earliest and latest of these dates for the use of Beaker pottery falls within the ranges *2580-2468 BC* and *2204-2052 BC* (*95% probability*).

The start and end dates predicted by Bayesian modelling for the currency of Beaker pottery in Ireland is strongly corroborated by the archaeological evidence (Figs. 8.3-8.4). The earliest high-quality Beaker-associated dates in Ireland are represented by radiocarbon determinations from Faughart Lower 6 (2850-2460 BC: Beta-217946; 4030±50 BP and 2860-2470 BC: Beta-217947; 4070±50 BP); Dunboyne 3 (2570-2340 BC: Beta-241273; 3960±40 BP); Mell (2470-2290 BC: WK-17457; 3906±33 BP); and Curraheen 1

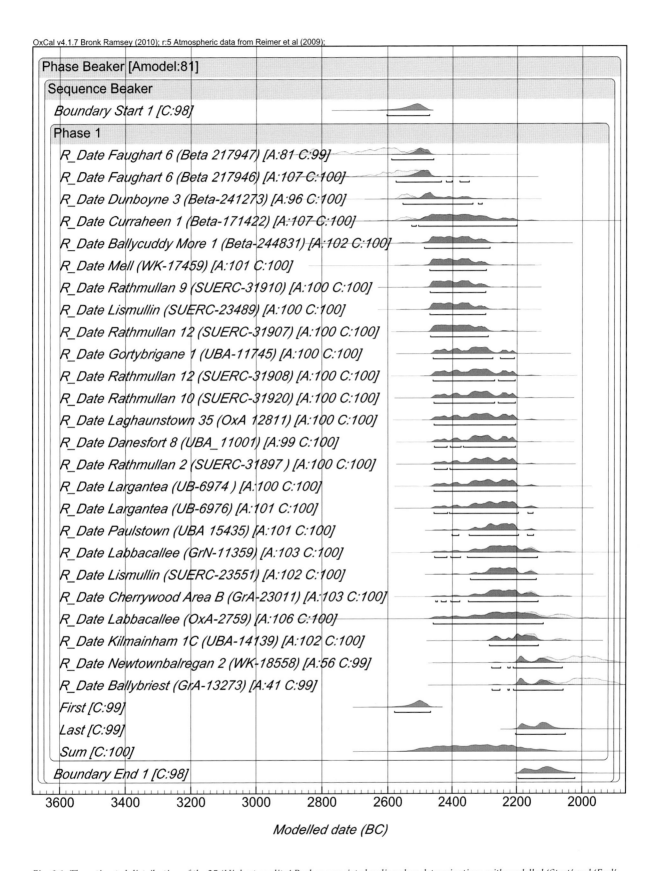

Fig. 8.1: The estimated distribution of the 25 'Highest quality' Beaker-associated radiocarbon determinations with modelled 'Start' and 'End' dates. These have been treated as a single broad phase of activity whose chronological sequence is unknown.

A TIME FOR BEAKERS? | 165

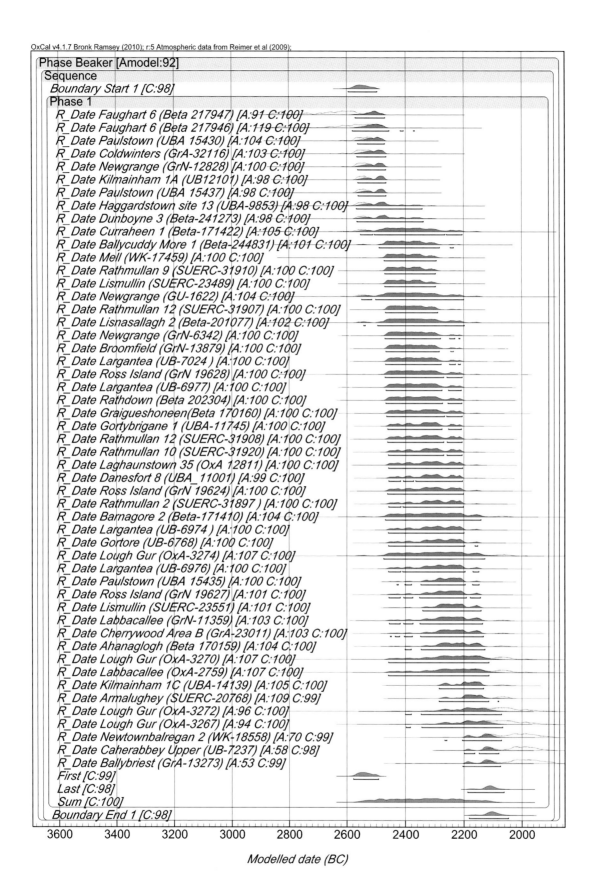

Fig. 8.2: Modelled distribution of all 61 'Highest quality' and 'Medium quality' dates treated as a broad phase of activity.

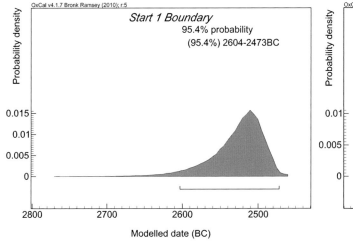
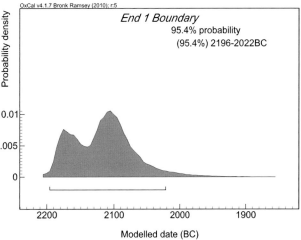

Fig. 8.3: Modelled 'Start' date for the earliest appearance of Beaker pottery in Ireland based upon the 25 'Highest quality' Beaker-associated radiocarbon determinations.

Fig. 8.4: Modelled 'End' date for Beaker pottery in Ireland based upon the 25 'Highest quality' Beaker-associated radiocarbon determinations.

(2580-2200 BC: Beta-171422; 3920±70 BP). Each of these was contextually associated with sherds from continental-style Beakers that were decorated with All-Over-Ornament or All-Over-Cord. These form part of a small group of vessels that display the earliest stylistic elements known to occur on Beaker pottery in Ireland and are thought to represent the first components of this tradition to appear on this island (see Section 3.1; Case 1993, 248; Brindley, A.L. 2004, 334; Grogan and Roche 2010, 36). On the continent, this style of All-Over-Ornament pottery is considered to have been in use c. 2450 BC (Brindley, A.L. 2007, 300) and these form part of a limited group of Beakers appearing in Britain at an early date during the twenty-fifth century BC (Clarke 1970; Lanting and Van der Waals 1972; Needham 2005, 179; Sheridan 2007a, 96, 99). This certainly accords with the results of the Bayesian analysis, which suggests that these pots were being deposited in Ireland by *2473 BC*.

The youngest 'Highest quality' or 'Medium quality' Beaker-associated radiocarbon dates in Ireland are almost certainly represented by the determinations from Ballybriest (2139-1830 BC: GrA-13273; 3630±50 BP) and Caherabbey Upper (2135-1914 BC: UB-7237; 3642±38 BP). Bayesian analysis reported that these determinations had a poor level of agreement (*e.g.* below 60%) with the rest of the modelled Beaker dates (Figs. 8.1-8.2). This suggests that these two determinations represent statistical outliers and should not be modelled as belonging to the same phase as all the other Beaker-associated dates. Both dates, however, were contextually associated with stylistically later Beakers, Case's Style 3/Group B2 (see Section 3.1; Hurl 2001; McQuade *et al.* 2009; Grogan and Roche 2010, 33), which is currently considered to

date from 2000-1950 BC in Ireland (Case 1995a, 23, 2004c; 375; Brindley, A.L. 2004, 334; 2007, 250, 300). In Britain, ceramics of this type have been variously categorised as Northern and Southern Beakers (Clarke 1970), Group B Beakers (Case 1995a; 2004a) as well as Long-Necked, Short-Necked and Weak-Carinated Beakers (Needham 2005), which have been shown to post-date 2250 BC (ibid., 188, 191, 195; Sheridan 2007a, 99; Wilkin 2009; Curtis and Wilkin 2012; Neil Wilkin, pers. comm.). Thus, the earlier part of the Ballybriest and Caherabbey Upper date ranges are exactly what one would expect them to be and seem to represent the very tail end of the Beaker phenomenon in Ireland (see below). There is very little evidence for the deposition of Beaker pottery after 2000 BC in Ireland and only a comparatively small quantity of late-style Beakers has been found here. This strongly corroborates the Bayesian modelled estimate that the deposition of Beakers in Ireland had ceased by the latter half of the twenty-first century BC. By implication, this suggests that late-style Beakers were probably only in use in Ireland for a short duration between 2200 and 2050 BC, indicating that they appeared and disappeared earlier in an Irish context than previously thought.

Utilising the query 'Sum' in OxCal provides summed probability ranges that produce an estimate for the frequency distribution of dated events in a given phase (see Bayliss, Bronk Ramsey *et al.* 2007, 11). A visual examination of these simple summed probability distributions for both the Irish Beaker datasets suggests that Beakers appeared in Ireland quite suddenly c. 2450 BC and gradually began to wane from c. 2200 BC until they disappeared c. 2050 BC (Figs. 8.5-8.6). Most of the dates (19 out of 29 from the 'Highest quality' dataset)

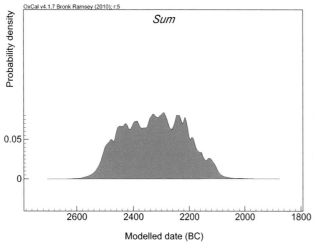

Fig. 8.5: Summed probability distribution for all 25 'Highest quality' Beaker-associated radiocarbon determinations which seems to indicate a relatively sudden appearance of Beakers.

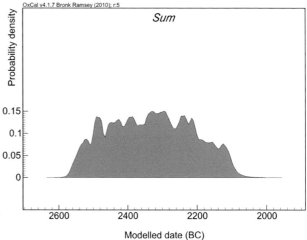

Fig. 8.6: Summed probability distribution of all 61 'Highest quality' and 'Medium quality' dates.

fall between 2450-2200 BC and it is clear that this period represents the main floruit of Beaker pottery in Ireland. This is entirely consistent with the fact that only a small number of continental-styled or late-styled Beakers have been found on this island (see Section 3.1). The majority of Irish Beaker pottery displays a typical Bell Beaker S-shaped profile, but with simple formal horizontally arranged zonal ornamentation (see below and above; also see Case 1993, 248; Brindley, A.L. 2004, 334; Grogan and Roche 2010, 36). Pottery of this kind can be classified as belonging to Clarke's (1970) European Bell Beaker, or his Wessex/Middle Rhine types; Stages 2 and 3 in Lanting and van der Waals (1972) scheme for the development of British Beakers (Brindley, A.L. 2004, 334); and Case's (1993; 1995a) Style 2, which are considered to date from c. 2450-2200 BC. These hybrid styles appear to have been produced across Ireland from a very early stage (Case 1993, 265; 1995a, 14, 23; Brindley, A.L. 2004; Grogan and Roche 2010).

Indeed, such was the scale of the early adoption of Beakers across Ireland, that it seems to have rapidly and completely replaced Grooved Ware by c. 2450 BC (Carlin and Brück 2012; Carlin and Cooney 2017). This suggests that the Irish production of Grooved Ware ceased much earlier than is claimed to be the case for southern Britain (Garwood 1999; Needham 2005). There is, however, strong evidence for continuity of practices over the course of the Later Neolithic–Chalcolithic transition in Ireland, with Beakers fulfilling many of the roles previously occupied by Grooved Ware (see Carlin and Brück 2012; Carlin and Cooney 2017). For example, Late Neolithic practices such as the deposition of pottery in pits or in the postholes of abandoned timber circles were sustained,

but with Beakers being used instead of Grooved Ware (see Chapters Six and Ten). While there are many similarities in the types of contexts in which these two ceramics were deposited, Grooved Ware and Beaker pottery have only occurred on the same site on 16 occasions (representing 16% of all Grooved Ware and 8% of all Beaker sites in Ireland) and Beaker has only been found in direct contextual association on three of these. Overall, there seems to be very little archaeological evidence for a sustained overlap in the duration of these two traditions. This argues in favour of the rapid adoption of Beakers in Ireland suggested by the Bayesian analysis.

Utilising the query 'Span' in OxCal on the 'Highest quality' datasets provides an estimate of 282-492 years for the span of activity associated with the deposition of Beaker pottery in Ireland (Fig. 8.7). This corresponds broadly with A.L. Brindley's (2007, 328, 250) suggestion that Beaker pottery was current for approximately 300 years before Bowls of the Food Vessel tradition began to be made c. 2160 BC (see Chapter Five). As stated above, the summed probability distributions indicate that the main currency of Beaker pottery in Ireland occurred from 2450-2200 BC and that the use of this ceramic steadily declined from 2200 until it disappeared completely c. 2050 BC. This is certainly borne out by the strong indications for a short overlap between the creation of Irish Food Vessels and a small number of late-style Beakers, which post-date the typical form of this pottery in Ireland (see Chapter Five). For example, Beakers and Food Vessels have been found together on at least 30 sites and there is evidence that they were used together or in very rapid succession. This is particularly so for Bowls, which have been found in close association with Beakers in the chambers of

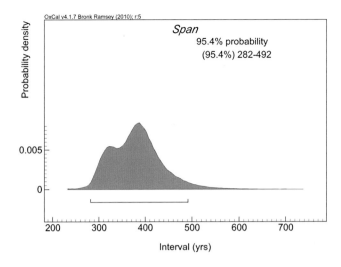

Fig. 8.7: Modelled use-span of Beaker pottery in Ireland based on the 25 'Highest quality' Beaker-associated radiocarbon determinations.

ly, the Bayesian modelling conducted here indicates that by 2000 BC at the very latest, Beaker pottery ceased to exist as a recognisable entity that was distinct from Food Vessels, the insular ceramic that completely replaced it in funerary, settlement and ceremonial contexts. The overall currency for Irish Beaker pottery therefore spans c. 2470-2050 BC.

It is not currently possible to identify regional differences in the dating of the Beaker phenomenon across Ireland. There simply are not enough suitable dates from all the various places where Beakers have been found across the country to accurately consider such fine-grained issues in an unbiased way. All that we can currently say is that there are equally early dates occurring in the south, east, north and west of the island. Although Beaker-associated copper mining was firmly established at Ross Island in the south-west by 2400 BC (Lanting 2004, 312-4), there is nothing to suggest that this ceramic was being used any earlier there than elsewhere in Ireland.

some wedge tombs, suggesting that only a small amount of time elapsed between the sequential deposition of these different ceramics (see Chapter Five). In some of these tombs, such as Aughrim, Co. Cavan (Channing 1993), these two ceramics have been found together in association with human bone in primary contexts, sealed beneath layers associated with the secondary re-use of the tombs (Brindley, A.L. 2007, 51).

The typo-chronological evidence also suggests that Beakers continued to be used for a short duration after the advent of Bowls, but had ceased to be made by the time that Vases of the Food Vessel tradition appeared in Ireland c. 2150-2020 BC (see Brindley, A.L. 2007). Beaker pottery seems to have influenced both ceramics, however, as indicated by the overlap in design traits shared between Beakers and Food Vessels, such as the inturned necks of Bowls, the extended necks of Vases, broad zonal geometric patterns, especially filled chevrons, lozenges, cross-hatching and dense fingernail impressions (Case 2004a, 375; Gibson, A. 2007). Indeed, A.L. Brindley (2007, 251) observes that the use of cross-hatching as a decorative fill on both late Beakers and late Irish Bowls indicates that Beaker pottery was still being made once in a while between 2000 and 1900 BC, but this may simply have been a motif that endured beyond the decline of Beakers. Alternatively, the translation of these Beaker motifs onto Food Vessels may have originally occurred in parts of northern Britain, where Beakers remained current for longer than in Ireland. For example, in a Scottish context there is much evidence for hybridisation between Beakers and Food Vessels around the end of the third millennium BC and for some time afterwards (Sheridan 2007a, 99; Wilkin 2014). Ultimate-

8.4 Dating depositional practices

It is difficult to determine the chronology of various Beaker-associated depositional practices in Ireland. This is due to the small number of suitable radiocarbon dates from each of the various contexts and the nature of the Beaker-associated depositional record, particularly the lack of secure well-defined short-life contexts containing datable materials that were genuinely associated with Beaker artefacts. For example, most of the Beaker finds from earlier Neolithic megaliths have been discovered in contexts where it is rarely possible to identify reliable associations between dateable materials and particular finds (see Chapters Two and Five). Many of the same problems affect the dating of Beaker deposits in cists, most of which were discovered during older excavations and are exceptionally poorly dated (see Section 5.6). Furthermore, except for Beaker pottery, most stereotypical Beaker-related objects were deposited in 'natural places' such as bogs, without any associated dateable materials (see Chapter Seven). The dating of this practice is therefore entirely dependent upon typological comparisons with similar objects from dated contexts in Britain or elsewhere. While these typological approaches inform our understanding of the date range of object-types, they are less suitable for refining our understanding of the duration of Beaker-associated deposition in 'natural places'. Despite all these problems, it is still possible to make some broadscale observations about the dating and duration of the various Beaker-associated depositional practices that formed part of the Irish Beaker phenomenon.

Most of the radiocarbon determinations in this study come from pit contexts, including the earliest and some of the latest dates associated with Beaker pottery in Ireland (see Tables 8.2-8.3). They also contain various earlier and later styles of Beaker, albeit in smaller quantities. Based on this, it seems that Beaker-pit deposition seems to have been practiced from the very start of the Beaker phenomenon in Ireland, c. 2470 BC, and to have continued until c. 2050 BC. However, most of the radiocarbon determinations seem to pre-date 2200 BC, thereby suggesting that this practice was at its peak between the years 2450 and 2200 BC, after which the deposition of Beakers in pits began to wane. This is supported by the very small amount of stylistically later Beaker pottery dating from 2200 to 2050 BC from pit contexts.

Only six radiocarbon determinations from Beaker-associated surface deposits meet the minimum standards necessary for inclusion in this analysis, all of which pre-date 2200 BC. Due the small size of this dataset and the formation processes associated with surface deposits such as spreads and middens, which generally contain derived materials that were aggregated at various different stages and contain assemblages of unknown time-spans (see Section 8.2), it is imprudent to attempt to propose a fine-grained start or end-date for this practice. Most of the Beaker pottery recovered from secure chronological contexts within spreads and middens is, however, of the stylistically earlier variety including some continental-type and Irish-style vessels (see above; Section 3.1). This suggests that the practice of collecting occupational debris in surface deposits may have been *en vogue* from as early as the twenty-fifth century. The paucity of late-style Beakers from these features suggests that this practice declined c. 2200 BC.

The results of Bayesian modelling by Schulting and colleagues (2008) estimated that the construction of wedge tombs began abruptly c. 2450 BC (see Section 5.2). The available radiocarbon dates from wedge tombs suggest that the deposition of Beaker pottery in association with human remains inside these megaliths began at this time and continued until c. 2050 BC (Table 5.4; Fig 5.9); Brindley and Lanting 1991/2, 25). This is supported by the presence of stylistically early Beakers dating broadly from c. 2450-2200 BC (*e.g.* Clarke's E and W/MR, Case's Group A) at Moytirra, Largantea and Cashelbane and later styles (*e.g.* Clarke's N and S groups; Case's Group B2) of Beaker pottery dating from 2200 and 2050 BC at Ballyedmonduff, Largantea, Loughash, Ballybriest and Carriglong (Table 5.6). While both Beaker-associated inhumations and cremations seem to have been deposited broadly contemporaneously, it was observed in Chapter Five that later forms of Beakers have only been found in tombs containing cremations. This suggests that while Beaker-associated cremations continued to be buried in wedge tombs until c. 2050 BC, the placement of unburnt burials with Beaker pottery in these monuments ceased c. 2150 BC, at which stage these began to be buried in small rectangular cist and pit graves and were accompanied by Irish Bowls, rather than Beakers.

Beaker pottery has only been found in definite association with a timber circle on two sites; Paulstown, Co. Kilkenny, and Armalughey, Co. Tyrone. In both cases, the Beakers were found in secondary contexts within the postholes of timber circles that had been constructed in the Late Neolithic (see Chapter Six). Just three radiocarbon determinations of suitable standard have been obtained from Beaker-associated deposits within these monuments. The two dates from Paulstown of 2617-2471 BC (UBA-15430; 4017±28 BP) and 2573-2467 BC (UBA-15437; 3989±27 BP) both suggest that Beaker materials were certainly placed in timber circles at an early stage in the development of the Beaker complex in Ireland. The date of 2290-2030 BC (SUERC-20768; 3750±30 BP) from Armalughey suggests that this form of deposition may have continued to be practised as late as 2200 BC. Against this, the absence of late-styled Beakers or Food Vessels from any of the likely timber circles in Ireland suggests that the deposition of Beakers in these monuments had certainly ceased by 2200 BC and was predominantly practiced in the twenty-fifth and twenty-fourth centuries BC. Very few firm conclusions can, however, be drawn from such a small dataset.

8.5 Comparing Ireland to Britain?

Due to the lack of intensive targeted dating programmes to address the chronology of the Irish version of the Beaker phenomenon, Irish archaeologists have relied heavily upon the results of such studies from Britain to estimate the date of developments in Ireland. The results of the analysis conducted here, however, indicates notable differences between the dating of the use of Beaker pottery in both places. In his widely accepted scheme, Stuart Needham (2005) proposed that the development of the Beaker phenomenon in Britain is best understood as a three-step process. The first stage lasted from 2500/2400-2250 BC during which time Grooved Ware was still in use but Beakers were quite uncommon and greatly resembled their continental counterparts. This was followed by a pinnacle phase (c. 2250-1950 BC), which Needham (2005, 171, 205) refers to as a 'fission horizon'. At this time, continental-style pots were adapted to create new regional forms of Beaker such as Wessex/Middle Rhine types, which became much more widely used throughout Britain. In conjunction with this transformation, the range of Beaker-associated artefacts also changed and Beaker burials became much more frequent and diverse. More recently, it has been argued based on analysis of newer radiocarbon dates, that this 'fission horizon' probably happened slightly earlier c. 2300 BC (Sheridan 2007a, 99; Barclay and Marshall 2011, 178;

Needham 2012, 5). Needham's last phase, dating from 1950-1750 BC, consisted of more radical changes to the form of Beaker pottery and its eventual decline in use.

There are several key differences between the Irish evidence and Needham's model. In Ireland, Grooved Ware pottery rapidly disappeared, and very soon after the first appearance of continental-style pots, by 2400 BC, insular hybrids such as Wessex/Middle Rhine Beakers were being deposited (see Case 1993, 265; Grogan and Roche 2010, 36). While it is difficult to provide hard evidence for this, it remains the case that very few early continental Beakers are known in Ireland. Where they have been found, almost all of them were in contextual association with insular-style Beakers. Some of the deposits containing both types have produced some of the earliest Beaker-associated radiocarbon dates on this island. For example, the early radiocarbon date of 2850-2460 BC from a pit deposit at Faughart Lower 6, Co. Louth, which contained sherds of AOC Beaker, as well as sherds from pots that are entirely typical of well-known Irish examples from Newgrange and Knowth, Co. Meath, and Lough Gur, Co. Limerick (Roche and Grogan 2006). Similarly, a pit deposit at Dunboyne 3, Co. Meath, which produced a radiocarbon date of 2570-2340 BC, contained sherds from an AOO Beaker and five other classically Irish-styled Beakers (Grogan and Roche 2007b: O Hara 2008). Notwithstanding the possibility that the assemblages in these pits are of unknown time-span, and that the strength of association between the various pot-types may be open to question (see above), it does seem that continental-style Beakers were rapidly replaced by other forms of Beaker pottery.

In Ireland, the floruit of Beaker pottery dates from c. 2450-2200 BC, whereas although some Beaker-associated burial activity clearly occurred in the twenty-fifth and twenty-fourth centuries in Britain, at places such as Boscombe Down, Wiltshire (Barclay and Marshall 2011; Parker Pearson *et al.* 2016), the quantities of burials with acceptable Beaker-associated radiocarbon determinations pre-dating 2300 BC in England or Scotland are quite small (Needham 2005; 2012; Sheridan 2007a; Fitzpatrick 2011, 195-6). Instead, the currency of Beakers in Britain reaches its pinnacle from 2300-2000 BC, shortly before Food Vessel usage began in Ireland. Irish Beakers went into decline during this time and the Irish Bowl was created to fulfil a very similar role in burial practices as some recently hybridised British Beakers (see Chapter Five). Ultimately, Beakers in Ireland completely disappeared c. 2000 BC, while they apparently continued to be produced until c. 1800 BC in parts of Britain. Notably, Beakers ceased to be placed with burials in Scotland by 2000 BC, suggesting that Beaker production may have ceased there around the same time as in Ireland (Parker Pearson *et al.* 2016).

While there are clear differences in the chronology of this phenomenon across Britain and Ireland, there is no unambiguous evidence that Beakers were adopted earlier in either Ireland or Britain. When comparing Beaker-associated radiocarbon dates from these islands, it is important to remember that these have predominantly been obtained from very different types of context and that this has strongly influenced the patterning present in the dates. British Beaker dates have almost exclusively been obtained from mortuary contexts, where very few occur before 2300 BC (Bayliss, McAvoy *et al.* 2007, 50). As an aside, in Britain it appears that this is part of a wider and longer trend of focusing on the data from mortuary settings; there has been a focus on obtaining radiocarbon dates from this context to the exclusion of any other, including settlements, resulting in a somewhat one-sided account. It remains possible that Beaker ceramics were used by at least a few generations in Britain before the adoption of the single inhumation rite (see Parker Pearson *et al.* 2007, 634-5). Although Needham (2012, 4) has argued that there is insufficient evidence to prove this, it remains entirely plausible that much greater evidence for Beaker-associated activity between 2500-2250 BC in Britain would be recognised if the radiocarbon dates from non-mortuary contexts such as pits and spreads were given more attention.

Perhaps the key finding to emerge from the chronological analysis conducted here is the very real and immediate need to undertake a detailed programme of targeted radiocarbon dating and Bayesian modelling for the Irish Chalcolithic. As we have seen, our current timelines operate in 250-500 year time-blocks, which prevents the recognition of gradual stepwise social transformations or persistent patterns of behaviour (Bayliss, Bronk Ramsey *et al.* 2007; Whittle and Bayliss 2007). This gives the false impression that past cultural innovations suddenly appeared and spread outwards together in space and time as part of preconceived 'transition moments' (Shryock and Smail 2011). To fully address this in a manner that takes account of the relational nature of change, it is necessary for future chronological studies to operate across a wider range of burial, ceremonial and settlement contexts that integrate the temporality of objects, sites, social practices and traditions (Harding, J. 2005; Roberts *et al.* 2013). This will provide finer-grained chronologies that come much closer to the human experience of change.

9

Everything in its right place?

9.1 Introduction

Beaker-related objects were seen as socially significant objects that both possessed and created values, and played an important part in the social lives of people (see Chapter Four). So far, we have examined the deposition of a wide variety of objects including Beaker pottery, polypod bowls, V-perforated buttons, wrist-bracers, copper tanged daggers, gold lunulae, discs, bands and basket-shaped ornaments, as well as stone battle axes, all within the framework of the contextual category in which that object occurred; settlement (Chapters Three and Four), funerary and ceremonial settings (Chapters Five and Six) and 'natural places' (Chapter Seven). Here we move beyond the obvious constraints of that analysis by examining the depositional treatment and spatial distributions of each of these artefact-types across all contexts. This involves examining aspects such as the quantities of each artefact occurring as single finds or as part of hoards, in wet or dry places. The depositional treatment of the various objects is then explored in relation to one another to reveal the social practices that were involved. This integrative approach reveals additional information about the highly selective and codified deposition of each of these object types in Ireland, providing the basis for new insights into the meanings of these things and their social roles.

When discussing the quantities of objects found in a particular context, we must be careful not to project our modern western economic value systems into the past by assuming that a greater number of things equalled greater worth. For example, both a single button and a group of buttons may reflect a single depositional act, but while the discovery of multiple V-perforated buttons together represents the composite remains of a single item such as a jacket or cloak or a necklace, the deposition of a solitary V-perforated button may have been considered fully representative of a larger set of these items and their cultural biography. Thus, a greater or lesser number of objects from a particular context-type should not be interpreted as a definitive indication that it represents a preferred depositional zone or greater wealth. Accordingly, to avoid biased value judgements it is important to contrast the number of objects deposited in a context with the number of depositions of that object-type in that kind of context.

9.2 Beaker Pottery

Earlier chapters revealed that apart from a few caves, Beaker pottery is completely absent from supernatural places like bogs, even though many of the other items belonging to the Beaker repertoire were deposited in those places (see Chapter Seven). We saw that a much greater amount of Beaker deposition occurred in funerary contexts or megalithic tombs or timber circles than previously realised. However, only small amounts of this ceramic were deposited infrequently in these 'monumental places' compared to pits and spreads where the overwhelming majority of Beaker pottery occurs (Fig. 9.1). We have seen that features such as pits or spreads defy broad-scale categorisations because they display evidence for both ceremonial and occupational activity and that it is not possible

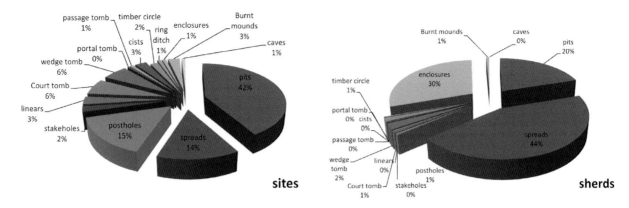

Fig. 9.1: The percentage of sites of different type to have produced Beaker pottery and the percentage of Beaker sherds found in each type.

to make clear-cut distinctions between social practices dating from the last half of the third millennium BC (see Chapters Three, Four, Five, Six and Seven). Considering this, it is appropriate to comparatively examine the deposition of Beakers in these features in relation to one another (even though this involves some revisitation of previous chapters).

We have seen that small amounts of Beaker pottery have been discovered in monuments such as wedge tombs and Late Neolithic timber circles and to a far lesser extent in contexts like cists, burnt mounds, caves and earlier Neolithic court or passage tombs. Though there are exceptional sites such as Cashelbane wedge tomb, where the remains of ten Beakers were recovered, the numbers of these sites and the quantities of Beaker pottery retrieved from them seems rather negligible compared to both pits and spreads, where large amounts of these ceramics were deposited (Fig. 9.1; Table 9.1). Indeed, the number of Beaker pits and sites that they occur on far outnumber all other Beaker-associated features. Undoubtedly, pits are the most common Beaker-associated feature excavated in Ireland indicating that this pottery was deposited in these features more often than any other (see Chapter Four). The quantity of Beakers (at least 4436 sherds from 472 vessels) recovered from pits dwarfs that discovered within most other context-types, but yet even this amount is relatively minor compared to that from spreads, despite only 39 having been excavated (see Chapter Four).

Clearly, the majority of Beaker pottery in Ireland was deposited above ground rather than below it and this almost certainly explains why Beakers are so commonly found in residual contexts. No evidence was found to uphold the highly dubious distinction between "settlement" and "ceremonial" surface deposits. Both represent related features that contain the same types of artefacts and were produced through a very similar set of actions (see Chapters Three, Four and Six). It was probably from these spreads or middens that smaller amounts of occupational debris were obtained for deposition within many other features. As we have seen, representational quantities of these curated materials were infrequently transferred to timber circles and court tombs, while pits represent the main context in which these materials were most often re-deposited in Ireland (see Chapters Three, Four, Five and Six).

While a large quantity of Beaker pottery has been found on multiple sites in Ireland, the range of objects discovered with this ceramic is quite restricted and predominantly consists of lithics. Beakers have been found in contextual association with 258 convex end scrapers on 30 different sites; 20 barbed and tanged or hollow-based arrowheads on 13 sites; eight polished stone axes on eight sites; nine polypod bowls on seven sites; two wrist-bracers from two different sites; a single necklace comprising 24 disc-beads; a gold disc; a lead rod which is thought to be of Chalcolithic date and a copper axe, as well as other items such as hammer-stones and large quantities of lithic debitage (which are not quantified here for reasons outlined in Chapter One). We can see that Beaker pottery is rarely discovered with other typical Beaker items such as wrist-bracers, and it has almost never been found with any others, such as gold ornaments, copper tanged daggers, or V-perforated buttons.

When we examine the contexts in which Beaker pottery occurs with any of these or other objects, patterning emerges that makes it clear the contextual isolation of these artefact types was deliberate. A restricted range of objects occur within pits and spreads, both of which predominantly received deposits of occupational debris comprising pot-sherds, lithics, debitage and a very small number of rare Beaker-associated items; convex end scrapers occur very frequently alongside Beakers, as do arrowheads and polypod bowls, but in much lower numbers (see Chapter Four). These are the only features in which the latter two object-types have been found with Beakers. Similarly, the only known occurrence of disc beads in direct association with Beakers was within a pit beside a timber circle at Paulstown. Spreads consist of very similar

Context	Number of sites	Number of features	Number of sherds	Number of vessels
Pits	91	177	4436	472
Spreads	30	39	9721	567
Postholes	34	19	132	31
Stakeholes	5	3	25	?
Linears	7	12	72	18
Court Tomb	14	14	103	19
Wedge tomb	13	13	509	51
Portal tomb	1	1	2	1
passage tomb	2	2	21	2
Cists	6	6	20	11
Timber circle	4	4	303	50
Ring ditch	2	2	62	8
Enclosures	2	2	6534	?
Burnt mounds	6	6	155	11
Caves	2	2	?	3

Table 9.1: The number of sites and features of different type to have produced Beaker pottery, as well as the numbers of sherds and vessels to occur in each of these types.

material to that found in pits, but they contain much larger quantities, as well as a wider range of artefacts, including rare examples of objects that are generally only found in 'natural places'. For example, the only known instances of a copper axe or gold discs occurring with Beaker pottery was within a spread at Lough Gur Site D (see Chapters Three and Four). Although an Early Bronze Age axe was also found in a surface deposit containing Beaker pottery at Newgrange. One of the only two wrist-bracers found with Beaker pottery in Ireland occurred in a spread at Rathmullan Site 10, Co. Meath. The discovery of these objects (albeit in small quantities) with Beakers in these contexts suggests that pits and spreads were suitable to occasionally receive such deposits and therefore, different from other types of contexts. This also highlights the diversity and complexity of depositional practices, whereby these kind of objects seem to have been deliberately selected and then placed among deposits of occupational debris in a very restricted range of settings.

Timber circles received comparable kinds of deposits to those often found in pits. This is consistent with the fact that pit-like depressions were dug into the remains of the rotting postholes that formed these wooden monuments and these holes were then backfilled with scoops of accumulated settlement debris comprising Beaker sherds, stone tools and debitage (see Chapter Six). However, other items that have been found in pits such as barbed and tanged arrowheads were completely excluded from deposition in timber circles.

Wedge tombs have produced far more Beaker pottery than any of the other classes of megalithic monument. This pottery seems to have been deposited as complete vessels, while most of the Beakers from other megaliths seem to have been deposited as sherds, except for the Beaker in the passage tomb at Knowth (see Section 5.4; Fig. 5.12). Indeed, it is within wedge tombs that the largest body of evidence for Beaker-associated burials have been found. The inclusion of complete vessels in these tombs was almost certainly related to ceremonies that were conducted exclusively within these monuments (see Chapters Five and Ten). Significantly, despite the discovery of many Beaker pots as well as several Beaker-associated burials in wedge tombs, only convex end scrapers, polished stone axes and barbed and tanged arrowheads were deposited in association with these burials. Thus, almost no stereotypical Beaker items other than arrowheads have been found within wedge tombs.

Within older megaliths, the deposition of Beaker material was just as circumscribed. For example, several V-perforated buttons have been found within passage tombs – one of only two human-made context-types that contained these ornaments – yet very few Beakers seem to have been placed within these megaliths. The paucity of Beaker pottery from passage tombs is more startling when one considers the very large quantities of Beaker sherds from the entrance areas of the tombs at both Knowth and Newgrange (see Chapters Three and Five). Very few objects have been found with Beaker pottery in court tombs, other than scrapers. This is also true of cists, caves, and burnt mounds, although, a wrist-bracer was found with this ceramic in the sub-megalithic cist at Longstone Furness (see below; Chapter Five). This confirms that, in most settings, Beaker ceramics were deliberately kept apart from most other Beaker-related objects; their depo-

Fig. 9.2: The distribution of polypod bowls in Ireland.

sition was highly codified like that of other Beaker-related objects including daggers and wrist-bracers. The quantity of pottery, the context in which it was deposited, the manner of its deposition (*e.g.* in sherds from spreads or as complete vessels) and the objects that it could be deposited with were all highly circumscribed. These sherds may have been perceived as relics or mementoes that were associated with the people who made and used them or with particular events (Brück 1999a, 319-21; 2006a, 303; Jones, A. 1999, 57; 2008, 331; 2012; Chapman 2000a; 2000b; Pollard 2001, 327; Woodward 2002, 1040-41). Either way, these ceramic fragments had acquired symbolic meanings over the course of their use-lives, which meant that they either required or were suitable for particular forms of depositional treatment (see Chapter Four). The social role of these sherds will be considered alongside other Beaker-related objects in Chapter Ten.

The aggregation of Beaker sherds and occupational detritus, in what appear to be the eroded remains of middens, seems to have fulfilled various practical, social and ceremonial functions. The almost-monumental nature of these deposits is indicative of a long-term attachment to place (see Brück 2006a, 299). These served as visible physical reminders of past events, activities and people, while also demarcating particular locations so that they endured as meaningful places. Regardless of whether the materials within each of these was generated during a small number of large-scale social gatherings and feasting or in the course of repeated smaller-scale everyday occupational activities, the accessible and visible nature of these deposits enabled ongoing engagement with the materials contained within them. This is indicated by the fact that debris seems to have been retrieved from these middens for deposition in other contexts such as pits, timber circles and megaliths (see Chapters Four, Five and Six).

The significance of these deposits is reinforced by the fact that a far greater range of artefacts, including metal axes, a gold disc and a wrist-bracer, occur with Beakers in these deposits than in any other context (see below). The gathering of occupational detritus into large piles formed an important role in social practices during the Chalcolithic. The aggregated materials may well have served as reminders of past events or activities. In doing so, they also functioned as physical metaphors for social relationships between people, places and things that facilitated the construction and reproduction of identities (see Chapter Four).

9.3 Polypod bowls

Polypod bowls are thought to have strong eastern European Bell Beaker and Corded Ware affinities (Case 2004a, 375). They occur mostly in central Europe, particularly in the Czech Republic and the Elbe-Saale region of Germany where they are found in both Corded Ware and Beaker assemblages (Harrison 1980, 26, 30, 39, 45; Piguet *et al.* 2007, 252-5). These also occur in smaller numbers as part of Beaker assemblages across much of Europe, in places such as Sicily, Sardinia; Italy; southern France, Austria, Hungary, Poland and the Netherlands in contexts primarily dating from 2500-2200 BC (Besse 2003; 2004; Piguet *et al.* 2007, 252-5, fig. 4). They most often have four or five feet and the bowls are often decorated. These occur quite frequently in central European funeral assemblages, where they seem to have been placed in graves instead of Beakers (Manby 1995, 83; Marc Vander Linden, pers. comm.).

In Ireland, the remains of at least 16 polypod bowls – ten ceramic and six wooden – have been discovered in 12 different locations. These have mainly been found in a restricted range of dryland human-made contexts consisting of spreads and pits, but also in wetland 'natural places' represented by bogs. Unsurprisingly, all ten ceramic versions have been retrieved from the former, while each wooden bowl has been found within bogs (see Chapter Seven). A wooden example from Tirkernaghan, Co. Tyrone, produced a radiocarbon date of 2870-2147 BC, suggesting that these are broadly contemporary with the ceramic forms (Earwood 1991/2). Both types exhibit a preference for four, five or six feet just like their continental counterparts, but the bowls of the Irish vessels are plain and undecorated. The wooden examples are slightly unusual in that only two other wooden polypod bowls have been found in Europe, both from a Corded Ware cemetery at Stedten in Germany (Clarke 1970, 90; Piguet *et al.* 2007, 253). This may, however, be more reflective of the material qualities of wood, which only survives in oxygen-free environments. Clarke (1970, 90) has argued that footed ceramic vessels may originally have been skeuomorphs of wooden bowls that occur in the Corded Ware complex. In an Irish context, Earwood has argued the opposite to be the case.

Polypod bowls were discovered across widely dispersed parts of the northern half of Ireland (Fig. 9.2). The ceramic examples, however, have only been found in the east of the country within areas where dense concentrations of Beaker sites and pottery are known. Ten of these bowls were discovered along the coastal fringe stretching from Dublin to Louth, with a very notable concentration of five bowls occurring at Newgrange, Rathmullan and Mell in the Boyne Valley. In contrast, the wooden bowls are predominantly known from the north-west counties of Roscommon, Fermanagh, Monaghan and Tyrone, where the wet or anaerobic conditions necessary for the survival of these wooden artefacts are common. Beakers have only rarely been found in these less well-drained areas, a fact that seems to be related to the non-deposition of this ceramic in bogs (see Section 7.2). Although two of the wooden polypod bowls have no recorded provenances, no footed bowls are currently known from the southernmost parts of the island, apart from a possible polypod from Longstone Cullen, Co. Tipperary (Grogan 1989; Case 1995a, 20), and a potentially related unfooted large decorated open bowl from Lough Gur Site D, Co. Limerick. The latter was recovered from a multi-period deposit, which included Beaker-associated habitation debris (see Chapter Three) and was included alongside polypod bowls by Clarke (1970, 89-92).

Most of the polypod bowls occurring in bogs were single finds and the only exception to this was the example from Tirkernaghan, which was found alongside two plain wooden bowls during peat cutting (Fig. 9.3; Earwood 1991/2). In contrast, most of those from pits and spreads occurred as multiple finds. The only ceramic polypod bowl to occur as a single find was discovered at Newtownbalregan 2, Co. Louth (see Chapter Four). This had been deposited intact in an upright position within a shallow pit beside a larger pit containing multiple Beakers. This is one of only two polypod bowls to have been discovered in pits. Sherds from a second example were found at Rathmullan Site 12, Co. Meath, within a large pit forming part of a pit cluster. The uppermost fill of that pit contained

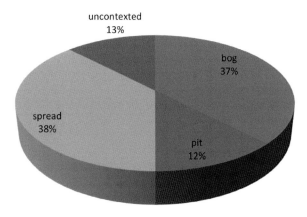

Fig. 9.3: The percentage of polypod bowls (n=16) found in each context type.

more than 500 sherds of Beaker pottery as well as a barbed and tanged arrowhead and burnt pig bone that produced a radiocarbon date of 2470-2280 BC (SUERC-31907; 3890±30 BP; Bolger 2011; Fintan Walsh, pers. comm.).

Six (of 16) polypod bowls have been found within four spreads at Newtownlittle, Co. Dublin, Newgrange, Mell and Rathmullan Site 10, Co. Meath (Fig. 9.3). It was predominantly within this type of context that we see these bowls occurring with other objects including occupational debris, predominantly consisting of fragmented Beakers and lithic debitage (see Chapter Four). The most well-known example comes from the so-called 'Beaker layers' outside the main passage tomb at Newgrange where the fragmentary remains of two polypod bowls occurred in a considerable concentration of pottery (Concentration No. 3) (Cleary, R. 1983, 74, fig. 25, group 15; O'Kelly *et al.* 1983, 24, 72-4). Other less monumental examples include Mell, where seven sherds, a foot and some smaller fragments of a polypod bowl came from a series of deposits that overlay one another. This spread also contained 354 sherds from a minimum of 26 Beakers, eight convex scrapers, a flint knife, a lead rod, fired clay pottery wasters, burnt bone and carbonised cereals (McQuade 2005). Similarly, at Newtownlittle the spread contained two rimsherds and two feet representing the remains of two polypod bowls, 350 sherds from at least 20 Beaker pots, including a Beaker dish and five pieces of flint debitage (Ward 2006). At Rathmullan, Site 10, only 60m from Site 12 mentioned above, a fragmented red wrist-bracer was also present in one of the spreads that contained the foot from a polypod bowl and Beaker pottery (Bolger 2001; 2012).

The deposition of ceramic polypods alongside Beaker pottery and other settlement debris in Ireland suggests that these bowls were seen as part of the Beaker ceramic assemblage. These were treated in accordance with the same conventions that governed the use of Beakers and have never been found in association with any other type of pottery such as Food Vessels. In contrast to their ceramic counterparts, the wooden polypod bowls seem to have been viewed differently, as indicated by their exclusive deposition within bogs, a context from which deposits of Beaker pottery were excluded. These wooden vessels provide an important link to the other items of the Beaker assemblage that were deliberately deposited in 'natural places'. Perhaps the wooden materiality of these bowls leant them a quality that made them suitable for deposition in wetlands in a way that the ceramic nature of pottery did not. What is more certain is that the complementary concentrations of wooden and ceramic examples indicate that there were strict preferences about the ways in which these polypod bowls could be deposited. Similarly, the higher quantities of ceramic polypod bowls in spreads than pits suggest that it was considered more appropriate for these vessels to remain deposited within these large-scale accumulations of material. Although the fact that much greater quantities of pottery occur in spreads compared to any other context is also likely to be a factor.

Apart from their very different contexts of discovery, the wooden bowls differ considerably from their ceramic counterparts; all six were deposited intact. In contrast, almost all of the ceramic-footed bowls seem to have been broken prior to deposition. The only exception to this is the nearly complete polypod from the pit at Newtownbalregan 2, which appears to have been intact when deposited (Grogan and Roche 2005a). In complete contrast to this, each of the other ceramic examples are represented by only a few fragmented sherds. The condition of these vessels is consistent with that of Beaker pottery in spreads and pits, most of which display evidence for considerable life-histories after their breakage but prior to their eventual deposition (see below; Chapter Four). It seems that the use-life of polypod bowls also continued post-fracture, with sherds being collected and stored in large aggregations prior to their final deposition.

The discovery of 16 polypod bowls in Ireland indicates that while rare, these were more common here than Britain or the Netherlands or elsewhere in Atlantic Europe, where very small numbers of polypod bowls are known. For example, fragments from just two bowls have been found in southern Britain, within disturbed contexts at Abingdon, Oxfordshire, and Inkpen, Berkshire (Clarke 1970, 89-92). Fitzpatrick (2015, 47) has recently suggested, however, that another potential example may have been found at Mount Pleasant henge, Dorset (Longworth 1979, P227). Although Case (2001, 361) has argued that Ireland was a melting pot, where the Atlantic Bell Beaker tradition and the north-west continental European Beaker tradition collided, the greater quantities of these pots found on this island is probably also reflec-

Context	Find place	No. of single finds	No. of buttons with other objects	No. of hoards	No. of buttons from hoards	Total find spots	Total finds
Bog	wet	1	0	2	24	3	25
Passage tomb	dry	4	2	0	0	4	6
Cist	dry	2	1	0	0	2	3
Mountain	dry	1	0	1	12	2	13
Unknown	unknown	0	0	0	0	0	12

Table 9.2: The contexts in which V-perforated buttons occur as single or multiple finds or as hoards, as well as the number of findspots and the number of buttons.

tive of the particular ways in which they were adopted and adapted. Nevertheless, they are not commonly found in Ireland, and the rarity of polypod bowls here and in most parts of north-western Europe, suggests that these were not everyday objects. This is also intimated by their deposition within bogs in Ireland, a treatment that was applied to contemporary supra-regional special-purpose objects (see below; Chapters Seven and Ten). The small numbers of these pot types, and the circumscribed nature of their deposition, suggests that they fulfilled a different function to Beaker pottery and carried different meanings for their users. Indeed, the concentration of these bowls in the Boyne Valley also suggests that these may have had a special role, but what this may have been requires further detailed study which is beyond the scope of this book.

9.4 V-perforated buttons

At least 59 V-perforated buttons have been found at 14 locations in the northern half of Ireland and their distribution is quite complementary to that of Beaker pottery (Fig. 9.4). The densest concentration of these is in the poorly drained northern midlands in present-day County Cavan. The most southerly examples occur at the passage tombs of Tara, Dowth and Loughcrew, all in County Meath. Their distribution suggests a regional preference for these objects in the north of the island and strong links between this area and the north of Britain.

The buttons found in Ireland are predominantly dark in colour, particularly black, and are mainly circular and flat based like Ian Shepherd's (2009) types 1 and 2 which date from approximately 2300-1900 BC (ibid., 343). Buttons of this type are predominantly found in northern Britain with concentrations occurring in Yorkshire and Derbyshire and to a lesser extent in the Scottish southern uplands, but also in Wessex in southern Britain. Most of these are made of Whitby jet from Yorkshire and so the concentration of discoveries in that area is unsurprising (Sheridan and Davis 1998; Shepherd, A.N. 2009, 337-40). Only a few of the buttons from Ireland appear to have been made of jet, such as those from Lissan and Lurgan (Harbison 1976), although a group of ten un-provenanced examples were made using albertite from Strathpeffer, Sutherland, in Scotland (see Shepherd, A.N. 2009, 341). While these examples were clearly made from non-local materials, most of the buttons from Ireland were made from an assortment of specially selected local materials including anthracite, steatite and mudstone. For example, anthracite has been mined in recent times in Counties Tipperary, Laois and Kilkenny. While these materials may have had symbolic values attached to them, it is also possible that they were chosen with reference to the British buttons made of Whitby jet. No amber examples have been found in Ireland, but specimens made from bone (species unknown) have been found; a single bone example came from a cist at Kinkit, Co. Tyrone, and a cache of ten bone buttons was retrieved from a bog at Skeagh, Co. Cavan. Unlike their stone counterparts, buttons made from bone are thought to pre-date 2300 BC (Schuhmacher *et al.* 2013; Woodward and Hunter 2015, 155).

The worn condition of some V-perforated buttons in Britain has been noted (Woodward and Hunter 2015, 148-72) and Ian Shepherd (2009, 348) observed that many buttons had been rebored or restrung. All of which suggests that these objects had a long use-life. While no scientific examination has yet been conducted on Irish V-perforated buttons, the edges of the three buttons from the Mound of the Hostages are certainly worn and chipped suggesting that they had lengthy histories of use (Fig. 5.13). There is no evidence to suggest that Irish V-perforated buttons did not have important social biographies just like their British counterparts and may have been used by multiple persons during their lifespan.

Although contextual details are lacking for 12 of the 59 V-perforated buttons known from Ireland, the available information indicates that these objects only occur within a restricted set of contexts (Table 9.2). At least 38 (65% of 59) buttons have been recovered from five 'natural places' representing a mix of wet and dry contexts, namely 25 (43% of 59) buttons from three bogs and 13 buttons from two mountainsides (see Chapter Six), while nine buttons (15% of 59) came from six human-made contexts represented by four

Fig. 9.4: The distribution of V-perforated buttons in Ireland.

passage tombs and two cists (see Chapter Five). These were mainly deposited as single finds or in 'hoards'.

Most of these buttons (61%: 36 out of 59) have been found in just three hoards in 'natural places', all of which were one-type hoards in bogs or mountainsides. It seems likely that the buttons in these 'hoards' actually represent the remains of a single button set or a composite item such as a jacket, cloak or necklace (Shepherd, A.N. 2009, 348). For example, 14 stone buttons were found in a bog at Drumeague, Co. Cavan, while a cache of 12 stone buttons was found on Ballyboley Mountain, Co. Antrim (Wood-Martin 1895, 534; Harbison 1976, 15). The absence of associated garments or cords at findspots where they could have been preserved if deposited suggests that the buttons were separated prior to deposition. This does require further research, however, such as the use-wear analysis conducted by Woodward and Hunter (2015) in Britain. Nevertheless, if we consider each of these 'hoards' as a single depositional act, then it becomes clear from the eight V-perforated buttons that have been discovered as single finds, that these ornaments were most often deposited singly (Table 9.2; Fig. 9.5).

The four passage tombs (Loughcrew Cairn R2, Co. Meath, Carrowmore Site 49, Co. Sligo, Dowth

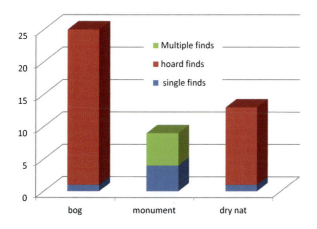

Fig. 9.5: The number of buttons from each context type.

and Mound of the Hostages, Co. Meath) produced six buttons, but it is difficult to discern if any of these were intended as funerary gifts or as ceremonial deposits. For example, within the central chamber of a simple passage tomb (Site 49) at Carrowmore, antiquarians discovered a steatite button along with oyster shells and three sherds of (unidentified) 'reddish pottery' in association with two burials (one cremated and one unburnt) (Wood-Martin 1888, 68; Harbison 1976, 14). An unusual starshaped V-perforated button made from jasper was recorded by Wilde (1857, 122) as being found "in the sepulchral caverns during the excavations of the tumulus" at Dowth. As detailed below, this material seems to have been specially selected for the manufacture of wrist-bracers. Similarly, an unperforated stone button (of unknown petrology) was found by an antiquarian (Rotherham 1895) within what seems to have been the chamber of a passage tomb (Cairn R2) at Loughcrew. Three buttons (two of anthracite and one of mudstone) were found within the chamber at the Mound of the Hostages, where at least one example made from anthracite appears to have been deposited with an Irish Bowl and a bronze awl as part of an Early Bronze Age inhumation burial (O'Sullivan, M. 2005, 104-9; see Chapter Five). In Chapter Five, we saw that this type of burial practice may represent a regional adaptation of the Beaker inhumation post-2200 BC.

It was only within three of the cists and passage tombs that V-perforated buttons were found in association with other objects. Three buttons have been discovered in two cists; Portanure, Co. Cavan (Waddell 1970, 110; Glover 1975, 151) and Kinkit, Co. Tyrone (Glover 1975). At the former, two buttons – presumably V-perforated – were found in a cist that was destroyed at the beginning of the twentieth century and the details are vague (Waddell 1970, 110; Glover 1975, 151). At Kinkit, a single bone button accompanied the cremated remains of two young adults along with a bone pin (Fig. 5.20). Significantly, this represents the only V-perforated button to have been found with a burial in a non-megalithic context in Ireland.

Notably, there are no records of any of these buttons ever being found with Beaker pottery in Ireland. This may be because these objects had slightly different chronological currencies, with the floruit of button use possibly occurring after that of Beaker ceramics. However given the circumscribed deposition of both Beakers and V-perforated buttons, the lack of association between these two artefact types may be better understood in another way. The emphasis on depositing buttons singly or in one-type hoards, often in 'natural places', suggests that a conscious effort was made to strategically deposit these buttons separately from Beaker pottery or any other stereotypical Beaker-related objects. The type of context that was suitable for buttons seems to have been deemed inappropriate for Beaker pottery. This is illustrated by the way that passage tombs are the only form of megalith to have produced V-perforated buttons, but this pottery is only rarely discovered inside passage tombs (see Chapter Five). For some reason, these ornaments were never placed in any other type of megalith, particularly those wedge tombs that received primary deposits (containing Beaker ceramics) that were contemporary with the use of V-perforated buttons. The particular social biographies of each of these items, and the values that they had become imbued with, seems to have strongly influenced their depositional treatment (see Chapter Ten). Although some buttons were made from non-local materials, most were made locally to resemble British and European examples; yet, it seems likely that they were all regarded as a supra-regional style of ornament that represented people, places and values relating to the use of these buttons in other regions.

9.5 Wrist-bracers

At least 112 wrist-bracers have been found throughout Ireland, however, 48 of these are unprovenanced single finds without any associations (Harbison 1976, 7), which means that only an incomplete distribution can be mapped (Fig. 9.6). Despite this, a pattern is potentially visible. There are large swathes of the country where no wrist-bracers have been found including the south-east, the south-west and much of the western seaboard. Nevertheless, many (55) are recorded within the northern part of the country including Counties Sligo, Donegal, Tyrone, Derry, Armagh and Down, with as many as 38 occurring within Antrim. Seven wrist-bracers have also been recovered from a band of land stretching across the middle of the island in Counties Galway, Westmeath, Kildare and Meath, four of which occur in the latter. Only three wrist-bracers have been discovered further south in Counties Tipperary and Limerick. As we have already seen and will discuss later, this distribution seems

Fig. 9.6: The distribution of wrist-bracers in Ireland.

to reflect regional differences in the kinds of objects that were used and deposited in the Chalcolithic.

The particularly dense concentration of wrist-bracers within County Antrim is very curious. Not least because many of these share the same provenance and are lacking exact details of location. While it might be tempting to dismiss these as modern fakes, many of these wrist-bracers have been broken in antiquity, thereby strongly suggesting that these are genuine objects (Ann Woodward, pers. comm.). Most of these wrist-bracers came from mid-Antrim, an area that also produced large amounts of Neolithic projectiles perhaps largely due to the prevalence of antiquarians and collectors operating in this area in the nineteenth and twentieth centuries (Woodman *et al.* 2006, 268-75, 309). It may be revealing for future studies to examine which wrist-bracers came from particular antiquarian collections, to explore the role of collectors in the creation of what seem to be archaeological hot-spots. Notwithstanding these issues, the number of wrist-bracers to have been discovered in Ireland is much larger than from other Atlantic regions. A total of 20 wrist-bracers are known from Portugal and 50 from the Netherlands. In France, 20 come from Brittany, six from the Paris Basin (Salanova 2004, 69-71) and 30 from the south-east (Guilaine *et al.*

182 | THE BEAKER PHENOMENON

Fig. 9.7: A selection of typical red jasper wrist-bracers from Ireland (Roe and Woodward 2009, Fig.1; reproduced here with the permission of Fiona Roe and Ann Woodward).

Context	Findplace	Total find spots	No. of bracers
Bog	wet	3	4
Spread	dry	1	1
Cist	dry	1	1
Megalith	dry	1	1
Other burials	dry	2	2

Table 9.3: The numbers of wrist-bracers from each context.

2001, 238). In neighbouring Britain, 95 (68 from England, 24 from Scotland) wrist-bracers have been found (Smith 2006; Woodward and Hunter 2011). As was the case with the polypod bowls, it is hard to explain why such large numbers have been found in Ireland.

The wrist-bracers found here seem to represent a melting pot of different styles that were combined to produce objects with a distinctively regional character. Irish wrist-bracers are typically tall and narrow with straight or tapered sides and a plano-convex profile with just two holes and fit within Atkinson's Types A and B (Fig. 9.7; Harbison 1976). Only a small number of the four-holed examples that are more common in northern or central Europe and Britain have been found here (Woodward *et al.* 2006, 534; Fokkens *et al.* 2008, 112). Two-holed wrist-bracers are known from the Netherlands and the middle Rhine area of Germany, but are predominantly found in Atlantic Europe in countries like Portugal, Spain, southern France and Brittany (Sangmeister 1964; 1974; Roe 2011; Woodward and Hunter 2011, 112). At least half of all Irish wrist-bracers are red in colour, although dark grey, brown or black examples also occur in smaller numbers (Harbison 1976, 6; Roe and Woodward 2009). This contrasts with the Atlantic façade, where wrist-bracers are mostly grey (Laure Salanova, pers. comm.), as well as Britain where these are mainly blue/grey or green/grey variations and only four red and four black wrist-bracers are known (Woodward *et al.* 2006, 534; Roe 2011, 107). The strong emphasis on both red and dark coloured wrist-bracers in Ireland may indicate links with central Europe where black and red colours were also preferred (Sangmeister 1964; Woodward and Hunter 2011, 112). In contrast to Ireland, however, on the continent in places like the Rhineland, red wrist-bracers usually have four perforations and black ones have just two.

Contextual details are only known for nine wrist-bracers in Ireland and these occur as single finds, multiple finds and as part of a hoard, within a mix of dryland human-made contexts and wetland 'natural places' represented by bogs (see Table 9.3). What is striking about these discoveries is that each one seems atypical and so the depositional treatment of wrist-bracers cannot be easily characterised. At least four wrist-bracers have been recovered from three bogs, including one from Ironpool, Co. Galway (Costello 1944), and another that was discovered a few centimetres from the base of the blanket bog at Carrowkeel Mountain, Co. Sligo, near the passage tomb complex (Watts 1960, 115; Harbison 1976, 24). The other two (one near-complete and one broken) were found within Corran bog, Co. Armagh, in a remarkable discovery consisting of a wooden box bound with a gold band, together with two gold discs and several jet beads, which are discussed individually below (Wilde 1857, 89; Case 1977b, 21).

Only five examples have been found in five dryland human-made contexts within a range of settings including a cist, a court tomb and a spread (see Table 9.3). As we saw in Section 5.2, three fragments of a wrist-bracer that may have been made of porphyry were discovered in a sub-megalithic cist located next to a standing stone at Furness, Co. Kildare. The bracer occurred with the cremated remains of two adults (a male and a possible female) and a sherd of possible 'domestic' Beaker pottery (Macalister *et al.* 1913; Macalister 1928). Elsewhere, a red-coloured stone object with a plano-convex section and a perforation at either end was found in the court tomb at Ballywholan, Co. Tyrone (Kelly, D. 1985, 162). This is now lost, but was almost certainly a (Type A) wrist-bracer. Its exact context and associations are unknown, but comparison with the deposition of Beaker-related objects in other earlier Neolithic megaliths suggests that its placement occurred during ceremonial practices that may not have involved human remains (see Chapter Five). At Drumstaple, Co. Derry, a vessel (of unknown type) containing cremated bone and a wrist-bracer was reported as having been discovered by a farmer; however, both the sherds and wrist-bracer are now lost (Harbison 1976, 7). At Longstone Cullen, Co. Tipperary, a two-holed Type A wrist-bracer that had been snapped in half was found with an Encrusted Urn. Although Beaker pottery was also present on this site, the contextual association of the wrist-bracer with this later form of pottery suggests that it was deposited as an heirloom (Helen Roche, pers. comm.). At Rathmullan Site 10, within the Boyne Valley, Co. Meath, a fragmented (Type A2 -2TPC; Fig. 4.22) wrist-bracer occurred within a spread of occupation debris along with 250 Beaker sherds, the foot of a polypod bowl and lithics (Bolger 2001; 2012). This wrist-bracer is loosely dated by the burnt longbone from a pig that produced a radiocarbon date of 2460-2200 BC (SUERC-31920; 3850±30 BP; Fintan Walsh, pers. comm.). This is the only radiocarbon date from a context containing a wrist-bracer in Ireland. Harbison (1976, 27, pl. 18: no. 94) catalogued a wrist-bracer found in a spread at Site C, Lough Gur, Co Limerick; however, this object is best interpreted as a pendant (Roe and Woodward 2009).

Another three wrist-bracers were discovered as unstratified stray finds, so it is not possible to decipher their original depositional context. Interestingly, two of these display a spatial association with passage tombs, like the example found in blanket bog near the Carrowkeel passage tomb cemetery. A fragmented (Type A2 -2SPC) wrist-bracer was discovered in topsoil 500m east of the passage tombs at Fourknocks (Fig. 5.14) and another (Type B2) was found within 400m of Cairn K at Lough Crew (Cooney 1987), both in County Meath. However, wrist-bracers have never been found in any passage tomb in Ireland.

That only five wrist-bracers have been discovered in the course of the high number of archaeological excavations conducted in Ireland, particularly from the late 1990s onwards (see Chapter 2), suggests that these were rarely deposited within archaeological features. Based on this, it seems likely that a large proportion of the 100 uncontexted wrist-bracers may have been found in 'natural places'. Although we cannot be certain of that, what is clear is that in Ireland, wrist-bracers have seldom been found with human remains as they so often are elsewhere in Europe. This is illustrated by the way that Beaker-associated burials have been recovered from wedge tombs, but no wrist-bracers have never been found in these monuments (see Chapter Five). This indicates that a deliberate choice was made not to deposit wrist-bracers in these tombs, or many other types of context. There does not seem to have been any context in Ireland in which it was appropriate to place wrist-bracers with human remains and/or Beaker pottery. This is proven by the fact that the two Rathmullan and Longstone discoveries represent the only time that Beakers have been found with wrist-bracers. The available evidence suggests that there were strict preferences in the way that these objects were treated and the known discoveries that we have discussed represent the exceptions that prove this rule. Wrist-bracers were predominantly deposited singly within 'natural places' rather than in humanly made contexts like pits or monuments or with other objects because of what these objects and places represented (see Chapter Seven). This raises the question of what meanings these objects must have had in order for them to be treated in this way?

Recent studies have found that most wrist-bracers from burials in Europe were not utilitarian. The materiality, size and form of many suggest that these could not have functioned as wrist-bracers (Fokkens *et al.* 2008, 117). When found with skeletons, these predominantly occur on the outside of the arm where they could be easily seen rather than on the inside where a functioning wrist-bracer would have been needed to guard the wrist (ibid., 112-6). Microscopic examinations of English wrist-bracers have revealed very little evidence for wear and many may never have been used before their deposition (Woodward *et al.* 2006). Furthermore, some are so finely made that they would have shattered upon any impact (ibid.). Impractical Irish examples include eight wrist-bracers that are less than 5cm long. Many of these were non-functional symbolic ornaments that may have formed part of a special uniform that was used in ceremonial activities (Fokkens *et al.* 2008; Woodward and Hunter 2011, 124). These had cosmological connotations and carried particular meanings that drew upon the symbolism of archery. It seems that these artefacts were predominantly deposited in graves or megaliths across various parts of Europe as gifts to the ancestors, part of the exchange of objects between people and the supernatural. This served to construct desirable forms of social identity for the deceased and to enact/reaffirm particular social values (Fokkens *et al.* 2008). In Ireland, although wrist-bracers rarely occur in graves, their treatment seems to have been as codified and circumscribed as elsewhere and it is possible that these objects and their deposition served much the same roles here as elsewhere (see Chapter Ten).

That a range of important meanings were being reproduced within and through these wrist-bracers is indicated not just by their circumscribed depositional treatment, but also by the selectivity involved in the creation of these objects. In a similar way to polished stone axes in the Neolithic, the manufacture of wrist-bracers from particular stone sources with specific colours would have resulted in them becoming imbued with special meanings. Roe and Woodward (2009) observed that only three main types of stone were used in the manufacture of Irish wrist-bracers; jasper, porcellanite and a mixture of fine-grained siltstones, mudstones and shales. The selective use of each of these stone types may have been motivated by the symbolic values that were already attached to these materials. This is illustrated by the manufacture of black/dark wrist-bracers using porcellanite from Tievebulliagh, Co. Antrim, which had traditionally been used to make polished stone axes (Cooney and Mandal 1998, Roe and Woodward 2009). Similarly, the brown and grey wrist-bracers were made from fine-grained sedimentary rocks such as siltstones, mudstones and shales that were also used in the manufacture of polished stone axes in Ireland.

This strongly parallels the use of historically significant stone types to make wrist-bracers in Britain (Woodward *et al.* 2006). At least 24% of 74 British wrist-bracers were made from the Langdale tuff that was used to make Group VI axes in the Neolithic. Another 38% were made from amphibolite, which seems to have been specially selected because it was considered similar to the material used to make classic Neolithic jadeite axeheads (Woodward and Hunter 2011, 116-26). Certain continental wrist-bracers also have highly distinctive geological sources (ibid., 119). In the case of the Irish examples made from jasper, whose red colour seems to have held special meanings for people in Ireland, this material also seems to have been historically significant. At Lambay Island, off the coast of Dublin, jasper outcrops were worked to produce beads and macehead pendants of the kind that have been found in passage tombs (Cooney *et al.* 2013, 415). While jasper also occurs in various parts of Ireland, including Counties Cavan, Galway, Tyrone and Waterford (Mitchell 2004, 265), the evidence from Lambay raises the possibility that this island was the source of the stone for the production of Chalcolithic and Neolithic cosmological ornaments. If so, the selection of jasper and porcellanite in Ireland and tuff from the Langdales would indicate that materials for making wrist-bracers were being obtained from places that were spatially removed from everyday life and probably perceived as being associated with the supernatural, or coming from the world of the ancestors (Helms 1988). Indeed, the skill and expertise involved in crafting these objects may have also been regarded as being given by the ancestors (ibid.). These perceptions of wrist-bracers as special or cosmologically derived could explain the very particular ways in which these objects were treated and deposited.

Harbison (1976, 4) observed that over one-third of all Irish wrist-bracers were damaged including some examples that had been broken, some of which were subsequently reworked to form smaller wrist-bracers or pendants. More recently, Roe and Woodward (2009) identified an even higher rate of pre-depositional breakage (61% of 43), reworking and repolishing. Compared to those made from other stone types, the jasper wrist-bracers display a much greater rate of breakage (60% of 27 red wrist-bracers, compared to 34% of 26 dark coloured wrist-bracers) and reworking. Indeed, at least 13 red, but only four dark-coloured wrist-bracers have been deliberately snapped or sawn exactly in half and it is clear that they were specially selected for this treatment (Roe and Woodward 2009). Broken wrist-bracers also occur in Britain but in far smaller numbers (ibid.; Woodward and Hunter 2011, 81). It has been suggested that these were deliberately broken so that they could be employed in processes of social enchainment whereby pieces were taken away by separate groups post-breakage as symbols of their shared relationships (Woodward *et al.* 2006, 536; Roe and Woodward 2009). Clearly, the production, fragmentation, reworking and eventual deposition that occurred throughout the long use-lives of some wrist-bracers implies that they were seen as highly symbolic objects that fulfilled important social functions (see Brück 2006b, 76).

9.6 Copper Daggers

Twenty copper daggers are known from Ireland, excluding the example from the Killaha hoard, Co. Kerry, which appears to post-date the main currency of Beakers in Ireland (see Chapter Seven). Ten of these are simple tanged blades (Type Knocknagur), while the other ten display rivet holes (Type Listack) (Harbison 1969a). A single copper tanged and riveted dagger from the Whitespots hoard was examined for use-wear by Katharina Becker (2006). She observed that this had a blunted tip and was quite damaged along one cutting edge (ibid., 89). Other copper daggers, such as that from the Silees River in County Fermanagh, show absolutely no signs of use (Sheridan and Northover 1993, 61).

Seventeen copper daggers were discovered as single finds, while three were deposited within two hoards from Knocknagur, Co. Galway, and Whitespots, Co. Down. While no contextual information is available for eight copper daggers, at least ten were discovered in wet 'natural places'; six (30%) have been found in bogs, while four (20%) were retrieved from three rivers (Fig. 9.8). The latter four examples, however, are of the tanged and riveted type (Listack) whose currency is of a slightly later date (see Chapter Seven) and represent part of a shift towards increased river deposition in Ireland post-2100 BC (Becker 2006, 85; 2013). Significantly, early copper

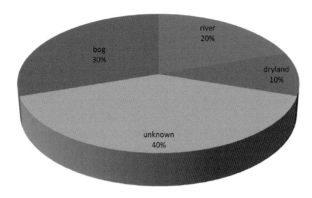

Fig. 9.8: The percentage of copper tanged daggers (n=17) found in each context type including those for which contextual information is missing.

daggers (Type Knocknagur) have overwhelmingly been found in bogs (see Chapter Seven).

As they mostly occur as single finds, daggers have no associations apart from the objects they were found alongside within the two hoards from Knocknagur and Whitespots, where they both occurred with copper thick-butted axes. The Knocknagur hoard was found in a bog and comprised a copper tanged dagger, three copper Lough Ravel thick-butted axes and three copper double pointed awls (Harbison 1969a, 10, 19). The hoard from Whitespots consisted of a copper tanged dagger, a copper tanged and riveted dagger and a copper Lough Ravel thick-butted axe that were found within a rock crevice (Case 1966, 162; Harbison 1969a, 7, 18). These two daggers represent the only known examples from a dryland context. Thus, these metal blades have not been found with Beaker pottery or recovered from any burials or other human-made contexts in Ireland, despite occurring regularly with this ceramic in graves in other regions such as Britain (Harbison 1979, 98).

These daggers have mainly been recovered from the present-day Counties Galway, Leitrim, Offaly, Meath, Cavan, and Fermanagh within central Ireland (Fig. 9.9). Although some northern and southern outliers are known, few to none occur in large parts of the island such as the south, south-east or north-east and west. The clear concentration of these in the less well-drained and boggy areas of the Irish midlands seems to reflect regional preferences. The distribution of daggers overlaps with that of Beaker pottery but is also somewhat complementary; Beakers are less commonly found in the midlands, while daggers are lacking from those areas where Beakers are most common. Perhaps this reflects a preference for the deposition of daggers within bogs in this region, rather than recycling them as probably occurred in other areas (see Bray and Pollard 2012).

The repeated occurrence of single daggers in supernatural places, often in bogs, indicates that their deposition was highly structured. It seems to have been important to maintain a separation between daggers and other objects, particularly Beaker pottery, and to deposit them in special places, away from settlements or burials. This is in stark contrast to the treatment of these blades in Britain and other parts of Europe, where they were deposited in male graves along with Beaker pottery (Needham 1988). Yet in both scenarios, the very particular ways in which these were deposited during collective ceremonial activities either in graves or in 'natural' places suggests that they were regarded as highly meaningful objects (see Chapter Ten).

Daggers were specially crafted from copper and seem to have been supra-regional objects of exchange that symbolised key values and played an important social role (see Salanova 1998b; 2007, 221; Vandkilde 2005; Sarauw 2008). Like wrist-bracers, their usefulness as tools or weapons has been questioned and they seem to have functioned primarily as symbolic representations of particular concepts (see Nielsen 2009). Debate continues as to whether daggers symbolised martial values (*e.g.* Sarauw 2007b; 2008) or recalled the qualities of a hunter and the use of blades to give the coup-de grâce to hunted game (Case 2004b, 29; Harding, A. 2006, 506-7). Either way, while the exact meanings of the copper tanged daggers remain unknown, it seems these were included in graves to act as gifts to the ancestors and also to construct a form of idealised identity for the deceased (Thomas 1999, 157-9; Case 2004b, 29 and b, 200; Vander Linden 2004, 41; 2006a; 2006b; Fokkens *et al.* 2008).

9.7 Sun-discs

At least 22 gold flat discs of broadly contemporary date with Beaker pottery have been found across much of Ireland (Fig. 9.10). This excludes two later examples from Ballydehob (Sparrogoda) and Ballyvourney, both in County Cork, which post-date the currency of Beakers in Ireland (Cahill 2005a, 260-74; 2015). Most of these 22 discs were decorated using a range of concentric circles and cruciform motifs resembling those found on the base of continental Beaker vessels such as those from Iberia and on the base of many Irish Bowls of the Food Vessel tradition (Cahill 2015; 2016). The 22 Irish discs predominantly occur in two distinct concentrations in Counties Armagh, Monaghan and Roscommon, all within the northern midlands and also along the southern coastline within Counties Cork and Wexford (Fig. 9.11). Outliers have also been found to the west in County Mayo and north in Donegal. The quantities found in Ireland far exceeds the ten examples known from Britain or the smaller numbers that have been recorded in France, Spain and Portugal, though in each place they tend to occur in pairs (Needham and Sheridan 2014; Cahill 2015; 2016). In Britain, these have been found to occur in graves with Beaker pottery as was the case at Mere and

Fig. 9.9: The distribution of copper tanged daggers in Ireland. Examples provenanced to county are represented by open symbols.

Fig. 9.10: Gold discs from Rappa, Co. Mayo (photograph reproduced with the permission of the National Museum of Ireland ©).

EVERYTHING IN ITS RIGHT PLACE? | 187

Fig. 9.11: The distribution of gold discs in Ireland.

at Farleigh Wick, both in Wiltshire (Eogan, G. 1994, 18; Needham and Sheridan 2014, 908). In Brittany, Spain, and Portugal, these have been found with secondary Beaker burials in earlier Neolithic megaliths (Taylor 1994, 45, 52).

In Ireland, these gold discs are mainly found in pairs (20 discs) within one-type hoards (16 discs). Single discs have only been recovered on two occasions; as an isolated find in Castle Treasure, Co. Cork (Case 1977b, 20), and a very small undecorated gold disc that occurred with many other objects, including Beaker pottery, within a multi-period spread of habitation debris at Lough Gur Site D (see Chapter Three). While no contextual information is available for nine discs, most of those (ten out of 13) for which details are known have been found in a mix of both wet (four out of ten) and dry (six out of ten) 'natural places' consisting of bogs and fields (Table 9.4). It may be significant to note that the golds discs from bogs occurred in two hoards that represent the only two instances in which these objects were found in association with other artefacts. These consisted of a pair of discs that were deposited with a lunula at Coggalbeg, Co. Roscommon (Fig. 7.1; Kelly and Cahill 2010) and another pair that were found with two wrist-bracers and jet beads in a wooden box at Corran, Co. Armagh (Case 1977b, 21). Apart from the aforementioned

Context	Findplace	No. of single finds	No. of hoards	No. of sundiscs from hoards	Total findspots	Total Finds
Bog	wet	0	2	4	2	4
Field	dry	0	3	6	3	6
Monument	dry	0	1	2	1	2
Spread	dry	1	0	0	1	1
Unknown	unknown	1	4	2	5	9

Table 9.4: The contexts in which sundiscs occur as single finds and as hoards, as well as the number of findspots and the number of sundiscs.

Lough Gur example, just two other discs were allegedly recovered from a human-made context, which represents the only instance of these objects occurring in a burial. Antiquarian accounts report that these were found as a pair with an inhumation in a cist at Ballyshannon, Co. Donegal, but further information to corroborate this is lacking (Case 1977b, 30-1; Eogan, G. 1994, 21). While most gold discs are in good condition, some such as the pair from Kilmuckridge, Co. Wexford (Cahill 1994; 2005a) or the single example from Lough Gur (Ó Ríordáin, S.P. 1954, 384-6, 410-11), display evidence for having been folded in a similar fashion to lunulae (see Section 9.8).

All of this suggests that the deposition of gold discs in Ireland was very structured. It was important to deposit them separately from other objects in particular locations away from settlements and burials. Presumably this was because of the qualities that they were thought to possess. It seems safe to assume that like many of the other Beaker-related objects, these discs were worn on the body and formed part of an individual's dress. This is supported by their discovery on the body in Beaker burials elsewhere. Their inclusion in these exceptional burials and their depositional treatment in Ireland suggest they were special objects, used to transform people's identities on special occasions. The evidence for folding on some discs, as well as their deposition in contexts such as dry places and bogs from which they could be retrieved, may indicate that some were temporarily stored and then resurrected episodically for ceremonial events. The fact that they were made from gold and do not occur in very large numbers also suggests that they functioned as symbolic ornaments that enabled the expression of various concepts that may have been related to people's cosmological beliefs. Whatever these concepts were, the presence of these objects across various parts of Europe suggest that these may have been shared by widely dispersed communities at this time and were in some way related to the use of Beaker pottery. Significantly, Mary Cahill (2015) has convincingly argued from the shape, material and decoration of these discs that they were symbols of the sun. Drawing on interpretations of Scandinavian Bronze Age rock art, she has highlighted how the repeated occurrence of discs as pairs may indicate they represented the day and the night sun.

9.8 Lunulae

A minimum of 92 crescent-shaped gold objects known as lunulae have been found in Ireland, although locational data is lacking for 61 of these objects and contextual information is only available for 31 examples. Based upon the available information, most lunulae (31%: 28 out of 91) have been found in 'natural places', mostly bogs. They were predominantly deposited as single finds (79%: 72 out of 91) with a far smaller proportion (21%: 19 out of 91) occurring in eight hoards (Table 9.5). These are overwhelmingly one-type hoards comprising pairs of lunulae, although groups of three or four have also been found. The only recorded instance of lunulae occurring with other types of objects was with a pair of gold discs within the Coggalbeg Hoard, which was discovered during peat cutting (see Section 9.7; Kelly and Cahill 2010).

At least 15 lunulae were recovered from 11 'natural' wet places; 14 came from ten boglands and one was found in a lake. This includes six single examples such as that found "under twenty feet of peat" near Enniskillen, Co. Fermanagh (Frazer 1897, 65) and another eight from four hoards, including the specimen from Coggalbeg and three folded lunulae that were recovered from Banemore bog, Co. Kerry (Cahill 1983, 78-80).

At least 11 (five single finds and six from two hoards) lunulae were retrieved from seven 'natural' dryland contexts (see Chapter Seven). Two lunulae were found on mountains underneath large boulders, one came from a quarry, another from a rocky context and three examples were retrieved from fields; one was found under a boulder at Carrickmore, Co. Tyrone (Frazer 1897), and two were found together under a boulder at Rathroeen, Co Mayo (Taylor 1970, 70; Cahill 2005b, 57). A hoard of four was retrieved from a spread of gravel at Dunfierth, Co. Kildare (Eogan, G. 1994, 34).

Four (5%) lunulae have allegedly been discovered at megaliths, but exact details of these unusual discoveries are lacking (Table 9.5). A hoard of three lunulae was reportedly found at a megalith at Cairnlochran, Magheramesk, Co. Antrim (Taylor 1980, 142), while a single lunula occurred within or near another megalith at Highwood, Co. Sligo (Wood-Martin 1888, 180-81; Cahill 2005a, 276). These two accounts represent the only discovery of lunulae in human-made contexts.

Context	Find place	No. of single finds	No. of hoards	No. of lunulae from hoards	Total findspots	Total finds
Bog	wet	6	4	8	10	14
Lake	wet	1	0	0	1	1
Field	wet	1	0	0	1	1
Megalith	dry	1	1	3	2	4
Gravel	dry	0	1	4	1	4
Mountain	dry	2	0	0	2	2
Quarry	dry	1	0	0	1	1
Rocky	dry	1	0	0	1	1
Field	dry	1	1	2	2	3
Unknown	unknown	59	1	2	60	61

Table 9.5: The contexts in which lunulae occur as single finds and hoards as well as the number of findspots and the number of lunulae.

The numbers of lunulae known from Ireland are far higher than elsewhere in Europe, where only a few examples are known from countries such as Britain, France and Belgium. Gold lunula-type ornaments that seem related to the Irish and British examples are also known from Denmark and Portugal (Needham and Sheridan 2014; Cahill 2015). The large numbers of lunulae found in Ireland suggest that it represents an Irish innovation. This is supported by the fact that two of the main types identified by Joan Taylor (1970), the Classical and the Unaccomplished lunulae, almost exclusively occur in Ireland. Although the start date for lunulae production is unknown, these seem to be slightly later in date than the earliest goldwork in Ireland, as represented by basket-shaped ornaments and gold flat discs. Thus, some examples probably post-date the currency of Beakers, while others such as that found in association with sun-discs as part of the Coggalbeg hoard may date to as early as 2300 BC (Kelly and Cahill 2010; Cahill 2015).

Lunulae seem evenly spread throughout much of the island of Ireland (Fig. 9.12), though they are notably lacking from the south-east of the country, where a single example occurs in County Wicklow. Although the distribution of lunulae and Beaker pottery overlaps, there are mutually exclusive clusters of both (see Fig. 9.2). This is exemplified by the situation in Wicklow and the other eastern coastal counties of Louth, Meath, and Dublin, where this ceramic is plentiful but very few lunulae have been recovered. Denser concentrations of lunulae occur across the central to northern midlands where 20 have been found and also in the south-west where eight lunulae have been recovered, four of which came from present-day northern Kerry. Significantly, all of these are areas where Beaker pottery has not been found in large amounts (see Section 3.1.1). Moreover, in the south-west of the island an oppositional relationship has also been observed between the find spots of lunulae and wedge tombs (O'Brien 2004, 570-2; Cahill 2005a, 277). This patterning is probably a reflection of the differential depositional treatment of Beakers and lunulae.

Unlike Beaker pottery (see below), lunulae were largely excluded from human-made contexts and so were generally deposited away from monuments, in 'natural places', particularly bogs. This is an issue to which we will return.

The depositional treatment of lunulae was very restricted in much the same way as the other objects examined here. Again, it seems to have been important to keep lunulae apart from Beaker pottery or other ornaments and to only deposit them in 'natural places' such as bogs. The marking of some lunulae deposits with boulders and their occurrence in contexts such as bogs from which they could be retrieved suggests that these may have been repeatedly hidden and reclaimed for use ceremonies (Cahill 2005b, 53-71; Becker 2008). This may be related to the way that some lunulae show evidence for having been rolled and unrolled or folded over (Fig. 9.13). Very few are recorded as having been found in a rolled position, which might suggest that this use-wear was pre-depositional, but the examples from the hoard from Carrickmore, Co. Tyrone, may still have been rolled up upon their discovery (see below). Other lunulae also seem to have been deposited in protective containers, such as that from Crossdoney, Co. Cavan, which was found in a wooden box, or those from the hoard found within a bog in County Sligo that seem to have been rolled and unrolled before being encased in leather or cloth (see Cahill 1994, 90).

The recurrent aspects of their deposition and the uniformity of the damage to lunulae indicate that these were being used in a consistently circumscribed fashion. These seem to have been special-purpose objects of ritual significance whose main function may have been symbolical. Indeed, these probably needed to be deposited in very specific ways within suitable places (on a permanent or temporary basis) at a distance from everyday activities because of their enduring potency as symbols. Drawing on the work of Fleming Kaul, Mary Cahill (2015) has convincingly argued that while lunulae were neck ornaments, they also functioned as symbolic representa-

Fig. 9.12: The distribution of lunulae in Ireland.

tions of boats that carried the sun on its nightly journey through the underworld. This interpretation is supported by the representation of a similar type of boat on the Nebra disc and images of two suns travelling on a boat (presumably representing the day and the night sun and the nocturnal journey of the latter) on Beaker vessels from Los Millares in Spain (ibid.). Cahill highlights that just like the Coggalbeg hoard, a lunula was found with a pair of gold discs at Cabeceiras de Basto, Braga, in Portugal. This strongly suggests that together with the gold discs, they formed elements of a Europe-wide solar cult and had widely shared cosmological connotations.

9.9 Gold bands and basket-ornaments

Just three gold basket-shaped ornaments have been found in Ireland; an unprovenanced pair and a single find from Benraw, Co. Down (a.k.a Deehommed or Dacomet) (Fig. 9.14; Taylor 1994, 46; O'Connor, B. 2004, 207-8). Unfortunately, contextual details are lacking for all three of these. Five decorated gold bands have also been found in Ireland. All of these were discovered in a hoard in a stream-bed that formed a tributary of the River Erne at Belville, Co. Cavan (Cahill 2005a, 267). These gold bands included two pairs of sub-rectangular plaques with round ends and central perforations (Fig. 9.15). Both Taylor

EVERYTHING IN ITS RIGHT PLACE? | 191

Fig. 9.13: Lunula from Trillick, Co. Tyrone (photograph reproduced with the permission of the National Museum of Ireland ©).

(1980, 237; 1994, 46) and Needham (2011, 133) have considered these plaques as a form of basket-ornament despite them missing a tang. The other Belville object was a single band composed of four fragments thought to represent a diadem (Case 1977b, 27; Eogan, G. 1994, 19). Collectively, all eight examples represent sheet gold objects that would have ornamented the forehead, hair or ears and in this regard, can be grouped together. Significantly, the basket-ornament from Benraw and the bands from Belville also show evidence of having been rolled or folded in a similar fashion to lunulae and gold discs (see Sections 9.7 and 9.8; Cahill 2005b).

The quantity of these ornaments from Ireland is much smaller than Britain, where as many as 22 examples of basket-shaped ornaments are now known, many of which have been found as a pair within Beaker burials (Needham 2011, 131-3; Needham and Sheridan 2014; 906-8; Fitzpatrick *et al.* 2016). Only a very small number are known from elsewhere in Atlantic Europe, occurring in Brittany, Spain and Portugal, a few of which were found with Beakers (Fitzpatrick *et al.* 2016). Despite being based on a continental idea, the Irish and British examples represent an insular style, which were made on these islands c. 2400-2200 BC, very soon after Beaker pottery was first adopted (Needham 2011; Needham and Sheridan 2014). The ornament from Deehommed (Benraw) seems to be an exception to this as it is generally regarded as an Iberian object that was brought to Ireland (Cahill 2015; Fitzpatrick *et al.* 2016). Despite the lack of contextual information for the Irish examples, it does seem that as per so many of the other objects, these too were deposited in a distinctively different fashion to elsewhere. They seem to have been placed apart from other objects in 'natural places' and there is no evidence for these being associated with burials or Beakers.

9.10 Battle Axes

A total of 32 early battle axes have been found in Ireland, all of which seem to have been discovered as single finds (Simpson 1990). Contextual information is only available for four of these; two came from the River Shannon, one was reputedly found within an old copper mine, somewhere in County Cork and one that is now lost was recovered from the chamber floor of a passage tomb at Sess Killgreen, Co. Tyrone (after Simpson 1990; 1996). There is no record of these occurring in any graves along with Beakers or Beaker-related materials in Ireland, as is commonly the case in Britain (see Simpson 1996). Nor indeed is there any evidence that these were ever deposited

Fig. 9.14: The gold basket-shaped "earrings" from 'Ireland' (photograph reproduced with the permission of the National Museum of Ireland ©).

Fig. 9.15: The gold diadem and the two pairs of sub-rectangular plaques found in a stream-bed at Belville, Co. Cavan (photograph reproduced with the permission of the National Museum of Ireland ©).

in association with Beaker pottery. The absence of these objects from hoards and their lack of associations suggest that they were deposited in a circumscribed fashion. Based on the treatment of the other supra-regional styled ornaments that form part of the so-called Beaker package in Ireland, it seems probable that the uncontexted battle axes were probably also deposited in 'natural places'.

9.11 Identifying depositional patterns and practices

So far, we have seen that the deposition of each Beaker artefact-type seems to have followed a set of overarching rules. The extent of this depositional patterning becomes even more obvious when we consider the treatment of the different objects all together. Like Beaker pottery, polypod bowls mainly occur as multiple finds. In contrast, wrist-bracers, battleaxes, lunulae and copper daggers mainly occur as single finds, whereas V-perforated buttons, gold basket-ornaments and sun-discs are chiefly found within hoards (Fig. 9.16). Most of these either rarely or never occur with other types of objects, and only a small quantity of a very restricted range of items, such as wrist-bracers, buttons and sun-discs, have ever been found with other artefacts, but these rarely include Beakers. Significantly, arrowheads and ceramic polypod bowls are the only items from the so-called 'Beaker package' to have been found alongside this pottery in Ireland with any kind of regularity, although two wrist-bracers and a disc bead necklace have also been recovered in association with Beakers (see Chapter Four). Not only were many Beaker-related objects deliberately kept separate from one another, but also the deposition of these items was contextually compartmentalised into various kinds of places.

Many objects including copper tanged daggers, gold discs, gold head ornaments, lunulae and V-perforated buttons are either exclusively or predominantly found in 'natural places' at a distance from settlements, graves and monuments. For example, copper daggers are exclusively recovered from bogs, rivers and 'natural' dryland places. Other objects, such as wrist-bracers, V-perforated buttons and gold discs, occur in a slightly wider array of settings including a few instances where they have been found within human-made archaeological features. Yet,

EVERYTHING IN ITS RIGHT PLACE? | 193

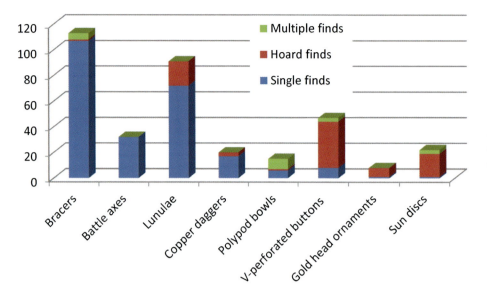

Fig. 9.16: The numbers of various Beaker objects occurring as single finds, multiple finds or in hoards.

these occur in such small numbers as to serve to be the exceptions that prove the general depositional rules. As highlighted in Chapter Seven, the treatment of many of these objects mirrors the type-specific deposition of contemporary copper axes and halberds, which are also mainly found as single finds within wet 'natural places', particularly bogs, although axes and halberds do occasionally occur in one-type hoards and roughly half of all the contexted copper axes that were found within hoards come from dry 'natural places' (based on information from Becker 2006).

It is striking that a much greater proportion of wristbracers, buttons, daggers and lunulae have been found in bogs than in any other context (see Table 9.6). Indeed, bogs seem to represent the preferred context for the deposition of most Beaker-related objects in Ireland, other than Beaker pottery, which seems to have been totally excluded from them (see Chapter Seven). Instead, Beaker pottery and lithics such as scrapers and debitage that were used in everyday occupational activities occur in human-made contexts, especially pits and spreads. The deposition of other objects with or without Beaker pottery in these contexts was also quite restricted. For example, no Beaker arrowheads have been discovered in timber circles, disc beads have only been found in pits and polypod bowls have been discovered in pits, spreads and bogs. All of this indicates that a clear contextual separation was maintained between various Beaker-related objects, particularly the pottery, whose deposition was just as circumscribed as the aceramic objects.

The treatment of Beaker pottery was regulated in terms of the contexts and manner in which Beaker-associated settlement debris was being deposited, including the types of objects that were included and excluded. Many of the deposits of Beaker pottery in pits and spreads occur alongside habitation debris but have a formal character, suggesting that there may have been a ceremonial aspect to their deposition. The placement of very similar deposits into a wide range of contexts, including megaliths and timber circles, complicates any interpretation of Beaker-related occupational deposits as simply representing settlement activity. No absolute division between 'domestic' and ritual activities seems to have existed for people at this time (see Brück 1999a; Bradley 2005a).

Settlement debris represented a meaningful cultural material that fulfilled an important social role and it seems obvious from their distinctive treatment that potsherds were seen as objects that both possessed and created meaning; they took on a life of their own that was independent of the vessels to which they once belonged. The symbolic materiality of pot-sherds is hardly surprising given that people construct and negotiate their social relationships, identities and worldview through their everyday material engagement with their world, including the routine production, use and disposal of objects. These sherds may have been seen as heirlooms or relics of certain people or past events that acted as physical metaphors for social relationships between people, places and things (see Woodward 2002, 1040-41). The fragmentation, curation and deposition of these quotidian items may also have been considered to be connected to various stages in the human life-cycle and to beliefs about fertility, renewal and regeneration (Case 1973; Pollard 2000; Cooney 2005) as well as transformation (Brück 1995). Such was the potency of these fragments of past times, that in most Beaker-associated depositional practices in Ireland, a small part of the pot often seems to have been just as suitable as a complete vessel, if not more so. This custom may partially explain the paucity of evidence for the deposition of whole Beakers (see Chapter Four).

	Pits	Spread	Wedge tomb	Court tomb	Portal tomb	Passage tomb	Cist	Timber circle	Cave	Burnt mound	Bog	River and lakes	Dry land (natural)
Beaker pots	472	567	51	19	1	2	6	50	3	11	0	0	0
Beaker sherds	4436	9721	509	103	2	21	?	303	?	155	0	0	0
Barb and tanged arrowhead	6	5	7	6	0	3	0	0	0	1	Yes	0	Yes
Hollow-based arrowhead	0	4	0	0	3	1	0	0	0	1	Yes	0	Yes
Disc beads	24	0	0	0	0	0	0	0	0	0	0	0	0
Ceramic Polypod Bowls	2	6	0	0	0	0	0	0	0	0	0	0	0
Wooden Polypod Bowls	0	0	0	0	0	0	0	0	0	0	6	0	0
Wrist bracer	0	1	0	1	0	0	1	0	0	0	4	0	0
Copper daggers	0	0	0	0	0	0	0	0	0	0	6	4	2
V-perforated buttons	0	0	0	0	0	6	3	0	0	0	25	0	13
Bone pin	0	0	1	0	0	0	0	0	0	0	0	0	0
Gold discs	0	1	0	0	0	0	1	0	0	0	4	0	6
Gold head ornaments	0	0	0	0	0	0	0	0	0	0	0	5	0
Lunulae	0	0	0	0	0	0	0	0	0	0	14	1	11

Table 9.6: The number of each artefact type found in each context type (all 24 discbeads are probably from the same necklace).

Clearly, the treatment of Chalcolithic ceramic and non-ceramic items was both multifaceted and very circumscribed. There seems to have been commonly-held ideas about the right contexts in which to deposit particular objects and the right ways of doing this. These ideas about the correct ways of depositing these objects relates directly to the social values that were attributed to each of them. This highlights just how important these meanings were and the key social roles that these objects played in the constitution of people's social reality. The highly selective and circumscribed treatment of these various objects also suggests that there must have been a performative aspect to their use and deposition, whereby the meanings associated with these objects were enacted during formal ceremonial activities that were conducted in sacred places (Needham 1988, 246). These are issues that will be explored further in the next chapter, but before concluding here, it is worth briefly highlighting an important implication of what has been established.

This very strong evidence for structured and selective deposition means that we are dealing with very partial assemblages. Thus, by its very nature, the depositional record only offers us a very biased picture regarding which objects were in circulation at the same time and whether these were used together (see Needham 2006; 2007). Similarly, the distribution patterns of the various types of objects do not necessarily reflect their actual distribution (Becker 2011, 460-61). In many cases, particular copper or gold artefacts may have been in use, but did not enter the depositional record, perhaps they were recycled instead (ibid.).

Recently, Stuart Needham (2016) has highlighted that the deposition of halberds in Britain, Ireland and the near continent took place at locations away from the areas where Beakers, contemporary Beaker materials and Beaker burials were deposited. This argument is of relevance here because as we have seen, many different Beaker items such as copper tanged daggers were deposited in Ireland in much the same way as halberds were in Britain, for example, not in graves and separate from other objects. This raises questions about how we define the Beaker package, a topic that we will explore in Chapter Ten. For now, we will focus on Needham's argument that this spatial separation is reflective of an opposition between the users of halberds and Beakers, whereby halberds were a symbol used by communities with a distinct non-Beaker identity who did not adopt/use Beaker pottery. Similarly, it has been observed that lunulae and wedge tombs have a mutually exclusive distribution in the south-west (O'Brien 2004, 570-72; Cahill 2005a, 277). This has prompted the suggestion that this scenario also represents the existence of different social groups; those who used wedge tombs but not Beakers, and those who used Beakers and lunulae (O'Brien 2004, 572).

In an Irish context, where no other ceramics other than Beakers were in use during the main currency of halberds and wedge tombs and only a very small number of Chalcolithic wooden vessels are known from bogs or other contexts, the idea of non-Beaker users seems highly improbable. Based on this, it can be assumed that the people who deposited these halberds and built some of these wedge tombs were indeed users of Beaker pottery. Needham (2016) and O'Brien are correct to highlight that there is a paucity of Beaker pottery from the Irish midlands where halberd deposition was concentrated and from parts of the south-west where wedge tombs are concentrated, but as argued above, these aspects of the archaeological record reflect the choices that were made in each region about how to do things.

Overall, we need to be careful not to make too much of the presence or absence of objects in particular areas. People were certainly using some of the same objects and doing similar things with many of these objects, as exemplified by the fact that Beakers occur in pits and spreads in all parts of the country where this pottery has been found. This suggests that people across the island were expressing shared identities in certain contexts. Yet, the spatial patterning in the distribution of certain objects does seem reflective of differences in practices across Ireland and gives us important insights into regionality. As we have seen, there are some areas where concentrations of certain object types occur and other locales where these are scarce. For example, polypod bowls and V-perforated buttons are exclusively found in the northern half of the country. In the case of the buttons, this may reflect the proximity of this part of Ireland to northern Britain. Similarly, copper tanged daggers mainly occur in the midlands. What we are probably seeing here in this discrete spatial patterning is evidence for complementary social practices. In some instances, we may be dealing with the same group of people who conducted different kinds of activities in different places. In others, we are probably looking at very similar social groups who share many of the same ideas, objects and values, but who have locally or regionally divergent customs and so did different things with different objects in different regions.

We can see these similarities and differences as expressions of local and non-local identities and as reflecting regionally divergent traditions, worldviews and practices (Cooney 2000a, 7). It may also be the case that broadly similar values were being expressed, or similar aims were achieved by these differing practices. For example, the deposition of a dagger in one region may have served a very similar purpose to the deposition of a halberd in another. For reasons that are hard to explain, the social values of a particular type of object in a particular region may have meant that it was seen as the most appropriate thing to deposit in a particular place. We see other evidence for regional differences in social practices when we consider the distribution of different site-types. This is exemplified by the paucity of wedge tombs in the east of the country, except for a few locations such as the Dublin Mountains. Similarly, Beakers have only been found in court tombs in the north of Ireland, where these Early Neolithic megaliths are especially common. The aim here has been to highlight that regional differences existed in depositional practices and site-types, but the subtleties of what these regional differences represented is an important topic that will hopefully be explored further in the future.

10

The Beaker phenomenon in Ireland and Beyond?

What can we say about the widespread and rapid transmission of the cultural novelties and material traits forming the Beaker phenomenon? We know that it likely indicates high levels of pan-European interconnectivity during the third millennium BC. The scale and extent of exchange networks and human mobility seems to have expanded considerably during this period. This was certainly the case in Ireland and Britain where the introduction of these innovations signalled a dramatic change in the level of archaeological evidence for inter-continental interactions. Frustratingly, no material traces of contacts between people in continental Europe and these islands are known from 3000-2500 BC, suggesting the unlikely scenario that interregional interactions were exclusively insular for approximately 500 years (Carlin and Brück 2012; Wilkin and Vander Linden 2015, 104). While it seems incredible that people stopped travelling between Ireland and continental Europe in the later Neolithic, there is no doubt that there was at least some small-scale movement of people between Ireland, Britain and continental Europe during the Chalcolithic. A good example of this is provided by the technological knowledge required for the earliest gold and copper metallurgy in Ireland c. 2500 BC; this knowledge would have been embodied and its inception required the arrival or return of people with the requisite level of expertise, some of whom may have been 'alien' (O'Brien 2004; Roberts 2008b, 35; 2008a, 364).

At the wider European level, it is hard to explain the distribution of some highly uniform material traits without some level of mobility of people who had knowledge of these widespread practices (see Vander Linden 2007a; 2007b). Confirmation that small-scale people movement was occurring among those who used Beaker-related objects has been provided by isotope analysis on various Beaker-associated burials across Europe such as the 'Amesbury Archer' and 'Boscombe Bowmen' from Wiltshire in southern England (*e.g.* Price *et al.* 1998; 2004; Bentley 2006; Evans *et al.* 2006; Sheridan 2008a and b; Parker Pearson *et al.* 2016). Examination of the isotopic composition of the teeth from the deceased individual known as the 'Amesbury Archer' indicated that he had spent time in continental Europe, possibly southern Germany, as a young man (Fitzpatrick 2009). While analysis on the Boscombe Bowmen indicate that these may have come to Wiltshire from Wales, Ireland or Brittany (Evans *et al.* 2006).

As outlined in Chapter Two, a recent paper by Reich, Olalde and colleagues detailed the results of a major new aDNA study of 226 individuals from Beaker-associated graves across Europe. This has revealed important new evidence regarding human mobility at this time. The authors of the paper claim to have identified a major westward migration of 'Steppe genes' from central Eurasia into north-west Europe, which occurred in tandem with the spread of Beaker-related material traits (Olalde *et al.* 2018). Beaker-associated burials with this particular genetic signature have been detected in countries including the Netherlands, Germany, the Czech Republic, southern France and northern Italy. The arrival of people with a different genetic composition is most evident in Britain, where apparently 90% of Britain's Neolithic gene pool was almost totally replaced by

Steppe genes over a few hundred years. This is assumed to have occurred in tandem with the introduction of Beaker-related material culture (ibid.). The same genetic ancestry as that of the Beaker-associated burials in Britain has also been identified in the aDNA of three individuals from burials dating to c. 2000 BC on Rathlin Island, off the coast of Northern Ireland (Cassidy and Bradley 2015; Cassidy *et al.* 2016). From this, it is asserted that people with these Steppe genes probably came to Ireland c. 2500 BC, in tandem with the introduction of Beaker-related material traits to these shores (Cassidy *et al.* 2016, 372).

10.1 The genomic transformation of north-west Europe?

Predictably, the results of such aDNA studies have led to a resurgence of interest in migratory explanations (*e.g.* Allentoft *et al.* 2015; Haak *et al.* 2015; Mathieson *et al.* 2015; Kristiansen *et al.* 2017). This includes debates about the character of human mobility in the third millennium BC and its relationship to the spread of the Beaker complex (*e.g.* Vander Linden 2016; Fultorf 2017; Callaway 2018). These papers raise important questions, including what does genomics tell us of the people who used, curated and experienced the things we have come to call the Beaker complex? In an Irish context, more insular questions emerge: what was the role of external or 'foreign' groups from other parts of Europe in the development of the Beaker complex in Ireland? What quantity of newcomers may have arrived in Ireland and what was their impact on the indigenous population and vice versa?

Lara Cassidy and Dan Bradley's (2016) claims of a Beaker-associated wave of genomic change in Ireland are not supported by the limited evidence they have published to date, which is based on as little as three burials post-dating the introduction of Beaker pottery by 500 years. However, the aDNA study conducted by David Reich, Iñigo Olalde and colleagues, in combination with results from isotope analysis and the archaeological evidence, do provide concrete evidence for human mobility over both shorter and longer distances. This confirms that people were certainly moving to and from Britain during the Chalcolithic, and importantly, it informs us that some of those people were newcomers with a very different genetic ancestry to the pre-existing British population. There is no reason to doubt that a similar change in genetic ancestry may have occurred in Ireland during the third millennium BC, as was the case in so many other parts of Europe. However, the scale of migration or mobility or the pace and duration of associated genetic changes at this time in Ireland or Britain is currently undetermined. Furthermore, we have little understanding of how or why this or any associated genetic change occurred in the way that it did.

A critical point that seems to have been overlooked in much of the discussion about the recent aDNA results is that significant gaps in our understanding of the spread and adoption of the Beaker phenomenon remain unexplained by mass migration or the spread of 'Steppe genes'. This is exemplified by the finding from Olalde *et al.*'s (2018) aDNA analysis of 37 Beaker-associated burials from Iberia, whose genes were shown to have very little affinity to those of the Beaker-associated individuals from north-western and central Europe. This means that the genetic composition of those who used Beaker-related objects is diverse, much like the complex itself, and that unlike Britain, migration does not seem to have been a major factor in interactions between people who used Beaker pottery in Iberia and north-western or central Europe.

Genetics provide us with much valuable information about the past including details on the origins of people's hereditary ancestors, biological relationships, the demography of past populations and mobility. All of which certainly contribute towards better understandings of the nature of cultural change. For example, it has previously been claimed that the exogamous exchange of female marriage partners played a key role in the spread of the Beaker complex to Britain (*e.g.* Brodie 1997; 2004; Needham 2005; 207-8; 2007, 43), but the results of the new aDNA analysis show that both men and women with 'Steppe' genes came to Britain and there does not seem to be clear evidence of gender patterning (Olalde *et al*, 2018, 193). This has also been independently confirmed by recent isotope analysis (Parker Pearson *et al.* 2016). However, genetics tells us little of the everyday experience and cultural practices of people living in the latter part of the third millennium BC, providing few insights into 'how' and 'why' people constructed their cultural and social identities (MacEachern 2000, 72; Hofmann 2015, 460; Horning 2018, 12).

Despite the presence of newcomers and the introduction of multiple cultural novelties from various parts of Europe in Ireland and Britain, we also see much evidence for a very strong insular Neolithic cultural legacy from 2500-2200 BC. As discussed below, this is indicated by the regionally distinctive ways in which the Beaker complex was adopted/adapted across Ireland, which have their origins in deeply-rooted local/regional customs. We see continuity of practices and places, as well as the reimagining of older insular traditions. The exact same situation is true of Britain (see Cleal and Pollard 2012; Curtis and Wilkin 2012; Wilkin and Vander Linden 2015). How do we reconcile this archaeological evidence for cultural continuity during the Chalcolithic with the idea that it occurred against the backdrop of large-scale population replacement, as has been claimed? Certainly, it is very difficult to envisage how a Neolithic cultural legacy could have developed in the way that it did if the indigenous people who enacted these transitions had been rapidly and almost completely replaced.

Resolving these issues is difficult, but this is at least partially because the scale, tempo, timing and character of the people movements that occurred in the Chalcolithic are very poorly understood. While this is not the place to discuss these issues in depth, it is important to highlight here that the interrelationships between people movement, population replacement, genetic variation and socio-cultural change are far more complex than has been assumed by Olalde *et al.* (2018) and by many others (see Müller 2013, Vander Linden 2016). The human remains from which genetic material was extracted are certainly part of the archaeological record and represent one aspect of the material culture of past people. The genetic patterning detectable within these bones occurred through sexual reproduction, which is strongly influenced by socio-cultural processes. Yet, genetic variation is subject to a series of biological mechanisms that are quite different from those associated with material culture. This is because people strategically used material culture as a symbolic form of communication to construct social identities (at both a personal and group level), to shape social relations and to create meaning in their lives (Hodder and Hutson 2003, 6).

Changes in genetics, demographics and culture can certainly overlap. Indeed, distinctive genetic signatures can provide proof of migration and it is often difficult to account for social change without some level of mobility. The movement of people or any resulting population change does not, however, explain how or why cultural change happened, and these things cannot be assumed to be closely or causally linked (see Vander Linden 2016, 8-11; Furholt 2017). People who are closely related genetically can display different material traits while those who were not part of the same biological population can share similar cultural practices. Importantly, both scenarios are evidenced by the results of Olalde *et al.*'s (2018) analysis. For example, this showed that people in Iberia as well as in northern and central Europe were all participating in the Beaker complex without being closely related in genetic terms, while groups in the Netherlands and Britain were genetically similar but had differing social practices and material culture. Similarly, immigrants often display considerable fluidity in their material traits upon reaching their new homeland, whereby they either retain their traditions, partially change them or completely replace their previous cultural practices (Burmeister 2000; Furholt 2017). Equally, indigenous groups can respond to newcomers in a variety of ways that are largely determined by choices, though this is not to deny that this agency is constrained by and enmeshed in social relations and context, occasionally to the extent that some choices may not have been that freely made (Hodder 1982; 1986, 74; Cameron 2013, 220).

In other words, culture is a complex human-made social phenomenon that results from the active choices through which groups create themselves in diverse ways across time and space (Robb and Miracle 2007). One's cultural identity is not fixed and there is most certainly not an inexorable biological connection between people's genes and their cultural traits. While the genetic changes that occurred after 2450 BC substantially increased the frequency of genetic variants associated with lighter skin and eye pigmentation in some of the British population (Olalde *et al.* 2018, 193-4), there was still likely to have been considerable diversity in the physical appearance of any newcomers (Tom Booth pers. comm). In a nutshell, it seems unlikely that people's genetic ancestry played a significant role in the construction of their social identity, given that how we define and recognise where we are from is itself socially and contextually defined. Indeed, shared social identities and alliances probably would have existed in the Chalcolithic between people who were not biologically related (Johannsen *et al.* 2017). For example, some people that were not blood-relatives may have been considered part of the same household or kinship group through formal social unions including love, allegiance or authority.

To summarise here, although Olalde *et al.* (2018) successfully identified a significant genetic change, they have too hastily linked this to the introduction of the Beaker phenomenon without having sufficient evidence to demonstrate that the two things were inextricably connected. The assumptions underlying this 'leap of faith' are worryingly reminiscent of the highly problematic approaches that characterised cultural-historical forms of archaeology and resulted in the construction of a mythical 'Beaker folk' (see Chapter Two). The Beaker complex was a regionally divergent socially constructed phenomenon, not a biological condition. The presence of people with a different (Steppe-related) genetic heritage in Britain or Ireland certainly does not explain the spread of Beaker pots to these islands or the adoption of new ideas, objects and practices in the third millennium BC. The continuation of pre-existing traditions after the adoption of Beakers suggests that the level of population replacement in Britain c. 2450-2200 BC may not have been as profound or as sudden as Olalde *et al.* (2018) claimed. However, neither can it be presumed that this continuity of customs indicates a static population that was insulated from external influences during this time-frame (see Robb and Miracle 2007). We must be cautious in our generalisations and give greater attention to the following facts; culture is always chosen, benignly or by force, and genetic transmission is only one part of a complicated range of biological, social and cultural interactions that occurred across Europe during the third millennium BC. Using appropriate methods, including aDNA studies that take account of the complexity and 'messiness' of the evidence, we need to carefully revisit this topic. This will allow us to gain a better understanding of when, what, how and why various socio-cultural interactions and processes resulted in the reproduction of society and culture in the ways that are evident from the genetic and archaeological records.

10.2 External influences?

Returning now to the archaeological evidence from Ireland, what might the style of the objects found here, or the nature of how they were used, reveal about their introduction or the role of newcomers in this process? It has long been suggested that the character of the Beaker phenomenon in Ireland reflects a very strong Atlantic European influence (see Chapter Two), but detailed analysis of the Beaker-related objects found on this island indicates a highly diverse range of extensive contacts between Ireland and various parts of Europe (Case 2004a, 361; Chapter Nine). Indeed, Humphrey Case (2001, 361) characterised Ireland as a 'melting-pot', where the Atlantic and the north-west continental European Beaker traditions collided. If parallels in material traits and social practices can be understood as traces or legacies of former interactions, then a very complex series of overlapping networks existed.

This is amply illustrated by the Irish Beaker ceramics, which show influences from France and Iberia, as well as central and northern Europe (Case 1995a; 2004a; Brindley, A.L. 2004, 335; Needham 2005, 179, see Chapter Three). Although it must be acknowledged that the identification of the style and form of many vessels is impeded by their highly fragmentary condition. Well-known examples of Beakers with a prominent Atlantic European resemblance include the remnants of an S-shaped vessel at Moytirra, Co. Sligo, which can be assigned to Clarke's (1970) European Bell Beaker type (Cremin Madden 1969, fig. 2, wk. 169-170) and another found at Dalkey Island, which has a low-bellied S-profile that is characteristic of Breton Beakers (Liversage 1968, 61, fig 9, sherds 73, 207; Case 1993, 254; Needham 2005, 179). Sherds from a vessel (No. 2) at Newtownlittle, Co. Dublin (Grogan 2005), are very similar to those at Moytirra. Two Beakers described as Maritime-type from Hill of Rath, Co. Louth (Brindley, A.L. 2000; Duffy 2002), may represent further examples. Many Irish Beakers display decorative aspects that reflect an Atlantic contribution including simple horizontal and comb impressed decoration, minor geometrical motifs and cordons (Case 1995a, 20; 2001, 374).

Equally, other Beaker pots display decorative treatments that reflect a central or northern European influence, including zig-zags, fringes, multiple chevrons, ermine decoration, finger nail and finger-tip impressions (Case 1995a, 23; 2004a, 375). This is reinforced by the discovery of a small number of early-style Beakers from sites such as Dalkey Island, Newgrange and Lough Gur (Clark 1970) which seem to display All-Over-Ornament or All-Over-Cord decoration more typical of central and northern European regions (Case 1993, 248; Brindley, A.L. 2004, 334; Grogan and Roche 2010, 36). As discussed in Chapter Nine, the discovery of over 16 polypod bowls in Ireland may also point towards a central European influence as these are found most frequently in the Czech Republic and the Elbe-Saale region of Germany, though they also occur sporadically across much of north-western Europe (Piguet *et al.* 2007).

Interestingly, the styles of many non-ceramic Beaker-related artefacts in Ireland show clear Atlantic affinities. Examples include, gold sun-discs, diadems or bands and basket-shaped ornaments (Case 2004a, 375). While most examples of the latter type from Ireland and Britain are distinctively insular in style, the basket-ornament from Benraw, Co. Down, is an import from Estremoz in Portugal (Taylor 1994; O'Connor, B. 2004). Lunulae seem to be an Irish innovation that also occur occasionally in Britain, France and Belgium, but related ornaments are also known from Denmark and Portugal (Taylor 1980; Needham and Sheridan 2014; Cahill 2015). Cahill (2015) has highlighted that the only other context where a lunula was found with a pair of gold discs, like in the Coggalbeg hoard, was at Cabeceiras de Basto, Braga, in Portugal.

The distinctive arsenical copper technology employed in early Irish metalwork is most comparable to that practiced in conjunction with the use of Beakers in Atlantic France and Iberia (Ambert 2001; O'Brien 2004, 557-61). This suggests that the necessary technological knowledge originated there (O'Brien 2004, 558-69). Copper thick-butted axes characteristic of Atlantic Europe are widely known in Ireland (Burgess 1979, 213), while close parallels to the Irish Lough Ravel axes are found in Iberia and Atlantic France (Harbison 1979, 103; Sheridan 1983, 16). Similarities between the character of Irish copper halberds and those in France and Iberia, which are of earlier date, suggest a direct sharing of ideas (Horn 2014; Needham *et al.* 2017, 48). In addition, copper thin-butted axes that are considered characteristic of northern Europe are also prevalent in Ireland and close parallels to the Irish Ballybeg-type copper thin-butted flat axes occur in Germany, the Netherlands and Scandinavia (Burgess 1979, 213; Mount 2000, 70; Case 2004a).

Chalcolithic arrowheads in Ireland include both barbed and tanged and hollow-based examples, indicating influences from Atlantic and Central Europe (Case 2004a). This fits with the fact that Irish wrist-bracers represent a unique mixture of different European wrist-bracer styles. As we saw in Chapter Nine, they are mainly red or black in colour like the four-holed wrist-bracers of central Europe, but the Irish examples are predominantly two-holed just like those from Atlantic Europe and a small number of black wrist-bracers from the Netherlands and Germany. Cumulatively, this stylistic evidence suggests a complex set of direct and indirect links between Ireland and various other regions during the Chalcolithic, but it is very clear that external ideas were being adopted and hybridised in uniquely insular ways. This is exemplified by the character of much of the Beaker pottery and the goldwork, especially the basket-shaped ornaments and the wrist-bracers (see Chapter Nine). Of course, this not that surprising given that a clear majority of Beaker-related objects found in Ireland were made there.

When we considered the various social practices that featured Beaker-related objects in Ireland, the differences between how people used and deposited these on that island, compared to other parts of Europe, became pronounced. Certainly, there is little evidence in Ireland for the classic crouched single inhumation burial with accompanying items from the Beaker assemblage, which is a recurrent feature of the Beaker phenomenon in much of north-western and central Europe (*e.g.* Strahm 1995; Turek 1998; Czebreszuk 2003; Vander Linden 2004). Despite the commonly held view that Beaker funerary practices in Ireland are comparable to that of the Atlantic façade, where collective burials were placed into Neolithic megaliths, examination of this in Chapter Five showed that this is clearly not the case. As discussed in Chapter Nine, far greater quantities of objects such as copper tanged daggers and wrist-bracers have been found in Ireland than other European regions like northern France or southern Portugal, suggesting that a very different approach was taken towards the manufacture and deposition of these objects in Ireland. This is entirely consistent with the very different depositional contexts in which these objects have been found in Ireland compared to other parts of Europe. In Chapter Seven, we saw that although the occurrence of Beaker artefacts in non-anthropogenic contexts has not been the subject of detailed examinations within other parts of Europe, this does not seem to have been a central feature of Beaker-associated practices in any of these regions in the way that it was in Ireland.

Interestingly, some of the closest parallels for Beaker-associated social practices in Ireland seem to be found in other areas that were located at the outer edges of the European continent. The character of the Beaker phenomenon in Denmark best illustrates this. Although different to Ireland, similarities are identifiable; Beaker pottery is found as occupational debris in settlement contexts, while the aceramic objects were often deposited in 'natural places' (Sarauw 2008, 30, 40; Vandkilde 2009). Although inhumation burials complete with flint daggers and arrowheads are present in Denmark, Beaker pottery, gold and metal objects, as well as wrist-bracers were totally excluded from burials (Vandkilde 2005, 27; Sarauw 2007b).

Contrary to traditional views of the Irish version of the Beaker phenomenon (see Chapter Two), this study shows that the best parallels for Beaker-related objects and social practices in Ireland are to be found with its nearest neighbour, Britain. This is not surprising given that people on these islands clearly interacted during the Neolithic (Sheridan 2004a and b); for example, very strong links developed c. 3200 BC, when local communities across the Irish Sea became interconnected through a shared cosmology and their use of Grooved Ware and related artefact types (Carlin 2017). These contacts continued after the appearance of the Beaker phenomenon in both places, clearly illustrated by the key role of Irish copper in early British metalwork, which was included in some southern British Beaker burials (Northover *et al.* 2001, 28; Needham 2004, 235; O'Brien 2004). There are clear stylistic similarities between other objects, including some of the Beaker pottery from Ireland, Wessex and northern Britain (Case 1995a, 20; 2004a, 375; see Chapter Three). Gold lunulae have also been found in Britain indicating the sharing of ideas between people on these islands. Most of these are of a distinctly regional form, but, a few examples of the classical Irish type that probably represent imports from Ireland have been found in Cornwall at Harlyn Bay and St. Juliot (Needham and Sheridan 2014, 911). Similarly, the V-perforated buttons found in Ireland point to links with northern Britain; some of these seem to be made from Yorkshire jet while others were made using albertite from Sutherland in Scotland (Harbison 1976; Shepherd, A.N. 2009, 341).

As we have seen in the earlier chapters, there are also clear similarities between Beaker-related social practices on these neighbouring islands. Just like the Irish settlement evidence, in Britain this mainly comprises pits and spreads containing Beaker-associated occupation debris (see Chapter Four). As is the case in Ireland, Late Neolithic ceremonial monuments including timber circles and henges continue to be used in much the same ways as before (see Chapter Six) and the deposit of Beakers at these and older Neolithic sites like the West Kennet long barrow, indicates a similar concern with historically important places (Cleal and Pollard 2012; see Chapter Six). Indeed, several Neolithic tombs in western and northern Britain were re-used in the mid/late third millennium BC for a variety of Beaker-associated depositional practices (see Chapter Five). Like in Irish court tombs, these do not seem to have been funerary in nature, instead the deposits placed within these tombs generally comprised Beaker sherds that had been obtained from spreads of occupational debris (see Wilkin 2016; Chapters Four and Five).

As discussed in Chapter Five, aspects of British funerary practises resemble those found in Ireland. A few classic early Beaker inhumations are present in some parts of Britain, but these and other forms of Beaker-associated burial are rare until after 2300 BC. Beaker-associated burial in Britain after this date shows considerable diversity of practice, some of which are directly comparable to what we see in Ireland at this time. This is especially obvious in the case of the construction and use of wedge tombs on the Hebrides and other related monuments including Clava cairns, entrance graves and recumbent stone circles (Bradley 2000b; 2005b; 2009).

This is not, however, to give a false picture of homogeneity between these islands as there are significant differences in Beaker-related material culture and practices across both. For example, unlike wrist-bracers in Ireland, those from Britain are dominated by green and grey four-holed types (Woodward *et al.* 2006; Hunter and Woodward 2015). Despite the similarities in some aspects of the funerary sphere on both islands, unlike Ireland, this still represents the context in which most Beaker-related objects in Britain have been found. Directly related to this is another key difference; deposition of Beaker-related objects in 'natural places' was not a prominent social practice in Britain, other than perhaps in north-eastern Scotland which was very closely linked to Ireland through the exchange of stone and metal axes throughout the fourth and third millennium BC (Sheridan 1986; Cowie 1988; Needham 2004, 239; 2007).

The similarities and differences between the Beaker complex in various parts of Ireland and Britain provide an apt illustration of the fact that culture is always chosen. For example, those people who used Irish copper throughout Britain predominantly chose not to emulate the social practices associated with that material in Ireland (Wilkin and Vander Linden 2015, 107). All of this suggests that this spatially discrete patchwork of similarities and differences represent the residues of various regional networks during the latter half of the third millennium BC. Interconnected communities in various parts of Ireland and western, south-western and northern Britain chose to share some materials and traditions of practice, as well as maintain social relations with each other (see Needham 2004; Curtis and Wilkin 2012; Wilkin 2016, 280). This is evidenced by discoveries such as that at Seafield West, near Inverness, where a burial with a distinctively Irish Bowl was located next to a second burial containing a bronze dagger made from Irish copper and a second Irish Bowl (Cressey and Sheridan 2003).

The Beaker complex in Ireland is clearly 'similar but different' to everywhere else. This brings us back to one of the points made in Chapter One, that although certain interregional artefact types and ideas were widely shared across Europe, these were adapted differently in each region to fit the local context and its pre-existing traditions (Salanova 2000; 2004; Vander Linden 2006a; 2007a; 2007b). Just like the Beaker phenomenon elsewhere, the exact range of Beaker-associated practices and material culture found in Ireland did not originate in a single European region. Instead, like elsewhere, different external and internal influences were rapidly combined at an early stage to produce a unique hybrid. Cumulatively, all of this suggests that in the latter half of the third millennium BC, Ireland was inhabited by a well-connected society capable of maintaining long-distance exchange networks and developing relationships with other people elsewhere in Europe. As part of this, people, things and ideas were moving to and from Ireland at various times within these different networks.

10.3 Continuity and change?

Turning now to consider these internal influences in more detail, we see that although there were some changes to practices, the adoption of Beaker-related cultural innovations in Ireland generally involved these being blended and balanced with long-standing depositional practices. As a result, these cultural novelties were often deployed in idiosyncratic ways that strongly continued or reflected the character of the Irish Neolithic. The rapid replacement of Late Neolithic Grooved Ware by Beaker pottery c. 2500-2400 BC occurred in tandem with an increase in the scale and range of pottery deposition (see Carlin and Brück 2012; Carlin and Cooney 2017). Some of the traditions associated with the manufacture and use of Irish Grooved Ware continued however. The high quantity of plain undecorated Beakers that occur in Ireland may be a direct reflection of the extent to which most of the Grooved Ware found there was also very plain with few decorative elements, unlike that from Britain (Grogan and Roche 2010, 34-6). Indeed, pre-existing social practices were largely sustained, and Beakers assumed many of the roles that Grooved Ware once fulfilled in highly similar depositional practices (see Chapter Eight). Just like Grooved Ware, most of the Beaker pottery in Ireland has been found in a highly fragmentary condition in deposits of occupational debris within pit clusters or spreads (Carlin and Cooney 2017, see Chapters Four and Nine). As we saw in Chapter Six, some Late Neolithic timber circles continued in use until 2200 BC, with Beakers being deposited at these monuments in the same ways as the Grooved Ware that it replaced (see Section 10.4 for further discussion).

Despite the slight changes in practices that we see occurring in tandem with the adoption of Beaker-related material culture, a definite interest in older monuments, places, people and practices was maintained. This is illustrated by the Newgrange and Knowth passage tombs, which continued as foci for largely unchanging forms of ceremonial practices over much of the third millennium BC (see Chapters Three, Five and Six). The deposition of large quantities of Beaker pottery – often in association with or in deposits overlying Grooved Ware – concentrated outside the entrances to these monuments formed part of a much longer sequence of ceremonial acts which emphasised their exterior. This tells us that ceremonial practices at these passage tombs did not change after the adoption of Beaker pottery. The ways in which the Beaker-associated activities echoed the previous activities conducted there is exemplified by the deposition of the Beaker pot beside human remains dating from 2912-2877 BC in the passage of Knowth Tomb 15. Significantly, this is the only Beaker pottery pre-dating 2200 BC known from the interior of an Irish passage tomb, signalling an awareness of the later Neolithic tradition of depositing materials outside rather than inside the tomb.

The apparent lack of highly formalised Beaker-associated burial activity (outside of wedge tomb contexts) can also be seen as a continuation of Late Neolithic practices and values (see below). In Ireland, Grooved Ware was rarely deposited in funerary contexts or with human remains and the deposition of burnt or unburnt human bone in a manner that left a clear and obvious archaeological trace declined as a practice after 2800 BC (Carlin 2017; Carlin and Cooney 2017). The character of Beaker-associated burial practices in Ireland, including the paucity of Beaker pottery or other Beaker-related objects within mortuary contexts and the continuation of cremation as a major burial rite, was almost certainly influenced by these pre-existing approaches. Although clearly there were also other forces at play; we do see both an increase in the level of evidence for burial activity as well as wider adoption of inhumation rites and the deposition of these unburnt human remains in a completely new type of megalith, the wedge tomb.

The ways in which metallurgy was developed and then used in Ireland was strongly influenced by Neolithic traditions, particularly those associated with the production and exchange of polished stone axes (Cooney and Mandal 1998; Carlin and Brück 2012). Similar to how the stone for those axes was often obtained from a very particular source (*e.g.* porphyry from Lambay Island), for several centuries copper ore was extracted from a single source by communities in the south-west (O'Brien 2004, 563). Furthermore, the products from the Ross Island mine were also widely distributed throughout Ireland and across the Irish Sea along the same exchange routes as the porcellanite stone axes from Antrim (Cooney 2000a, 204; Needham 2004, 235). This is most visible in north-eastern Scotland, where a significant concentration of porcellanite axes have been found (Sheridan 1986, 2) and the earliest known metal objects are copper thick-butted flat axes from Ireland (Cowie 1988, 7). The Migdale-Marnoch bronze metalwork tradition, which used Irish copper and Cornish tin, subsequently developed in this region (Needham 2004, 235).

Some of the copper from Ross Island may have been exchanged and circulated in the form of axes or axe-shaped ingots, large numbers of which have been found in north-eastern Ireland (Harbison 1969b, 22-24; but see Schmidt and Burgess 1981, 30). If so, this would have also strongly mirrored the exchange of stone axes between people in parts of Ireland and Scotland. The discovery of a single polished stone axe within the spread of occupational debris and ore processing spoil at the Ross Island copper mine (O'Brien 2004, 358) and a cache of polished stone axes in another Early Bronze Age copper mine at Ballyrisode, near Goleen, Co. Cork (O'Brien 2003, 53-4), also underlines the vital role played by these objects in the acceptance of copper technology (Roberts *et al.* 2009).

This seems to reflect the longstanding significance of polished stone axes in Irish prehistory. These played a prominent role in social life during the Mesolithic and Neolithic and this continued after the adoption of Beakers in Ireland (Cooney and Mandal 1998, 34; Cooney and Grogan 1999, 231; Cooney 2004, 39). Numerous polished stone axes have been found in association with Beaker pottery in a very wide range of contexts. Furthermore, evidence for their manufacture by people using this pottery was recorded at Cloghers, Co. Kerry, and Roughan Hill, Co. Clare (see Chapters Three, Four, Five and Six). Axes retained their special role in society, despite the change in the material from which they were made c. 2500 BC (Carlin and Brück 2012). This is evidenced by the exceptionally strong emphasis on both the production and deposition of copper flat axeheads; these form the main component (78%) of Ireland's early copper assemblage with over 450 copper axes found throughout the entire island compared to 20 of the copper tanged daggers, which are considered to typify the Beaker complex elsewhere (Harbison 1969b; Becker 2006, 80).

The depositional treatment of these copper axes, as well as halberds and many of the aceramic Beaker novelties, respected the pre-existing Neolithic custom on this island of predominantly depositing supra-regional stone axeheads in natural wet places in one-type hoards (Cooney 2004, 39; Carlin and Brück 2012). While polished stone axes come from a wide variety of contexts that include settlements and burials, a large proportion (57%) have been recovered from watery locations, with many (45%) coming from rivers and a lesser amount (12%) from bogs (Cooney and Mandal 1998, 34-8; Cooney 2004, 38-9). Significantly, it was the large finely made or highly polished stone axes, particularly those from distant places, which were deposited in wet locales.

A large proportion (43%) of the Langdale stone axes from Cumbria and most of the exotic Alpine jadeite axes that were brought to Ireland in the fourth millennium BC were deposited in wetland environs (see Cooney and Mandal 1998; Bradley 2000a, 86; Pétrequin *et al.* 2008; 2009; Alison Sheridan, pers. comm.). Unlike other more local or everyday objects, these axes had a special significance, which meant that they needed to be treated in a particularly formal manner, including their deposition in distinctive and discrete contexts that were removed from the everyday world (Cooney and Mandal 1998, 34; Bradley 2000a, 120-21). These supra-regional polished stone axes represented value-laden symbols of exchange that served to negotiate and reproduce collective values and underpin social relations (Cooney and Mandal 1998; Cooney and Grogan 1999, 231; Wentink and van Gijn 2008, 35).

The depositional treatment of Chalcolithic objects with a special significance in Ireland followed on from this practice of keeping value-laden objects spatially and contextually separate, but in an even more restricted and rule-bound manner. This is illustrated by the recovery from bogs of half of the 400 contexted copper flat axes (after Becker 2006). Similarly, copper tanged daggers, V-perforated buttons, wrist-bracers, gold discs and lunulae are predominantly found in bogs as single finds or within one-type hoards (see Chapters Seven and Nine). These objects appear to have assumed many of the roles previously occupied by certain forms of polished stone axes, especially in depositional ceremonies that we understand as relating to the expression and constraint of identities, relationships and social values on this island.

This is certainly evidenced by wrist-bracers. As we saw in Chapter Nine, most of the main types of stone that these were manufactured from, including fine-grained siltstones, mudstones, shales and Antrim porcellanite, had previously been source materials for Neolithic polished stone axes in Ireland (Cooney and Mandal 1998, 58, 81; Roe and Woodward 2009). While the red wrist-bracers were made from jasper, a material that had been previously used in the production of the macehead pendants and beads that were deposited in passage tombs c. 3200-3000 BC. These probably came from Lambay Island, which was also the location of a porphyritic andesite axe quarry during the Neolithic (Cooney *et al.* 2013, 415). Incidentally, this matches with the use of historically significant stone types to make wrist-bracers in Britain, including Langdale tuff that had previously been a major source material for stone axes (Woodward *et al.* 2006; Woodward and Hunter 2011).

Based on the distribution of various discoveries across Ireland, the people who lived there (whether newly arrived and/or longer-term inhabitants) adopted and adapted various new ideas and practices within quite a short timescale. Yet, as is exemplified by the distinctive ways in which early metallurgy was practised here, they did so in a way that fitted within the local or regional cosmologies of the Neolithic population (Carlin and Brück 2012). This is unsurprising given that it has been widely recognised that people adopt cultural innovations when and if they are compatible with their local culture, value systems and social structures (Rogers 2003, 10; Fokkens 2008, 18; Roberts 2008a, 365-6).

Yet what we see in Ireland is not as simple as this might suggest. Also evident are the development of new practices in conjunction with the introduction of the Beaker complex, such as the occasional deposition of inhumations. Much of this new form of activity did, however, reference older traditions and places that had declined by 3000 BC. As discussed in Chapter Five, the placement of Beaker-associated deposits of occupational debris into portal and court tombs c. 2450 BC denotes a resurgence of interest in earlier Neolithic megalithic structures that had not been foci for depositional activity in the Late Neolithic. These Beaker deposits seem to represent a rebirth of an earlier Neolithic tradition of depositing occupational materials into megaliths during interactions between the communities of the living and their past ancestors who were embodied by these monuments (see Case 1969; 1973). Whether the people depositing the Beakers were descended from these ancestors or simply imagined themselves as such may not have been of crucial importance.

We also see the construction of a new megalithic monument type; wedge tombs in which burnt and unburnt human remains were deposited in association with Beaker pottery. These began to be constructed quite suddenly c. 2450 BC after a 500-year-long hiatus in tomb building. These represent a reinvention of the Neolithic megalithic tradition in Ireland as evidenced by how their design was strongly influenced by the architecture of pre-existing megaliths, which they were occasionally sited beside (Chapter Five). These new megaliths provided a special kind of place to deposit Beaker pots and arrowheads with the remains of a select group of dead people to enable the transformation of their identities (see Chapter Five). Importantly, wedge tombs represent the only context in which we find complete Beaker pots with human remains. Perhaps these monuments needed to be created to facilitate the adoption of such a new form of social practice in a manner that accorded with traditional insular values. By referencing earlier Neolithic monuments, an older tradition was re-imagined in a way that reproduced ancestral social relations. This is supported by the deliberate exclusion of other supra-regional styled Beaker-related objects, the deposition of which would not have transformed the identity of the specially selected

Fig. 10.1: Excavations at Parknabinnia wedge tomb on the Burren, Co. Clare, during the summer of 2017 by The Irish Fieldschool of Prehistoric Archaeology (photo reproduced by permission of Ros Ó Maoldúin).

dead or established relationships between the living and the ancestors in the correct manner (see Fokkens 1997; Fontijn 2008, 102).

This strong concern with insular traditions, whether reinvented or continued, represents a recurrent aspect of social practices in Chalcolithic Ireland. We have seen much evidence for material engagements that metaphorically connected people back to other people, places, events and values in the near and distant past. Creating and maintaining relationships with the ancestral in these ways seems to represent efforts on the part of newcomers and/or indigenes to construct or emphasise a shared local or insular social identity in certain contexts. This may have been a high priority as this was a time of increasingly wider inter-regional links, whereby more non-local people may have been visiting or staying on the island than had previously been the case. There was also an increased range and quantity of artefacts that referred to other people and places that were spatially remote. Turning to 'tradition' in the ways people did may have functioned as a powerful framework that enabled the new and the old to be successfully integrated together in a way that fitted with extant cultural conventions (Osborne 2008, 284).

This is certainly the case for wedge tombs, which enabled the adoption of new ideas and values relating to the deposition of inhumations (Fig. 10.1). This was clearly a contentious issue and as we have seen throughout the book, the small number of inhumations known from the Chalcolithic indicated a strong resistance to the uptake of the stereotypical crouched single inhumation with accompanying pottery and other grave-gifts. It was not until the creation in Ireland c. 2200 BC of a completely new and distinctly insular special purpose funerary ceramic – Irish Bowls of the Food Vessel tradition – that pottery or other objects like daggers began to be buried with inhumations on a more widespread basis within pits, cists and older megaliths. As detailed in Chapter Five, these Bowls represent the Irish version of British funerary Beakers whose development enabled the widespread adoption of the practices that had previously been resisted.

10.4 Beaker pots: commemorating the domestic

As we saw earlier in the book, Ireland has long been seen as a place where Beaker pottery predominantly occurs in settlement or 'domestic' contexts, but this does not match the complexity of the Irish evidence. These characterisations were originally founded upon a misreading of a small number of well-known discoveries, particularly those from *Brú na Bóinne* and Lough Gur. One of the main reasons why it seems to have persisted, however, is because so much of the deposits containing Beaker pottery have a strongly 'domestic' character. This situation was compounded by the lack of attention given to Beaker-associated ceremonial practices in Ireland and the false assumption that there was a clear and distinct division between ceremonial and domestic activity.

One of the points that has been made throughout this book is about how people strategically used material culture to symbolically negotiate, reproduce and communicate social values, identities and relationships. This is highly pertinent for understanding Beaker-related social practices in Ireland because so much of the Irish Chalcolithic archaeological record comprises deposits in pits, spreads, megaliths, timber circles, *fulachtaí fia* and 'natural places'. Even though many of these deposits seem to have been made during routine actions, they were highly selective and intentional acts that enacted and reflected ideological values in materially-specific ways, rather than directly representing how things were in the past (Fontijn 2002; Pollard 2002; Bradley 2003, 6-12; 2005a, 208-9).

This is relevant because so many of these Beaker-associated deposits are so similar. These frequently include what appears to be habitation debris, including fragmented sherds of Beaker pottery but few of the other stereotypical Beaker-related objects. Despite their uniformity, they were placed with varying degrees of formality into a diverse range of contexts including pits, spreads, megalithic tombs and timber circles. This epitomises the highly intertwined nature of Chalcolithic ritual and domestic activity, but thwarts the interpretation of any of these deposits, making it exceptionally difficult to assess whether any pits or spreads signify the poorly preserved remains of settlement activity in those locations. This is further complicated by the fact that houses from the mid-third millennium BC do not appear to have left a lasting trace and only a few examples, such as Graigueshoneen, Co. Waterford, have been identified.

Perhaps the key finding from the earlier chapters to highlight here is that the Chalcolithic record exists (in the way that it does) precisely because these deposits were performed in a structured and culturally prescribed manner with a heightened degree of formality that resulted in the creation of a recognisable archaeological trace (see Bradley 2005a, 208-9). Clearly, many of these deposits of occupational debris were made in a highly ritualised manner that fulfilled various practical, social and ceremonial functions for the community who seem to have participated and witnessed these acts. That is not to say that these deposits were conducted in complete isolation from everyday life. Instead, they seem to form part of a spectrum of social practices that formed a continuum ranging from the sacred to the profane (see Brück 1999a). Indeed, many of these Beaker-associated deposits seem to represent interactions (such as gift exchanges) between the social groups of the living and that of the ancestors. This involved conducting everyday activities in a much more formalised or dramatic manner than usual and making material statements that deliberately emphasised 'domestic' aspects of life (see Bradley 2005a, 32-6).

By depositing Beaker pottery in this way, people drew upon the symbolism of the home in accentuated ways that commemorated collective everyday 'domestic' activities and recalled the virtues of an idealised community. This involved ritualising the customs of daily life so that the materials being deposited acted as metaphorical representations of the various shared activities and social ties that bound people, places and their ancestors together in their everyday world. Their deposition physically removed them from daily life so that by their absence the meanings associated with these artefacts, as well as the life stories of the people and the places associated with them, would have been recalled and reproduced (Rowlands 1993, 146; Thomas 1996, 197; Fontijn 2007, 76-7; 2008, 102). This seems to have been a social strategy that served to construct and emphasise a shared group identity, based around the idea of mutual membership of a household (see Lévi-Strauss 1983; Carsten and Hugh-Jones 1995; Thomas 2010).

The ways in which this operated shows a very strong concern with both the creation and the commemoration of shared memories. Across the wide-range of contexts in which Beaker-associated deposits occur, there is compelling evidence for a material engagement with people, places and things from the recent and more distant past. Pre-existing ceremonial foci including earlier Neolithic megaliths and Late Neolithic timber circles, as well as other places with long histories of inhabitation, consistently attracted a considerable degree of Beaker-associated depositional activity. As we have seen here, these deposits were generally conducted in a manner that was consistent with the past traditions associated with each of these places.

By placing Beaker-associated habitation materials into ancient monuments such as Early Neolithic court tombs, people may have been conducting exchanges with those they perceived as their ancestors or as founders of the group in a manner that celebrated the 'domestic', but also demonstrated kinship and descent (Helms 1998,

15; Fokkens 1999, 41; Fontijn 2008, 94). This served to construct and maintain the group's local identity and their sense of belonging to a specific place (see Chapter Five). Similarly, the deposition of Beaker-associated occupational debris into the postholes of Late Neolithic timber circles was highly commemorative of these monuments, the ways they had been used before and the people who used them. How these deposits were placed within these monuments created and reasserted a shared connection between those involved in this activity and their predecessors. Significantly, the Beaker-associated practice in Ireland of conducting depositional activity that emphasised the homeplace is a direct continuation of the strong emphasis that was placed on the domestic household in Late Neolithic ceremonial activity (see Chapter Six). This chimes with the point made above about how, in Ireland, Late Neolithic ceremonial traditions were clearly echoed by Beaker-associated depositional practices.

10.5 The meanings of Beaker-related objects?

Non-ceramic Beaker-related artefacts in Ireland can be rather frustrating because so many of these occur as stray or single finds within 'natural places', particularly bogs. This sense of frustration often feels more acute when we contrast the Irish evidence with that from other European regions, where many of these objects occur together with Beaker pottery and often accompanying burials. The examination of the context and condition of Beaker-related objects, however, demonstrates that there were highly selective and uniform ways of treating different artefacts throughout much of the island. In Ireland, as elsewhere, the people who used these cultural innovations consistently chose characteristic ways of depositing these artefacts that were type-, context- and place-specific. Importantly, this indicates that these deposits are not the product of random acts. Instead, the depositional treatment of these objects is directly reflective of the social practices and belief systems of that time and place, as well as the complex meanings and values that had become attached to these objects. This is exemplified by the uniformity evident in the treatment of some lunulae and red wrist-bracers. Common ideas seem to have been broadly shared regarding the correct life-path for particular object types, which resulted in so many of the metal objects being deposited in particular ways rather than recycled.

Each of these object types seem to have functioned as very important symbols whose meanings were commonly understood by many people across Ireland. Of course, this is not to say that Beaker artefacts represented the same thing to everyone at all times; the meanings attached to these items were highly dynamic and varied from person to person, context to context and were strongly influenced by the biography of each object. This plurality of meanings is evidenced by occasional divergences in the depositional treatment of these artefacts such as the deposition of the wrist-bracer in the cist at Furness (see Section 9.5), but these occurrences are exceptional. In fact, these exceptions highlight how widely shared the cultural treatment of these objects must have been. It leads us to assume that the values ascribed to these objects must also have been widely recognised across Ireland. Naturally, this brings us on to the question of what were these values or meanings and how did they come to be ascribed to these objects?

Traditionally, Beaker-related objects have been understood as representations of personal wealth that were competitively exchanged and displayed as part of a prestige goods economy (*e.g.* Clarke *et al.* 1985; Needham 2004; Heyd 2007; Sheridan 2008b). As we saw in Chapter Two, the prestige-based interpretation of the Beaker phenomenon is based on analysis of Beaker-associated graves and the idea that these objects were the personal possessions of the deceased individual within them and that they inform us about their social status in life. Many aspects of these various interpretations are, however, highly problematic and hard to reconcile with the evidence before us (Brück 2004b; 2006a and b; Fowler 2004; 2013; see Chapters One and Two).

According to these prestige-based viewpoints of Chalcolithic and Bronze Age Europe, objects were deemed economically valuable because of their scarcity (*e.g.* Kristiansen and Larsson 2005; for critique see Fokkens 1999; 2012b). There is, however, little to suggest that there was any scarcity of Beakers or Beaker-related objects in Ireland, or that this was the source of their value. A putative prestige goods economy would have been based on the control of the exchange of foreign or rare exotica, but there is little evidence for such in Ireland because almost all the Beaker-related objects found on this island were made here, often through local community-based enterprise. Furthermore, it is difficult to argue that the highly codified deposition of single finds or pairs of insular objects, as was typical of the Irish Chalcolithic, represented a lavish act of conspicuous consumption designed to impact upon a political economy.

Indeed, the idea that wealth or rank was the driving force behind the acquisition, use or deposition of these objects does little to account for the highly structured nature of Chalcolithic deposition in Ireland, such as the tendency to keep particular object types apart and only deposit them in specific ways in certain kinds of places. Equally, it does not explain why the same selective range of objects were repeatedly included in Beaker-associated graves in other parts of Europe in restricted quantities, combinations and location in relation to the body (Fokkens 2012b, 120; Fowler 2013, 99). The highly standardised ways that these objects were deposited in

Ireland or in European Beaker graves seems unrelated to either personal wealth or economics. Instead, their treatments suggest that these objects were regarded as highly symbolic, representing what must have been widely shared values and beliefs that were of key ideological significance for the community (see Fokkens 2012b, 120-23). So, we are left with the questions of what, where, or who specifically, did these objects represent that made them so valued? What resulted in them being treated in such a circumscribed manner?

10.6 Personhood and 'personal possessions'

The prestige-based interpretation of the Beaker phenomenon is based on upon a western capitalist conception of objects as passive and anonymous inanimate things that were primarily traded or exchanged for economic gain, which overlooks the evidence indicating that objects were often treated the same way as humans (See Section 2.11; Brück and Fontijn 2013; Fowler 2013, 87) This interpretation falsely imposes a modern-day distinction between people, places and things as well as gifts and commodities into the past (Brück 2016). It ignores the widely accepted view that gift exchange was fundamental to Chalcolithic and Bronze Age societies, particularly in terms of the creation and maintenance of interpersonal and intergroup relations (see Bradley and Edmonds 1993; Godelier 1999; Needham 2008; Brück and Fontijn 2013). In short, it divides the social from the economic and then privileges the latter over the former (Barrett and Needham 1988).

Objects played a key role in negotiating and representing social values and relationships, as well as constituting the person, both as an individual and as a member of the wider society (Weiner 1992; Latour 1996; Gell 1998). One of the main ways in which identities and relationships were constructed was by the entanglement of the biographies of people and things through gift exchange (cf. Maus 1990; Weiner 1992; Godelier 1999). In gift exchange, things become inalienably imbued with human values, particularly those of the giver, to the extent that objects come to personify that person or persons (Appadurai 1986; Mauss 1990; Weiner 1992). As a result, objects may have been regarded as possessing life and thereby having a life-cycle with a correct form of beginning and end (Jones, A. 2008, 331). Over the course of their lives, multiple social values and meanings would have been attributed to objects based on biographical factors, such as where they came from, who made them, who they previously belonged to and how they were acquired (Kopytoff 1986; Hoskins 1998; Gosden and Marshall 1999, 170; Hodder and Hutson 2003, 192).

At significant life-stages, such as birth, adulthood, marriage and death, the various qualities and aspects that constituted pre-modern personhood were often gifted by other people, gods or ancestors (Fokkens 1999; 2012b; Brück and Fontijn 2013). The exchange of ideas, people and things also tied people together across space and time to geographically distant people or to their predecessors (Latour 1996; Gell 1998; Brück 2006b; Chapman 2008). Beaker-related objects would almost certainly have been seen as active animate social entities that were of moral, social and cultural importance because of the people, places and things they represented and the key roles that they played in the construction of a social reality (see Hodder and Hutson 2003, 6)

The assumption that the Beaker-related objects found in graves alongside individuals were personal possessions of the deceased that reflected their social ranking is highly problematic (Brück 2004b; 2006b; Fowler 2004; 2013). It imposes a very modern western conception of personhood as a bounded, autonomous subject into the past (Brück 2001; 2004; Fowler 2004). This makes a false distinction between the self and other, which overlooks the fact that identity is inherently relational rather than fixed. In other words, a person's identity would have been socially constructed over the course of their life through their exchanges and relationships with other people, places and things and this would have varied over time and space (Fokkens 1999; Fontijn 2002, 81; Brück and Fontijn 2013).

10.7 Transformation rituals

The funerary realm represents one arena in which social identities and relationships were constructed in very particular ways through a series of transformation rituals. These rituals represented rites of passage that transformed the deceased into a different kind of person or entity with a new social identity (such as an ancestor) (Fowler 2004; Garwood 2011; 2012, 300). Rather than belonging to the deceased, the Beaker-related objects that we are so familiar with are more likely to be gifts that were given by the community to the ancestors or the dead during these transformation rituals (Brück 2004b; 2006b; Fowler 2013). These gifts served to construct, negotiate and underline relationships (of kinship, indebtedness, authority and allegiance) between the communities of the living, the dead and the ancestors or supernatural, as well as between people and places (Mizoguchi 1993; Barrett 1994, 116-23; Woodward 2000, 113-15; Brück 2004a; 2004b, 180).

It has previously been argued that the types of objects like halberds, lunulae or axes that have almost exclusively been deposited in 'natural places' were 'communal', in contrast to those found with burials, which were deemed 'personal' (*e.g.* Needham 1988; Vandkilde 1996; Fontijn 2002, 83). Rather than being related to individual's social identities, these were unsuitable for inclusion in burials because they were so closely interlinked with the wider groups of people who used these in communal ceremonies to mark critical events (Needham 1988; Fontijn 2002). In an Irish context, this would mean that so many objects typically considered 'personal', such as copper daggers, stone wrist-bracers and gold ornaments, must have been 'communal' objects, just like copper axes, because they were all excluded from graves and not linked with individuals. This scenario, however, illustrates that this distinction between 'personal' daggers or wrist-bracers and 'communal' daggers or wrist-bracers rests upon the problematic assumption that the objects found with individuals were personal possessions of the person in the grave. The objects deposited in graves are the product of a series of activities that focused on a specific body and place, but that were performed by and for a community. Indeed, this body and the assemblage within the grave may well have been regarded as both belonging to and representing the community (Fowler 2004; 2013, 100-102). Their deposition constructed and depicted that community's relationships, as well as their shared values and beliefs, not just those of the deceased.

The deposition of these same objects in 'natural places' in Ireland suggest that it may also have been another form of gift exchange that similarly involved the community of the living giving away highly symbolic objects, presumably also to the ancestors or the supernatural, to establish social relationships and constitute personhood (Fokkens 1999; Fontijn 2002, 275). By ceremonially removing these objects from the sphere of the living, the values and ideas associated with them were enacted and memorised (Rowlands 1993, 146; Fontijn 2007, 76-7; 2008, 102). This means that the deposition of objects in graves and those in 'natural places' may be more strongly related than previously realised. Both represent communal ceremonial activities that enabled communities to construct and depict their values, relationships, identities and categories of places (see Barrett and Needham 1988, 129; Fontijn 2008, 98). The ways in which various kinds of social identities in both scenarios were articulated and transformed seems to have differed however. As is discussed later, deposition of Beaker-related objects in 'natural places' may reflect the deconstruction of social personas.

Most of the Beaker-related artefacts that are found in 'natural places' in Ireland, but in burials elsewhere in Europe, seem to have been predominantly non-utilitarian symbolic items (see Chapter Nine). The craftwork involved in the manufacture of some of these objects such as wrist-bracers or gold discs suggests that visual display must have been an important aspect of their use. Many seem to represent bodily adornments or dress ornaments relating to a person's physical appearance. Again, we are still left with the questions of what were the important values, ideals or qualities that were attributed to these objects and how did these objects acquire these properties?

In other parts of Europe, the recurrent association of a restricted selection of objects together in graves suggests that these may have formed part of a special outfit or costume that was used in very specific kinds of funerary contexts to ritually transform the appearance and identity of a restricted proportion of the population after their death (Fokkens 2012b; Garwood 2012, 301). Rather than being elites, these probably comprised esteemed members of the community, who upon their death, were transformed into a specific category of person or ancestor with a new idealised social persona epitomising the essential characteristics of a good person or ancestor (Thomas 1991; Fokkens 2012b; Garwood 2012; Fowler 2013). All of this suggests that these objects may not accurately represent the way that people usually dressed at this time (Barrett 1994, 117-9; Thomas 1999, 157-9; Fokkens *et al.* 2008), but we cannot be certain of this. While age and sex seem to have influenced the way in which these burials were constituted, the recurrent inclusion of objects such as gold ornaments, wrist-bracers or daggers in male graves certainly suggest that some of these idealised personal qualities seem to have been related to craftsworking, hunting or martiality (Thomas 1999, 157-9; Case 2004b, 29; Vander Linden 2004, 41; 2006a; 2006b; Fokkens *et al.* 2008; Fokkens 2012b).

In Ireland, the presence of a broadly similar range of objects (outside of burials) suggests that these may have also been used to ritually transform people's identities, but in a slightly different way within a very dissimilar setting. Even though these objects were predominantly deposited apart from each other in Ireland, it seems likely that prior to deposition, they were worn together as part of a costume. The most convincing evidence for this is provided by the discovery of the wooden box at Corran bog containing pairs of sun-discs, wrist-bracers, and jet beads. A striking parallel for this is provided by the hoard of similar dress items all found together at Migdale in Scotland. This is a point to which we will return.

10.8 Supra-regional cosmologies?

All these objects in an Irish context were made in a supra-regional style using new techniques that seem to represent new ideas and referred to other people and places. Most of these were made using local materials, but it has recently been argued that the lead isotopes in Irish gold objects may be more likely to match with an unknown source in south-western England rather than in north-eastern Ireland as previously thought (Warner *et al.* 2009; 2010; Standish *et al.* 2014; 2015). The key thing here seems to be that the objects, whether they were made using Irish materials or not, referred to places or people that were spatially remote and were perceived as external by local communities (Helms 1988; Fontijn 2002, 218, 229; Fokkens 2012b). This is entirely characteristic of the wider Beaker complex across Europe. The relevance of this can be interpreted in two separate ways, neither of which needs to exclude the other.

Fontijn (2002, 81-2) has observed that the classic Beaker graves did not contain local-style objects that reflected local identities, instead they generally included supra-regional styled objects that resulted in the burials being "dressed in internationality". These objects enabled groups in different regions to demonstrate their participation within a wide and complex interaction network by constructing and expressing a shared group identity based on being members of imagined non-local communities (Fontijn 2002, 230-2; 2008, 96; Vandkilde 2009). Like Benedict Anderson's (1991) concept of socially constructed "imagined communities", the people in this collective would recognize themselves as belonging to a larger group even though they may only rarely have actual physical contact with other members of that group (Vandkilde 2009). Certainly, this view fits well with the growing body of highly complex evidence for the movement, interaction and exchange of people, things and ideas across various parts of Europe at this time (Vander Linden 2007a and b; 2016, 8-11; Furholt 2017).

A community or group identity is generally constructed in relation to a wider social world, in terms of both similarity and difference (see Cohen 1985, 12). This accounts for the ways in which widely shared Beaker-related material traits were often locally integrated in a manner that was 'similar but different'. Beaker-related supra-regional innovations enabled mutual forms of material engagement that could be adhered to or modified to varying extents through regionally specific practices and traditions. Interaction in Beaker-related networks enabled different groups to simultaneously emphasise their similarities with and differences from each other and to construct shareable worlds to which they could belong, while remaining separate (Helms 1988, 22; Barth 1992; Barrett 1994, 97-107; Vander Linden 2007b, 349-50).

The non-local character of Beaker-related material culture is also important because in pre-modern societies, objects, ideas and know-how that are perceived as coming from a temporally or spatially distant or esoteric source beyond the everyday may have been from another world. Mysterious objects or technologies were regarded as being cosmologically charged with supernatural powers and/or of being of mythical or ancestral origin (Helms 1988; 1993). This certainly seems to have applied in different ways to the gold, copper and stone used to make these Beaker-related objects, which were seen as coming from special places. This is exemplified by the porcellanite wrist-bracers made with stone from the top of Tievebulliagh Mountain, which was the source material for most Neolithic polished stone axes in Ireland. It may be that the objects themselves, the materials they were made from, or the knowledge of how to obtain the materials, as well as the craftworking skill to make them and use them correctly, were all seen as being sacred or divine in origin (Godelier 1999). This helps us to understand the widespread interest in transferable transformative technologies and why craftwork appears to have been so valued during the latter part of the third millennium BC (Needham 2004, 218).

In short, many Beaker-related objects, materials, ideas and know-how may have been regarded as gifts from the gods or ancestors that originated in the otherworld. This is significant because gifts retain aspects of their giver(s) (Mauss 1990). Therefore, objects gifted by supernatural forces would have been imbued with supernatural powers or qualities, which would in turn have been shared with its user (Godelier 1999). This explains why these objects were considered so valuable, treated in such circumscribed ways and perhaps also why they were all worn on the body or next to the skin.

From this perspective, it seems that the objects that form the Beaker assemblage and adorned Beaker-associated burials in certain regions had very particular cultural biographies. It was these biographies and their relationship to a greater set of commonly held cosmological beliefs that resulted in these objects being deemed part of a cosmological outfit. Although some aspects of this were flexible enough to enable regional adaptation, various aspects of the outfit were widely shared across Europe. We have already seen that some of these related to the symbolic expression of the qualities of martiality and of being from a different time and/or place. But, perhaps the most obvious of these were connected to the rising and setting of the sun at the beginning and end of its diurnal journey across the sky.

A strong concern with the daily movement and position of the sun in the sky is most evident in the recurrent alignments (east–west, facing south or north–south, facing east) of many Beaker graves across Europe (Harrison and Heyd 2007, 2-6-7; Shepherd, A.N 2012). It is also indicated by the decorative motifs depicting the sun, including crosses and concentric circles, that occur on so many different Beaker-related objects in Ireland and various other parts of Europe, including on the base of Beaker pots, gold discs and V-perforated buttons (Pazstor 2006; Cahill 2015, 2016; McVeigh 2017). As discussed in Chapter Five, this is also referenced in the orientation of wedge tombs on the setting midwinter sun. The sun may have been regarded as a source of life, growth and fertility. The sun's highly observable daily and annual cycles provided a very tangible representation of the passing of the seasons and the cyclical regeneration of life. The sun's daily (east–west) journey from day to night demonstrated that the death of the sun at the end of one day results in its regeneration at the start of the next. This provided a metaphorical illustration of the way that birth and death are inextricably interlinked parts of the same transformative cycle, so that the death of a person may result in their rebirth or the birth of another (Brück 2006a, 305). All of this suggests that the sun played a key role in people's belief systems and their understanding of the world across Europe at this time, just as much as it did in the later Bronze Age (Brück 2011, 388-93; Goldhahn 2012; 251-3). This highlights the extent to which Beaker related objects and practices embodied the cosmological values of the society in which they had an active function.

Of course, this is not surprising and there is little to suggest that this fascination with the sun was a radically new preoccupation that was instigated or spread exclusively in association with the use of Beaker pottery in the third millennium BC. Many of the cosmological principles that were expressed and mediated through Beaker-related material culture were long-lived and widely shared. For example, the same interest in the sun is certainly evident in the Irish Neolithic as indicated by the construction of passage tomb chambers that were aligned on the midwinter sunrise and sunset (Prendergast 2011), as well as the presence of solar motifs on the pottery associated with Linkardstown burials. Furthermore, versions of the same cosmological concepts including a preoccupation with the sun can be seen in aspects of Corded Ware and Yamnaya complexes such as the orientation and position of individual burials, as well as the inclusion of objects displaying sun motifs or referencing the use of weaponry and consumption of food and drink (Harding, A. 2000; Harrison and Heyd 2007; Fokkens 2012b, 123; Furholt 2014, 10).

Bringing together some of the previous points, we have seen that many of the Beaker-related objects had particular cultural biographies that imbued them with important social and cosmological values. On the one hand, these facilitated people to express new forms of collective ties with a wider community and to mediate the shifting social boundaries that defined their world. On the other hand, these objects possessed supernatural qualities due to being sacred in origin and formed part of a cosmologically-charged outfit that transformed the identity of their wearer into a different kind of social entity. The social identities expressed through these various objects (whether in Ireland or beyond) were always temporary and context-specific and their construction and/or deconstruction occurred through transformational rituals, which in most European regions were conducted in a funerary setting.

Although in Ireland these objects are found in 'natural places' rather than with burials, we have seen that both depositional scenarios reflect differing forms of transformation rituals that involved their exchange with the ancestors/supernatural. In both cases, these objects played a key role in instigating and indicating people's transition from one life-stage or social persona to another in a way that modified and reproduced personal and communal social identities (Fontijn 2002, 146; 2008, 89). Though this is not to deny that the ways in which social identities were articulated and transformed in these distinct settings was quite different. It may be that what we are seeing traces of in Ireland, is the deconstruction of a social persona that had previously been created and demarcated through the wearing of this same costume. Whether such acts of disassembly occurred upon the costume-wearer changing social persona or reaching a different life-stage, perhaps even death, is very unclear.

The details of the acts associated with constructing this persona are even less clear because no traces of this activity survive. Indeed, this is not unique to Ireland. At a European level, we are limited in what we can say about the wearing of these costumes and whether or how the social identities associated with them were expressed in most settings; much of our evidence results from the very circumscribed set of treatments that effectively ended the use of these objects by humans within a very restricted set of contexts. We do know that some of these objects such as wrist-bracers had extensive use-lives prior to their final deposition (see Chapter Nine) and this suggests these are complex issues that warrant further attention.

Leaving that aside, much of the deposition of Beaker-related objects in Ireland certainly seems to result from the shedding of this specific identity. It is possible that the costume was associated with a role that was only required episodically, perhaps on ceremonial occasions (Brück and Fontijn 2013, 209). If so, transformational rituals would have been required before and after, to change the identity of the wearer into and out of that which was associated with the costume (Fontijn 2002, 230-2). After the use of this cosmological regalia, it must have been necessary to deposit at least some of the various dress objects in very particular and formalised ways that removed the costume, both from the wearer and the everyday world. This certainly seems to be represented by the objects found together in Corran bog and Coggalbeg bog in Ireland and possibly also the Migdale hoard in Scotland. Despite the differences between this process and those relating to the inclusion of these objects with a burial in a very different kind of context, both similarly marked the transformation of relationships between the community conducting the deposition, the person undergoing the rite of passage and the gods or ancestors, regardless of whether this occurred during or at the end of the person's life. In those cases, where only one of the wider range of Beaker-related objects has been deposited, whether in a bog or with a burial, it may be that this part was considered wholly representative of the wider ensemble and its associated cultural biography (see Chapman 2000b).

10.9 Rites of passage in sacred places?

While we cannot be certain about what the complex cultural biographies of these non-local style objects meant, there is no doubt that there was a correct and socially appropriate life-course for such objects to follow. As gifts from the ancestors/gods, it may have been necessary to return these inalienable sacred objects through deposition in the correct context (Fokkens 1999; Godelier 1999; Fontijn 2002, 232; Needham 2008, 319-20). This would, however, have varied regionally in accordance with local traditions and cosmologies. In Ireland, the objects were removed from the domain of the living by depositing them in 'natural places', while in other regions across Europe this was generally done by burying them with a particular kind of person. As discussed above, in both scenarios, these objects were exchanged with the ancestors, but social identities were articulated and transformed differently in these distinct settings. In the case of the stereotypical Beaker burial, where a new social persona was constructed for a deceased person at the end of their lives by adorning their body in this outfit, these objects remained in direct association with each other and the human remains. This contrasts with the ceremonies conducted in Ireland in 'natural places', particularly bogs, which resulted in these same objects becoming physically disassociated with their previous wearer.

Clearly, people in Ireland had a belief system that required these objects be excluded from funerary settings, largely kept apart and deliberately deposited (either temporarily or permanently) at the edges of the lived landscape, generally in bogs. Yet this brings us back to some of the issues raised in Chapter Seven; why were Beaker-related objects deposited in 'natural places' in Ireland? This question is more answerable now that we have established that these objects formed part of a cosmological uniform whose deposition in 'natural places' represents the deconstruction of the special identity that they constituted and the returning of these cosmologically charged objects to the supernatural entities with whom they were associated (Fontijn 2002, 230-2). As we saw in Chapter Seven, distinctive features of the physical landscape such as hilltops, caves, rivers, bogs and lakes seem to have been viewed as sacred places or entities that served as entrances to the otherworld (Bradley 2000a; Fontijn 2002, 265). As such, they may also have been conceived of as suitable places for interacting with the supernatural and conducting transformational activities such as the deconstruction of social personae.

There also seems to have been some ambiguity surrounding the novel ideas and foreign values that these Beaker-related objects represented. While the non-local characteristics of these objects were valued at certain times and places, the extent to which these supra-regional style objects represented relationships with foreign people/ entities and places may have resulted in them being regarded as powerful or threatening symbols that needed to be contextually constrained or preserved (Fontijn 2008, 101). As we have seen, this could be achieved by depositing these transformative objects in spatially discrete and liminal places like bogs, where these objects were kept apart from each other and from local, traditional or everyday objects, including Beaker pottery. Bogs were particularly suitable for concealing and perhaps protecting such ambiguous objects because of their unique mixture of wet and dry land that was located away from settlements or funerary sites (Fontijn 2002, 279; 2008, 98-104). By maintaining these depositional separations between the local and the foreign, the conflicting yet mutually reinforcing values and ideas associated with Beaker-related objects could be expressed.

While people clearly treated some of the non-ceramic Beaker-related objects and the pottery differently, the intention here has not been to suggest a domestic/ritual dichotomy. All these artefacts were regarded as special objects, but they were deposited differently to enact contrasting social values and qualities. Within certain settings, people may have constructed and expressed identities relating to being members of a much wider community, interlinked through exchange and the sharing of objects. Inside the context of the household, the funerary and the monumental, however, they may have redefined themselves by expressing more local identities. In these settings, people accentuated their shared local ancestry and long-standing attachments to place by depositing occupational debris associated with the home and everyday activities such as food consumption. At this time, the household still operated as a powerful metaphor for the well-established ties that connected people, places and their ancestors together to form a 'domestic' community. Although the presence of Beakers in these deposits may also have referred to links with the wider cultural world, the fragmented and used condition of the pottery may have served to diminish this aspect by emphasising its quotidian character in a way that enabled groups to reassert their local communal identities and preserve their shared sense of belonging.

Only a very small proportion of Beaker pottery has come from burials compared to the amount found in non-funerary contexts. People here do not seem to have been wholly comfortable with placing Beaker pottery and objects with human remains. Beaker sherds played such an important social role in the depiction of household-based kinship that perhaps it was rarely deemed acceptable for Beakers to accompany the dead. It may have been feared that the deposition of Beakers in funerary places might dilute the associations of this pottery with the home place. Indeed, it may be speculated that the need to preserve this connection between the Beaker pot and the 'domestic' community ultimately resulted in the creation of a new pot type – the Irish Bowl – that was almost exclusively associated with the dead. The reluctance of people to deposit classic supra-regional objects such as copper tanged daggers and wrist-bracers with human remains may also be understood in terms of a desire to express a local identity in this setting by emphasising their ancestral membership of the local group rather than their international connections.

Bogs may also have been deliberately chosen for the removal of these things from the social world precisely because these depositional locales were generally unmarked. Bog deposits were invisible in contrast to the deposition of materials in highly visible places like monuments, which would have served as visual markers or *aides de memoire* for the deposits made within them and their associated intentions. The values and meanings of these objects would have been celebrated during their deposition, so that the life stories of people, objects and places were tied together (Fontijn 2008, 102). This meant that the significance of these objects and their deposition became fixed through their absence and could only be remembered through the recollection or repetition of similar practices (Rowlands 1993; Fontijn 2007, 76-7; Garwood 2007). The act of deposition may have been an important occasion for a community, during which they constructed and expressed communal and personal identities, while witnessing the burial of these active agents that were linked with other people and events (Fontijn 2008, 98; see Chapter Ten).

As a final thought on these issues, it is striking that the various points made here are united by the concept of sacred travel or pilgrimage. As we have seen, the objects forming this cosmological costume were regarded as being of supernatural or ancestral origin. Some of the objects symbolised the journey of the sun, while others expressed idealised qualities that drew upon the symbolism of martiality, but all of them referred to spatially or temporally distant places that had to be journeyed to. Travel, whether actual or mythological, seems to have held deeply cosmological connotations that were connected to beliefs about the otherworld and the journey of the sun, such as those depicted in the Scandinavian Bronze Age (*e.g.* Kaul 1998; 2004). This kind of journeying, which would have involved real or metaphorical trips to liminal or otherworldly places, probably formed an essential part of a rite of passage undertaken by some members of the community upon reaching a specific life-stage (van Gennep 1960; Helms 1988). If so, in dressing the person as a cosmological traveller, they were transformed into someone who could, would or previously had undertaken a voyage to a liminal space/place. Equally, the removal of this costume would have transformed the voyager back into a regular member of society, who upon return from their travels could then re-join their community.

In other words, the actions of putting this costume on and subsequently taking it off would have played a central role in the different stages of this rite of passage. This interpretation certainly fits well with the contrasting archaeological evidence just discussed for the transformation of identities. While the adorned Beaker burials that we see in various parts of Europe seem to represent the voyager on a journey, it seems that much, if not all the archaeological evidence that we have from Ireland relates to the disassembly of this costume at the end stage of such a journey or rite of passage. By removing and then depositing these highly transformative magical objects in sacred places within bogs, the costumes otherworldly powers were preserved, but also contained and therefore restricted from entering more everyday spheres of life.

10.10 The Beaker transformation?

As we near the end of the book, it is appropriate to reflect on the implications of all that has been discussed here in terms of our understanding of the Beaker phenomenon in Ireland and beyond. Clearly, the extent and the consequences of changes in Ireland that have been attributed to the introduction of novel Beaker-associated material culture, and the metallurgical technologies for making these objects, has been exaggerated. Neither the introduction of the Beaker phenomenon nor metallurgy to Ireland caused or represented major changes. Instead, we have seen that during the Chalcolithic there was a broad range of ongoing changes in material culture and in social practices too, albeit to a lesser degree, but evidence for large-scale significant cultural transformation or social reconfiguration is lacking.

One of these changes, which occurred c. 2450 BC, was the introduction of copper metallurgy and this has often been viewed as the defining development of this time. Yet, while this new technology was certainly harnessed to produce functional items, early metal objects did not offer many advantages over stone-tools and the lives of people were certainly not radically transformed by its introduction (O'Brien 2004, 515; Roberts 2008a, 365; Bartleheim 2012, 92; Carlin and Brück 2012). Some commentators have reprised Childe's (1925; 1930) technological determinism in suggesting that continental Beaker-using immigrants prospecting for new sources of metal ore were responsible for the expansion of the Beaker phenomenon to Ireland and Britain (*e.g.* Sheridan 2007a, 104-5; 2008a, 64; 2008b; Fitzpatrick 2009). Problematically, this falsely attributes the transmission of these cultural innovations to a few colonising individuals. The way that copper and other Beaker-related items on this island were produced, exchanged, and deposited, as well as their widespread distribution, suggests that local insular communities and their long-standing traditions of practice played a considerable role in the inception of these changes.

Copper metalworking was a community-based enterprise; the laborious processes associated with it could not have been conducted without the support of local groups (Roberts 2008a, 365-6; Carlin and Brück 2012). The co-occurrence of Beaker pottery and early metalwork in Ireland and Britain been seen as culturally synonymous, but the fact that metallurgy pre-dates the Beaker complex in most European regions indicates that this is not necessarily the case (Roberts 2008a). Very few metal sources were actually exploited during the early phases of the Beaker phenomenon and Beaker pottery was also spread to many non-metal bearing regions including southern England (Needham 2007, 42). There is little to suggest that the motivations underlying the spread and adoption of the Beaker phenomenon were in any way directly related to a desire for copper technology on the part of insular or continental European populations. Most importantly perhaps, these hypotheses concerning pioneering migratory Beaker-using smiths suffer from all the problems of the prestige goods model because they rest upon the highly problematic assumptions that metal was desirable as a source of financial wealth (see below; Chapter Two).

For decades, the spread of the Beaker complex and the inception of metallurgy has been widely considered to indicate the emergence of a hierarchical society in which individual status was attained by the competitive exchange and display of exotic Beaker ornaments as part of a prestige goods economy (*e.g.* Renfrew 1974; Thorpe and Richards 1984; Heyd 2007; Sheridan 2008a). While the highly problematic basis of this was discussed in Chapter Two and is returned to below, it is also worth highlighting here again that convincing evidence to link the development of the Beaker complex in Ireland with an institutionalised elite or a prestige goods economy is lacking. As discussed above, the very circumscribed treatment of Beaker-related items of bodily adornment indicates that these were socially important objects that played important roles for the wider community. These certainly would have differentiated the wearer from the rest of the population, but they did not passively reflect personal wealth. Instead, these temporarily dressed certain individuals as extraordinary or special kinds of persons at particular times and places. The subsequent deposition of the objects provided a way for people to establish and maintain a shared identity, as well as to negotiate and reproduce social relations and cultural ideals. In a comparable way, the deposition of the bodies of a very restricted proportion of the population in wedge tombs indicates that selected individuals were specially chosen by the community to receive this transformational treatment, presumably because they were valued members of their society, but it is wrong to infer from this that they were wealthy or powerful (see Chapter Five). The ubiquity of Beaker ceramics in Ireland indicates that from an early stage this pottery was extensively used for a wide range of both every day and special purposes that were not restricted to elites. Furthermore, there is no evidence for any kind of settlement hierarchy such as the presence of high-status buildings.

The use of these cultural novelties in Ireland is due to ongoing meaningful relations and interactions between people from this island and other parts of Europe, which must have occurred both within and beyond Irish shores. For the reasons that we have explained, as well as others which we do not yet fully understand, Beaker-related material culture fulfilled the distinctive needs of the communities who inhabited the island during this time, at least some of whom were newcomers. These objects played a vital role in the reproduction of society by facilitating the expression and constraint of both personal and group identities. We see that various aspects of this material culture were used in regionally distinctive ways to express both local and non-local characteristics and values. People in Ireland were participating in social networks that operated at a variety of scales ranging from the very local to further afield. As a result, their frames of reference were simultaneously focused upon the local and the global. We can understand this to reflect how the concept of 'community' is a relational idea that implies both similarity and difference (see Cohen 1985, 12). While supra-regional Beaker-associated artefacts enabled people on this island to consider themselves part of a wider international community, a distinctively local identity was also constructed by treating these objects differently.

Overall, the alterations that occurred in conjunction with the appearance of Beakers in Ireland were a cumulative combination of both gradual and rapid developments involving both continuities in and reinventions of insular 'traditions'. This meant that new people, practices, technologies, things and ideas were hybridised and integrated to produce something that was similar but different to what had gone before. It is important to remember that the adoption of these cultural innovations forms part of a longer sequence of gradual and incremental material changes relating to strategies for formation of identities and relationships, as well the negotiation and reproduction of social values in Ireland throughout the fourth and third millennia BC. This is illustrated by the way that widely separated groups across Britain and Ireland participated in an interregional social network associated with the use of Grooved Ware and other objects and ideas from 3200-2450 BC that referred to other people, places and values (Thomas 2010; Carlin 2017).Long-distance travel and exchange between Ireland and Britain was an integral element of this, as epitomised by the evidence for boat journeys of over 450km between the Boyne Valley and the Orkney Islands (Wilkin and Vander Linden 2015, 101; Carlin 2017). There is every reason to believe that people movement (between different locales) might have been as much of a reality during the first half of the third millennium BC as it was during the latter, but for various complex reasons relating to the nature of the Late Neolithic archaeological record in Ireland and Britain, this is not archaeologically, genetically or isotopically obvious. This is a key point that is worth emphasising because it so often seems to be forgotten.

While the scale, character and detectability of mobility c. 2500 BC distinguishes the Chalcolithic in Ireland and Britain from what went before, this kind of mobility is neither enigmatic nor abnormal. Increasingly, new scientific techniques are revealing that regular and repeated human movement was a much greater feature of life than we had assumed (Greenblatt 2010). Small-scale seasonal movements between the continent and Britain and Ireland of the kind suggested by Humphrey Case (1969a; 1998, 410; 2004a) certainly represent an archaeological reality that enabled the transmission, sharing and adaption of new objects, ideas, and genes during the Neolithic (Cassidy *et al.* 2016; Olalde *et al.* 2018). The widespread distribution of specific prominent artefacts or practices that are characteristic of the Beaker complex is entirely consistent with much of the interconnectivity that occurred throughout European prehistory (Greenblatt 2010). Arguably, similar archaeological phenomena with characteristic ceramics and burial practices were present across much of Europe during the third millennium BC (Harding, A. 2000; Fokkens 2012b, 123; Furholt 2014). This returns us to the points made at the start of the book, that exchanges and social interactions are necessary for biological, social and material reproduction (Mauss 1990; Lévi-Strauss 1949; 1987, 47).

10.11 The Beaker Phenomenon?

From the perspective that mobility, exchange and interaction had been part of the human story for millennia before the dawn of the Copper Age, we can see that approaches to the Beaker phenomenon have exaggerated the strangeness of its character. This brings us back full circle to some of the points made in Chapters One and Two, particularly those prompted by the work of David Clarke (1976, 460), who suggested that the Beaker 'problem' is a construct that we made for ourselves through a combination of our situated knowledge and the flawed approaches that have been taken towards trying to explain it. As highlighted at the outset, the Beaker label is a historical classification that was originally created by archaeologists who reductively conflated the diverse sets of material traits that they applied it to. These include a dynamic collection of novel materials, objects, ideas and practices that originated in various regions and were circulated through the movement of people and overlapping exchange networks. As a culture or package, this assemblage lacks unity or coherency outside of certain burial contexts, whose representativeness has been over emphasised. Much of this, including the exaggeration of the uniformity of the character of this complex and reification of the Beaker pot is a direct legacy of problematic cultural-historical migratory explanations that have never been fully forsaken. This is exemplified by the recent upsurge in interest in the movement of genes in the latter half of the third millennium BC and the assumption that these were inherently linked to the use of Beaker pottery.

The things that were happening across Europe in this millennium involved a complex range of social processes that cannot be explained by a single cause or attributed to a single social group. The so-called Beaker phenomenon was a set of overlapping multi-directional ideas, beliefs, practices and symbols that were shared to varying extents through multiple interlinked networks of affiliation and were selectively adopted and adapted in very diverse regional settings. The material patterning created by these networks are archaeologically confusing, but we have made it far more complicated than it needs to be. We need to be careful of this if we wish to better understand how and why so many people in so many places adopted and adapted such similar ideas and items in such distinctive ways.

As a concluding thought, I wonder can we ever truly understand why or how the idea of the Beaker pot, or the other items which we consider to be Beaker-related, came to be used in Ireland? Undoubtedly, shared cosmologies, values and relationships seem to be part of the answer, but I am inclined to answer this question with another: why have we consistently found the way that people did these things to be so strange? What does that say about us? In many ways, groups in the mid-third millennium BC were just doing what people have always done. They were obtaining novel objects and using them to create meanings, negotiate values, construct and maintain identities and relationships and make sense of their lives, as well as the world in which they lived. Indeed, this seems very similar to what we continue to do to this day.

Bibliography

Abercromby, J., *1902*. The oldest Bronze Age ceramic type in Britain, its close analogies on the Rhine, its probable origin in central Europe. *Journal of the Anthropological Institute*, 32, 373-397.

Abercromby, J., 1912. *A Study of the Bronze Age Pottery of Britain and Ireland and its associated Grave-goods*. Oxford: Clarendon Press.

Allen, M. J., 2005. Beaker settlement and environment on the chalk downs of southern England. *Proceedings of the Prehistoric Society*, 71, 219-245.

Allentoft, M. E., Sikora, M., Sjögren, K.-G., Rasmussen, S., Rasmussen, M., Stenderup, J., et al., 2015. Population genomics of Bronze Age Eurasia. *Nature*, 522, 167-172.

Ambert, P., 2001. La place de la métallurgie campaniforme dans la première métallurgie française. In: F. Nicolis (ed.) *Bell Beakers today. Pottery, People, Culture, Symbols in Prehistoric Europe. Proceedings of the International Colloquium Riva del Garda (Trento, Italy) 11-16 May 1998*. Trento: Ufficio Beni Archeologici, 577-588.

Anderson, B., 1991. *Imagined Communities. Reflections on the Origin and Spread of Nationalism*. Rev. ed. London: Verso.

Anon., 2006. *Key Recommendations from the Royal Irish Academy Forum – Archaeology in Ireland: A Vision for the Future*. Dublin: Royal Irish Academy.

Anon., 2007. *A Review of Research Needs in Irish Archaeology. A Report Prepared by the Heritage Council for the Minister for the Environment, Heritage and Local Government*. Kilkenny: The Heritage Council

Appadurai, A. (ed.), 1986. *The Social Life of Things*. Cambridge: Cambridge University Press.

Apsimon, A. M., 1969. The Earlier Bronze Age in the North of Ireland. *Ulster journal of Archaeology*, 32, 28-72.

Apsimon, A. M., 1976. Ballynagilly and the beginning and end of the Irish Neolithic. In: Sigfried J. de Laet (ed.) *Acculturation and Continuity in Atlantic Europe mainly during the Neolithic Period and Bronze Age*. Brugge: Dissertationes Archaeologicae Gandenses, 15-38.

Apsimon, A.M., 1986. Chronological contexts for Irish megalithic tombs. *Journal of Irish Archaeology*, 3, 5-15.

Ashmore, P., 1999. Radiocarbon dating: avoiding errors by avoiding mixed samples. *Antiquity*, 73, 124-130.

Bamford, H., 1971. Tullywiggan. *Excavations 1971*. Belfast: Association of Young Irish Archaeologists, 24-25.

Barclay, A. & Marshall, P., with Higham, T. F. G., 2011. Chronology and the radiocarbon dating programme. In: A.P. Fitzpatrick (ed.) *The Amesbury Archer and the Boscombe Bowmen: Bell Beaker burials at Boscombe Down, Amesbury, Wiltshire (Wessex Archaeology 27)*. Salisbury: Wessex Archaeology, 167-184.

Barclay, G., 1983. Sites of the third millennium BC to the first millennium AD at North Mains, Strathallan, Perthshire. *Proceedings of the Society of Antiquaries of Scotland*, 113, 122-281.

Barker, C.T., 1992. *The Chambered Tombs of South-West Wales. A Re-assessment of the Neolithic Burial Monuments of Carmarthenshire and Pembrokeshire. Oxbow Monograph 14*. Oxford: Oxbow Books.

Barrett, J. C., 1994. *Fragments from Antiquity. An Archaeology of Social Life in Britain, 2900-1200 BC*. London: Blackwell.

Barrett, J. C., 2012. Are models of prestige goods economies and conspicuous consumption applicable to the archaeology of the Bronze to Iron Age transition in Britain?. In: A. M. Jones, J. Pollard, M. J. Allen & J. Gardiner (eds) *Image, Memory and Monumentality: Archaeological Engagements with the Material World*. Oxford: Oxbow, 6-17.

Barrett, J. C. & Needham, S., 1988. Production, circulation and exchange: problems in the interpretation of Bronze Age metalwork. In: J. C. Barrett & I. Kinnes (eds) *The Archaeology of Context in the Neolithic and Bronze Age: Recent Trends*. Sheffield: Department of Archaeology and Prehistory, University of Sheffield, 127-140.

Barrett, J. C. & Fewster, K. J., 1998. Stonehenge: is the medium the message? *Antiquity*, 72, 847-852.

Bayley, D., 2005. *Stratigraphic report of Excavations at site 127 Carn More 5, Co. Louth*. Unpublished Report for Irish Archaeological Consultancy Ltd on behalf of Louth County Council and the National Roads Authority.

Bayley, D., 2009a. *Site 113: Newtownbalregan 5*. Final Report for Irish Archaeological Consultancy Ltd on behalf of Louth County Council and the National Roads Authority.

Bayley, D., 2009b. *Site 112: Newtownbalregan 2*. Final Report for Irish Archaeological Consultancy Ltd on behalf of Louth County Council and the National Roads Authority.

Bayley, D., 2010. *Final Report on Archaeological Excavation of Kilmainham 1B, A029/054, E3142. M3 Clonee-North of Kells*. Unpublished Report for Irish Archaeological Consultancy Ltd on behalf of Meath County Council and the National Roads Authority.

Bayliss, A., Bronk Ramsey, C., Van der Plicht, J. & Whittle, A., 2007. Bradshaw and Bayes: towards a timetable for the Neolithic. *Cambridge Archaeological Journal*, 17(1), 1-28.

Bayliss, A., McAvoy, F. & Whittle, A., 2007. The world recreated: redating Silbury Hill in its monumental landscape. *Antiquity*, 81, 26-53.

Bayliss, A., Whittle, A. & Wysocki, M., 2007. Talking about my generation: the date of the West Kennet long barrow. *Cambridge Archaeological Journal*, 17, 85-101.

Bayliss, A. & O'Sullivan, M., 2013. Interpreting chronologies for the Mound of the Hostages, Tara, and its contemporary contexts in Neolithic and Bronze Age Ireland. In: M. O'Sullivan, C. Scarre & M. Doyle (eds) *Tara From the Past to the Future*. Dublin: Wordwell, in association with the UCD School of Archaeology, 26-104.

Beatty, W. & Collins, A. E. P., 1955. A bog find from Co. Donegal. *Ulster Journal of Archaeology*, 18, 117.

Becker, K., 2006. *Hoards and Deposition in Bronze Age Ireland*. Dublin: Unpublished PhD thesis, University College Dublin.

Becker, K., 2008. Left but not lost. *Archaeology Ireland*, 22 (1), 12-15.

Becker, K., 2011. The Irish Iron Age: continuity, change and identity. In: T. Moore & X. Armada (eds) *Atlantic Europe in the First Millennium BC*. Oxford: Oxford University Press, 449-467.

Becker, K., 2013. Transforming identities – New approaches to Bronze Age deposition in Ireland. *Proceedings of The Prehistoric Society*, 79, 1-39.

Becker, K., Armit, I. & Swindles, G. T., 2017. New perspectives on the Irish Iron Age: the impact of NRA development on our understanding of later prehistory. In: M. Stanley, R. Swan & A. O'Sullivan (eds) *Stories of Ireland's Past*. Dublin: Transport Infrastructure Ireland, 85-100.

Bendrey, R., Thorpe, N., Outram, A. & van Wijngaarden-Bakker, L. H., 2013. The origins of domestic horses in north-west Europe: new direct dates on the horses of Newgrange, Ireland. *Proceedings of the Prehistoric Society*, 79, 70-103.

Besse, M., 2003. Les céramiques communes des Campaniformes européens. *Gallia Préhistoire*, 45, 205-258.

Besse, M., 2004. Bell Beaker common ware during the third millennium BC in Europe. In: J. Czebreszuk (ed.) *Similar but Different. Bell Beakers in Europe*. Poznan: Adam Mickiewicz University, 127-148.

Bintliff, J., 1979. Archaeological science: science and archaeology, or a science of archaeology?. *Symposium on Archaeological Sciences*, 68-75.

Bolger, T., 2001. Three sites on the northern motorway at Rathmullan, Co. Meath. *Ríocht Na Midhe*, VII, 8-17.

Bolger, T., 2012. *00E0813 Rathmullan 10 Final Report*. Unpublished final report to the National Monuments Service, Department of the Environment, Heritage and Local Government, Dublin.

Bolger, T., 2011. *01E0294: Rathmullan 6 (site 12) Final report*. Unpublished final report to the National Monuments Service, Department of the Environment, Heritage and Local Government, Dublin.

Bradley, R., 1982. The destruction of wealth in later prehistory. *Man*, 17, 108-122.

Bradley, R., 1984. *The Social Foundations of Prehistoric Britain*. Harlow: Longman.

Bradley, R., 1990. *The Passage of Arms*. Cambridge: Cambridge University Press.

Bradley, R., 2000a. *An Archaeology of Natural Places*. London: Routledge.

Bradley, R., 2000b. *The Good Stones: a New Investigation of the Clava Cairns*. Edinburgh: Society of Antiquaries of Scotland.

Bradley, R., 2003. A life less ordinary: the ritualization of the domestic sphere in later prehistoric Europe. *Cambridge Archaeological Journal*, 13(1), 5-23.

Bradley, R., 2005a. *Ritual and Domestic Life in Prehistoric Europe*. London: Routledge.

Bradley, R., 2005b. *The Moon and the Bonfire: An Investigation of Three Recumbent Stone Circles in North-east Scotland*. Edinburgh: Society of Antiquaries of Scotland.

Bradley, R., 2006. *Bridging the Two Cultures: Commercial Archaeology and the Study of British Prehistory*. Unpublished paper to the Society of Antiquaries of London on 12th January 2006.

Bradley, R., 2007. *The Prehistory of Britain and Ireland*. Cambridge: Cambridge World Archaeology.

Bradley R., 2009. Missing links and false relations: architecture and ideas in Bronze Age Scotland and Ireland. In: G. Cooney, K. Becker, J. Coles, M. Ryan & S. Sievers (eds) *Relics of Old Decency: Archaeological Studies in Later Prehistory. Festschrift for Barry Raftery*. Bray: Wordwell, 221-232.

Bradley, R. & Edmonds, M., 1993. *Interpreting the Axe Trade: Production and Exchange in Neolithic Britain*. Cambridge: Cambridge University Press.

Bradley, R., Haselgrove, C., Vander Linden, M. & Webley, L., 2016. *The Later Prehistory of North-west Europe: The Evidence of Development-led Fieldwork*. Oxford: Oxford University Press.

Braithwaite, M., 1984. Ritual and prestige in the prehistory of Wessex c. 2,200-1400 BC: a new dimension to the archaeological evidence. In: D. Miller & C. Tilley (eds) *Ideology, Power and Prehistory*. Cambridge: Cambridge University Press, 93-110.

Bray, P. & Pollard, A., 2012. A new interpretative approach to the chemistry of copper-alloy objects: source, recycling and technology. *Antiquity*, 86, 853-867.

Bremer, W., 1928. Notes on some objects in the National Collection of Irish Antiquities. *Proceedings of the Royal Irish Academy*, 38C, 39.

Brennan, J., Briggs, C.S. & Apsimon, A. M., 1978. A giant beaker from Cluntyganny townland, Co. Tyrone. *Ulster Journal of Archaeology*, 41, 33-37.

Briard, J., 1984. *Les Tumulus d'Armorique. Collection : « L'Âge du Bronze en France » vol. 3*. Paris : Picard.

Briard, J. & Roussot-Larroque, J., 2002. Les débuts de la métallurgie dans la France Atlantique. In: M. Bartelheim, E. Pernicka & R. Krause (eds) *The Beginnings of Metallurgy in the Old World*. Rahden: Verlag Marie Leidorf, 135-160.

Brindley, A. L., 1995. Radiocarbon, chronology and the Bronze Age. In: J. Waddell & E. Shee Twohig (eds) *Ireland in the Bronze Age*. Dublin: Stationery Office, 4-13.

Brindley, A. L., 1999. Irish Grooved Ware. In: R. Cleal & A. MacSween (eds) *Grooved Ware in Britain and Ireland. Neolithic Studies Group Seminar Papers 3*. Oxford: Oxbow, 23-35.

Brindley, A. L., 2004. The prehistoric mine: specialist studies. In: W. O'Brien (ed.) *Ross Island. Mining, Metal and Society in Early Ireland*. Galway: Dept of Archaeology, NUIG, 331-338.

Brindley, A. L., 2007. *The Dating of Food Vessels and Urns in Ireland*. Galway: Galway University Press.

Brindley, A. L. & Lanting, J. N., 1991/2. Radiocarbon dates from wedge tombs. *Journal of Irish Archaeology*, 6, 19-26.

Brindley, A. L., Lanting, J. N. & Mook, W. G., 1987/8. Radiocarbon dates from Moneen and Labbacallee, County Cork. *Journal of Irish Archaeology*, 4, 13-19.

Brindley, A. L., Lanting, J. N. & van der Plicht, J., 2005. Appendix 7: Radiocarbon-dated samples from the Mound of the Hostages. In: M. O'Sullivan (ed.) *Duma na nGiall. The Mound of the Hostages, Tara*. Dublin: Wordwell, 281-298.

Brindley, A. L., 2000. Pottery report from excavations in the townlands of Mell and Hill of Rath. Unpublished report.

Brindley, J., 1984. Petrological examination of Beaker pottery from the Boyne Valley sites. In: G. Eogan (ed.) *Excavations at Knowth 1*. Dublin: Royal Irish Academy, 330-346.

Brodie, N. J., 1994. *The Neolithic-Bronze Age Transition in Britain: A Critical Review of Some Archaeological and Craniological Concepts. BAR British Series 238*. Oxford: Tempus Reparatum.

Brodie, N. J., 1997. New perspectives on the Bell Beaker Culture. *Oxford Journal of Archaeology*, 16, 297-314.

Brodie, N. J., 1998. British Bell Beakers: twenty-five years of theory and practice. In: M. Benz & S. van Willigen (eds) *Some New Approaches to The Bell Beaker Phenomenon. Lost Paradise...? Proceedings of the 2nd Meeting of the "Association Archéologie et Gobelets", Feldburg, 18th-20th April 1997. BAR International Series 690*. Oxford: Tempus Reparatum, 43-56.

Brodie, N. J., 2004. Technological frontiers and the emergence of the Beaker culture. In: F. Nicolis (ed.) *Bell Beakers Today. Pottery, People, Culture, Symbols in Prehistoric Europe. Proceedings of the International Colloquium at Riva del Garda*. Trento: Servizio Beni Culturali, Ufficio Beni Archeologici, 487-496.

Bronk Ramsey, C., 1995. Radiocarbon calibration and analysis of stratigraphy: the OxCal program. *Radiocarbon*, 37(2), 425-430.

Bronk Ramsey, C., 1998. Probability and dating. *Radiocarbon*, 40 (1), 461-74.

Bronk Ramsey, C., 2001. Development of the radiocarbon calibration program. *Radiocarbon*, 43 (2), 355-63.

Bronk Ramsey, C., 2009. Dealing with outliers and offsets in radiocarbon dating. *Radiocarbon*, 51(3), 1023-1045.

Brophy, K. & Noble, G., 2012. Henging, mounding and blocking: the Forteviot henge group. In: A. Gibson (ed.) *Enclosing the Neolithic: Recent studies in Britain and Europe. BAR International Series 2440.* Oxford: Archaeopress, 21-35.

Brophy, K. & Barclay, G., 2009. *Defining a Regional Neolithic: The Evidence from Britain and Ireland. Neolithic Studies Group Seminar Papers 9.* Oxford: Oxbow.

Brudenell, M. & Cooper, A., 2008. *Post-middenism: depositional histories on Later Bronze Age settlements at Broom, Bedfordshire. Oxford Journal of Archaeology,* 27, 15-36.

Brück, J., 1995. A place for the dead: the role of human remains in Late Bronze Age Britain. *Proceedings of the Prehistoric Society,* 61, 245-277.

Brück, J., 1999a. Ritual and rationality: some problems of interpretation in European archaeology. *Journal of European Archaeology,* 2(2), 313-344.

Brück, J., 1999b. Houses, lifecycles and deposition on Middle Bronze Age settlements in Southern England. *Proceedings of the Prehistoric Society,* 65, 145-166.

Brück, J., 1999c. The nature of the upper secondary fill in the outer ditch, Trench B: the case for more rapid deposition and continued significance of the enclosure. In: A. Whittle, J. Pollard & C. Grigson (eds) *The Harmony of Symbols: The Windmill Hill Causewayed Enclosure.* Oxford: Oxbow, 375-380.

Brück, J., 2001. Body metaphors and technologies of transformation in the English Middle and Late Bronze Age. In: J. Brück (ed.) *Bronze Age Landscapes: Tradition and Transformation.* Oxford: Oxbow, 149-160.

Brück, J., 2004a. Early Bronze Age burial practices in Scotland and beyond: differences and similarities. In: I. A. G. Shepherd & G. J. Barclay (eds) *Scotland in Ancient Europe: The Neolithic and Early Bronze Age of Scotland in their European Context.* Edinburgh: Society of Antiquaries of Scotland, 179-186.

Brück, J., 2004b. Material metaphors: the relational construction of identity in Early Bronze Age burials in Ireland and Britain. *Journal of Social Archaeology,* 4(3), 307-333.

Brück, J., 2006a. Fragmentation, personhood and the social construction of technology in Middle and Late Bronze Age Britain. *Cambridge Archaeological Journal,* 16(2), 297-315.

Brück, J., 2006b. Death, exchange and reproduction in the British Bronze Age. *European Journal of Archaeology,* 9(1), 73-101.

Brück, J., 2009. Women, death and social change in the British Bronze Age. *Norwegian Archaeological Review,* 42(1), 1-23.

Brück, J., 2011. Fire, earth, water: an elemental cosmography of the European Bronze Age. In: T. Insoll (ed.) *Oxford Handbook of the Archaeology of Ritual and Religion.* Oxford: Oxford University Press, 387-404.

Brück, J., 2015. The value of archaeology. *Current Swedish Archaeology,* 23, 33-36.

Brück, J., 2016. Hoards, fragmentation and exchange in the European Bronze Age. In: S. Hansen, D. Neumann & T. Vachta (eds) *Raum, Gabe und Erinnerung: Weihgaben und Heiligtümer in prähistorischen und antiken Gesellschaften.* Berlin: Edition Topoi, 75-92.

Brück, J. & Fontijn, D., 2013. The myth of the chief: prestige goods, power and personhood in the Bronze Age, In: A. Harding & H. Fokkens (eds) *The Oxford Handbook of the European Bronze Age.* Oxford: Oxford University Press, 197-215.

Brück, J. & Goodman, M., 1999. Introduction: themes for a critical archaeology of prehistoric settlement. In: J. Brück and M. Goodman (eds) *Making Places in the Prehistoric World: Themes in Settlement Archaeology.* London: UCL Press, 1-19.

Buckley, L., 2001. The human bone from Corbally, Co. Kildare. Unpublished specialist report.

Burgess, C., 1979. The background of early metalworking in Ireland and Britain. In: M. Ryan (ed.) *The Origins of Metallurgy in Atlantic Europe: Proceedings of the Fifth Atlantic Colloquium.* Dublin: Stationary Office, 207-247.

Burgess, C., 1980. *The Age of Stonehenge.* London: Dent.

Burgess, C. & Shennan, S., 1976. The Beaker phenomenon: some suggestions. In: C. Burgess & M. Miket (eds) *Settlement and Economy in the Third and Second Millennia BC. BAR British Series 238.* Oxford: Tempus Reparatum, 309-331.

Burl, H. A. W., 1984. Report on the excavation of a Neolithic mound at Boghead, Speymouth Forest, Fochabers, Moray, 1972 and 1974. *Proceedings of the Society of Antiquaries of Scotland* ,114, 35-73.

Burmeister, S., 2000. Archaeology and migration. Approaches to an archaeological proof of migration. *Current Anthropology,* 41, 539-567.

Butler, J. & Fokkens, H., 2005. From stone to bronze. Technology and material culture. In: L. P. Louwe Kooijmans, P. W. van den Broeke, H. Fokkens & A. L. van Gijn (eds) *The Prehistory of the Netherlands, Volume 1.* Amsterdam: Amsterdam University Press, 371-399.

Cahill, M., 1983. Irish prehistoric gold-working. In: M. Ryan (ed.) *Treasures of Ireland. Irish Art 3000 B.C. – 1500 A.D.* Dublin: Royal Irish Academy, 8-23.

Cahill, M., 1994. Mr Anthony's bog oak case of gold antiquities. *Proceedings of the Royal Irish Academy,* 94C, 53-109.

Cahill, M., 2005a. John Windele's golden legacy–prehistoric and later gold ornaments from Co. Cork and Co. Waterford. *Proceedings of the Royal Irish Academy,* 106C, 219-337.

Cahill, M., 2005b. Roll your own lunula. In: T. Condit & C. Corlett (eds) *Above and Beyond: Essays in Memory of Leo Swan.* Dublin: Wordwell, 53-62.

Cahill, M., 2015. Here comes the sun. *Archaeology Ireland,* 29(1), 26-33.

Cahill, M., 2016. A stone to die for. *Archaeology Ireland,* 30(3), 26-29.

Callaway, E., 2018. Divided by DNA: the uneasy relationship between archaeology and ancient genomics. *Nature, 555(7698), 573-557.*

Cameron, C.M. 2013. How People Moved among Ancient Societies: Broadening the View. American Anthropologist, 115(2), 218-31.

Carlin, N., 2005a. *A Study of Beaker Associated Settlement in Leinster.* Unpublished M.A. Thesis. Queens University Belfast.

Carlin, N., 2005b. Some findings from a study of Beaker settlement in Leinster. *Proceedings of the Annual Conference of the Association of Young Irish Archaeologists 2006.* Cork: Association of Young Irish Archaeologists, 12-23.

Carlin, N., 2006. Summary and discussion of the Beaker activity at Ballyclogh North. In: Y. Whitty (ed.) *Final Report on Excavations at Ballyclogh North, Co. Wicklow.* Unpublished final report for Irish Archaeological Consultancy Ltd on behalf of Wicklow County Council and the National Roads Authority.

Carlin, N., 2010. The Grooved Ware and Beaker discoveries at Armalughey in context. In: K. Dingwall (ed.) *Final Report on excavations at Site 4, Armalughey, Co. Tyrone.* Unpublished report by Headland U.K.

Carlin, N., 2011a. *A Proper Place for Everything: The Character and Context of Beaker Depositional Practice in Ireland.* Unpublished PhD thesis, University College Dublin.

Carlin, N., 2011b. Into the West: placing Beakers within their Irish contexts. In: A. M. Jones & G. Kirkham (eds) *Beyond the Core: Reflections on Regionality in Prehistory.* Oxford: Oxbow, 87-100.

Carlin, N., 2013. "Keep going, sure it's grand": understanding the Irish Late Neolithic – Early Bronze Age. In: K. Cleary (ed.) *The Archaeology of Disaster and Recovery. Proceedings of the IAI Autumn 2012 Conference.* Dublin: Institute of Archaeologists of Ireland, 18-27. Available at: http://www.iai.ie/wp-content/uploads/2016/03/Proceedings-of-the-IAI-Autumn-2012-Conference-2.pdf [Accessed May 2015].

Carlin, N., 2016. The timber circle and the Grooved Ware and Beaker discoveries at Armalughey. In: V. Ginn (ed.) *Road to the West: The Archaeology of the A4 / A5 Road Improvements Scheme from Dungannon to Ballygawley.* Belfast: Lagan Ferrovial and Northern Archaeological Consultancy for Transport NI, 193-210.

Carlin, N., 2017. Getting into the groove: exploring the relationship between Grooved Ware and developed passage tombs in Ireland c. 3000-2700 BC. *Proceedings of the Prehistoric Society,* 83, 155-188.

Carlin, N. & Brück, J. 2012. Searching for the Chalcolithic: continuity and change in the Irish Final Neolithic/Early Bronze Age. In: M. J. Allen, J. Gardiner, A. Sheridan & D. McOmish (eds) *Is there a British Chalcolithic? People, Place and Polity in the later 3rd millennium. Prehistoric Society Research Paper No. 4.* Oxford: Oxbow, 191-208.

Carlin, N., O'Connell, T. J. & O'Neill, N., 2015. The Neolithic discoveries on the Carlow Bypass. In: T. Bolger, C. Moloney & D. Shiels (eds) *A Journey along the Carlow Corridor: the Archaeology of the M9 Carlow Bypass. NRA Scheme Monographs 16.* Dublin: National Roads Authority, 95-109.

Carlin, N. & Cooney, G., 2017. Transforming our understanding of Neolithic and Chalcolithic society (4000-2200 cal BC) in Ireland. In: M. Stanley, R. Swan & A. O'Sullivan (eds) *Stories of Ireland's Past: Knowledge gained from NRA Roads Archaeology. TII Heritage 5.* Dublin: Transport Infrastructure Ireland, 23-56.

Carlin, N., Walsh, F. & Clarke, L. ,2008. *The M4 Kilcock-Enfield-Kinnegad Roadway: The Archaeology of Life and Death on the Boyne Floodplain.* Dublin: National Roads Authority.

Carsten, J. & Hugh-Jones, S., 1995. Introduction. In: J. Carsten & S. Hugh-Jones (eds) *About the House: Lèvi-Strauss and Beyond.* Cambridge: Cambridge University Press, 1-46.

Case, H., 1961. Irish Neolithic pottery: distribution and sequence. *Proceedings of the Prehistoric Society,* 9, 174-233.

Case, H., 1966. Were Beaker people the first metallurgists in Ireland? *Palaeohistoria,* 12, 141-177.

Case, H., 1969a. Settlement patterns in the Neolithic in the North Irish Neolithic. *Ulster Journal of Archaeology,* 32, 3-7.

Case, H., 1973. A ritual site in the North-East of Ireland. In: G. Daniel & P. Kjaerum (eds) *Megalithic Graves and Ritual. Papers Presented at the III Atlantic Colloquium, Moesgård 1969.* Copenhagen: Jutland Archaeological Society Publications, 173-196.

Case, H., 1977a. The Beaker Culture in Britain and Ireland. In: R. Mercer (ed.) *Beakers in Britain and Europe. BAR International Series 26.* Oxford: Tempus Reparatum, 71-89.

Case, H., 1977b. An early accession to the Ashmolean Museum. In: V. Markotic (ed.) *Ancient Europe and the Mediterranean*. Warminster: Aris and Phillips Ltd, 18-34.

Case, H., 1993. Beakers: Deconstruction and After. *Proceedings of the Prehistoric Society*, 59, 241-268.

Case, H., 1995a. Irish Beakers in their European context. In: J. Waddell & E. Shee Twohig (eds) *Ireland in the Bronze Age*. Dublin: Stationery Office, 14-29.

Case, H., 1995b. Some Wiltshire Beakers and their contexts. *Wiltshire Archaeological and Natural History Magazine*, 88, 1-17.

Case, H., 1998. Où en sont les Campaniformes de l'autre côté de la Manche. *Bulletin de la Société Préhistorique Française*, 95, 403-411.

Case, H., 2004a. The Beaker culture in Britain and Ireland: groups, European contacts and chronology. In: F. Nicolis (ed.) *Bell Beakers Today. Pottery, People, Culture, Symbols in Prehistoric Europe. Proceedings of the International Colloquium at Riva del Garda*. Trento: Servizio Beni Culturali, Ufficio Beni Archeologici, 361-377.

Case, H., 2004b. Beakers and the Beaker culture. In: J. Czebreszuk (ed.) *Similar but Different. Bell Beakers in Europe*. Poznan: Adam Mickiewicz University, 11-35.

Case, H., 2004c. Beaker burial in Britain and Ireland. A role for the dead. In: M. Besse & J. Desideri (eds) *Graves and Funerary Rituals during the Late Neolithic and the Early Bronze Age in Europe*. Oxford: Archeopress, 195-201.

Cassidy, L. M., & Bradley, D., 2015. Ancient DNA and Irish human prehistory: uncovering the past through palaeogenomics. *Journal of Irish Archaeology*, 24, 1-18.

Cassidy, L. M., Martiniano, R., Murphy, E., Teasdale, M. D., Mallory, J., Hartwell, B. & Bradley, D. G., 2016. Neolithic and Bronze Age migration to Ireland and establishment of the insular Atlantic genome. *Proceedings of the National Academy of Sciences*, 113 (2), 368-373.

Chambon, P. & Salanova, L., 1996. Chronologie de sépultures du IIIe millénaire dans le Bassin de la Seine. *Bulletin de la Société Préhistorique Française*, 93, 103-118.

Channing, J., 1993. Aughrim. In: I. Bennett (ed.) *Excavations 1992*. Wicklow: Wordwell, 4.

Chapman, J., 2000a. Pit digging and structured deposition in the Neolithic and Copper Age of Central and Eastern Europe. *Proceedings of the Prehistoric Society*, 61, 51-67.

Chapman, J., 2000b. *Fragmentation in Archaeology: People, Places and Broken Objects in the Prehistory of South Eastern Europe*. London: Routledge.

Chapman, J., 2008. Approaches to trade and exchange in earlier prehistory (Late Mesolithic – Early Bronze Age). In: A. Jones (ed.) *Prehistoric Europe. Theory and practice*. Oxford: Wiley-Blackwell, 333-355.

Cherry, S., 1990. The finds from Fulachta Fiadh. In: V. Buckley (ed.) *Burnt Offerings. International Contributions to Burnt Mound Archaeology*. Dublin: Wordwell, 49-54.

Childe, V. G., 1925. *The Dawn of European Civilization*. New York: Knopf.

Childe, V. G., 1930. *The Bronze Age*. New York: Biblo and Tannen.

Childe, V. G., 1949. *Prehistoric Communities of the British Isles*. 3rd ed. London: Kegan Paul.

Childe, V. G., 1950. *Prehistoric Migrations in Europe*. Oslo: H. Aschehoug and Co.

Childe, V. G., 1958. *The Prehistory of European Society*. Harmondsworth: Penguin.

Chitty, L. F., 1933. A Beaker-like vessel from Bushmills, Co. Antrim. *Antiquaries Journal*, 13, 259-265.

Clarke, D. L., 1968. *Analytical Archaeology*. London: Methuen.

Clarke, D. L., 1970. *Beaker Pottery of Great Britain and Ireland*. Cambridge: Cambridge University Press.

Clarke, D. L., 1976. The Beaker network – social and economic models. In: J. Lanting & J. van der Waals (eds) *Glockenbecker Symposion Oberried 1974*. Haarlem, Fibula-Van-Dischoeck, 459-477.

Clarke, D. V., Cowie, T. G. & Foxon, A., 1985. *Symbols of Power at the Time of Stonehenge*. Edinburgh: HMSO

Cleal, R. & Pollard, J., 2012. The revenge of the native: monuments, material culture, burial and other practices in the third quarter of the 3rd millennium BC in Wessex. In: M. J. Allen, J. Gardiner, A. Sheridan & D. McOmish (eds) *Is there a British Chalcolithic? People, Place and Polity in the later 3rd millennium. Prehistoric Society Research Paper No. 4*. Oxford: Oxbow, 317-332.

Cleary, K., 2007. *Irish Bronze Age Settlements: Spatial Organisation and the Deposition of Material Culture*. Unpublished PhD Thesis, University College Cork.

Cleary, K., 2016. Burial practices in Ireland during the late third millennium BC connecting new ideologies with local expressions. In: J. Koch & B. Cunliffe (eds) *Celtic from the West 3: Atlantic Europe in the Metal Ages–Questions of Shared Language*. Oxford: Oxbow, 139-179.

Cleary, K., 2017. Broken bones and broken stones: exploring fragmentation in Middle and Late Bronze Age settlement contexts in Ireland. *European Journal of Archaeology*, 21(3), 1-25.

Cleary, R., 1980. *The Late Neolithic/Beaker Period Ceramic Assemblage from New Grange, Co. Meath, Ireland: a Study*. Unpublished M.A thesis. University College Cork.

Cleary, R., 1983. The ceramic assemblage. In: M. J. O'Kelly, R. Cleary & D. Lehane (eds) *Newgrange, Co. Meath, Ireland: the Late Neolithic-Beaker Period Settlement. BAR International Series 190*. Oxford: Tempus Reparatum, 58-108.

Cleary, R., 1984. Bone tempered Beaker potsherd. *Journal of Irish Archaeology*, 2, 73-75.

Cleary, R., 1993. The Later Bronze Age at Lough Gur: filling in the blanks. In: E. Shee Twohig & M. Ronayne (eds) *Past Perceptions: The Prehistoric Archaeology of South-west Ireland*. Cork: Cork University Press, 114-120.

Cleary, R., 1995. Later Bronze Age settlement and prehistoric burials, Lough Gur, Co. Limerick. *Proceedings of the Royal Irish Academy*, 95C, 1-92.

Cleary, R., 2003. Enclosed Late Bronze Age habitation site and boundary wall at Lough Gur, Co. Limerick. *Proceedings of the Royal Irish Academy*, 103C, 97-189.

Cleary, R., 2015. Excavation at Grange Stone Circle (B), Lough Gur, Co. Limerick, and a review of the dating. *Journal of Irish Archaeology*, 24, 51-77.

Cleary, R. & Jones, C., 1980. A cist-burial at Ballynagallagh, near Lough Gur, Co. Limerick. *North Munster Antiquarian Journal*, 22, 3-7.

Coghlan, H.H. & Case, H.J., 1957. Early metallurgy of copper in Ireland and Britain. *Proceedings of the Prehistoric Society*, 23, 91-123.

Cohen, A. P., 1985. *The Symbolic Construction of Community*. London: Tavistock (now Routledge).

Collins, A. E. P., 1954. The excavation of a double horned cairn at Audleystown, Co. Down. *Ulster Journal of Archaeology*, 17, 7-56.

Collins, A. E. P., 1956. A horned cairn at Ballynichol, Co. Down. *Ulster Journal of Archaeology*, 19, 115-20.

Collins, A. E. P., 1957. Some recent finds of flint arrowheads. *Ulster Journal of Archaeology*, 20, 42-43.

Collins, A. E. P., 1959. Two hollow-based arrowheads in carboniferous chert. *Ulster Journal of Archaeology*, 22, 42.

Collins, A. E. P., 1966. Barnes Lower court cairn, Co. Tyrone. *Ulster Journal of Archaeology*, 29, 43-75.

Condit, T. & O'Sullivan, A., 1999. Landscapes of movement and control: interpreting prehistoric hillforts and fording places on the River Shannon. In: *Discovery Programme Reports 5*. Dublin: Royal Irish Academy, 25-39.

Condit, T. & Simpson, D., 1998. Irish hengiform enclosures and related monuments: a review. In: A. Gibson & D. Simpson (eds) *Prehistoric Ritual and Religion*. Stroud: Sutton, 45-61.

Cooney, G., 1987. *North Leinster in the Earlier Prehistoric Period*. Unpublished PhD Thesis, National University of Ireland.

Cooney, G., 1995. Theory and practice in Irish archaeology. In: P. Ucko (ed.) *Theory in Archaeology: A World Perspective*. London: Routledge, 263-277.

Cooney, G., 1996. Building the future on the past: archaeology and the construction of national identity in Ireland. In: M. Diaz-Andreu & T. Champion (eds) *Nationalism and Archaeology in Europe*. London: UCL Press, 143-163.

Cooney, G., 1997a. Images of settlement and the landscape in the Neolithic. In: P. Topping (ed.) *Neolithic Landscapes*. Oxford: Oxbow, 23-31.

Cooney, G., 1997b. The excavation of the portal tomb site at Melkagh, Co. Longford. *Proceedings of the Royal Irish Academy*, 97C, 195-244.

Cooney, G., 2000a. *Landscapes of Neolithic Ireland*. London: Routledge

Cooney, G., 2000b. Recognising regionality in the Irish Neolithic. In: A. Desmond, G. Johnson, J. Sheehan & E. Shee Twohig (eds) *New Agendas in Irish Prehistory*. Dublin: Wordwell, 49-65.

Cooney, G., 2003. Rooted or routed? Landscapes of Neolithic settlement in Ireland. In: I. Armit, E. Murphy, E. Nelis & D. Simpson (eds) *Neolithic Settlement in Ireland and Western Britain*. Oxford: Oxbow, 47-55.

Cooney, G., 2004. Performance and place: the hoarding of axeheads in Irish prehistory. In: H. Roche, E. Grogan, J. Bradley, J. Coles & B. Raftery (eds) *From Megaliths to Metal. Essays in Honour of George Eogan*. Oxford: Oxbow, 38-44

Cooney, G., 2005. Stereo porphyry: quarrying and deposition on Lambay Island, Ireland. In: P. Topping & M. Lynott (eds) *The Cultural Landscape of Prehistoric Mines*. Oxford: Oxbow, 14-29.

Cooney, G., 2006. Newgrange – A view from the platform. *Antiquity*, 80, 696-710.

Cooney, G., 2007. In retrospect: Neolithic activity at Knockadoon, Lough Gur, 50 years on. *Proceedings of the Royal Irish Academy*, 107C, 215-225.

Cooney, G., 2014. The role of cremation in mortuary practice in the Irish Neolithic. In: I. Kuijt, C. P. Quinn & G. Cooney (eds) *Transformation by Fire: The Archaeology of Cremation in Cultural Context*. Tucson: University of Arizona Press, 198-206.

Cooney, G., 2017. Interpreting the mortuary practices. In: G. Eogan & K. Cleary (eds) *Excavations at Knowth 6: The Great Mound at Knowth (Tomb 1) and its Passage Tomb Archaeology*. Dublin: Royal Irish Academy.

Cooney, G., & Grogan, E. 1998. People and place during the Irish Neolithic: exploring social change in time and space. In: M. Edmonds & C. Richards (eds) *Understanding the Neolithic of North-Western Europe*. Glasgow: Cruithne Press, 456-480.

Cooney, G. & Grogan, E., 1999. *Irish Prehistory: A Social Perspective*. 2nd ed. Dublin: Wordwell.

Cooney, G. & Mandal, S., 1998. *The Irish Stone Axe Project. Monograph 1*. Dublin: Wordwell.

Cooney, G., O'Sullivan, M. & Downey, L., 2006. *Archaeology 2020: Repositioning Irish Archaeology in the Knowledge Society – A Realistically Achievable Perspective*. The School of Archaeology UCD and The Heritage Council.

Cooney, G., Warren, G. & Ballin, T., 2013. Island quarries, island axeheads, and the Neolithic of Ireland and Britain. *North American Archaeologist*, 34(4), 409-431.

Coughlan, T., 2010. *Excavations at Cappydonnell, Co. Offaly*. Unpublished report.

Cowie, T., 1988. *Magic Metal: Early metalworkers in the North-east*. Aberdeen: Anthropological Museum, University of Aberdeen.

Cowie, T., 2004. Special places for special axes? Early Bronze Age metalwork from Scotland in its landscape setting. In: I. Shepherd & G. Barclay (eds) *Scotland in Ancient Europe: The Neolithic and Early Bronze Age of Scotland in their European Context*. Edinburgh: Society of Antiquaries of Scotland, 247-261.

Coyne, F., 2002. *Excavations at Ballyvollane II, Co. Limerick*. Unpublished report.

Crellin, R., J. 2014. *Changing Times: The Emergence of a Bronze Age on the Isle of Man*. Unpublished PhD Thesis. Newcastle University.

Cremin Madden, A., 1968. Beaker pottery in Ireland. *Journal of the Kerry Archaeological and Historical Society*, 1, 9-24.

Cremin Madden, A., 1969. The Beaker wedge tomb at Moytirra, Co. Sligo. *Journal of the Royal Society of Antiquaries of Ireland*, 99, 151-159.

Cressey, M. & Sheridan, A., 2003. The excavation of a Bronze Age cemetery at Seafield West, near Inverness, Highland. *Proceedings of the Society of Antiquaries of Scotland*, 133, 47-84.

Crooke, E., 2000. *Politics, Archaeology and the Creation of a National Museum in Ireland: an expression of national life*. Newbridge: Irish Academic Press.

Curtis, N. G. W & Wilkin, N. C. A., 2012. The regionality of beakers and bodies in the Chalcolithic of north-east Scotland. In: M. J. Allen, J. Gardiner, A. Sheridan & D. McOmish (eds) *Is there a British Chalcolithic? People, Place and Polity in the later 3rd millennium. Prehistoric Society Research Paper No. 4.* Oxford: Oxbow, 237-256.

Curtis, N. G. W. & Wilkin, N. C. A., 2017. Beakers and bodies: north-east Scotland in the first age of metal. *British Archaeology*, 17, 36-42.

Curtis, N. G. W & Wilkin, N. C. A., In press. Beakers and bodies in north-east Scotland: a regional and contextual study. In: M. Parker Pearson, A. Chamberlain, M. Jay, M. Richards, A. Sheridan & J. Evans (eds) *The Beaker People: Isotopes, Mobility and Diet in Prehistoric Britain. The Prehistoric Society Research Paper No. 7.* London: The Prehistoric Society.

Czebreszuk, J., 2003. Bell Beakers from West to East. In: P. Bogucki & P. J. Crabtree (eds) *Ancient Europe. 8000 B.C.-A.D. 1000. Volume I. The Mesolithic to Copper Age. Encyclopedia of the Barbarian World*. New York: Thomson and Gale, 476-485.

Czebreszuk, J. (ed.) 2004. *Similar but Different. Bell Beakers in Europe*. Poznan: Adam Mickiewicz University

Danaher, E., 2003. *A Final Report on the Excavation of an Early Neolithic House and Three Bronze Age Pits at Barnagore, Ballincollig, Co. Cork*. Unpublished final report for Archaeological Consultancy Services Ltd on behalf of Cork County Council.

Danaher, E., 2005. *Excavations at Ballinaspig More 5, Ballincollig, Co. Cork*. Unpublished final report issued to Duchas, The Heritage Service.

Danaher, E., 2007. *Monumental Beginnings: Archaeology of the N4 Sligo Inner Relief Road*. Dublin: National Roads Authority.

Darvill, T., 1996. Neolithic Buildings in England, Wales and the Isle of Man. In: T. Darvill & J. Thomas (eds) *Neolithic Houses in Nortwest Europe and Beyond*. Oxford: Oxbow, 76-111.

Darvill, T., 2010. *Prehistoric Britain*. 2nd edition. London: Routledge.

Darvill, T. C., Marshall, P., Parker Pearson, M. & Wainwright, G. J., 2012. Stonehenge remodeled. *Antiquity*, 86, 1021-1240.

Davies, O., 1937. Excavations at Ballyrenan, Co. Tyrone. *Journal of the Royal Society of Antiquaries of Ireland*, 67, 89-100.

Davies, O., 1938. Excavation of a horned cairn at Aghanaglack, Co. Fermanagh. *Journal of the Royal Society of Antiquaries of Ireland*, 69, 21-38.

Davies, O., 1939a. Excavations at the Giant's Grave, Loughash. *Ulster Journal of Archaeology*, 2, 254-268.

Davies, O., 1940. Cairn at Legland, Co. Tyrone. *Journal of the Royal Society of Antiquaries of Ireland*, 70, 206-207.

Davies, O. & Mullin, J. B., 1940. Excavation of Cashelbane Cairn, Loughash, Co. Tyrone. *Journal of the Royal Society of Antiquaries of Ireland*, 70, 143-163.

de Paor, L. & Ó h-Eochaidhe, M., 1956. Unusual group of earthworks at Slieve Breagh, Co. Meath. *Journal of the Royal Society of Antiquaries of Ireland*, 86, 97-101.

de Paor, M., 1961. Notes on Irish Beakers. In: G. Bersu (ed.) *Bericht über den V. Internationalen Kongress für Vor- und Frühgeschichte, Hamburg vom 24. bis 30. August 1958*. Berlin: Gebr. Mann, 653-660.

De Valera, R., 1951. A group of 'horned cairns' near Ballycastle, Co. Mayo. *Journal of the Royal Society of Antiquaries of Ireland*, 81, 161-197.

De Valera, R., 1960. The court cairns of Ireland. *Proceedings of the Royal Irish Academy*, 60C, 9-140.

De Valera, R. & Ó Nualláin, S., 1961. *Survey of the megalithic tombs of Ireland, Vol. I* Dublin: Stationery Office.

Delaney, D., 2001. *Excavations at Leopardstown Road, Rocklands.* Unpublished report.

Devine, E., 2006. *Preliminary Report. Archaeological Excavations (A003/055, E3466) Frankfort Site 1. N11 Gorey to Arklow Link, Co. Wexford.* Unpublished report for Valerie J. Keeley Ltd.

Dillon, F., 1997. Lithic assemblage of the Beaker complex. In: G. Eogan & H. Roche (eds) *Excavations at Knowth, 2.* Dublin. Royal Irish Academy, 161-184, 193-196.

Dingwall, K., 2010. *Final Report on Excavations at Site 4, Armalughey 2, Co. Tyrone.* Unpublished report by Headland U.K.

Douglas, M., 1966. *Purity and Danger. An Analysis of Concepts of Pollution and Taboo.* London: Routledge & Kegan Paul.

Dowd, M. A., 2004. *Caves: Sacred Places on the Irish Landscape.* Unpublished thesis, University College Cork.

Dowd, M. A., 2015. *The Archaeology of Caves in Ireland.* Oxford: Oxbow.

Doyle, I., Jennings, D. & MacDermott, J., 2002. *Unpublished Excavations in the Republic of Ireland 1930-1997.* Kilkenny: The Heritage Council.

Duffy, C., 2002. *Excavations in the Townlands of Mell and Hill of Rath.* Unpublished Final Report for Valery J. Keeley Ltd.

Earwood, C., 1991/2. A radiocarbon date for the Early Bronze Age wooden polypod bowls. *Journal of Irish Archaeology*, 4, 27-28.

Elliott, R., 2009. *Excavations at Paulstown, Co. Kilkenny.* Unpublished report by Irish Archaeological Consultancy Ltd on behalf of Kilkenny County Council and the National Roads Authority.

Eogan, G., 1983. *Hoards of the Irish Later Bronze Age.* Dublin: University College Dublin.

Eogan, G., 1984. *Excavations at Knowth*, 1. Dublin: Royal Irish Academy.

Eogan, G., 1991. Prehistoric and Early Historic culture change at Brugh na Boinne. *Proceedings of the Royal Irish Academy*, 91C, 105-132.

Eogan, G., 1994. *The Accomplished Art: Gold and Gold-working in Britain and Ireland during the Bronze Age (c.2300-650 B.C).* Oxford: Oxbow.

Eogan, G. & Cleary, K., 2017. *Excavations at Knowth 6: The Great Mound at Knowth (Tomb 1) and its Passage Tomb Archaeology.* Dublin: Royal Irish Academy.

Eogan, G. & Roche, H., 1997. *Excavations at Knowth 2.* Dublin: Royal Irish Academy.

Eogan, J., 2002. Excavations at a cairn at Coolnatullagh townland, County Clare. *North Munster Antiquarian Journal*, 42, 113-150.

Eogan, J., 2004. The construction of funerary monuments in the Irish Early Bronze Age: a review of the evidence. In: H. Roche, E. Grogan, J. Bradley, J. Coles & B. Raftery (eds) *From Megaliths to Metals: Essays in Honour of George Eogan.* Oxford: Oxbow, 56-60.

Eogan, J. & O'Brien, R., 2005. *Final Report of Excavations at Rathdown Upper, Greystones, Co. Dublin.* Unpublished Report by ADS Ltd.

Evans, E. E., 1939. Excavations at Carnanbane, Co. Londonderry: a double horned cairn. *Proceedings of the Royal Irish Academy*, 45C, 1-12.

Evans, E. E., 1953. *Lyles Hill: A Late Neolithic Site in County Antrim.* Belfast: HMSO.

Evans, E. E., 1968. Archaeology in Ulster since 1920. *Ulster Journal of Archaeology*, 31, 3-8.

Evans, E. E., 1981. *Personality of Ireland: Habitat, Heritage and History.* Belfast: Blackstaff.

Evans, E. E. & Megaw, B. R. S., 1937. The multiple cist cairn at Mount Stewart, Co. Down, Northern Ireland. *Proceedings of the Prehistoric Society*, 8, 29-42.

Evans, J. A. & Chenery, C. A., 2011. Isotope studies. In: A. P. Fitzpatrick (ed.) *The Amesbury Archer and the Boscombe Bowmen: Bell Beaker burials at Boscombe Down, Amesbury, Wiltshire. Wessex Archaeology 27.* Salisbury: Wessex Archaeology, 32.

Evans, J. A., Chenery, C. A. & Fitzpatrick, A.P., 2006. Bronze Age childhood migration of individuals near Stonehenge, revealed by strontium and oxygen isotope tooth enamel analysis. *Archaeometry*, 48, 309-321.

Frankenstein, S., & Rowlands, M., 1978. The internal structure and regional context of early Iron Age society in south-western Germany. *Bulletin of the Institute of Archaeology London*, 15, 73-112.

Fitzgerald, M., 2006. Archaeological discoveries on a new section of the N2 in Counties Meath and Dublin. In: J. O'Sullivan & M. Stanley (eds) *Settlement, Industry and Ritual: Proceedings of a Public Seminar on Archaeological Discoveries on National Road Schemes.* Dublin, National Roads Authority, 29-42.

Fitzpatrick, A. P., Delibes de Castro, G., Velasco Vázquez, J. & Guerra Doce, E., 2016. Bell Beaker connections along the Atlantic façade: the gold ornaments from Tablada del Rudrón, Burgos, Spain. In: E. Guerra Doce & C. Liesau von Lettow-Vorbeck (eds) *Analysis of the Economic Foundations supporting the Social Supremacy of the Beaker Groups.* Oxford: Archaeopress, 37-54.

Fitzpatrick, A. P., 2009. In his hands and in his head: the Amesbury Archer as a metalworker. In: P. Clarke (ed.) *Bronze Age Connections: Cultural Contact in Prehistoric Europe.* Oxford: Oxbow, 177-189.

Fitzpatrick, A. P., 2011. *The Amesbury Archer and the Boscombe Bowmen: Bell Beaker burials at Boscombe Down, Amesbury, Wiltshire. Wessex Archaeology 27.* Salisbury: Wessex Archaeology.

Fitzpatrick, A. P., 2015. The earlier Bell Beakers: migrations to Britain and Ireland. In: M. P. Prieto Martínez & L. Salanova (eds) *The Bell Beaker Transition in Europe. Mobility and Local Evolution During the 3rd Millennium BC.* Oxford: Oxbow, 41-56.

Fokkens, H., 1997. From barrows to urnfields: economic crisis or ideological change?. *Antiquity,* 71, 373.

Fokkens, H., 1999. Cattle and martiality. Changing relations between man and landscape in the Late Neolithic and the Bronze Age. In: C. Fabech & J. Ringtved (eds) *Settlement and Landscape. Proceedings of a conference in Århus, Denmark, May 4-7 1998.* Århus: Århus University Press, 31-38.

Fokkens, H. 2012a. Background to Dutch Beakers. A critical review of the Dutch model. In: H. Fokkens & F. Nicolis (eds.) *Background to Beakers. Inquiries in Regional Cultural Backgrounds to the Bell Beaker Complex.* Leiden: Sidestone Press, 1-27.

Fokkens H., 2012b. Dutchmen on the move? A discussion of the adoption of the Beaker package. In: M. J. Allen, J. Gardiner, A. Sheridan & D. McOmish (eds) *Is there a British Chalcolithic? People, Place and Polity in the later 3rd millennium. Prehistoric Society Research Paper No. 4.* Oxford: Oxbow, 113-123.

Fokkens, H., 2016. *Farmers, Fishers, Fowlers, Hunters. Knowledge generated by development-led archaeology about the Late Neolithic, the Early Bronze Age and the start of the Middle Bronze Age (2850 – 1500 cal BC) in the Netherlands. Nederlandse Archeologische Rapporten no. 53.* Amersfoort: Rijksdienst voor het Cultureel Erfgoed.

Fokkens, H. & Arnoldussen, S., 2008. *Bronze Age Settlements in the Low Countries.* Oxford: Oxbow.

Fokkens, H., Achterkamp, Y. & Kuijpers, M., 2008. Bracers or bracelets? About the functionality and meaning of Bell Beaker wrist-guards. *Proceedings of the Prehistoric Society,* 74, 109-140.

Fontijn, D. R., 2002. *Sacrificial landscapes: cultural biographies of persons, objects and 'natural' places in the Bronze Age of the southern Netherlands, c. 2300-600BC. Analecta Praehistorica Leidensia 33/34.* Leiden: University of Leiden

Fontijn, D. R., 2007. The significance of 'invisible' places. *World Archaeology,* 39, 70-83.

Fontijn, D. R., 2008. Everything in its right place? On selective deposition, landscape and the construction of identity in later prehistory. In: A. Jones (ed.), *Prehistoric Europe. Theory and Practice.* London: Willey-Blackwell, 86-106.

Fontijn, D. R. & Van Reybrouck, D., 1999. The luxury of abundance: Syntheses of Irish prehistory. *Archaeological Dialogues,* 6(1), 55-73.

Fowler, C., 2004. *The Archaeology of Personhood: An Anthropological Approach.* London: Routledge.

Fowler, C., 2005. Identity politics: personhood, kinship, gender and power in Neolithic and Early Bronze Age Britain. In: E. Casella & C. Fowler (eds) *The Archaeology of Plural and Changing Identities: Beyond Identification.* New York: Kluwer Academic Press, 109-134.

Fowler, C., 2013. *The Emergent Past: A Relational Realist Archaeology of Early Bronze Age Mortuary Practices.* Oxford: Oxford University Press.

Fowler, C. & Wilkin, N., 2016. Early Bronze Age mortuary practices in north-east England and south-east Scotland: using relational typologies to trace social networks. In: R. Crellin, C. Fowler & R. Tipping (eds) *Prehistory without Borders: Prehistoric Archaeology of the Tyne-Forth Region.* Oxford: Oxbow, 112-135.

Frazer, W., 1897. On Irish gold ornaments. Whence came the gold and when?. *The Journal of the Royal Society of Antiquaries of Ireland,* 7(4), 359-370.

Frieman, C. J., 2014. Double edged blades: revisiting the British (and Irish) flint daggers. *Proceedings* of the *Prehistoric Society,* 79, 33-65.

Furholt, M., 2014. *Upending a 'Totality'*: re-evaluating Corded Ware variability in Late Neolithic Europe. *Proceedings of the Prehistoric Society,* 80, 67-86.

Furholt, M., 2017. Massive migrations? The impact of recent aDNA studies on our view of third millennium Europe. *European Journal of Archaeology,* 21(2), 159-191.

Garrow, D., 2006. *Pits, Settlement and Deposition during the Neolithic and Early Bronze Age in East Anglia. BAR British Series 414.* Oxford: Archaeopress.

Garwood, P., 1999. Grooved ware in Southern Britain: chronology and interpretation. In: R. Cleal & A. MacSween (eds) *Grooved Ware in Britain and Ireland. Neolithic Studies Group Papers 3.* Oxford: Oxbow, 145-176.

Garwood, P., 2007. Before the hills in order stood: chronology, time and history in the interpretation of Early Bronze Age round barrows. In: J. Last (ed.) *Beyond the Grave: New Perspectives on Barrows.* Oxford: Oxbow, 30-52.

Garwood, P., 2011. Rites of passage. In: T. Insoll (ed.) *The Oxford Handbook of the Archaeology of Ritual and Religion. Oxford: Oxford University Press,* 261-284.

Garwood, P., 2012. The present dead: the making of past and future landscapes in the British Chalcolithic. In: M. J. Allen, J. Gardiner, A. Sheridan & D. McOmish (eds) *Is there a British Chalcolithic? People, Place and Polity in the later 3rd millennium. Prehistoric Society Research Paper No. 4.* Oxford: Oxbow, 238-316.

Gell, A., 1998. *Art and Agency: An Anthropological Theory.* Oxford: Clarendon Press.

Gibson, A., 1980. Pot beakers in Britain?. *Antiquity,* 54, 219-221.

Gibson, A., 1982. *Beaker Domestic Sites: A Study of the Domestic Pottery of the Late Third and Early Second Millennia B.C in the British Isles. BAR British series 107*. Oxford: Tempus Reparatum.

Gibson, A., 1987. Beaker domestic sites across the North Sea: a review. In: J. C. Blanchet (ed.) *Les Relations entre le Continent et les Iles Britanniques à l'Age du Bronze: Actes du Colloque de Lille dans le Cadre du 22e Congrès Préhistorique de France*. Revue Archéologique de Picardie Supplément, 7-16.

Gibson, A., 1996. The Later Neolithic structures at Trelystan, Powys, Wales: ten Years on. In: T. Darvill & J. Thomas (eds) *Neolithic Houses in Nortwest Europe and Beyond*. Oxford: Oxbow, 133-141.

Gibson, A., 1999. *The Walton Basin Project: Excavation and Survey in a Prehistoric Landscape 1993-7*. York: Council for British Archaeology.

Gibson, A., 2004. Burials and Beakers: seeing beneath the veneer in late Neolithic Britain. In: J. Czebrezuk (ed.) *Similar but Different: Bell Beakers in Europe*. Poznan: Adam Mickiewicz University, 173-192.

Gibson, A., 2005. *Stonehenge and Timber Circles*. Stroud: Tempus.

Gibson, A., 2007. Book Reviews: The Dating of Food Vessels and Urns in Ireland, by A.L. Brindley. Available at: http://www.ucl.ac.uk/prehistoric/reviews/07_08_brindley.htm_[Accessed July 2018].

Gibson, A., 2010. Excavation and survey at Dyffryn Lane henge Complex, Powys, and a reconsideration of the dating of henges. *Proceedings of the Prehistoric Society,* 76, 213-248.

Gibson, C., 2013. Beakers into bronze: tracing connections between Western Iberia and the British Isles 2800-800 BC. In: J. T. Koch & B. Cunliffe (eds) *Celtic from the West 2: Rethinking the Bronze Age and the Arrival of Indo-European in Atlantic Europe*. Oxford: Oxbow, 71-99.

Ginn, V., 2014. *Settlement Structure in Middle – Late Bronze Age Ireland*. Unpublished PhD thesis, Queen's University Belfast.

Ginn, V. 2016. *Mapping Society: Settlement Structure in Later Bronze Age Ireland*. Oxford: Archaeopress.

Glover, W., 1975. Segmented cist grave in Kinkit Townland, County Tyrone. *Journal of the Royal Society of Antiquaries of Ireland,* 105, 141-144 and 150-155.

Godelier, M., 1977. *Perspectives in Marxist Anthropology*. Cambridge: Cambridge University Press.

Godelier, M., 1999. *The Enigma of the Gift*. Chicago: University of Chicago Press.

Gosden, C., 1985. *Gifts and kin in Early Iron Age Europe.* Man, 20, 475-493.

Gosden, C. & Marshall, Y., 1999. The cultural biography of objects. *World Archaeology,* 31(2), 169-178.

Gowen, M., 1988. *Three Irish Gas Pipelines: New Archaeological Evidence in Munster*. Dublin: Wordwell.

Graeber, D., 2001. *Towards an Anthropological Theory of Value. The False Coin of our own Dreams*. New York: Palgrave.

Green, H.S., 1980. *The Flint Arrowheads of the British Isles. BAR British Series 75*. Oxford: Tempus Reparatum.

Greenblatt, S. (ed.) 2010. *Cultural Mobility: A Manifesto*. Cambridge: Cambridge University Press.

Grogan, E., 2004. Middle Bronze Age burial traditions in Ireland. In: H. Roche, E. Grogan, J. Bradley, J. Coles & B. Raftery (eds) *From Megaliths to Metals: Essays in Honour of George Eogan*. Oxford: Oxbow, 61-70.

Grogan, E., 1980. *Houses of the Neolithic Period in Ireland and Comparative Sites in Britain and on the Continent*. Unpublished M.A. thesis, University College Dublin.

Grogan, E., 1989. *The Early Prehistory of the Lough Gur Region*. Unpublished PhD Thesis, National University of Ireland.

Grogan, E., 1991. Radiocarbon dates from Brúgh na Bóinne. In: G. Eogan (ed.) Prehistoric and Early Historic culture change at Brú na Bóinne. *Proceedings of the Royal Irish Academy,* 91C, 105-132.

Grogan, E., 1996. Neolithic Houses in Ireland. In: T. Darvill & J. Thomas (eds) *Neolithic Houses in Nortwest Europe and Beyond*. Oxford: Oxbow, 41-60.

Grogan, E., 2002. Neolithic houses in Ireland: a broader perspective. *Antiquity,* 76, 517-525.

Grogan, E., 2004a. The implications of Irish Neolithic houses. In: I. A. G., Shepherd & G. J. Barclay (eds) *Scotland in Ancient Europe. The Neolithic and Early Bronze Age of Scotland in their European Context*. Edinburgh: Society of Antiquaries of Scotland, 103-114.

Grogan, E., 2004c. *The Prehistoric Pottery Assemblage from Charlesland, Co. Wicklow. Sites 1B, J, K, R.M.P, and G.C1*. Unpublished report.

Grogan, E., 2005a. *The North Munster Project. Volume 1. The Later Prehistoric Landscape of South-east Clare. Discovery Programme Monographs 6*. Dublin: Wordwell.

Grogan, E., 2005b. *The North Munster Project. Volume 2: The Prehistoric Landscape of North Munster. Discovery Programme Monographs, No. 6*. Dublin: Wordwell.

Grogan, E., 2005c. *The Prehistoric Pottery Assemblage from Kilgobbin, Co. Dublin*. Unpublished report.

Grogan, E., 2005d. Appendix C. The pottery from Mooghaun South. In: E. Grogan (ed.) T*he North Munster Project. Volume 1. The Later Prehistoric Landscape of South-east Clare. Discovery Programme Monograph 6*. Dublin: Wordwell, 317-328.

Grogan, E., 2006. *The Prehistoric Pottery from Glebe, Balrothery, Co. Dublin*. Unpublished report.

Grogan, E., 2008. *The Prehistoric Pottery from Curragh More, Co. Galway.* Unpublished report.

Grogan, E., 2017. The Bronze Age: a surfeit of data? In: M. Stanley, R. Swan & A. O'Sullivan (eds) *Stories of Ireland's Past: Knowledge Gained from NRA Roads Archaeology. TII Heritage 5*. Dublin: Transport Infrastructure Ireland, 57-85.

Grogan, E. & Eogan, G., 1987. Lough Gur Excavations by Sean. P. Ó Ríordáin: further Neolithic and Beaker habitations on Knockadoon. *Proceedings of the Royal Irish Academy*, 87C, 229-506.

Grogan, E. & Roche, H., 2005a. *The Prehistoric Pottery from Newtownbalregan 2, Co. Louth.* Unpublished report.

Grogan, E. & Roche, H., 2005b. *The Prehistoric Pottery from Newtownlittle, Co. Dublin.* Unpublished report.

Grogan, E. & Roche, H., 2005c. Prehistoric Pottery Analysis. In: E. Danaher (ed.) *Excavations at Carrigrohane 4, Ballincollig, Co. Cork.* Unpublished final report issued to Duchas, the Heritage Service.

Grogan, E. & Roche, H., 2005d. *The Prehistoric Pottery from Carnmore 5, Co. Louth.* Unpublished report.

Grogan, E. & Roche, H., 2005e. *The Prehistoric Pottery from Newtownbalregan 5, Co. Louth.* Unpublished report.

Grogan, E. & Roche, H., 2006. *The Prehistoric Pottery Assemblages from the N8 Cashel Bypass, Co. Tipperary.* Unpublished report for the National Roads Authority.

Grogan, E. & Roche, H., 2007a. *The Prehistoric Pottery Assemblages from the N11 Rathnew – Arklow Project. Ballyclogh North, Co. Wicklow (A022/046).* Unpublished report for Irish Archaeological Consultancy Ltd on behalf of Wicklow County Council.

Grogan, E. & Roche, H., 2007b. *The Prehistoric Pottery Assemblages from the M3 Clonee – North of Kells, Co. Meath. Ardsallagh 1, Ardsallagh 2, Ardsallagh 4, Johnstown 3, Pace 1 and Dunboyne 3.* Unpublished report for Archaeological Consultancy Services Ltd on behalf of Meath County Council.

Grogan, E. & Roche, H., 2008. *The Prehistoric Pottery Assemblage from Frankfort, Co. Wexford (A003/055, E3466). N11 Gorey – Arklow Link Road, Co. Wexford.* Unpublished report for Valery J. Keeley Ltd on behalf of Wexford County Council.

Grogan, E. & Roche, H., 2009a. *The Prehistoric Pottery Assemblage from Paulstown 2, Co. Kilkenny (AR146, E3632). N9/N10 Rathclogh to Powerstown.* Unpublished report for Irish Archaeological Consultancy Ltd.

Grogan, E. & Roche, H., 2009b. *The Prehistoric Pottery Assemblages from Lismullin 1 (E3074). The M3 Clonee – North of Kells, Co. Meath.* Unpublished report for Archaeological Consultancy Services Ltd.

Grogan, E. & Roche, H., 2009c. *The Prehistoric Pottery Assemblage from Kilmainham 1B, Co. Meath.* Unpublished report for Irish Archaeological Consultancy Ltd.

Grogan, E. & Roche, H., 2010. Clay and fire: the development and distribution of pottery traditions in prehistoric Ireland. In: M. Stanley, E. Danaher & J. Eogan (eds) *Creative Minds. Archaeology and the National Roads Authority Monograph Series 7.* Dublin: National Roads Authority, 27-45.

Grogan, E. & Roche, H., 2011. *The Prehistoric Pottery Assemblage from Rathmullan 12, Co. Meath (01E0294). M1 Northern Motorway.* Unpublished Report for Irish Archaeological Consultancy Ltd.

Grogan, E., O'Donnell, L. & Johnson, P., 2007. *Bronze Age Landscapes of the Gas Pipeline to the West. An Integrated Archaeological and Environmental Assessment.* Dublin: Wordwell.

Guilaine, J., Claustre, F., Lemercier, O. & Sabatier, P., 2001. Campaniformes et environnement culturel en France méditerranéenne. In: F. Nicolis (ed.) *Bell Beakers today. Pottery, People, Culture, Symbols in Prehistoric Europe. Proceedings of the International Colloquium Riva del Garda (Trento, Italy) 11-16 May 1998.* Trento: Ufficio Beni Archeologici, 229-275.

Haak, W., Lazaradis, I., Patterson, N., Rohland, N., Mallick, S., Llamas, B., Brandt, G., et al., 2015. Massive migration from the steppe was a source for Indo-European languages in Europe. *Nature*, 522, 207-211.

Hackett, L., 2010. *Final Report on Archaeological Investigations at Site E2980, in the Townland of Moone, Co. Kildare. Archaeological Services Contract No. 5- Resolution, Kilcullen to Moone and Athy Link Road. N9/N10 Kilcullen to Waterford Scheme Phase 3: Kilcullen to Carlow (A021/173).* Unpublished report.

Hagen, I., 2005. *Excavations at Kilgobbin, Co. Dublin.* Unpublished final report.

Hall, M. & Brück, J., 2010. Women, death and social change in the British Bronze Age. Comments by Mark Hall. *Norwegian Archaeological Review*, 43 (1), 77-85.

Harbison, P., 1969a. *The Daggers and the Halberds of the Early Bronze Age in Ireland. Prähistorische Bronzefunde 6.* Munchen: C.H. Beck.

Harbison, P., 1969b. *The Axes of The Early Bronze Age in Ireland. Prähistorische Bronzefunde 9.1.* Munchen: C.H. Beck.

Harbison, P., 1973. The Earlier Bronze Age in Ireland. *Journal of the Royal Society of Antiquaries of Ireland*, 103, 93-152.

Harbison, P., 1975. The coming of the Indo-Europeans to Ireland: an archaeological view point. *Journal of Indo-European studies*, 3, 101-119.

Harbison, P., 1976. *Bracers and V-perforated Buttons in the Beaker and Food Vessel Cultures of Ireland. Archaeologica Atlantica Research Report 1.* Bad Bramstedt: Moreland.

Harbison, P., 1979. Who were Ireland's first metallurgists?. In: M. Ryan (ed.) *The Origins of Metallurgy in Atlantic Europe. Proceedings of The Fifth Atlantic Colloquium*. Dublin: Stationary Office, 97-105.

Harbison, P., 1978 A flat-tanged dagger from Co. Tyrone Now in the Monaghan County Museum. *Clogher Record*, 9 (3), 333-335.

Harbison, P., 1988. *Pre-Christian Ireland*. London: Thames & Hudson.

Harding, A., 2006. What does the context of deposition and frequency of Bronze Age weaponry tell us about the function of weapons?. In: T. Otto, H. Thrane & H. Vandkilde (eds) *Warfare and Society. Archaeological and Anthropological Perspectives*. Aarhus: Aarhus University Press, 505-525.

Harding, A., 2000. *European Societies in the Bronze Age*. Cambridge: Cambridge University Press.

Harding, J., 2005. Rethinking the Great Divide: long-term structural history and the temporality of event. *Norwegian Archaeological Review*, 38(2), 88-101.

Harding, J., 2006. Pit-digging, occupation and structured deposition on Rudston Wold, Eastern Yorkshire. *Oxford Journal of Archaeology*, 25, 109-126.

Harrison, R. & Heyd, V., 2007. The transformation of Europe in the 3rd Millennium BC: the example of 'Le Petit-Chasseur I + II' (Sion, Valais, Switzerland). *Prähistorische Zeitschrift*, 82, 129-214.

Harrison, R. J., 1980. *The Beaker Folk, Copper Age Archaeology in Western Europe*. London: Thames & Hudson.

Hartnett, P. J., 1971. The excavation of two tumuli at Fourknocks (Sites II and III), Co. Meath. *Proceedings of the Royal Irish Academy*, 71C, 35-89.

Hartwell, B., 1998. The Ballynahatty complex. In: A. Gibson & D. Simpson (eds) *Prehistoric Ritual and Religion*. Stroud: Sutton Publishing, 32-44.

Hartwell, B., 2002. A Neolithic ceremonial timber complex at Ballynahatty, Co. Down. *Antiquity*, 76, 526-532.

Hawkes, A., 2014. The beginnings and evolution of the Fulacht fia tradition in early prehistoric Ireland. *Proceedings of the Royal Irish Academy*, 114C, 89-139.

Hawkes, A., 2015. Fulachtaí fia and Bronze Age cooking in Ireland: reappraising the evidence. *Proceedings of the Royal Irish Academy*, 115C, 47-77.

Hawkes, J. H. & Hawkes, C. F. C., 1947. *Prehistoric Britain*. Rev and enlarged ed. London: Chatto and Windus.

Hayes, A., 2007. *Archaeological Excavation of Pit Features at Site 134, Faughart Lower 6, Dundalk, Co. Louth*. Unpublished final report for Aegis Archaeology Ltd.

Heise, M., 2016. Heads North or East? A Re-Examination of *Beaker*. Burials in Britain. Unpublished PhD Thesis. University of Edinburgh.

Helms, M. W., 1988. *Ulysses' Sail. An Ethnographic Odyssey of Power, Knowledge, and Geographical Distance*. Princeton: Princeton University Press.

Helms, M. W., 1993. *Craft and the Kingly Ideal. Art, Trade and Power*. Austin: University of Texas Press.

Helms, M. W., 1998. *Access to Origins. Affines, Ancestors and Aristocrats*. Austin: University of Texas Press.

Hencken, H. O., 1935. A cairn at Poulawack, Co. Clare. *Journal of the Royal Society of Antiquaries of Ireland*, 65, 191-222.

Hencken, H. O., 1939. A long cairn at Creevykeel, Co. Sligo. *Journal of the Royal Society of Antiquaries of Ireland*, 69, 53-98.

Hensey, R. & Shee Twohig, E., 2017. Facing the cairn at Newgrange, Co. Meath. *Journal of Irish Archaeology*, 26, 57-76.

Henshall, A. S. & Wallace, J. C., 1964. The excavation of a chambered cairn at Embo, Sutherland. *Proceedings of the Society of Antiquaries of Scotland*, 96, 9-36.

Henshall, A. S., 1968. *Scottish dagger graves*. In: J. M. Coles &. D. D. A. Simpson (eds.) *Studies in Ancient Europe. Essays Presented to Stuart Piggott*. Leicester: Leicester University Press, 173-196.

Henshall, A., 1972. *The Chambered Tombs of Scotland, Vol. 2*. Edinburgh: Edinburgh University Press.

Herity, M., 1966. Excavation near Ballinskelligs, Co. Kerry. *North Munster Archaeological Journal*, 10(1), 67.

Herity, M., 1967. Excavation near Derrynane, Co. Kerry. *North Munster Archaeological Journal*, 10 (2), 218.

Herity, M., 1970. The prehistoric peoples of Kerry: a programme of investigation. *Journal of the Kerry Archaeological and Historical Society*, 4, 3-14.

Herity, M., 1974. *Irish Passage Graves: Neolithic Tomb-builders in Ireland and Britain, 2500 BC*. Dublin: Irish University Press.

Herity, M., 1982. Irish Decorated Neolithic Pottery. *Proceedings of the Royal Irish Academy*, 82C, 247-404.

Herity, M., 1987. The finds from Irish court tombs. *Proceedings of the Royal Irish Academy*, 87C, 103-281.

Herity, M. & Eogan, G., 1977. *Ireland in Prehistory*. London: Routledge.

Herring, I., 1938. The cairn excavation at Well Glass Spring, Largantea, Co. Londonderry. *Ulster Journal of Archaeology*, 1, 164-188.

Herring, I. & May, A., 1937. The Giants Grave, Kilhoyle, Co. Londonderry. *Proceedings of the Belfast Natural History and Philosophical Society*, 1(3), 34-48.

Herring, I. & May, A.M., 1940. Cloghnagalla cairn, Boviel, Co. Londonderry. *Ulster Journal of Archaeology*, 3,164-168.

Heyd, V., 2007. Families, prestige goods, warriors and complex societies: Beaker groups of the third millennium cal BC along the Upper and Middle Danube. *Proceedings of the Prehistoric Society*, 73, 321-370.

Hill, J. D., 1995. *Ritual and Rubbish in the Iron Age of Wessex – A Study of the formation of a specific archaeological record. BAR British Series 242.* Oxford: Tempus Reparatum.

Hodder, I., 1982. *Symbols in Action: Ethnoarchaeological Studies of Material Culture.* Cambridge: Cambridge University Press.

Hodder, I., 1986. *Reading the Past: Current Approaches to Interpretation in Archaeology.* Cambridge: Cambridge University Press.

Hodder, I. & Hutson, S., 2003. *Reading the Past: Current Approaches to Interpretation in Archaeology.* 3rd ed. Cambridge: Cambridge University Press.

Hofmann, D., 2015. "What Have Genetics Ever Done for Us? The Implications of aDNA Data for Interpreting Identity in Early Neolithic Central Europe." European Journal of Archaeology 18 (3): 454-476. doi:10.1179/1461957114Y.0000000083.

Horning, A. 2018. Constructing selves, constructing others: Approaching identities in Ireland. In E. Campbell, E. FitzPatrick, & A. Horning (eds) *Becoming and Belonging in Ireland 1200-1600,* 1-15, Cork: Cork University Press.

Hoskins, J., 1998. *Biographical Objects: How Things Tell the Stories of People's Lives.* London & New York: Routledge.

Hughes, I., 1988. Megaliths: space, time and the landscape – a view from the Clyde. *Scottish Archaeological Revew,* 5, 41-58.

Hunt, J., 1967. Prehistoric burials at Caherguillamore, Co. Limerick. In: E. Rynne (ed.) *North Munster Studies: Essays in Commemoration of Monsignor Micheal Moloney.* Limerick: Thomond Archaeological Society, 20-42.

Hurl, D., 2001. Excavation of a wedge tomb in Ballybriest townland, Co. Londonderry. *Ulster Journal of Archaeology,* 60, 9-31.

Ixer, R., 2004. The petrography of prehistoric pottery from Ross Island mine. Appendix 7. In: W. O'Brien (ed.) *Ross Island, Mining, Metal and Society in Early Ireland.* Galway: Department of Archaeology, NUIG, 643-650.

Johannsen N. N., Larson G., Meltzer D. J., & Vander Linden, M., 2017. *A composite window into human history. Science,* 356(6343),1118-1120.

Johnston, P. & Carlin, N. Forthcoming. The significance of the prehistoric settlement and communal places. In: P. Johnston & J. Kiely (eds) *Hidden Voices. The Archaeology of the M8 Fermoy – Mitchelstown Motorway. TII Heritage Series.* Dublin: Transport Infrastructure Ireland.

Johnston, P. & Kiely, J., Forthcoming. *Hidden Voices. The Archaeology of the M8 Fermoy – Mitchelstown Motorway. TII Heritage Series.* Dublin: Transport Infrastructure Ireland.

Johnston, P., Kiely, J. & Tierney, J., 2008. *Near the Bend in the River: The Archaeology of the N25 Kilmacthomas Realignment.* Bray: NRA monographs/Wordwell.

Jones, A., 1999. The world on a plate: ceramics, food technology and cosmology in Neolithic Orkney. *World Archaeology,* 31, 55-77.

Jones, A. M., 2005. *Cornish Bronze Age ceremonial landscapes c.2500-1500 BC, BAR 394.* Oxford: Archaeopress.

Jones, A. M., 2008. How the dead live: mortuary practices, memory and ancestors in Neolithic and Early Bronze Age Britain and Ireland. In: J. Pollard (ed.) *Prehistoric Britain.* Oxford: Blackwell, 177-201.

Jones, A. M., 2012. *Prehistoric Materialities. Becoming Material in Prehistoric Britain and Ireland.* Oxford: Oxford University Press.

Jones, A. M. & Quinnell, H., 2006. Cornish Beakers: new discoveries and perspectives. *Cornish Archaeology,* 45, 31-70.

Jones, A. M. & Thomas, C., 2010. Bosiliack Carn and a reconsideration of entrance graves. *Proceedings of the Prehistoric Society,* 76, 271-296.

Jones, C., 1996. Prehistoric Farmstead at Kilnaboy. *The Other Clare,* 20, 17-19.

Jones, C., 1998a. *Excavations of Mound Walls and an Associated Final Neolithic / Early Bronze Age Settlement on Roughan Hill, Co. Clare.* Unpublished manuscript.

Jones, C., 1998b. The discovery and dating of the prehistoric landscape of Roughan Hill in Co. Clare. *Journal of Irish Archaeology,* 9, 27-43.

Jones, C., 2015. Dating ancient field walls in karst landscapes using differential bedrock lowering. *Geoarchaeology,* 21. 77–100. https://doi.org/10.1002/gea.21531.

Jones, C., 2008. *Roughan Hill prehistoric landscape. Burren Landscape and Settlement.* Unpublished final report.

Jones, C., Carey, O. & Hennigar, C., 2010. Domestic production and the political economy in prehistory: evidence from the Burren, Co. Clare. In: E. FitzPatrick & J. Kelly (eds) Domestic Life in Ireland. *Proceedings of the Royal Irish Academy,* 111C, 33-58.

Jones, C., McVeigh, T. & Ó Maoldúin, R., 2015. Monuments, landscape and identity in Chalcolithic Ireland. In: K. D. Springs (ed.) *Landscape and Identity: Archaeology and Human Geography. BAR International Series 2709.* Oxford: Archeopress, 3-25.

Jones, C., Walsh, P., & Ó Cearbhaill, P., 1996. Recent discoveries on Roughaun Hill, County Clare. *The Journal of the Royal Society of Antiquaries of Ireland,* 126, 86-107.

Jones, S., 1997. *The Archaeology of Ethnicity: Constructing Identities in the Past and the Present.* London & New York: Routledge.

Kaul, F., 1998. *Ships on Bronzes: A Study in Bronze Age Religion and Iconography*. Copenhagen: National Museum of Denmark.

Kaul, F., 2004. *Bronzealderens Religion. Studier af den Nordiske Bronzealders Ikonografi. Nordiske Fortidsminder, Serie B, bind 22*. Copenhagen: Det Kongelige Nordiske Oldskriftselskab.

Keeley, V., 1989. Taylorsgrange portal tomb. In: C. Manning & D. Hurl (eds) Excavation bulletin 1980-4. *Journal of Irish Archaeology*, 5, 74.

Kelly, D., 1985. A possible wrist-bracer from County Tyrone. *Journal of the Royal Society of Antiquaries of Ireland*, 115, 162.

Kelly, E. P., 1978. A reassessment of the dating evidence for Knockadoon Class II pottery. *Irish Archaeological Research Forum*, V, 23-26.

Kelly, E. P., 2006. Secrets of the bog bodies: the enigma of the Iron Age explained. *Archaeology Ireland*, 20(1), 26-30.

Kelly, E. P. & Cahill, M., 2010. Safe secrets 1 – an early Bronze Age detective story from County Roscommon. *Archaeology Ireland*, 24(2), 5-6.

Kiely, J. & Dunne, L., 2005. Recent archaeological excavations in the Tralee area. In: M. Connolly (ed.) *Past Kingdoms: Recent Archaeological Research, Survey and Excavation in County Kerry*. Tralee: The Heritage Council/ Kerry County Council, 39-64.

King, H. A., 1999. Excavations on the Fourknocks Ridge, Co. Meath. *Proceedings of the Royal Irish Academy*, 99C, 157-198.

Kinnes, I., Gibson, A., Ambers, J., Bowman, S., Loese, M. & Boast, R., 1991. Radiocarbon dating and British Beakers: the British museum programme. *Scottish Archaeological Review*, 8, 35-68.

Knowles, W. J., 1885. Proceedings. *The Journal of the Royal Historical and Archaeological Association of Ireland*, 7(63), 126-128.

Kopytoff, I., 1986. The cultural biography of things: commoditization as process. In: A. Appadurai (ed.) *The Social Life of Things*. Cambridge: Cambridge University Press, 64-91.

Kristiansen, K., 2015. The decline of the Neolithic and the rise of Bronze Age society. In: C. Fowler, J. Harding & D. Hofmann (eds) *The Oxford Handbook of Neolithic Europe*. Oxford: Oxford University Press, 1093-1017.

Kristiansen, K. & Larsson, T., 2005. *The Rise of Bronze Age Society: Travels, Transmissions and Transformations*. Cambridge: Cambridge University Press.

Kristiansen, K., Allentoft, M. E., Frei, K. M., Iversen, R., Johannsen, N. N., Kroonen, G., Pospieszny, Ł., Price, T. D., Rasmussen, S., Sjögren, K-G; Sikora, M. & Willerslev, E., 2017. Re-theorising mobility and the formation of culture and language among the Corded Ware Culture in Europe. *Antiquity*, 91, 334-347.

Kytmannow, T., 2008. *Portal Tombs in the Landscape: The Chronology, Morphology and Landscape Setting of the Portal Tombs of Ireland, Wales and Cornwall. BAR British Series 455*. Oxford: Archaeopress.

Lanting, J. & van der Waals, J. D., 1972. British Beakers as seen from the Continent. *Helenium*, 12, 20-46.

Lanting, J. N. & van der Plicht, J., 2001. De 14C-chronologie van de Nederlandse pre- en protohistorie IV: bronstijd en vroege ijzertijd. *Palaeohistoria*, 43-44, 117-262.

Larsson, L., 2001. South Scandinavian wetland sites and finds from the Mesolithic and Neolithic. In: B. Purdy (ed.) *Enduring Records: The Environmental and Cultural Heritage of Wetlands*. Oxford: Oxbow, 158-171.

Leask, H. & Price, L., 1936. The Labbacallee Megalith, Co. Cork. *Proceedings of the Royal Irish Academy*, 43C, 77-101.

Lehane, D., 1983. Part III: The Flint Work. In: M. J. O'Kelly, R. M. Cleary & D. Lehane (eds) *Newgrange, Co. Meath: The Late Neolithic / Beaker Period Settlement. BAR International Series 190*. Oxford: Tempus Reparatum, 118-167.

Lehmann, L. Th., 1965. Placing the potbeaker. *Helinium*, 5, 3-31.

Leonard, K., 2015. *Ritual in Late Bronze Age Ireland: Material Culture, Practices, Landscape Setting and Social Context*. Oxford: Archaeopress.

Lévi-Strauss, C., 1949. *Les Structures Elémentaires de la Parenté*. Paris: PUF.

Lévi-Strauss, C., 1983. *The Way of the Masks*. London: Jonathan Cape.

Lévi-Strauss, C., 1987. *Antropología e structural*. Barcelona: Paidós Studio Básica.

Little, A. & Warren, G., 2017. Stone tool assemblage from Knowth. In: G. Eogan & K. Cleary (eds) *Excavations at Knowth 6: The Passage Tomb Archaeology of the Great Mound at Knowth*. Dublin: Royal Irish Academy, 471-485.

Liversage, G. D., 1968. Excavations at Dalkey Island, Co. Dublin, 1956-1959. *Proceedings of the Royal Irish Academy*, 66C, 53-233.

Lochrie, J. & Sheridan J. A., 2010. The prehistoric pottery. In: K. Dingwall (ed.) *Final Report on Excavations at Site 4, Armalughey, Co. Tyrone*. Unpublished report for Headland U.K.

Long, P. & O'Malley, M., 2008. *Gortybrigane Site 1, E2487, Co. Tipperary. Preliminary Excavation Report. N7 Limerick to Nenagh High Quality Dual Carriageway Archaeological Resolution Project*. Unpublished report for Limerick County Council by Headland Archaeology Ltd.

Lucas, A. T., 1966. National Museum of Ireland: Archaeological Acquisitions in the year 1963. *Journal of the Royal Society of Antiquaries of Ireland*, 96, 7-28.

Lynch, A., 2014. *Poulnabrone: An Early Neolithic Portal Tomb in Ireland. Archaeological Monograph Series: 9*. Dublin: Stationery Office.

Lynch, R., 1998. *Excavations at Taylorsgrange, Dublin*. Unpublished report by Margaret Gowen and Co. Ltd.

Macalister, R. A. S., *1921. Ireland in Pre-Celtic Times.* Dublin: Maunsel and Roberts Ltd.

Macalister, R. A. S., 1928. *The Archaeology of Ireland*. London: Methuen.

Macalister, R. A. S. 1949. *The Archaeology of Ireland*. 2nd ed., revised and rewritten. London: Methuen.

Macalister, R. A. S., Armstrong, E. C. R, & Praeger, R., 1913. A Bronze Age interment near Naas. *Proceedings of the Royal Irish Academy*, 30C, 351-360.

MacDermott, M., 1949. Two Barrows at Ballingoola. *Journal of the Royal Society of Antiquaries of Ireland*, 79, 139-145.

MacEachern, S., 2000. Genes, tribes and African history. *Current Anthropology*, 41(3), 357-384.

Mahr, A., 1937. New aspects and problems in Irish prehistory: presidential address for 1937. *Proceedings of the Prehistoric Society*, 11, 261-436.

Mallory, J. P., Nelis. E. & Hartwell, B., 2011. *Excavations on Donegore Hill, Co. Antrim*. Dublin: Wordwell.

Manby, T. G., 1995. Skeuomorphism: some reflections of leather, wood and basketry in Early Bronze Age pottery. In: I. Kinnes & G. Varndell (eds) *Unbaked Urns of Rudely Shape*. Oxford: Oxbow, 81-88.

Mathieson, I., Lazaradis, I., Rohland, N., Mallick, S., Patterson, N., Alpaslan Roodenberg, S., Hardney, E., *et al.*, 2015. Genome-wide patterns of selection in 230 ancient Eurasians. *Nature*, 528, 499-503.

Mauss, M., 1990. *The Gift: The Form and Reason for Exchange in Archaic Societies*. London & New York: Routledge.

May, A. McL., 1947. Burial mound, circles and cairn, Gortcorbies, Co. Londonderry. *Journal of the Royal Society of Antiquaries of Ireland*, 77, 5-22.

McAuliffe, M., 2014. The Unquiet Sisters. Women, politics and the Irish Free State Senate, 1922-1936. In: M. McAuliffe & C. Fischer (eds) *Irish Feminisms; Past, Present and Future*. Dublin: Arlen House, 47-70.

McCarthy, M., 2000. Hunting, fishing, and fowling in late prehistoric Ireland: the scarcity of the bone record. In: A. Desmond, G. Johnson, J. Sheehan & E. Shee Twohig (eds) *New agendas in Irish Prehistory*. Dublin: Wordwell, 107-119.

McCormick, F., 2007. Mammal bones from prehistoric Irish sites. In: E. M. Murphy & N. J. Whitehouse (eds) *Environmental Archaeology in Ireland*. Oxford: Oxbow, 76-101.

McDermott, C., 1998. The prehistory of the Offaly peatlands. In: W. Nolan & T. P. O'Neill (eds) *Offaly History and Society*. Dublin: Geography Publications, 1-28.

McIntosh, S. K. (ed.) 1999. *Beyond Chiefdoms: Pathways to Complexity in Africa*. Cambridge: Cambridge University Press.

McKeon, J. & O'Sullivan, J. (eds) 2014. *The Quiet Landscape: Archaeological Investigations on the M6 Galway to Ballinasloe National Road Scheme. NRA Scheme Monographs 15*. Dublin: National Roads Authority.

McLoughlin, C., 2002. *Excavations at Kerlogue, Wexford*. Unpublished report by Stafford Mc Loughlin Archaeology Ltd.

McLoughlin, G., 2009. *Final Report on Archaeological Excavation at Site 13, Haggardstown, County Louth*. Unpublished report for Irish Archaeological Consultancy Ltd.

McQuade, M., 2005. Archaeological excavation of a multi-period prehistoric settlement at Waterunder, Mell, Co. Louth. *County Louth Archaeological and Historical Journal*, 26, 31-66.

McQuade, M., Molloy, B. & Moriarty, C., 2009. *In the Shadow of the Galtees. Archaeological Excavations along the N8 Cashel – Mitchelstown Road Improvement Scheme. NRA Monographs Number 4*. Dublin: National Roads Authority/Wordwell.

McSparron, C., 2008. Have you no homes to go to?. *Archaeology Ireland*, 22(3), 18-21.

McVeigh, T., 2017. *Calendars, Feasting, Cosmology and Identities: Later Neolithic-Early Bronze Age Ireland in European Context*. Unpublished PhD Thesis, NUI Galway.

Mercer, R. (ed.) 1977. *Beakers in Britain and Europe. BAR International Series 26*. Oxford: Tempus Reparatum.

Mercer, R., 1981. The excavation of a Late Neolithic Henge-type enclosure at Balfarg, Markinch, Fife, Scotland, 1977-78. *Proceedings of the Society of Antiquaries of Scotland*, 111, 63-171.

Milliken, S., 2005. The lithics report. In: I. Hagen (ed.) *Excavations at Kilgobbin, Co. Dublin*. Unpublished final report.

Mitchell, G. F. & Ó Ríordáin, S. P., 1942. Early Bronze Age pottery from Rockbarton, Co. Limerick. *Proceedings of the Royal Irish Academy*, 48C, 255-272.

Mitchell, W. I. (ed.) 2004. *The Geology of Northern Ireland: Our Natural Foundation*. Belfast: Geological Survey of Northern Ireland.

Mizoguchi, K., 1993. Time in the reproduction of mortuary practices. *World Archaeology*, 25(2), 223-235.

Moore, H. L., 1982. The interpretation of spatial patterning in settlement residues. In: I. Hodder (ed.) *Symbolic and Structural Archaeology*. Cambridge: Cambridge University Press, 74-79.

Moore, H. L., 1986. *Space, Text and Gender*. Cambridge: Cambridge University Press.

Moore, M., 1987. *Archaeological Inventory of County Meath*. Dublin: Government Publications Office.

Mount, C., 1994. Aspects of ritual deposition in the Late Neolithic and Beaker periods at Newgrange, Co. Meath. *Proceedings of the Prehistoric Society*, 60, 433-443.

Moore, M., 1999. *Archaeological Inventory of County Waterford*. Dublin, The Stationery Office for Dúchas, The Heritage Service.

Mount, C., 1995. New Research on Irish Early Bronze Age cemeteries. In: J. Waddell & E. Shee Twohig (eds) *Ireland in the Bronze Age*. Dublin: Stationery Office, 97-112.

Mount, C., 1997a. Early Bronze Age burial in south-east Ireland in the light of recent research. *Proceedings of the Royal Irish Academy*, 97C, 101-193.

Mount, C., 1997b. Adolf Mahr's excavations of an Early Bronze Age cemetery at Keenoge, County Meath. *Proceedings of the Royal Irish Academy*, 97C, 1-68.

Mount, C., 2000. Exchange and communication: the relationship between Early and Middle Bronze Age Ireland and Atlantic Europe. In: J.C Henderson (ed.) *The Prehistory and Early History of Atlantic Europe, BAR S861*. Oxford: Archaeopress, 57-72.

Mount, C. 2012. A note on some Beaker period pit burials in Ireland. *Journal of Irish Archaeology*, 21, 1-6.

Müller, A., 2004. Gender differentiation in burial rites and grave-goods in the Eastern or Bohemian-Moravian Group of the Bell Beaker Culture. In F. Nicolis (ed.) *Bell Beakers Today: Pottery, People, Culture, Symbols in Prehistoric Europe. Proceedings of the International Colloquium at Riva del Garda (Trento, Italy) 11-16 May 1998*. Trento: Ufficio Beni Archeologici, 589-599.

Müller, J., 2013. Kossinna, Childe and aDNA. Comments on the construction of identities. *Current Swedish Archaeology*, 21, 35-37.

Müller, J. & van Willigen, S., 2004. New radiocarbon evidence for European Bell Beakers and the consequences for the diffusion of the Bell Beaker Phenomenon. In: F. Nicolis (ed.) *Bell Beakers Today: Pottery, People, Culture, Symbols in Prehistoric Europe. Proceedings of the International Colloquium at Riva del Garda 11-16 May 1998*. Trento: Ufficio Beni Archeologici, 59-80.

Mullin, J. B. & Davies, O., 1938. Excavations at Carrick East. *Ulster Journal of Archaeology*, 1, 98-107.

Munro, R., 1902. Notes on a set of five jet buttons found on a hill in Forfarshire. *Proceedings of the Society of Antiquaries of Scotland*, 36, 463-487.

Murphy, E. M., 2001. Cremated human bone report. In: D. P. Hurl (ed.) Excavation of a Wedge Tomb in Ballybriest townland, Co. Londonderry. *Ulster Journal of Archaeology*, 60, 9-31.

Murray, C., 2002. *Ballybeg Bog, Co. Offaly 01E0663: Archaeological Survey Report*. Unpublished report by the Irish Archaeological Wetland Unit.

Murray, C., 2004. The Barrysbrook Bowstave. *Past*, 46. Available at: https://www.le.ac.uk/has/ps/past/past46.html#Bowstave [Accessed July 2018].

Needham, S., 1988. Selective deposition in the British Early Bronze Age. *World Archaeology*, 20, 229-248.

Needham, S., 1996. Chronology and periodisation in the British Bronze Age. *Acta Archaeologia*, 67, 121-140.

Needham, S., 1998. Radley and the development of early metalworking in Britain. In: G. Barclay & C. Halpin (eds) *Excavations at Barrow Hills, Radley, Oxfordshire. The Neolithic and Bronze Age Monuments Complex*. Oxford: Oxbow, 186-192.

Needham, S., 2000a. Power pulses across a cultural divide: cosmologically driven exchange between Armorica and Wessex. *Proceedings of the Prehistoric Society*, 66, 151-207.

Needham, S., 2001. When expediency broaches ritual intention: the flow of metal between systemic and buried domains. *Journal of the Royal Anthropological Institute*, 7(2), 275-298.

Needham, S., 2002. Analytical implications for Beaker metallurgy in north-west Europe. In: M. Bartelheim, E. Pernicka & R. Krause (eds) *Die Anfänge der Metallurgie in der Alten Welt*. Rahden: Verlag Marie Leidorf, 99-133.

Needham, S., 2004. Migdale-Marnoch: sunburst of Scottish metallurgy. In: I. A. G. Shepherd & G. J. Barclay (eds) *Scotland in Ancient Europe: The Neolithic and Early Bronze Age of Scotland in their European Context*. Edinburgh: Society of Antiquaries of Scotland, 217-245.

Needham, S., 2005. Transforming Beaker culture in north-west Europe; processes of fusion and fission. *Proceedings of the Prehistoric Society*, 71, 171-217.

Needham, S., 2006. Bronze makes a Bronze Age? Considering the systemics of Bronze Age metal use and the implications of selective deposition. In: C. Burgess, P. Topping & F. M. Lynch (eds) *In the Shadow of the Age of Stonehenge: Papers in Honour of Colin Burgess*. Oxford: Oxbow, 278-287.

Needham, S., 2007. Isotope aliens: Beaker movement and cultural transmissions. In: M. Larsson & M. Parker Pearson (eds) *From Stonehenge to the Baltic: Living with Cultural Diversity in the Third Millennium BC. BAR International Series 1692*. Oxford: Archaeopress, 42-46.

Needham, S., 2008. Exchange, object biographies and the shaping of identities, 10,000 – 1,000 BC. In: J. Pollard (ed.) *Prehistoric Britain*. London: Blackwell, 310-329.

Needham, S., 2011. Gold basket-shaped ornaments from graves 1291 (Amesbury Archer) and 1236. In: A. Fitzpatrick (ed.) *The Amesbury Archer and the Boscombe Bowmen: Bell Beaker Burials at Boscombe Down, Amesbury, Wiltshire.* Salisbury: Wessex Archaeology Report, 129-138.

Needham, S., 2012. Case and place for the British Chalcolithic. In: M. J. Allen, J. Gardiner, A. Sheridan & D. McOmish (eds) *Is there a British Chalcolithic? People, Place and Polity in the later 3rd millennium. Prehistoric Society Research Paper No. 4.* Oxford: Oxbow, 1-26.

Needham, S., 2016. The lost cultures of the halberd bearers: a non-Beaker ideology in later 3rd millennium Atlantic Europe. In: J. Koch & B. Cunliffe (eds) *Celtic from the West 3: Atlantic Europe in the Metal Ages–Questions of Shared Language.* Oxford: Oxbow, 40-82.

Needham, S. & Spense, T., 1996. *Refuse and Disposal at Area 16 East, Runnymede.* London: British Museum Press.

Needham, S. & Sheridan, J. A., 2014. *Chalcolithic and Early Bronze Age goldwork from Britain: new finds and new perspectives.* In: H. Meller, R. Risch & E. Pernicka (eds) *Metalle der Macht – Frühes Gold und Silber / Metals of power – Early Gold and Silver. 6. Mitteldeutscher Archäologentag vom 17. bis 19. Oktober 2013 in Halle (Saale).* Halle: Landesamt für Denkmalpflege und Archäologie Sachsen-Anhalt, 903-929.

Needham, S., Kenny, J., Cole, G., Montgomery, J., Jay, M., Davis, M., & Marshall, P., 2017. Death by combat at the dawn of the Bronze Age? Profiling the dagger-accompanied burial from Racton, West Sussex. *The Antiquaries Journal,* 97, 65-117.

Nelis, E., 2009 Lithics report. In: D. Bayley (ed.) *Site 112: Newtownbalregan 2.* Unpublished final report for Irish Archaeological Consultancy on behalf of Louth County Council and the National Roads Authority.

Nicolas, C., 2017. Arrows of power from Brittany to Denmark (2500-1700 BC). *Proceedings of the Prehistoric Society,* 83, 247-287.

Nielsen, N. V. S., 2009. Flint and metal daggers in Scandinavia and other parts of Europe: a re-interpretation of their function in the Late Neolithic and Early Copper and Bronze Age. *Antiquity,* 83, 349-358.

Northover, J. P., 1999. The earliest metalworking in southern Britain. In: A. Hauptmann, E. Pernicka, T. Rehren & U. Yalcin (eds) *The Beginnings of Metallurgy.* Bochum: Deutsches Bergbau-Museum, 211-226.

Northover, P., O'Brien, W. & Stos, S., 2001. Lead isotopes and metal circulation in Beaker/Early Bronze Age Ireland. *Journal of Irish Archaeology,* 10, 25-48.

O' Carroll, E. & Mitchell, F. J. G., 2013. Seeing the woods for the trees: unravelling woodland resource usage in the Irish midlands over the last five millennia. In: B. Kelly, N. Roycroft & M. Stanley (eds) *Futures and Pasts: Archaeological Science on Irish Road Schemes. Archaeology and the National Roads Authority Monograph Series No. 10.* Dublin: National Roads Authority, 111-120.

Ó Floinn, R., 1988. Irish bog bodies. *Archaeology Ireland,* 2, 94-97.

Ó Floinn, R., 1995. Recent research into Irish bog bodies. In: R. C. Turner & R. G. Scaife (eds.) *Bog Bodies: New Discoveries and New Perspectives.* London: British Museum Press, 137-145.

O Hara, R., 2008. *The Archaeological Excavation of Dunboyne 3, Co. Meath.* Unpublished final report for ACS Ltd.

O hEochaidhe, M., 1957. Portal dolmen at Kiltiernan, Co. Dublin. *Proceedings of the Prehistoric Society,* 23, 221.

Ó Maoldúin, R., 2014. *Exchange in Chalcolithic and Early Bronze Age (EBA) Ireland: Connecting People, Objects and Ideas.* Unpublished PhD Thesis, NUI Galway.

Ó Néill, J., 2000. *Cherrywood, Co. Dublin, Area B.* Unpublished report by Margaret Gowen and Co. Ltd.

Ó Néill, J., 2009. *Burnt Mounds in Northern and Western Europe: A Study of Prehistoric Technology and Society.* Saarbrücken: VDM Verlag.

Ó Néill, J., 2013. Being prehistoric in the Irish Iron Age. In: M. O'Sullivan, C. Scarre & M. Doyle (eds) *Tara: From the Past to the Future.* Dublin: Wordwell, 256-266.

Ó Nualláin, S., 1998. Excavation of the smaller court-tomb and associated hut sites at Ballyglass, Co. Mayo. *Proceedings of the Royal Irish Academy,* 98C, 125-175.

Ó Nualláin, S. & Walsh, P., 1986. A reconsideration of the Tramore passage-tombs. *Proceedings of the Prehistoric Society,* 52, 25-29.

Ó Nualláin, S., Greene, S. & Rice, K., Forthcoming. *Excavation of a Centre Court Tomb and Underlying House Site at Ballyglass, Co. Mayo.* Dublin: UCD School of Archaeology/Wordwell.

Ó Ríordáin, B., 1967. A prehistoric burial site at Gortnacargy, Co. Cavan. *Journal of the Royal Society of Antiquaries of Ireland,* 97, 61-73.

Ó Ríordáin, B., 1961. Neolithic vessel from Bracklin, Co. Westmeath. *Journal of the Royal Society of Antiquaries of Ireland,* 91, 43-45.

Ó Ríordáin, S. P., 1947. Excavation of a barrow at Rathjordan, Co. Limerick. *Journal of the Cork Archaeological and Historical Society,* 52, 1-4.

Ó Ríordáin, S. P., 1948. Further barrrows at Rathjordan, Co. Limerick. *Journal of the Cork Archaeological and Historical Society,* 53, 19-31.

Ó Ríordáin, S. P., 1950. Lough Gur excavations: Ballingoola V. *Journal of the Royal Society of Antiquaries of Ireland,* 80, 262-263.

Ó Ríordáin, S. P., 1951. Lough Gur excavations: the great stone circle (B) in Grange townland. *Proceedings of the Royal Irish Academy,* 54C, 37-74.

Ó Ríordáin, S. P., 1954. Lough Gur excavations: Neolithic and Bronze Age houses on Knockadoon. *Proceedings of the Royal Irish Academy*, 56C, 297-459.

Ó Ríordáin, S. P. & De Valera, R., 1952. Excavation of a megalithic tomb at Ballyedmonduff, Co. Dublin. *Proceedings of the Royal Irish Academy*, 55C, 61-81.

Ó Ríordáin, S. P. & Ó h-Iceadha, G., 1955. Lough Gur excavations: the megalithic tomb. *Journal of the Royal Society of Antiquaries of Ireland*, 85, 34-50.

O'Brien, E., 1988. A find of Beaker pottery from Broomfield, Ballyboghil, Co. Dublin. *Journal of the Royal Society of Antiquaries of Ireland*, 118, 118-123.

O'Brien, E., 1984. Late prehistoric – early historic Ireland: the burial evidence reviewed. Unpublished M.Phil. submitted to the Departments of Archaeology and Early Irish History, National University of Ireland.

O'Brien, R., 2014. Monadreela 13. Unpublished final report to the National Monuments Service, Department of the Environment, Heritage and Local Government, Dublin.

O'Brien, W., 1994. *Mount Gabriel. Bronze Age Mining in Ireland*. Galway: Galway University Press.

O'Brien, W., 1999. *Sacred Ground: Megalithic Tombs in Coastal South-West Ireland. Bronze Age Studies 4*. Galway: Dept. of Archaeology, NUI Galway.

O'Brien, W., 2002. Megaliths in a mythologised landscape: south-west Ireland in the Iron Age. In: C. Scarre (ed.) *Monuments and Landscape in Atlantic Europe: Perception and Society During the Neolithic and Early Bronze Age*. London, Routledge, 152-176.

O'Brien, W., 2003. The Bronze Age copper mines of the Goleen area, County Cork. *Proceedings of the Royal Irish Academy*, 103C, 13-59.

O'Brien, W., 2004. *Ross Island. Mining, Metal and Society in Early Ireland. Bronze Age Studies 6*. Galway: Dept. of Archaeology, NUI Galway.

O'Brien, W., 2012. The Chalcolithic in Ireland: a chronological and cultural framework. In: M. J. Allen, J. Gardiner, A. Sheridan & D. McOmish (eds) *Is there a British Chalcolithic? People, Place and Polity in the later 3rd millennium. Prehistoric Society Research Paper No. 4*. Oxford: Oxbow, 211-225.

O'Brien. W., 2016. *Prehistoric copper mining in Europe: 5500-500 BC*. Oxford: Oxford University Press.

O'Connell, A., 2009. *Lismullin 1 E3074 Final Report*. Unpublished final report.

O'Connell, A., 2013. *Harvesting the stars: a pagan temple at Lismullin, Co. Meath. NRA Scheme Monographs 11*. Dublin: National Roads Authority.

O'Connor, B., 2004. The earliest Scottish metalwork since Coles. In: I. Shepherd & G. Barclay (eds) *Scotland in Ancient Europe: the Neolithic and Early Bronze Age of Scotland in their European Context*. Edinburgh: Society of Antiquaries of Scotland, 205-216.

O'Connor, D., 2005. *Preliminary Report on the Archaeological Excavation at Site 19, Harlockstown, Co. Meath*. Unpublished report by CRDS on behalf of Meath County Council National Road Design Office.

O'Donoghue, J., 2010. Final excavation report of a Neolithic house at Gortore, Co. Cork. *Eachtra Journal 6*. Available at: http://eachtra.ie/index.php/journal/a014-003-gortore-co-cork/ [Accessed July 2018]

O'Donovan, E., 2002. Rathbane South. In: I. Bennett (ed.) *Excavations 2000*. Bray: Wordwell, 200-201.

O'Flaherty, R., 1993. *An Analysis of Irish Early Bronze Age Hoards*. Unpublished MA thesis, Department of Archaeology, National University of Ireland.

O'Flaherty, R., 1995. An analysis of Irish Early Bronze Age hoards containing copper or bronze objects. *Journal of the Royal Society of Antiquaries of Ireland*, 125, 10-45.

O'Flaherty, R., 2002. *A Consideration of the Early Bronze Age Halberd in Ireland*. Dublin: Unpublished PhD thesis, University College Dublin.

O'Kelly, M. J., 1952. Excavation of a Cairn at Moneen, Co. Cork. *Proceedings of the Royal Irish Academy*, 54C, 121-159.

O'Kelly, M. J., 1958. A wedge-shaped gallery-grave at Island, Co. Cork. *Journal of the Royal Society of Antiquaries of Ireland*, 88, 1-23.

O'Kelly, M. J.,1959. A wedge-gallery grave at Baurnadomeeny, County Tipperary: preliminary notice. *North Munster Antiquarian Journal*, 2, 63a-c.

O'Kelly, M. J., 1960. A wedge-shaped gallery grave at Baurnadomeeny, Co. Tipperary. *Journal of the Cork Historical and Archaeological Society*, 65, 85-115.

O'Kelly, M. J., 1982. *Newgrange, Archaeology, Art, and Legend*. London: Thames & Hudson.

O'Kelly, M. J., 1989. *Early Ireland: An Introduction to Irish Prehistory*. Cambridge: Cambridge University Press.

O'Kelly, M. J. & Shell, C., 1979. Stone objects and a Bronze Age axe from Newgrange, Co. Meath. In: M. Ryan (ed.) *The Origins of Metallurgy in Atlantic Europe, Fifth Atlantic Colloquium*. Dublin: Stationary Office, 127-144.

O'Kelly, M. J., Cleary, R. & Lehane, D., 1983. *Newgrange, Co. Meath, Ireland: The Late Neolithic-Beaker Period Settlement. BAR International Series 190*. Oxford: Tempus Reparatum.

O'Kelly, M. J., Lynch, F. & O'Kelly, C., 1978. Three passage graves at Newgrange, Co. Meath. *Proceedings of the Royal Irish Academy*, 78C, 249-352.

O'Neill, T., 2007. *The Archaeological Excavation of Parknahown 5, Co. Laois* Unpublished interim report for ACS Ltd.

O'Sullivan, A., 1996. Neolithic, Bronze Age and Iron Age woodworking techniques. In: B. Raftery (ed.) *Trackway Excavations in the Mountdillon Bogs, Co. Longford, 1985-1991. Transactions of the Irish Archae-*

ological Wetland Unit. 3. Dublin. Crannóg Publications, 291-342.

O'Sullivan, A., 2007. Exploring past people's interactions with wetland environments in Ireland. *Proceedings of the Royal Irish Academy,* 107C, 147-203.

O'Sullivan, M., 2005. *Duma na nGiall. The Mound of the Hostages, Tara*. Dublin: UCD School of Archaeology/Wordwell.

O'Hare, M. B., 2005. *The Bronze Age Lithics of Ireland*. Unpublished PhD Thesis. Queen's University Belfast.

Olalde, I., Brace, S., Allentoft, M. E., Armit, I., Kristiansen, K., Rohland, N., Mallick, S., Booth, T., Szécsényi-Nagy, A., Mittnik, A., Altena, E., Lipson, M., Lazaridis, I., Patterson, N. J., Broomandkhoshbacht, N., Diekmann, Y., Faltyskova, Z., Fernandes, D. M., Ferry, M., Harney, E., de Knijff, P., Michel, M., Oppenheimer, J., Stewardson, K., Barclay, A., Alt, K. W., Fernández, A. A., Bánffy, E., Bernabò-Brea, M., Billoin, D., Blasco, C., Bonsall, C., Bonsall, L., Allen, T., Büster, L., Carver, S., Navarro, L. C., Craig, O. E., Cook, G. T., Cunliffe, B., Denaire, A., Egging Dinwiddy, K., Dodwell, N., Ernée, M., Evans, C., Kuchařík, M., Farré, J. F., Fokkens, H., Fowler, C., Gazenbeek, M., Pena, R. G., Haber-Uriarte, M., Haduch, E., Hey, G., Jowett, N., Knowles, T., Massy, K., Pfrengle, S., Lefranc, P., Lemercier, O., Lefebvre, A., Maurandi, J. L., Majó, T., McKinley, J. I., McSweeney, K., Mende B. G., Modi, A., Kulcsár, G., Kiss, V., Czene, A., Patay, R., Endródi, A., Köhler, K., Hajdu, T., Cardoso, J. L., Liesau, C., Parker Pearson, M., Włodarczak, P., Price, T. D., Prieto, P., Rey, P-J., Ríos, P., Risch, R., Rojo Guerra, M. A., Schmitt, A., Serralongue, J., Silva, A. M., Smrčka, V., Vergnaud, L., Zilhão, J., Caramelli, D., Higham, T., Heyd, V., Sheridan, A., Sjögren, K-G., Thomas, M. G., Stockhammer, P. W., Pinhasi, R., Krause, J., Haak, W., Barnes, I., Lalueza-Fox, C., Reich, D., et. al., 2018. The Beaker phenomenon and the genomic transformation of northwest Europe. *Nature*, 555(7695), 190-196.

Osborne, R., 2008. Introduction: for tradition as an analytical category. *World Archaeology*, 40(2), 281-294.

Parker Pearson, M., Chamberlain, A., Jay, M., Richards, M., Sheridan, A., Curtis, N., Evans, J., Gibson, A., Hutchison, M., Mahoney, P., Marshall, P., Montgomery, J., Needham, S., O'Mahoney, S., Pellegrini, M., Wilkin, N., 2016. Bell Beaker people in Britain: migration, mobility and diet. *Antiquity,* 90, 620-637.

Parker Pearson, M., Chamberlain, A., Jay, M., Richards, M., Sheridan, A. & Evans, J. (eds) In press. *The Beaker People: Isotopes, Mobility and Diet in Prehistoric Britain. The Prehistoric Society Research Paper No. 7*. London: The Prehistoric Society.

Parker Pearson, M., Cleal, R., Marshall, P., Needham, S., Pollard, J., Richards, C., Ruggles, C., Sheridan, A., Thomas, J., Tilley, C., Welham, K., Chamberlain, A., Chenery, C., Evans, J., Knüsel, C., Linford, N., Martin, L., Montgomery, J., Payne, A. & Richards, M., 2007. The age of Stonehenge. *Antiquity,* 81, 617-639.

Parker Pearson, M., Pollard, J., Richards, C., Thomas, J., Tilley, C., Welham, K. & Albarella, U., 2006. Materiality and Stonehenge: the Stonehenge Riverside Project and new discoveries. *Journal of Material Culture,* 11, 227-261.

Parker Pearson, M., Sharples, N. & Symonds, J., 2004a. *South Uist: Archaeology and History of a Hebridean Island*. Stroud: Tempus.

Parker Pearson, M., Richards, C., Allen, M., Payne, A. & Welham, K., 2004b. The Stonehenge Riverside Project: research design and initial results. *Journal of Nordic Archaeological Science,* 14, 45-60.

Pétrequin, P., Cassen, S., Errera, M., Gauthier, E., Klassen, L., Pailler, Y., Pétrequin, A-M. & Sheridan, A., 2009. L'unique, la paire, les multiples. À propos des dépôts de haches polies en roches alpines en Europe occidentale pendant les cinquième et quatrième millénaires. In : S. Bonnardin, C. Hamon, M. Lauwers & B. Quilliec (eds) *Du Matériel au Spirituel. Réalités Archéologiques et Historiques des 'Dépôts' de la Préhistoire à nos Jours. XXIXe rencontres Rencontres Internationales d'Archéologie et d'Histoire d'Antibes*. Antibes: Éditions APDCA, 417-427.

Pétrequin, P., Sheridan, A., Cassen, S., Errera, M., Gauthier E., Klassen, L., Le Maux, N. & Pailler, Y., 2008. Neolithic Alpine axeheads from the Continent to Great Britain, the Isle of Man and Ireland. In: H. Fokkens, B. J. Coles, A. L. van Gijn, J. P. Kleijne, H. H. Ponjee & C. G. Slappendel (eds) *Between Foraging and Farming: An Extended Broad Spectrum of Papers Presented to Leendert Louwe Kooijmans. Analecta Praehistorica Leidensia 40*. Leiden: University of Leiden, 261-281.

Phelan, S., 2004. *Charlesland, Co. Wicklow, Sites 1C and D*. Unpublished report for Margaret Gowen and Co. Ltd.

Pollard, J., 1999. "These places have their moments: thoughts on settlement practices in the British Neolithic. In: J. Brück & M. Goodman (eds) *Making Places in the Prehistoric World: Themes in Settlement Archaeology*. London: UCL Press, 76-93.

Pollard, J., 2000. Neolithic occupation practises and social ecologies from Rinyo to Clacton. In: A. Ritchie (ed.) *Neolithic Orkney and Its European Context*. Cambridge: McDonald Institute, 363-369.

Pollard, J., 2001. The aesthetics of depositional practice. *World Archaeology,* 33, 315-333.

Pollard, J., 2002. The nature of archaeological deposits and finds assemblages. In: A. Woodward & J. Hill (eds) *Prehistoric Britain: The Ceramic Basis*. Oxford: Oxbow, 22-33.

Pollard, C. J., Garwood, P., Parker Pearson, M., Richards, C., Thomas, J. & Welham, K., 2017. Remembered and imagined belongings: Stonehenge in the age of first metals. In: P. Bickle, D. Hofmann, V. Cummings & J. Pollard (eds) *The Neolithic of Europe: Papers in honour of Alasdair Whittle*. Oxford: Oxbow, 279-297.

Powell, T., 1941. Excavation of a Megalithic Tomb at Carriglong, Co. Waterford. *Journal of the Cork Archaeological and Historical Society*, 46, 55-62.

Powell, T., 1973. Excavation of the chambered cairn at Dyffryn Ardudwy, Merioneth, Wales. *Archaeologia*, 104, 1-49.

Price, T. D., Grupe, G. A. & Shröter, P., 1998. Migration in the Bell Beaker period of Central Europe. *Antiquity*, 72, 405-412.

Price, T. D., Knipper, C., Grupe, G. & Smrcka. V., 2004. Strontium isotopes and prehistoric human migration: the Bell Beaker period in central Europe. *European Journal of Archaeology*, 7, 9-40.

Pryor, F., 1992. Discussion: the Fengate/Northey landscape. *Antiquity*, 66, 518-531.

Pryor, F., 1995. Abandonment and the role of ritual sites in the landscape. *Scottish Archaeological Review*, 9/10, 96-109.

Purcell, A., 2002. Excavation of three Neolithic houses at Corbally, Kilcullen, Co. Kildare. *Journal of Irish Archaeology*, 11, 31-75.

Purcell, A., 2005a. *Excavations at Ballinure, Co. Cork*. Unpublished report

Purcell, A., 2005b. *Archaeological Excavation at Kilbane, Castletroy, Co Limerick*. Unpublished interim report

Raftery, B., 1996. *Trackway Excavations in the Mountdillon bogs, Co. Longford, 1985-1991. Transactions of the Irish Archaeological Wetland Unit 3*. Dublin: Crannóg Publications.

Reimer, P. J., Baillie, M. G. L., Bard, E., Bayliss, A., Beck, J. W., Bertrand, C. J. H., Blackwell, P. G., Buck, C. E., Burr, G. S., Cutler, K. B., Damon, P. E., Edwards, R. L., Fairbanks, R. G., Friedrich, M., Guilderson, T. P., Hogg, A. G., Hughen, K. A., Kromer, B., McCormac, G., Manning, S., Bronk Ramsey, C., Reimer, R. W., Remmele, S., Southon, J. R., Stuiver, M ., Talamo, S ., Taylor, F. W., van der Plicht, J. & Weyhenmeyer, C. E., 2004. IntCal04 terrestrial radiocarbon age calibration, 0-26 cal yr BP. *Radiocarbon*, 46(3), 1029-1058.

Renfrew, C., 1973. Monuments, mobilization and social organization in Neolithic Wessex. In: C. Renfrew (ed.) *The Explanation of Culture Change: Models in Prehistory*. London: Duckworth, 539-558.

Renfrew, C., 1976. Megaliths, territories and populations. In: S. J. De Laet (ed.) *Acculturation and Continuity in Atlantic Europe Mainly during the Neolithic Period and Bronze Age. Papers presented at the IV Atlantic Colloquium, Ghent 1975*. Brugge: De Tempel, 199-220.

Renfrew, C., 1977. Space, time and polity. In: J. Friedman & M. J. Rowlands (eds) *The Evolution of Social Systems*. London: Duckworth, 89-112.

Rice, K., 2006. *The Prehistory of Piperstown. A Reassessment of an Upland Landscape*. Unpublished M.A thesis. University College Dublin.

Richards, C. & Thomas, J., 1984. Ritual activity and structured deposition in later Neolithic Wessex. In: R. Bradley & J. Gardiner (eds) *Neolithic Studies. A Review of Some Current Research. BAR 133*. Oxford: Tempus Reparatum, 189-218.

Robb, J., 1999. Hegemonic megaliths: changing the Irish prehistoric. *Irish Studies Review*, 7.1, 5-11.

Robb, J. & Miracle, P., 2007. Beyond "migration" versus "acculturation": new models for the spread of agriculture. In: A. Whittle & V. Cummings (eds) *Going Over the Mesolithic-Neolithic Transition in North-West Europe*. London: The British Academy, 99-115.

Roberts, B. W., 2008a. Creating traditions and shaping technologies: understanding the emergence of metallurgy in Western Europe, *c*. 3500-2000 BC. *World Archaeology*, 40(3), 354-372.

Roberts, B. W., 2008b. Migration, craft expertise and metallurgy: analysing the 'spread' of metal in Europe. *Archaeological Review from Cambridge*, 23(2), 27-45.

Roberts, B. W. 2009. Production networks and consumer choice in the earliest metal of western Europe. *Journal of World Prehistory*, 22(4), 461-481.

Roberts, B. W., Thornton, C. P. & Pigott, V. C., 2009. Development of metallurgy in Eurasia. *Antiquity*, 83(322), 1012-1022.

Roberts, B. W. & Vander Linden, M., 2011. Investigating archaeological cultures: material culture, variability, and transmission. In: *B. W. Roberts & M. Vander Linden* (eds) *Investigating Archaeological Cultures Material Culture, Variability, and Transmission*. New York: Springer, 1-22.

Roberts, B., Uckelmann, M. & Brandherm, D., 2013. Old Father Time: the Bronze Age chronology of Western Europe. In: A. Harding & H. Fokkens (eds) *The Oxford Handbook of the European Bronze Age*. Oxford: Oxford University Press, 17-46.

Roche, H., 1995. *Style and Context for Grooved Ware in Ireland with Special Reference to the Assemblage at Knowth, Co. Meath*. Dublin: Unpublished. MA thesis, University College Dublin.

Roche, H., 1999. *Parknabinnia, Co. Clare. Pottery Report*. Unpublished specialist report.

Roche, H., 2004. The dating of the embanked stone circle at Grange, Co. Limerick. In: H. Roche, E. Grogan, J. Bradley, J. Coles & B. Raftery (eds) *From Megaliths to Metals: Essays in Honour of George Eogan*. Oxford: Oxbow, 109-116.

Roche, H. & Eogan, G., 2001. Late Neolithic activity in the Boyne Valley, Co. Meath. In : C. T. L. Roux (ed.) *Du Monde des Chasseurs à celui des Métallurgistes: Hommage Scientifique à la Mémoire de Jean L'Helgouach et Mélanges Offerts à Jacques Briard*. Revue Archéologique de l'Ouest, Supplement 9, 125-140.

Roche, H. & Grogan, E., 2005. Appendix A. The prehistoric pottery from Mell, County Louth. In: M. McQuade (ed.) Archaeological Excavation of a Multi-Period Prehistoric Settlement at Waterunder, Mell, Co. Louth, *County Louth Archaeological and Historical Journal*, 26, 54-63.

Roche, H. & Grogan, E. 2006. *The Prehistoric Pottery Assemblage from Faughart Lower 6*. Unpublished report.

Roche, H. & Grogan, E. 2008. *The Prehistoric Pottery from Gortmakellis (E2816), Co. Tipperary. M8/N8 Cullahill – Cashel Road Improvement Scheme*. Unpublished report for V.J. Keeley Ltd.

Roche, H. Forthcoming. The prehistoric pottery. In: S. Ó Nualláin, S. Greene & K. Rice (eds) *Excavation of a Centre Court Tomb and Underlying House Site at Ballyglass, Co. Mayo*. Dublin: UCD School of Archaeology/Wordwell.

Roe, F., 2011. Bracers from the grave of the Amesbury Archer. In: A. Fitzpatrick (ed.) *The Amesbury Archer and the Boscombe Bowmen*. Salisbury: Wessex Archaeology, 103-111.

Roe, F. & Woodward, A., 2009. Bits and pieces: Early Bronze Age stone bracers from Ireland. *Internet Archaeology*, 26.

Rogers, E. M., 2003. *Diffusion of Innovations*. New York: Free Press.

Roscoe, P., 2009. On the 'pacification' of the European Neolithic: ethnographic analogy and the neglect of history. *World Archaeology*, 41, 578-588.

Rotherham, E. C., 1895. On the excavation of a cairn on Slieve-na-Callighe, Loughcrew. *Journal of the Royal Society of Antiquaries of Ireland*, 25, 311-316.

Rowlands, M., 1980: Kinship, alliance and exchange in the European Bronze Age. In: J. Barrett & R. Bradley (eds) *Settlement and Society in the British Later Bronze Age. BAR British Series 83*. Oxford: Tempus Reparatum, 15-55.

Rowlands, M., 1993. The role of memory in the transmission of culture. *World Archaeology*, 25(2), 141-151.

Rynne, E., 1972. Tanged dagger from Derrynamanagh, Co. Galway. *Journal of the Royal Society of Antiquaries of Ireland*, 102, 240-243.

Rynne, E. & O'hAéilidhe, P., 1965. A group of prehistoric sites at Piperstown, Co Dublin. *Proceedings of the Royal Irish Academy*, 64C, 61-84.

Salanova, L., 1998a. A long way to go…The Bell Beaker chronology in France, Some new approaches to the Bell Beaker 'phenomenon'. Lost paradise…?. In: M. Benz & S. van Willigen (eds) *Some New Approaches to The Bell Beaker Phenomenon. Lost Paradise…? Proceedings of the 2nd Meeting of the Association "Archéologie et Gobelets", Feldburg, 18th-20th April 1997. BAR International Series 690*. Oxford: Tempus Reparatum, 1-13.

Salanova, L., 1998b. Le statut des assemblages campaniformes en contexte funéraire: la notion de "bien de prestige". *Bulletin de la Société Préhistorique Française*, 95(3), 315-326.

Salanova, L., 2000. *La Question du Campaniforme en France et dans les Iles Anglo-Normandes: Productions, Chronologie et Rôles d'un Standard Céramique*. Paris: CTHS/Société Préhistorique Française.

Salanova, L., 2002. Fabrication et circulation des céramiques campaniformes. In: J. Guilaine (ed.) *Matériaux, Productions, Circulations du Néolithique à l'Age du Bronze. Séminaires du Collège de France*. Paris : Éditions Errance, 151-166.

Salanova, L., 2003a. Les sépultures mégalithiques et le phénomène campaniforme. In: V. S. Gonçalves (ed.) *Muita Gente, Poucas Antas? Origens, Espaços e Contextos do Megalitismo. Actas do II Coloquio Internacional sobre Megalitismo 25*. Instituto Portugues de Arqueologia: Trabalhos de Arqueologia, 385-393.

Salanova, L., 2003b. Heads north: analysis of Bell Beaker graves in Western Europe. *Journal of Iberian Archaeology*, 5, 163-169.

Salanova, L., 2004. The frontiers inside the western Bell Beaker block. In: J. Czerbreszuk (ed.) *Similar but Different: Bell beakers in Europe*. Poznan: Adam Mickiewicz University, 63-75.

Salanova, L., 2007. Les sépultures campaniformes: lecture sociale. Le Chalcolithique et la construction des inégalités. In: J. Guilaine (ed.) *Le Chalcolithique et la Construction des Inégalités*. Paris: Éditions Errance, 213-228.

Salanova, L., 2016. Behind the warriors: Bell Beakers and identities in Atlantic Europe (3rd millennium BC). In: J. T. Koch & B. Cunliffe (eds) *Celtic from the West 3. Atlantic Europe in the Metal Ages: Questions of Shared Language*. Oxford: Oxbow, 13-39.

Salanova, L., In press. The Bell Beaker Complex in France. In: L. Mcfadyen & C. Marcigny (eds) *Prehistoric France*. Cambridge: Cambridge University Press.

Sangmeister, E., 1964. Die schmalen 'Armschutzplatten'. In: R. van Uslar (ed.) *Studien aus Alteuropa: Kurt Tackenberg zum 65. Geburtstag am 30. Juni 1964. Bonner Jahrbücher 10*. Köln: Böhlau Verlag, 93-122.

Sangmeister, E., 1966. Die Datierung des Rückstroms der Glockenbecher und ihre Auswirkungen auf die Chronologie der Kupferzeit in Portugal. *Palaeohistoria*, 12, 395-407.

Sangmeister, E., 1972. Sozial-ökonomische Aspekte der Glockenbecherkultur. *Homo*, 23, 188-203.

Sangmeister, E., 1974. Zwei neufunde der Glockenbecherkultur in Baden-Württemberg. *Fundberichte aus Baden-Württemberg*, 1, 103-156.

Sarauw, T., 2007a. Male symbols or warrior identities? The 'archery burials' of the Danish Bell Beaker culture. *Journal of Anthropological Archaeology*, 26(1), 65-87.

Sarauw, T., 2007b. On the outskirts of the European Bell Beaker phenomenon – the Danish case. *Journal of Neolithic Archaeology*. Available at: http://www.jna.uni-kiel.de/index.php/jna/article/view/23 [Accessed July 2018].

Sarauw, T., 2008. Early Late Neolithic dagger production in northern Jutland. Marginalised production or source of wealth? *Bericht der Römisch-Germanischen Kommission*, 87, 252-272.

Schmidt, P. K., 1978. Beile als Ritualobjekte in der Altbronzezeit der Britischen Inseln. *Jahresbericht des Insituts für Vorgeschichte der Universität Frankfurt an Main*, 311-320.

Schofield, A. J., 1991. Interpreting artefact scatters: an introduction. In: A. J. Schofield (ed.) *Interpreting Artefact Scatters: Contributions to Ploughzone Archaeology*. Oxford: Oxbow, 3-8.

Schuhmacher, T. X., Banerjee, A., Dindorf, W., Sastri, C., & Sauvage, T., 2013. The use of sperm whale ivory in Chalcolithic Portugal. *Trabajos de Prehistoria*, 70(1), 185-203.

Schulting, R. J., 2014. The dating of Poulnabrone, Co. Clare. In: A. Lynch (ed.) *Poulnabrone, Co. Clare: Excavation of an Early Neolithic Portal Tomb in Ireland*. Dublin: The Stationery Office, 93-113.

Schulting, R. J., Bronk Ramsey, C., Reimer, P. J., Eogan, G., Cleary, K., Cooney, G. & Sheridan, A., 2017. Dating the human remains from Knowth. In: G. Eogan & K. Cleary (eds) *Excavations at Knowth 6: The Passage Tomb Archaeology of the Great Mound at Knowth*. Dublin, Royal Irish Academy, 331-386.

Schulting, R., Sheridan, A., Clarke, S. & Bronk Ramsey, C., 2008. Largantea and the dating of Irish wedge tombs. *Journal of Irish Archaeology*, 17, 1-18.

Schulting, R. J., Murphy, E., Jones, C. & Warren, G., 2012. New dates from the north, and a proposed chronology for Irish court tombs. *Proceedings of the Royal Irish Academy*, 112C, 1-60.

Scott, B.G., 1977a. Dancing, drink or drugs? Comments on the "Beaker Cult-Package" hypothesis. *Irish Archaeological Research Forum*, 2, 29-34.

Scott, B.G., 1977b. Notes on the introduction of non-ferrous metal technology to Ireland and the transition from stone-use to indigenous non-ferrous metal use. *Irish Archaeological Research Forum*, 2, 7-15.

Seaver, M., 2004a. From mountain to sea – excavations at Laughanstown/Glebe. *Archaeology Ireland*, 66, 8-12.

Seaver, M., 2004b. Laughanstown, site 78. In: I. Bennet (ed.) *Excavations 2002*. Dublin: Wordwell, 173-174.

Seaver, M., 2005. *Final Report on Excavations at Site 78, Laughanstown, Co. Dublin*. Unpublished report.

Seaver, M., 2008. *Final Report on Archaeological Monitoring and Excavation in Field 7, Oldbridge, County Meath on the route of the proposed Oldbridge-Sheephouse By-Pass on behalf of Meath County Council by CRDS Ltd*. Unpublished report.

Seaver, M. & Keeley, V.J., 2003. *Final Report on the Archaeological Excavation of an Archaeological Complex, Laughanstown Townland, Co. Dublin*. South Eastern Motorway. Unpublished report.

Shanks, M. & Tilley, C. Y., 1987. *Re-constructing Archaeology: Theory and Practice. New studies in Archaeology*. Cambridge: Cambridge University Press.

Shell, C., 2000. Metalworker or shaman: Early Bronze Age Upton Lovell G2a burial. *Antiquity*, 74, 271-272.

Shennan, S., 1976. Bell beakers and their context in central Europe. In: J. N. Lanting & J. D. van der Waals (eds) *Glockenbechersymposium Oberried 1974*. Harlem: Bussum, 231-239.

Shennan, S., 1977. The appearance of the Bell Beaker assemblage in Central Europe. In: R. Mercer (ed.) *Beakers in Britain and Europe: four studies. BAR British Series 26*. Oxford: Tempus Reparatum, 51-70.

Shennan, S., 1978. Archaeological "cultures": an empirical investigation. In: I. Hodder (ed.) *The Spatial Organisation of Culture*. London: Duckworth, 113-140.

Shennan, S., 1982. Ideology, change and the European Early Bronze Age. In: I. Hodder (ed.) *Symbolic and Structural Archaeology*. Cambridge: Cambridge University Press, 155-161.

Shennan, S., (ed.) *1989. Archaeological Approaches to Cultural Identity*. London: Routledge.

Shennan, S., 1993. Settlement and social change in central Europe, 3500-1500 BC. *Journal of World Prehistory*, 7, 121-161.

Shepherd, A. N., 1989. A note on the orientation of beaker burials in north-east Scotland. In: M. K. Greig, C. Greig, A. N. Shepherd & I.A.G. Shepherd (eds) A beaker cist from Chapelden, Tore of Troup, Aberdour, Banff and Buchan District, with a note on the orientation of beaker burials in north-east Scotland. *Proceedings of the Society of Antiquaries of Scotland*, 119, 73-81.

Shepherd, A. N., 2012. Stepping out together: men, women, and their Beakers in time and space. In: M. J. Allen, J. Gardiner, A. Sheridan & D. McOmish (eds) *Is there a British Chalcolithic? People, Place and Polity in the later 3rd millennium. Prehistoric Society Research Paper No. 4*. Oxford: Oxbow, 257-280.

Shepherd, I. A. G., 2009. The v-bored buttons of Great Britain and Ireland. *Proceedings of the Prehistoric Society*, 75, 335-369.

Sheridan, J. A., 1983. A reconsideration of the origins of Irish metallurgy. *Journal of Irish Archaeology*, 1, 11-19.

Sheridan, J. A., 1986. Megaliths and megalomania: an account, and interpretation, of the development of passage tombs in Ireland. *Journal of Irish Archaeology*, 3, 17-30.

Sheridan, J. A., 1995. Irish Neolithic Pottery: the story in 1995. In: I. Kinnes & G. Varndell (eds) *Unbaked Urns of Rudely Shape. Essays on British and Irish Pottery for Ian Longworth*. Oxford: Oxbow, 3-21.

Sheridan, J. A., 2004a. Going round in circles? Understanding the Irish Grooved Ware 'complex' in its wider context. In: H. Roche, E. Grogan, J. Bradley, J. Coles & B. Raftery (eds) *From Megaliths to Metals: Essays in Honour of George Eogan*. Oxford: Oxbow, 26-37.

Sheridan, J. A., 2004b. Neolithic connections along and across the Irish Sea. In: V. Cummings & C. Fowler (eds) *The Neolithic of the Irish Sea: Materiality and Traditions of Practice*. Oxford: Oxbow, 9-21.

Sheridan, J. A., 2007a. Scottish Beaker dates: the good, the bad and the ugly. In: M. Larsson & M. Parker Pearson (eds) *From Stonehenge to the Baltic: Living with Cultural Diversity in the Third Millennium BC. BAR S1692*. Oxford: Archaeopress, 91-123.

Sheridan, J. A., 2008a. Towards a fuller, more nuanced narrative of Chalcolithic and Early Bronze Age Britain 2500-1500 BC. *Bronze Age Review*, 1, 57-78.

Sheridan, J. A. 2008b. Upper Largie and Dutch-Scottish connections during the Beaker period. In: H. Fokkens, B. J. Coles, A. L. van Gijn, J. P. Kleijne, H. H. Ponjee & C.G. Slappendel (eds) *Between Foraging and Farming: An Extended Broad Spectrum of Papers Presented to Leendert Louwe Kooijmans. Analecta Praehistorica Leidensia 40*. Leiden: University of Leiden, 247-260.

Sheridan, J. A., 2012. *A Rumsfeld reality vheck: what we know, what we don't know and what we don't know about the Chalcolithic in Britain and Ireland*. In: M. J. Allen, J. Gardiner, A. Sheridan & D. McOmish (eds) *Is there a British Chalcolithic? People, Place and Polity in the later 3rd millennium. Prehistoric Society Research Paper No. 4*. Oxford: Oxbow, 40-55.

Sheridan, J. A. & Northover, J. P., 1993. A beaker period copper dagger blade from the Sillees River near Ross Lough, Co. Fermanagh. *Ulster Journal of Archaeology*, 56, 61-69.

Sheridan, J. A. & Davis, M., 1998. 'The Welsh 'jet set' in prehistory: a case of keeping up with the Joneses?. In: A. M. Gibson & D. D. A. Simpson (eds) *Prehistoric Ritual and Religion*. Stroud: Sutton, 148-162.

Shryock, A. & Smail, D. L. (eds) 2011. *Deep History: The Architecture of Past and Present*. Berkeley: University of The University of California Press.

Simpson, D. D. A., 1971. Beaker houses and settlements in Britain. In: D. D. A Simpson (ed.) *Economy and settlement in Neolithic and Early Bronze Age Britain and Europe*. Leicester: Leicester University Press, 131-153.

Simpson, D. D. A., 1988. The stone maceheads of Ireland. *Journal of the Royal Society of Antiquaries of Ireland*, 118, 27-52.

Simpson, D. D. A., 1989. The stone maceheads of Ireland part II. *Journal of the Royal Society of Antiquaries of Ireland*, 119, 113-126.

Simpson, D. D. A., 1990. The stone battle axes of Ireland. *Journal of the Royal Society of Antiquaries of Ireland*, 120, 5-40.

Simpson, D. D. A., 1996. Irish perforated stone implements in context. *Journal of Irish Archaeology*, 7, 65-76.

Schmidt, P. K. & C. B. Burgess., 1981. *The Axes of Scotland and Northern England. Prähistorische Bronzefunde IX.7*. Munich: Beck.

Smith, A. G., Pearson, G. W. & Pilcher, J. R., 1974. Belfast radiocarbon dates VII. *Radiocarbon*, 16, 269-276.

Smith, J., 2006. Early Bronze Age stone wrist-guards in Britain: Archer's bracer or social symbol?. Available at: https://www.academia.edu/5713702/Early_Bronze_Age_Stone_Wrist-Guards_in_Britain_archers_bracer_or_social_symbol [Original host platform no longer available] [Accessed July 2018].

Smyth, J., 2007. *Neolithic Settlement in Ireland: New Theories and Approaches*. Unpublished PhD thesis, University College Dublin.

Smyth, J., 2009. *Brú na Bóinne World Heritage Site Research Framework*. Kilkenny: The Heritage Council.

Smyth, J., 2010. The house and group identity in the Irish Neolithic. *Proceedings of the Royal Irish Academy*, 110C, 1-31.

Smyth, J., 2014. *Settlement in Neolithic Ireland: new discoveries on the edge of Europe. Prehistoric Society Research Paper 6*. Oxford: Prehistoric Society.

Spriggs, M., 2008. Ethnographic parallels and the denial of history. *World Archaeology*, 40, 538-552.

Standish, C. D., Dhuime, B., Chapman, R. J., Hawkesworth, C. J., & Pike, A. W. G., 2014. The genesis of gold mineralisation hosted by orogenic belts: A lead isotope investigation of Irish gold deposits. *Chemical Geology*, 378-379, 40-51.

Standish, C. D., Dhuime, B., Hawkesworth, C. J., & Pike, A. W. G., 2015. A non-local source of Irish Chalcolithic and Early Bronze Age gold. *Proceedings of the Prehistoric Society*, 81, 149-177.

Stanley, M., Swan, R. & O'Sullivan, A. (eds) 2017. *Stories of Ireland's Past: Knowledge Gained from NRA Roads Archaeology. TII Heritage 5.* Dublin: Transport Infrastructure Ireland.

Stanley, M., 2003. Archaeological survey of Irish bogs: information without understanding. *Journal of Wetland Archaeology,* 3, 61-74.

Stout, G., 1991. Embanked enclosures of the Boyne region. *Proceedings of the Royal Irish Academy,* 91C, 245-284.

Stout, G. & Stout, M., 2008. *Newgrange.* Cork: Cork University Press.

Strahm, C. (ed.) 1995. *Das Glockenbecher-Phänomen: Ein Seminar. Freiburger Archäologische Studien 2.* Freiburg: Institut für Ur- und Frügeschichte der Universität Freiburg.

Strahm, C., 1998. Le Campaniforme: phénomène et culture. In: C. Dargent (ed.) *Rhône-Alpes A404 : L'Énigmatique Civilisation Campaniforme, Hors-série d'Archéologia, no 9,* 6-13.

Strahm, C., 2004. Das Glockenbecher-Phänomen aus der Sicht der Komplementär- Keramik. In: J. Czebreszuk (ed.) *Similar but Different: Bell Beakers in Europe.* Poznan:Adam Mickiewicz University, 101-126.

Sweetman, P. D., 1971. An earthen enclosure at Monknewtown, Slane, Co. Meath: Preliminary report. *Journal of the Royal Society of Antiquaries of Ireland,* 101, 135-140.

Sweetman, P. D., 1976. An earthen enclosure at Monknewtown, Slane, Co. Meath. *Proceedings of the Royal Irish Academy,* 76C, 25-72.

Sweetman, P. D., 1985. A Late Neolithic/Early Bronze Age pit circle at Newgrange, Co. Meath. *Proceedings of the Royal Irish Academy,* 85C, 195-221.

Sweetman, P. D., 1987. Excavation of a Late Neolithic/Early Bronze Age Site at Newgrange, Co. Meath. *Proceedings of the Royal Irish Academy,* 87C, 238-298.

Sweetman, P. D., Alcock, O. & Moran, B., 1995. *Archaeological inventory of County Laois.* Dublin. Dublin Stationary Office.

Taylor, J. J., 1970. Lunulae reconsidered. *Proceedings of the Prehistoric Society,* 36, 38-81.

Taylor, J. J., 1980. *Bronze Age Goldwork of the British Isles.* Cambridge: Cambridge University Press.

Taylor, J. J., 1994. The first golden age of Europe was in Ireland and Britain (*c.* 2400-1400 BC). *Ulster Journal of Archaeology,* 57, 37-60.

Thomas, J., 1991. Reading the body: Beaker funerary practice in Britain. In: P. Garwood, D. Jennings, R. Skeates & J. Toms (eds) *Sacred and Profane.* Oxford: Oxford University Committee for Archaeology Monographs, 33-42.

Thomas, J., 1996. *Time, Culture and Identity: An Interpretive Archaeology.* London: Routledge.

Thomas, J., 1999. *Understanding the Neolithic.* London: Routledge.

Thomas, J., 2000. Death, identity and the body in Neolithic Britain. *Journal of the Royal Anthropological Institute,* 6, 603-617.

Thomas, J., 2002. Taking power seriously. In: M. O'Donovan (ed.) *The Dynamics of Power.* Carbondale: Southern Illinois University Press, 35-50.

Thomas, J., 2004a. *Archaeology and Modernity,* London & New York: Routledge.

Thomas, J., 2004b. The later Neolithic architectural repertoire: the case of the Dunragit complex. In: R. Cleal & J. Pollard (eds) *Monuments and Material Culture: Papers on Neolithic and Bronze Age Britain in Honour of Isobel Smith.* East Knoyle: Hobnob Press, 98-108.

Thomas, J., 2007. The internal features at Durrington Walls: investigations in the Southern Circle and. Western Enclosures 2005-6. In: M. Larsson & M. Parker Pearson (eds) *From Stonehenge to the Baltic: Living with Cultural Diversity in the Third Millennium BC. BAR International Series 1692.* Oxford: Archaeopress, 145-157.

Thomas, J., 2010. The return of the Rinyo-Clacton folk? The cultural significance of the Grooved Ware complex in Later Neolithic Britain. *Cambridge Archaeological Journal,* 20(1), 1-15.

Thorpe, I. J. & Richards, C., 1984. The decline of ritual authority and the introduction of Beakers into Britain. In: R. Bradley & J. Gardiner (eds) *Neolithic Studies: A Review of Some Current Research. BAR British Series 133.* Oxford: Tempus Reparatum, 67-84.

Topp, C., 1962. The Portal Dolmen of Drumanone- Co. Roscommon. *Bulletin of the Institute of Archaeology London,* 3, 38-46.

Tuckwell, A. N., 1975. Patterns of burial orientation in the round barrows of East Yorkshire. *Bulletin of the Institute of Archaeology,* 12, 95-123.

Turek, J., 1997. The first evidence of Bohemian Corded Ware settlements and the question of their economy. In: P. Siemen (ed.) *Early Corded Ware Culture: The A-horizon. Fiction or Fact? International Symposium in Jutland, 2-7 May 1994.* Esbjerg: Esbjerg Museum, 233-242.

Turek, J., 1998. The Bell Beaker Period in north-west Bohemia. In: M. Benz & S. van Willigen (eds) *Some New Approaches to The Bell Beaker Phenomenon. Lost Paradise…? Proceedings of the 2nd Meeting of the Association Archeologie et Goblets, Feldburg, 18th-20th April 1997. BAR International Series 690.* Oxford: Tempus Reparatum, 107-119.

Turek, J., 2013. Echoes and traditions of the Bell Beaker phenomenon. In: M. Bartelhei, J. Peška, J. Turek (eds) *From Copper to Bronze. Cultural and Social Transformations at the Turn of the 3rd/2nd Millennia B. C. in*

Central Europe. Gewidmet PhDr. Václav Moucha, CSc. anlässlich seines 80. Geburtstages. Beitrage zur Ur-und Frühgeschichte Mitteleuropas 74. Langenweissbach: Archäologische Fachliteratur, 9-23.

Turek, J., 2015. Bell Beaker stone wrist-guards as symbolic male ornament. The significance of ceremonial warfare. In: M. P. Prieto Martínez (ed.) *The Bell beaker transition in Europe: mobility and local evolution during the 3rd millennium BC*. Oxford: Oxbow, 28-40.

van der Beek, Z. & Fokkens, H., 2001. 24 years after Oberried: The 'Dutch Model' reconsidered. In; F. Nicolis. (ed.) *Bell Beakers Today. Pottery, People, Culture, Symbols in Prehistoric Europe. Proceedings of the International Colloquium, Riva del Garda (Trento, Italy), 11-16 May 1998*. Trento: Ufficio Beni Archeologici, 301-308.

Vander Linden, M., 2003. Competing Cosmos. On the relationships between Corded Ware and Bell Beaker mortuary practice. In: J. Czebreszuk & M. Szmyt (eds) *The Northeast Frontier of Bell Beakers. BAR International Series 1155*. Oxford: Archaeopress, 155-181.

Vander Linden, M., 2004. Polythetic networks, coherent people: a new historical hypothesis for the Bell Beaker phenomenon. In: J. Czebresuk (ed.), *Similar but Different. Bell Beakers in Europe*. Poznan: Adam Mickiewicz University, 35-62.

Vander Linden, M., 2006a. *Le Phénomène Campaniforme dans l'Europe du 3éme Millénaire avant notre Ère. BAR International Series 1470*. Oxford: Archaeopress.

Vander Linden, M., 2006b. For whom the bell tolls: social hierarchy vs social integration in the Bell Beaker culture of southern France. *Cambridge Archaeological Journal*, 16, 317-332.

Vander Linden, M., 2007a. For equalities are plural: reassessing the social in Europe during the third millennium BC. *World Archaeology*, 39(2), 177-193.

Vander Linden, M., 2007b. What linked the Bell Beakers in third millennium BC Europe? *Antiquity*, 81, 343-352.

Vander Linden, M., 2012. Demography and mobility in north-western Europe during the third millennium BC. In: C. Prescott & H. Glörstad (eds), *Becoming European. The Transformation of Third Millennium Northern and Western Europe*. Oxford: Oxbow, 19-29.

Vander Linden, M., 2013. A little bit of history repeating itself: theories on the Bell Beaker phenomenon. In: H Fokkens & A. Harding (eds) *The Oxford Handbook of the European Bronze Age*. Oxford: Oxford University Press, 68-81.

Vander Linden, M., 2015. Bell Beaker pottery and society. In: C. Fowler, J. Harding & D. Hofmann (eds) *The Oxford Handbook of Neolithic Europe*. Oxford: Oxford University Press, 605-620.

Vander Linden, M., 2016. Population history in the third millennium BC Europe: assessing the contribution of genetics. *World Archaeology*, 48(5), 714-728.

Vandkilde, H., 1996. *From Stone to Bronze. The Metalwork of the Late Neolithic and Earliest Bronze Age in Denmark*. Højbjerg: Jutland Archaeological Society.

Vandkilde, H., 2004. Beaker representation in the Danish late Neolithic. In: F. Nicolis (ed.) *Bell Beakers Today. Pottery, People, Culture, Symbols in Prehistoric Europe. Proceedings of the International Colloquium at Riva del Garda 11-16 May 1998*. Trento: Ufficio Beni Archeologici, 333-360.

Vandkilde, H., 2005. A review of the Early Late Neolithic Period in Denmark: Practice, identity and connectivity. *Journal of Neolithic Archaeology*. Available at: http://www.jna.uni-kiel.de/index.php/jna/article/view/13 [Accessed July 2018]

Vandkilde, H., 2009. Communities with Bell Beaker transculture – a commentary. *Norwegian Archaeological Review*, 41(2), 74-83.

van Gennep, A., 1960. *The Rites of Passage*, trans. M. B. Vizedom and G. L. Caffee. Chicago: University of Chicago Press.

van Wijngaarden-Bakker, L. H., 1974. The animal remains from the Beaker settlement at Newgrange, Co. Meath: first report. *Proceedings of the Royal Irish Academy*, 74C, 313-383.

van Wijngaarden-Bakker, L. H., 1986. The animal remains from the Beaker settlement at Newgrange, Co. Meath: Final report. *Proceedings of the Royal Irish Academy*, 86C, 17-111.

Waddell, J., 1970. Irish Bronze Age Cists: A Survey. *Journal of the Royal Society of Antiquaries of Ireland*, 100, 91-139.

Waddell, J., 1974. On some aspects of the Late Neolithic and Early Bronze Age in Ireland. *Irish Archaeological Research Forum*, 1, 32-38.

Waddell, J., 1976. Cultural interaction in the insular early Bronze Age: Some ceramic evidence. In: S. J. de Laet (ed.) *Acculturation and Continuity in Atlantic Europe mainly during the Neolithic Period and Bronze Age*. Brugge: Dissertationes Archaeologicae Gandenses, 284-295.

Waddell, J., 1978. The invasion hypothesis in Irish Prehistory. *Antiquity*, 52, 121-128.

Waddell, J., 1990. *The Bronze Age Burials of Ireland*, Galway: Galway University Press.

Waddell, J., 1991. The Irish Sea in Prehistory. *Journal of Irish Archaeology*, 6, 29-40.

Waddell, J., 1998. *The Prehistoric Archaeology of Ireland*. Galway: Galway University Press.

Waddell, J., 2005. *Foundation Myths: The Beginnings of Irish Archaeology*. Bray: Wordwell.

Waddell, J., 2007. A Professional Profession. Address to the Institute of Archaeologists of Ireland Autumn Conference, Galway. October 2007.

Waddell, J. 2010. *The Prehistoric Archaeology of Ireland*. 3rd ed. Dublin: Wordwell.

Wainwright, G. J. & Longworth, I. J., 1971. *Durrington Walls: Excavations 1966-1968: Report of the Research Committee of the Society of Antiquaries of London 29*. London: Society of Antiquaries of London.

Wallace, P. F., 2008. Irish archaeology and the recognition of ethnic difference in Viking Dublin. In: J. Habu, C. P. Fawcett & J. M. Matsunga (eds) *Evaluating Multiple Narratives: Beyond Nationalist, Colonialist, Imperialist Archaeologies*. New York: Springer, 166-183.

Walsh, F., 2009. *Final Report on Archaeological Excavation of Kilmainham 1C. A029/022, E3140, M3 Clonee-North of Kells*. Unpublished report for Irish Archaeological Consultancy Ltd.

Walsh, P., 1995. Structure and deposition in Irish wedge tombs: an open and shut case. In: J. Waddell & E. Shee Twohig (eds) *Ireland in the Bronze Age*. Dublin: Stationery Office, 113-127.

Ward, K., 2006. *Excavations at Newtownlittle, Co. Dublin*. Unpublished report.

Waterbolk, H. T., 1971. Working with radiocarbon dates. *Proceedings of the Prehistoric Society*, 37, 15-33.

Waterson, R., 1995. Houses and hierarchy in island SE Asia. In: J. Carsten & S. Hugh – Jones (eds) *About the House; Lévi – Strauss and Beyond*. Cambridge: Cambridge University Press, 47-68.

Watts, W., 1960. C-14 Dating and the Neolithic in Ireland. *Antiquity*, 34, 111-116.

Weiner, A. B., 1992. *Inalienable Possessions; The Paradox of Keeping-While-Giving*. Berkeley: University of California Press.

Wentink, K. & van Gijn, A. L., 2008. Neolithic depositions in the Northern Netherlands. In: C. Hamon, B. Benedicte & B. Quillec (eds) *Hoards from the Neolithic to the Metal Ages: Technical and Codified Practices. Session of the XIth Vol. 1758*. Oxford: Archaeopress, 29-43.

Whitehouse, N. J., Schulting, R. J., McClatchie, M., et al., 2014. Neolithic agriculture on the European western frontier: the boom and bust of early farming in Ireland. *Journal of Archaeological Science*, 51, 181-205.

Whittle, A., 1981. Later Neolithic society in Britain: a realignment. In: C. Ruggles & A. Whittle (eds) *Astonomy and Society in Britain during the Period 4000-1500 BC*. Oxford: Tempus Reparatum, 297-342.

Whittle, A. & Bayliss, A., 2007. The times of their lives: from chronological precision to kinds of history and change. *Cambridge Archaeological Journal*, 17(1), 21-28.

Whittle, A., Pollard, J. & Grigson, C., 1999. *The Harmony of Symbols: The Windmill Hill Causewayed Enclosure*. Oxford: Oxbow.

Whitty, Y., 2006. *Ballymoyle A22/019 Preliminary Report. N11 Rathnew to Arklow Road Improvement Scheme*. Unpublished report for Wicklow County Council/National Roads Authority. Irish Archaeological Consultancy Ltd.

Wilde, W. R., 1857. *A Descriptive Catalogue of the Antiquities of Stone, Earthen and Vegetable Materials in the Museum of the Royal Irish Academy Dublin*. Dublin: Royal Irish Academy.

Wilkin, N., 2009. *Regional Narratives of the Early Bronze Age. A Contextual and Evidence-led Approach to the Funerary Practices of East-Central Scotland*. Unpublished M.Phil thesis, Institute of Archaeology and Antiquity, University of Birmingham.

Wilkin, N., 2014. *Food Vessel Pottery from Early Bronze Age Funerary Contexts in Northern England: A Typological and Contextual Study*. Unpublished PhD thesis, University of Birmingham.

Wilkin, N., 2016. Pursuing the penumbral: the deposition of Beaker pottery at Neolithic monuments in Chalcolithic and early Bronze Age Scotland. In: K. Brophy, G. MacGregor & I. B. M. Ralston (eds) *The Neolithic of Mainland Scotland*. Edinburgh: Edinburgh University Press, 261-318.

Wilkin, N. & Vander Linden, M., 2015. What was and what would never be: Changing patterns of interaction and archaeological visibility across North West Europe from 2500 to 1500 cal. BC. In: H. Anderson-Whymark, D. Garrow & F. Sturt (eds) *Continental Connections: Exploring Cross-channel Relationships from the Mesolithic to the Iron Age*, Oxford: Oxbow, 99-121.

Wilkins, B., 2010. When the Celtic Tiger roared: the golden years of commercial archaeology in Ireland. *Current Archaeology*, 247, 12-19.

Woodham, A. A. & Woodham, M. F., 1957. The excavation of a chambered cairn at Kilcoy, Ross-shire. *Proceedings of the Society of Antiquaries of Scotland*, 90, 102-115.

Woodman, P., 1992a. Filling in the spaces in Irish prehistory. *Antiquity*, 66, 295-314.

Woodman, P., 1992b. Irish archaeology today: a poverty among riches. *Irish Review*, 12, 34-39.

Woodman, P., 1993. A sense of place in Irish prehistory. *Antiquity*, 67, 639-641.

Woodman, P., Finlay, N. & Anderson, E., 2006. *The Archaeology of a Collection: The Keiller-Knowles Collection of the National Museum of Ireland. National Museum of Ireland Monograph Series 2*. Dublin: Wordwell.

Wood-Martin, W. G., 1888. *The Rude Stone Monuments of Ireland (Co. Sligo and the Island of Achill)*. Dublin: Hodges and Figgis.

Wood-Martin. W. G., 1895. *Pagan Ireland, An Archaeological Sketch. A Handbook of Irish Pre-Christian Antiquities.* London: Longmans.

Woodward, A., 2000. *British Barrows. A Matter of Life and Death.* Stroud: Tempus.

Woodward, A., 2002. Beads and Beakers: heirlooms and relics in the British Early Bronze Age. *Antiquity,* 294, 1040-1047.

Woodward, A. & Hunter, J., 2011. *An Examination of Prehistoric Stone Bracers from Britain.* Oxford: Oxbow.

Woodward, A. & Hunter, J., 2015. *Ritual in Early Bronze Age Grave Goods: An Examination of Ritual and Dress Equipment from Chalcolithic and Early Bronze Age Graves in England.* Oxford: Oxbow.

Woodward, A., Hunter, J., Ixer, R., Roe, F., Potts, P. J., Webb, P. S., Watson, J. S. & Jones, M., 2006. Beaker age bracers in England: sources, function and use. *Antiquity,* 80, 530-543.

Wylie, A., 1993. A proliferation of new archaeologies: "beyond objectivism and relativism". In: N. Yoffee & A. Sherratt (eds). *Archaeological Theory: Who Sets the Agenda?.* Cambridge: Cambridge University Press, 20-27.

Yates, D. & Bradley, R., 2010. Still water, hidden depths: the deposition of Bronze Age metalwork in the English Fenland. *Antiquity,* 84, 405-415.